RINGO STARR
A LIFE

Printed in the United Kingdom by MPG Books Ltd, Bodmin

Published by Sanctuary Publishing Limited, Sanctuary House, 45-53 Sinclair Road,
London W14 0NS, United Kingdom

www.sanctuarypublishing.com

Distributed in the US by Publishers Group West

While the publishers have made every reasonable effort to trace the copyright owners
for any or all of the photographs in this book, there may be some omissions of credits,
for which we apologise.

ISBN: 1-86074-647-0

RINGO STARR
A LIFE

ALAN CLAYSON

Sanctuary

About The Author

Described by *The Western Morning News* as the "AJP Taylor of pop", Alan Clayson is the author of many books on music, including the best-selling *Backbeat*, subject of a major film. He has contributed to journals as disparate as *Record Collector*, *The Independent*, *The Beat Goes On*, *Mojo*, *Mediaeval World*, *The Times*, *Folk Roots*, *The Guardian* and, as a teenager, the notorious *Schoolkids Oz*. He had also written and presented programmes on national radio and has lectured on both sides of the Atlantic.

Before he became better known as a pop historian, he led the legendary Clayson And The Argonauts and was thrust to "a premier position on rock's Lunatic Fringe" (*Melody Maker*). Today, his solo cabaret act remains "more than just a performance; an experience" (*Village Voice*). "It is difficult to explain to the uninitiated quite what to expect," adds *The Independent*. There is even an Alan Clayson fan club, which dates from a 1992 appearance in Chicago.

Alan Clayson's cult following has continued to grow, along with demand for his production skills in the studio and the number of versions of his compositions by such diverse acts as Dave Berry – in whose Cruisers he played keyboards in the mid 1980s – and (via a collaboration with Yardbird Jim McCarty) Jane Relf and new age outfit Stairway. He has also worked with the Portsmouth Sinfonia, Wreckless Eric, Twinkle and Screaming Lord Sutch, among others.

Born in Dover in 1951, Alan Clayson lives near Henley-on-Thames with his wife, Inese, and sons, Jack and Harry.

"You will tell me no doubt that Mrs Patrick Campbell cannot act. Who said she could – and who wants her to act? Who cares twopence whether she possesses that or any other second-rate accomplishment? On the highest plane, one does not act, one is."

George Bernard Shaw

To Tinkerbelle

Contents

Prologue

"I've Never Really Done Anything To Create What Has Happened"

During a soundcheck in a theatre in Wales, the timpanist of the Portsmouth Sinfonia was addressed as "Oi, Ringo!" by a janitor who wished him to shift his bloody junk away from the safety curtain. In 1984, a British tabloid wrung a news item from a cockroach who'd been named Ringo by the duty officer after it had been brought into a Yorkshire police station by a greengrocer who'd found it amongst his turnips. In countless such trivial occurrences, former Beatle Ringo Starr is fulfilling an early wish to "end up sort of unforgettable".[1]

To the man in the street, his will always be the Beatle name more likely to trip off the tongue than those of John Lennon, Paul McCartney and George Harrison, none of whom assumed a permanent stage alias. Nevertheless, Ringo – born plain Richard Starkey – seemed the least altered of all of them by the scarcely believable years of Beatlemania and its aftermath. Not quite losing the air of an eternal Scouser who'd hit the big time, he'd confess, "I've never really done anything to create what has happened. It created itself, and I'm only here because it did happen."[2]

Yet, however peripheral he might have been to the group artistically, "ex-Beatle" remains an adjective more attributable to Starr than the "mystic" Harrison; McCartney, still basking in the limelight; and Lennon, in the legion of the lost. Back in Liverpool, another ex-Beatle, Pete Best – the one whom Ringo replaced – seemed content until recently as a civil servant, part-time drummer and prized guest speaker at Beatle Conventions.

Pete's first autobiography appeared in 1985. In that same year, it was reported that Ringo was to write one, too. This was not the sole such rumour, nor the only time that Starr had rejected six-figure sums to relate his side of it. "It would take three volumes up to when I was ten," he explained, "and they really only want to know about eight years of my life. So that's why I said no. They want just the juicy bits, just like you."[3]

He's underestimating himself – or he's over-estimating the tired old story of the Fab Four. The sagas of Ringo's sojourn with Rory Storm And The Hurricanes up until 1962 and his career in the 20 years since The Beatles are at least as funny, poignant, turbulent and scandalous as those of that more exalted and chronicled era.

Without much hope, I attempted to elicit Starr's assistance for my account, but all he gave me was a polite refusal via his secretary. This was regrettable but by no means disastrous. After all, a recent biographer of Alfred the Great hadn't interviewed his subject, either. Also, treating Ringo like a historical figure, footnotes and all, I waded through oceans of archive material and screwed myself up to talk to complete strangers about matters that took place up to 40 years ago.

As his profile assumed a sharper definition, Starr surfaced as an admirable man in many ways, although some of my findings shattered minor myths. He was not, for example, the originator of the film title *A Hard Day's Night*, as had been previously supposed.[4] His conscious tendency in interview to "hear myself saying the same things over again"[5] also emerged, and, while it got on my nerves slightly, it was useful for confirmation of personal information and opinions. Unlike Alfred the Great's annalist, I didn't have to arrive at a divergent conclusion but simply choose which of Ringo's remarks about the same matter was most interesting.

For most of my secondary research and consultation, I went first and last to Ian Drummond, who was always at hand at a moment's notice in his capacity as a Beatle scholar of the highest calibre.

I am also very grateful to Peter Doggett for his help with this project, and indeed with other ventures, quixotic and otherwise, over the years.

Special thanks are in order, too, for Susan Hill, Amy Sohanpaul, Carys Thomas, Amanda Marshall – and Helen Gummer, whose patience and understanding went beyond the call of duty as original commissioning editor. The same applies to Penny Braybrooke, who authorised this updated reissue, as well as Jeffrey Hudson, Alan Heal, Eddy Leviten, Dan Froude, Chris Bradford and Michelle Knight. I would also like to say a big hello to Hilary Murray.

Let's have a big round of applause, too, for Dave and Caroline Humphreys for accommodating me whenever I was on Merseyside and for Dave's skill and imagination as a photographer.

For their advice and for trusting me with archive material, particular debts are owed to Pete Frame, Bill Harry, Paul Hearne, Spencer Leigh, Steve Maggs, Allan Jones, Fraser Massey, Steve Morris of *Brumbeat*, Charles and Deborah Salt, Maggie Simpson of *Melody Maker* and John Tobler.

I have also drawn from conversations with the following musicians: Ian "Tich" Amey, Christina Balfour, Roger Barnes, Andre Barreau, Alan Barwise, Cliff Bennett, Dave Berry, Barry Booth, Bruce Brand, Louis Cennamo, Billy Childish, Jeff Christopherson, Frank Connor, Ron Cooper, Pete Cox, Tony Crane, Dave Dee, Wayne Fontana, Gary Gold, "Wreckless" Eric Goulden, David Hentschel, Penny Hicks, Malcolm Hornsby, Garry Jones, Billy Kinsley, Graham Larkbey, Dave Maggs, Jim McCarty, Jill Myhill, Ray Pinfold, Brian Poole, Reg Presley, Mike Robinson, Jim Simpson, Norman Smith, the late Lord David Sutch, Mike Sweeney, Geoff Taggart, John Townsend, Paul Tucker, Val Wiseman and Fran Wood.

It may be obvious to the reader that I have received much information from sources that prefer not to be mentioned. Nevertheless, I wish to express my gratitude towards them.

Thanks are also due in varying degrees to Andy Anderton, B&T Typewriters, Robert Bartel, Colin Baylis, Carol Boyer, Rob Bradford, Eva Marie Brunner, Stuart and Kathryn Booth, Gordon and Rosemary Clayson, Kevin Delaney, Greg and Debi Daniels, Doreen Davidson, Nancy Davis, Helen Drummond, Tim and Sarah Fagan, Kathi and Rick Fowler, Tom Hall (of the Spinning Disk), Sarah

Knake, Yvonne Lambourne, Mark and Carol Lapidos, Brian Leafe, Bill Mielenz, Coy Ness, Carolyn Pinfold, Andrea Tursso and Ted Woodings – plus Inese, Jack and Harry, who preferred Luddite rage at irrecoverable disasters while I taught myself to work a word processor to the incessant clacking of a typewriter by a paterfamilias strung out on Tipp-Ex, man.

Alan Clayson, July 2001

1 "I Was Just One Of Those Loony Teddy Boys"

In 1962, the plug was pulled and Richard Starkey was sucked into a vortex of events, places and situations that hadn't belonged even to speculation when, on 7 July 1940 – a week late and a month after the Dunkirk evacuation – he was born in the front bedroom of 9 Madryn Street, a three-up/three-down terrace in the Dingle. As it had been with most of his immediate forebears, unless tempted by the Merchant Navy or compelled by the government to fight foreign foes, nothing suggested that Richard too would not dwell until the grave around this Merseyside suburb that backed onto docklands carved from a plateau of sandstone and granite on the trudging river's final bend before it swept into the Irish Sea.

Since at least the construction of Madryn Street a century earlier, the Starkey name and many of those with whom the family intermarried – Cunningham, Parkin, Bower, Johnson, Parr, Gleave – had been imprinted upon census rolls pertaining to the mean streets of the Dingle-Toxteth area's main thoroughfares, where dray horses still dragged coal for the rusty ships in Gladstone Dock, with its cast-iron bollards. A combination of Victorian custom and hit-or-miss birth-control methods had resulted in many branches of the clan. Particularly prolific were Richard's maternal grandparents, who filled their Toxteth Park home with 14 children. With the port dominating their employment as boiler-makers, tinsmiths, engine-drivers and similar unlettered professions, the Starkey men might have aspired – as Richard would – "to have a semi in a posh part of Liverpool",[1] as his cousins the Fosters did in Crosby.

For the brief time they were together, he and his father were known parochially as Big Richie and Little Richie. Elsie Gleave and Big Richie's eyes had first locked among the cakes and tarts of the bakery where they both worked. Little Richie was the only issue of an unhappy seven-year espousal which began in his Starkey grandparents' house at 59 Madryn Street and ended in divorce in 1943, when Elsie was 29.

Little if any explanation could be offered the boy for why his daddy walked out, but his opinion of the shadowy figure that he was to see henceforth only infrequently was jaundiced to the degree that, on some of the occasions they met, "I wouldn't speak to him. I suppose my mother filled me up with all the things about him."[2] Other than the regular maintenance allowance that he sent, Richard Starkey Senior might as well have been lost in the hostilities that had caused Ministry of Transport officials to remove signposts and direction indicators that might have assisted invading Germans. A few weeks after Little Richie's birth, flares illuminated the sky as the Luftwaffe pounded the docks and the civilian population scurried for shelter.

Sooty foxgloves might have sprung up on the resulting bomb sites, but the Dingle had long been totally unrecognisable as the arcadian meadows where a Viking *thing* ("conclave of elders") had once assembled. One of the seediest districts of the blackened city, it was a huddled land of few illusions – of finger-crushing mangles in communal backyards, rubbish sogging behind railings, outside lavatories, skinny and ferocious cats and corner-shop windows barricaded with wire mesh. Inside the poky brick tangles, naked lightbulbs were coated in dust, damp plaster crumbled at a touch from cold walls, margarine was spread instead of butter and noisy copper geysers hung above sinks in which a wife would both bathe babies and wash up dishes from a Sunday lunch on a newspaper tablecloth. While her spouse slept it off in the cramped living room, the children could be heard beneath sepia skies, hopscotching, footballing and catcalling in the coarsest glottal intonation of a region where even the most refined speakers sounded ambiguously alien and common to anyone south of Birmingham.

"Things were pretty tough for Elsie, as I've always called my mother," Richie would recollect from a decade when a "wacker" accent became exotic. "She tried to bring me up decently. We were poor, but never in rags. I was lucky. I was her only child. She could spend more time with me."[3] Her husband's rancorous departure might have hardened Mrs Starkey's resolve to ensure that Richie was as comfortable and contented as her deprived station would allow. If rather worn, his clothes were always clean, and she'd tuck in his shirt, shine his shoes and brush his hair prior to delivering him to whatever nearby relation or friend was scheduled to mind him while she made ends meet. Four years older than Richie, one such minder, Marie Maguire, became the closest to a sister that he'd ever know while Elsie was busy with diverse menial jobs, such as pulling pints of Tetley's ale behind the bar of the narrow Empress pub, a promontory but a few convenient yards from both 9 Madryn Street and 10 Admiral Grove, where, for its cheaper rent, she and Richie were obliged to move in 1944.

Before overcrowding and subsequent urban renewal caused their borders to overlap, such neighbourhoods saw themselves as a race apart from the rest of Liverpool. *Race* is a crucial word in this most cosmopolitan of settlements, where West Indian immigrants gravitated towards a cluster of Toxteth streets named after Dickensian characters – the Nook pub in Chinatown served the vicinity with English beer, and a Greek Orthodox church stood opposite the Rialto Ballroom in the city centre, then a clattering 20-minute tram ride from Toxteth Dock terminus. The populace was so vulnerable to mixed marriages that the Catholic Information Centre placed boxed warnings in *The Liverpool Echo* about their inherent dangers.

Territorial identity and loyalty sprang from the greater municipal pride that bonded Liverpudlians more firmly than inhabitants of, say, Exeter or Norwich. When a grimy pivot of Victorian commerce, it almost as palpably forged opportunities for cultural development, with Augustus John teaching at the Art School and Dickens giving readings within the imposing Greek façade of the Institute next door. However, by the mid 20th century, a Merseyside artist was regarded as a contradiction in terms, unless a music-hall buffoon like "Big-Hearted Little" Arthur Askey or ukulele-plinking George Formby.

Once pre-eminent in transatlantic and tropical trade, Liverpool had been outflanked economically since the gouging of the Manchester ship canal. With demand for labour at rock bottom in the docks, clerking offices and mills that processed imported raw materials, the only visible reminders of former glory were promenade edifices such as the statue of Edward VII staring towards the hazy hills of North Wales. In between flowed the Mersey, which more than ever lived up to the Old English translation of *Liverpool* as "the place at the pool with thick water", as it was suffused with a soup of industrial pollutants and sewage. A species indigenous to the river was a brown, floating lump known euphemistically as a "Mersey trout". It was often encountered on day trips on the ferry to New Brighton, when, as well as a whirl at the fair, a pleasure-seeker yet chanced a dip in the dung-coloured waters.

Like every other British conurbation, Merseyside was a realm of queues as the country paid for its war with "Utility goods" and rationing that lasted well into the 1950s. Food tablets were available for families like the Starkeys, for whom a meal with chicken – before the grim advent of battery farms – was a most unlikely luxury. Some items were so scarce that you could only get them with weeks of saved-up ration coupons. A Mars bar, for instance, was such an expensive treat then that a knife would divide it between maybe five slavering children.

Less inviting were the third-pint bottles of lukewarm milk provided at morning playtime at school, courtesy of the Welfare State, which also encouraged a massive advertising campaign – centred on Norman Wisdom, the peaked-capped "little man" of British film comedy – to get people to drink more of the stuff for its calcium and vitamins. One of the most loathed desserts of many a late-1940s childhood, milk pudding was very much part of each week's menu.

With geometrically-patterned linoleum the only hint of frivolity in many homes, this drab era was epitomised in Liverpool by the middle-class male from Woolton who, after hours at a ledger in a dark business suit, would relax over a post-dinner crossword in quiet cardigan and baggy trousers. Through lace curtains, his adolescent – *not* teenage – son would glower and wonder if this was all there was. No parent or careers advisor had ever intimated that there might be openings other than in secure but dull jobs like Dad's, with El Dorado a bonus in your wage packet. Perish the thought, but you might be better off as the offspring of some unrespectable Toxteth navvy who didn't frown should you ask to go to the cinema on Sunday and wouldn't disinherit you if you dared to come downstairs in an American tie.

GIs on passes would burst upon the fun-palaces of Liverpool in garb in which, until the foundation of their base at Burtonwood, only blacks, London spivs and the boldest homosexuals would be seen dead – padded shoulders on double-breasted suits with half-belts at the back, "spearpoint" collars, black-and-white shoes and those contentious hand-painted ties with Red Indians or baseball players on them. To the ordinary Scouser, the United States seemed the very wellspring of everything glamorous, from the Coca Cola "Welcoming A Fighting Man Home From The Wars" – so its hoarding ran – to The Ink Spots, whose humming polyphony would enrapture the Liverpool Empire in April 1947. Priscilla White, a docker's daughter who knew the Starkeys, was typical of many young Liverpudlians who "lived in a world where the model of all that was good in life was in a Doris Day movie".[4]

As well as Barkis remarking that Mrs Peggotty "sure knows her cookin'" in a US cartoon-strip edition of David Copperfield, almost as incredible were the Wild West films that Richie came to absorb up to three times a week. He was certain that no one in the Dingle, even in the whole of England, ever talked *thataway*. Neither would an Empress barmaid not bat an eyelid if some *hombre* was plugged full of daylight in the lounge bar. A god descended on Liverpool once when "Singing Cowboy" Roy Rogers rode Trigger from the Adelphi

Hotel down Lime Street to the Empire, but Richie's hero was Gene Autrey, "the Yodelling Cowboy", who was "my first musical experience as a kid. I remember getting shivers up my back when he sang 'South Of The Border'. He had three Mexican guys behind him singing 'Ay-yi-yi-yi...' and he had his guitar."[5]

Cowboy music was more prevalent on Merseyside than anywhere else in England, probably because of the transatlantic seamen, who, as well as importing crew-cuts, "classics" in comic form and Davy Crockett mock-coonskin hats, were as knowledgeable about the Red Foleys, Webb Pierces, Ernest Tubbses and Cowboy Copases of North America as the better known Slim Whitmans, Tennessee Ernie Fords and Tex Ritters. Keeping abreast of new developments in country and western, the Dansette record players of Liverpool crackled with Hank Snow's 'I'm Movin' On', 1952's 'The Wild Side Of Life' by Hank Thompson And His Brazo Valley Boys and 'Down On The Corner Of Love' from Buck Owens, while the rest of the country were still coping with the Davy Crockett craze, 'The Yellow Rose Of Texas', Doris Day riding the Deadwood stage and the clippety-clop offerings of Frankie Laine and Vaughan 'Ghost Riders In The Sky' Monroe.

'Ghost Riders In The Sky' was definitely more exciting to Richie and his St Silas' Church of England Primary School classmates than any native music aired on the British Broadcasting Corporation's three national radio stations, which – with limited needle time – meant Kathleen Ferrier, *The Pirates Of Penzance* and *Melody Time* with the Midland Light Orchestra. Apart from junior geography, the only trace of Americana within the school's Victorian portals was in 'Git Along Little Dogies', 'Polly Wolly Doodle' and other selections from the *Singing Together* pupils' handbook distributed by the monitor during cross-legged music lessons around the upright piano in the main hall, which also served as gymnasium, dining room and for religious assemblies, which were conducted either by the head or by the vicar of the church – also named after the first-century minor apostle – in which Richie's parents had been wed.

The school was a five-minute dawdle from Admiral Grove. Mid-morning passers-by would catch multiplication tables chanted mechanically *en masse* by the older forms, perhaps to the rap of a bamboo cane on a teacher's ink-welled desk. Richie found arithmetic the most trying subject of all the "rubbish shoved into you at school – all those figures".[6]

He didn't endure St Silas' infants for long because of the first serious manifestation of the digestive maladies that were to blight his life. Possibly this delicateness was hereditary, for, like Big Richie, he would always be nauseated by any dish with the vaguest tang of onion or garlic. One afternoon, when he was six, "I felt an awful stab of pain. I remember sweating and being frightened for a while,"[7] when, to the agitated clang of an ambulance bell and clutching his abdomen, he was hastened to the Royal Children's Infirmary on the junction of Myrtle Street, beneath the shadow of the Roman Catholic cathedral, where most of the city's chief medical, penal and higher-educational establishments were clotted.

What was diagnosed initially as a ruptured appendix led to an inflamed peritoneum. In the thick of the inserted tubes and drips after the first operation, there seemed almost no hope of survival as Richie subsided into a coma in the intensive-care cubicle. However, although that pitiful, helpless life could have been taken without effort, Death decided to spare Richard Starkey, although his waxen face would remain pale and silent for nearly two worrying months afterwards. As parental visits were restricted, he was not spoon-fed with familiar sounds, and from more anaesthetised sessions under the scalpel and their painful aftermaths, he surfaced as a persistently poorly old-young creature whose surroundings seemed to fill him with melancholy reflections. Inwardly, however, "I didn't mind too much. I made a lot of friends. Too bad they always got better and left me alone."[7]

His formal education was hampered through the difficulties of running a school in hospital where blackboard work was generally impractical for immobile patients of different ages and abilities, and no new activity could be instigated without a doctor's permission. Much the same applied to the continuance of organisations such as Wolf Cubs and Brownies, as well as occupational therapy like basket-weaving, sketching and participation in the ward band. Richie's would, apparently, be the first hand to shoot up when the teacher sought volunteers to hit a drum as rhythmic pulse to 'Donkey Riding' or 'Down In Demerara'. He'd also be recalled once rat-a-tat-tatting a tin drum in an Orange Day parade. "When he was very young, he always wanted to make a noise on something, empty boxes and suchlike,"[8] Elsie would tell you when the myth gripped harder.

While she visited Myrtle Street whenever she was allowed, his father "came once to see me in hospital with a little notebook to ask me if I wanted anything".[2] On his seventh birthday, and with discharge in sight, Richie – with Grandad Starkey gazing fondly – unwrapped a bright-red toy bus "and drove it 'round and 'round my huge, high bed. When he left, the boy in the next bed looked so sad and lonely, I thought it would be nice to give him my red bus to cheer him up."[9] Leaning over, Richie tumbled to awake from concussed oblivion with burst stitches and the prospect of the rest of 1947 in hospital intensifying his growing inferiority complex.

Back in time to enter St Silas' junior department, he was nicknamed "Lazarus" by some of those who didn't mistake him for a new student. He was still virtually illiterate and would suffer the eventual indignity of being taught with children a year his junior. Among them was a Billy Hatton and – fleetingly – Billy's best friend, Ronnie Wycherley, who was destined to confinements in hospital with rheumatic fever and the damaged heart that would kill him.

Even the Dingle's most godless accorded an outward respect for its priesthood, and if neither St Silas nor his mother turned Richie into a devout churchgoer then he would adhere to a belief in life after death, even when he no longer "prayed and sung hymns. I've done everything our religion talks about, but it doesn't mean all that for me."[10] In a word-association game years later, Richie's reaction to "Christmas" was "happy times...food and drink... It doesn't mean anything religious to me".[11] Without the usual companionships nurtured during an uninterrupted school regime, he grew pensive and rather solitary, weeping when scolded or emotionally moved. His appearance suited him – shortish and hangdog, with flexible thick lips, crooked nose, droopy Pagliacci eyes and grey streaks in his brown hair and right eyebrow. His appearance was also more than faintly comical, and that also suited him. Like Tommy Cooper and Ken Dodd, "I have a face which seems to make people laugh."[1] Verbally, he was comparable to Dr William Spooner, in that he didn't have to try to be funny. Rather than conscious narrative jokes, his attempts to nutshell oral discussions in class and on the playground were often inadvertently hilarious because, although his wits would creak, quiver and jolt into life, his thoughts would emerge from his lips almost as mangled as a Stanley Unwin monologue. People amused themselves by getting him to talk.

At St Silas' and, next, Dingle Vale Secondary Modern, he was as well known for this quirk as bullies and cricket captains were in their spheres. Elsie had paid Marie Maguire to help him catch up with his reading with twice-weekly exercises from a primer, but, despite her conscientious efforts, Richie – by no means bookish and forever an unorthodox speller – had still been ineligible to even sit the Eleven Plus examination to determine whether he'd move up to a grammar school or instead go to a secondary modern, where the "failures" went.

As laughable as it was that he should sit with clever Billy Hatton at the Bluecoat Grammar School in Wavertree, unblinking in the monotony of Euclid's knottier theorems and Caesar's Gallic Wars, Richie found his own level at Dingle Vale, where he was judged "a quiet, thoughtful type, although working rather slowly. Academic work will no doubt improve in time, as he is trying to do his best."[12] Positioned academically around the middle of the lowest stream, he was poor at music, which was then taught as a kind of mathematics, in which a dotted crotchet was expressed diagramatically by "three of the little milk-bottles you have at school".[13] However, Starkey of 2C wasn't too bad at art, while at drama he "takes a real interest and has done very well".[12] He was also discovered to possess an aptitude for mechanics, so much so that later he'd have no qualms about dismantling a car engine and putting it back together again.

In one 1952 term, Richard was absent on 34 occasions, not all of which were through illness. His "A" standard for conduct implies that teachers were ignorant of his bouts of truancy with their *leitmotif*s of petty shop-lifting and smutty stories over communal cigarettes. Indeed, a legacy of these delinquent days was the smoking that he'd never have the will to stop. He'd already promoted his first alcoholic black-out "when I was nine. I was on my knees, crawling drunk. A friend of mine's dad had the booze ready for Christmas, so we decided to try all of it out. I don't remember too much."[14] An appalled Elsie would always remember, but she never knew then that he sometimes spent his dinner-money on "a few pennyworth of chips and a hunk of bread and save the rest for the fairground or the pictures".[7]

Revelling in his wickedness, Richie and his cronies would seek refuge in cinemas outside Dingle Vale's catchment area. While denouncing Roy Rogers, Hopalong Cassidy *et al* as "kids' stuff", there was still much to please Starkey in this escapist post-war epoch of Martians, robots and outer space things, although he inclined towards the more thought-provoking movies of this genre, such as *The Day The Earth Stood Still*, in which spaceman Michael Rennie lands in Washington, DC, to curb the Earthlings' self-destructive tendencies. During other idle hours, an acned youth would slobber over Hollywood's platinum blondes and identify with lonesome anti-heroes like narcissistic and defeatist James Dean or the more mature Victor Mature, whom Richie preferred as "tough but likeable – a guy for the lads of 15 to look up to".[15] With an intelligent rather than intellectual passion for the flicks, he "admired people like Elizabeth Taylor, Marlon Brando, Burt Lancaster and Fred Astaire. They never give bad performances."[15]

In another field of entertainment, Richie was also a fan of "Prince of Wails" Johnnie Ray, who anticipated the exhibitionism that would pervade rock 'n' roll. The intrinsic content of his stage repertoire, however, was much the same as that emitted from lustier throats during the merrier evenings in the Empress, when drinkers would be drawn into 'Sonny Boy', 'Bye Bye Blackbird', Doris Day's 'Sentimental Journey', 'Night And Day' and more cosy unison singalongs about roses and stardust. Furthermore, like contemporaries such as Cab Calloway, Jo Stafford, Guy Mitchell and The Platters, who also included Liverpool Empire on their European tour itineraries, Ray's spot was preceded by jugglers, trick cyclists, comedians and other variety turns. Nevertheless, in his mid 20s, Johnnie was the wildest act going in an age when popular vocalists were generally approaching middle life before achieving worthwhile recognition.

Against the heavily masculine images of the Tennessee Ernie Ford school of singers, frail Ray was as unlikely a star as, well, Richard Starkey; but, with his hearing-aid visible from the audience during the 'cry-guy' hamminess of 'The Little White Cloud That Cried' – his own composition – and the thwarted eroticism of 'Such A Night', women had hysterics and circle stalls buckled wherever he went. Nonetheless, Johnnie became dismayingly human to Richie, who was among the rapt crowd watching him *sip coffee* in a window of the Adelphi. "He was eating in fancy restaurants and waving at people from big hotels, and I thought, 'There! That's the life for me.'"[16]

Sucking on a Woodbine with either Johnnie Ray crackling from the Dansette or Vic Mature before him on the fleapit screen, Richie might have declared, had he read Wordsworth, that "to be young was very heaven" – although not for long, even if domestic conditions had improved after Elsie was able to give up work on marrying – with her son's approval – a painter and decorator from Romford whom she'd met via the Maguires. Of mild disposition and steady character, Harry Graves came to be accepted by a community not that removed from what he'd known back in the Cockney end of Essex.

During a half-term holiday in 1953, the new "stepladder" – so Richie in his gobbledegook dubbed Harry – took his wife and stepson over the edge of the world for a few days with his parents in Romford, where the obstinate 13-year-old refused to don a raincoat when caught in a thunderstorm of Wagnerian intensity. A simple sniff chilled to chronic pleurisy and another spell in Myrtle Street before lung complications necessitated Richie's transfer to the cleaner air of Heswall Children's Hospital in the rural Wirral.

Again, his schooling suffered, and it was officially over by 1955, when he'd regained sufficient strength to go home (where there was now a black-and-white television). All that remained was the formality of returning to Dingle Vale "to get the certificate to prove I'd left. You needed that to get a job. They didn't even remember I'd been there."[17] More humbling was an interview at the Youth Employment Office, where, if he agreed to a secondment to Riverside Technical College to complete basic education, there was a vacancy for a delivery boy with British Rail. It wasn't exactly the Pony Express but, if he stuck at it, he could finish up half a century later as a retired station master with a gold watch.

Whatever the secrets behind doors marked "Private" on every main platform, little intrigued Starkey after a week or so of errands that a child could run. Vanity demanded a uniform to be worn with negligent importance, but, in order to signify that here was a man engaged in man's work, he was given a mere *kepi*, as "you had to do 20 years to get the rest. Anyway, I failed their medical and left after a couple of months."[2]

In the regulation-issue, two-tone jacket of a barman/waiter, his next job was on a passenger steamer pottering between George's Landing Stage and New Brighton. He bumped up his wages of £3 and ten shillings wages with tips picked up mostly during peak hours, when he had hardly a second to himself, dashing from table to table with a trayful of drinks.

He played hard, too, especially when someone's parents were away for the weekend and "we had parties [where] everyone gets drunk and passes out".[18] With all but miniatures beyond individual pockets, spirits were not so much in evidence as Newcastle Brown and Devon cider in living rooms transformed into dens of iniquity by dimming table lamps with headscarves and pushing back armchairs to create an arena for smooching as a prelude to snogging and attacks of "desert sickness".[19] The soundtrack to this effused from the 78rpm discs that would be scattered around the Dansette in the corner.

Not so brittle were the plastic 45s that started to supersede 78s in 1955, a streamlining that was an apt herald of the "teenager", a word now coined to donate all those 'twixt twelve and 20 who were deciding whether or not they wished to grow up. Yet, even after the generation gap widened and the new breed received as independent "consumers", the BBC – as a universal aunt with its stranglehold over the nation's electric media – gave the public only that music that it ought to want, hence *The Black And White Minstrel Show*, the veletas and tangos of Victor Sylvester's *Come Dancing*, *Spot The Tune* with Marion Ryan and Cy Grant's calypsos during his slot on Cliff Michelmore's topical *Tonight* magazine.

Some supposed that the "square" sounds they picked up on the Light Programme were because they were listening on a cheap wireless, but from new Braun transistor to cumbersome radiogram it was the same on all of them, for also directed at the over-30s were shows monopolised by such as The Beverley Sisters and Donald Peers ("The Cavalier Of Song"), as well as musical interludes in those built around the ilk of ventriloquist's dummy Archie Andrews, "Mr Pastry" and Lancastrian "schoolboy" Jimmy Clitheroe. "Not one of my favourite comedians,"[16] said Richard Starkey.

The search for anything teenage was just as fruitless on Independent Television (ITV) when it began in 1956 with weekly spectaculars headlined by North America's Patti Page ("The Singing Rage") and, straight from fronting some palais bandstand, Dickie Valentine in stiff evening dress. While *Round About Ten* was a bit racy in its embrace of Humphrey Lyttelton's Jazz Band, the inclusion of The Teenagers – a winsome boy-girl troupe – in Vera Lynn's *Melody Cruise* was something of a false dawn.

Bandleader Ted Heath didn't "think rock 'n' roll will come to Britain. You see, it is primarily for the coloured population."[20] However, penetrating the BBC and its rival's snug little kingdoms as 1955 mutated into 1956 was a cover version of black rhythm and blues combo Sonny Dae And The Knights' 'Rock Around The Clock' by Bill Haley And The Comets, a paunchy US dance group. "When [Haley] came out," noticed Richie, "he was about 28, but when you're about 14 or 15 anyone at 28 is like your dad."[21] Nevertheless, the record was a hit with teenagers after adult blood ran cold at its metronomic clamour. Incited by the newspapers, girls jived in gingham and flat ballet shoes while pen-knives slit cinema seats when

Haley's movie of the same name – "the old backstage plot spiced with the new music",[22] quoth *Picturegoer* – reached these islands. Priscilla White was "told off for getting my school blazer ripped. Everybody was going mad and jumping about the aisles, and that was only for a film. I put sugar and water on my hair to get a Bill Haley kiss-curl. I tried milk as well, because that is supposed to dry the hair up. It was quite big, wasn't it, that kiss curl cut?"[23]

Haley would tender apologies at press conferences for his Comets' knockabout stage routines, but what with this "rock" nonsense going so well it'd have been bad business not to have played up to it, wouldn't it? Anyway, one of the band had served under Benny Goodman. Even with five concurrent entries in the newly established *New Musical Express* record-sales chart (or "hit parade"), Bill was more harmless than Johnnie Ray had proved to be. However, even as "the Creep", hula-hooping and the cha-cha-cha were proffered as the next short-lived fads, rock 'n' roll put forward a more suitable champion in a Tennessean named Elvis Presley, who dressed as a hybrid of amusement-arcade hoodlum and nancy boy. With an electric guitarist shifting from simple fills to full-blooded clangorous solo, Presley's first single had been a jumped-up treatment of a negro blues. From then on, his embroidered shout-singing and sulky balladeering had become both adored and detested throughout the free world.

Reports of Presley's unhinged go-man-go sorcery in concert caused Methodist preacher (and jazz buff) Dr Donald Soper to wonder "how intelligent people can derive satisfaction from something which is emotionally embarrassing and intellectually ridiculous".[24] Of the new sensation's debut UK release, 'Heartbreak Hotel', the staid *NME* wrote, "If you appreciate good singing, I don't suppose you'll manage to hear this disc all through."[25] What more did Elvis need to be the rage of teenage Britain? "It was all so new and exciting," enthused Richie. "No one believes what an effect that had on my life, just this lad with sideboards and shaking his pelvis and being absolutely naughty, [although] if you look back on those photos now he had big baggy trousers and it was all a bit weird."[26]

Although Tin Pan Alley's nose was put out of joint at the proportionally meagre sheet music sales, when it transpired that 60 per cent of the RCA record company's output for 1956 was by Elvis the hunt was up for similar money-making morons. Needless to say, these sprouted thickest in the States, where countless talent-scouts thought that all that was required was a lop-sided smirk and gravity-defying cockade. Many saw Jerry Lee Lewis as just an Elvis who substituted piano for guitar and hollered arrogance for hot-potato-in-the-mouth mumbling. While Capitol was lumbered with a pig in a poke in crippled, unco-operative Gene Vincent ("The Screaming End"), Acuff-Rose would snare two for the price of one in The Everly Brothers. There were black Presleys in Chuck Berry and shrieking Little Richard, female ones like Wanda Jackson and Janis Martin and a mute one in guitarist Duane Eddy. After Carl Perkins – an unsexy one – came bespectacled Buddy Holly and unsexy and bespectacled Roy Orbison with his eldritch cry and misgivings about the up-tempo rockers he was made to record by Sam Phillips, owner of Sun, the Memphis studio where Elvis had first smouldered onto tape.

Just as uncomfortable an Elvis was Tommy Steele, his innocuous English "answer", who, before abdicating to make way for Cliff Richard, had his effigy waxed for Madame Tussaud's and was sent up by Peter Sellers – of BBC Radio's *Goon Show* – as "Mr Iron", who "doesn't want to bite the fretboard that fed me". Despite finding rock 'n' roll objectionable, powers at the BBC were obliged to cater for Steele, Presley and their sort's disciples when the continental commercial station Radio Luxembourg began broadcasting pop showcases in English and ITV broke the tacit "toddler's truce" by filling what was previously a blank screen between 6pm and 7pm. The Corporation countered with *Six-Five Special* to keep teenagers out of trouble between the football results and *Dixon Of Dock Green* while their parents put younger siblings to bed.

Dr Soper might have watched it "as a penance"[24] but *Six-Five Special* sought to preserve a little decency by employing such upstanding interlocutors as disc jockey Pete Murray – who abhorred Elvis – and former boxing champion Freddie Mills. Comedy sketches, string quartets and features on sport and hobbies were inserted between the pop, which – as well as "rock 'n' roll" by such as trombonist Don Lang and his Frantic Five – was made to encompass Dickie Valentine, Joe "Mr Piano" Henderson plus traditional jazz and its by-product, skiffle – which was ruled by singing guitarist Lonnie Donegan, an ex-serviceman who reviled rock 'n' roll as "a gimmick. Like all gimmicks, it is sure to die the death. Let's hope it will happen soon. Nothing makes me madder than to be bracketed with those rock 'n' roll boys."[22]

Despite himself, Lonnie would be remembered as a more homogenously British equivalent of Elvis than Tommy Steele through his vibrant fusion of black rhythms and the music hall, especially after he broadened his appeal with 'Have A Drink On Me' and other gems from the golden days of the Empire. Moreover, anyone who'd mastered basic techniques could attempt skiffle. In fact, the more home-made your sound the better, for no one howled with derision if an amateur skiffle group included broom-handle-and-tea-chest bass, washboards tapped with thimbles and perhaps dustbin-lid cymbals. These and chords slashed on acoustic guitars were at the core of its contagious backbeat. Over this, certain outfits found a unique style even with 'The Grand Coolee Dam', 'Midnight Special' and other set works. "That's where half the enjoyment lies," pontificated one of skiffle's lesser icons, Bob Cort, "in experimenting with ideas."[27]

You had to be sharp to discriminate between them, but there evolved regional shades of skiffle, with Merseyside leaning – as might be expected – towards country and western. As well as an emulation of Nashville's Grand Ole Opry at Liverpool's Philharmonic Hall in 1955, there would be more than 40 local cowboy groups operational in what was christened "the Nashville of the North" by the late 1950s. All looking as if they'd cut their teeth on a branding iron, the likes of Johnny Goode And His Country Kinfolk, Phil Brady And The Ranchers and – still going strong 40 years later – Hank Walters And His Dusty Road Ramblers plundered the North American motherlode, covering all waterfronts from Slim Whitman's falsetto "sweetcorn" to the hard country of Hank Williams, with its unusual absorption with rhythm.

Also with names as homely as hitching posts, there grew younger splinter groups, many defying licensing laws concerning minors when playing the 300-odd venues affiliated to the Liverpool Social Clubs Association. Not old enough to quaff even a cherryade in these taverns, Billy Hatton moonlighted in such a band while his friend Brian O'Hara was guitarist in Gerry Marsden's Skiffle Group, an outfit connected genealogically to Hank Walters' bunch. Modelling themselves more on Flint McCullough, scout with BBC's *Wagon Train*, or half-breed "Cheyenne" Bodie over on ITV, some traded under fiercer nomenclatures: Clay Ellis And The Raiders, The James Boys – after pistol-packin' Jesse – and, later, Johnny Sandon and The Searchers (from a John Wayne movie).

With National Service soon to be abolished, "everyone took up guitars instead of guns",[10] generalised Richie, and too real was the boom in demand for the instruments in central Liverpool music shops like Rushworth's and Hessy's. Even Eddie Miles, the Starkeys' next door neighbour's teenage son, had purchased one. Nevertheless, as Richie had lost interest when once a member of an accordion band that practised in the drill hall opposite St Silas Church, so he lacked the application to teach himself to strum a guitar – although from somewhere or other he'd absorb a rudimentary three-chord trick in A major, and the same on piano, but in C. Such a knack was, however, incidental to his self-image as "just one of those loony Teddy Boys standing on the corner".[28]

Undersized, homely and of depressed circumstance, he was ripe to "run about with gangs in the Dingle as a tearaway with a Tony Curtis haircut, crêpe shoes and drape with a velvet collar".[3] Along with the sports coat and sensible shoes, mothballed forever were the cavalry twills, as around his legs now were circulation-impeding drainpipes tapering into fluorescent socks with a rock 'n' roll motif. His short back and sides now only a recollection, his longer tresses were now teased into a quiffed glacier of Brilliantine.

Out for more than boyish mischief these days, he was typical of many formerly tractable young men who, bored silly by slide-shows and ping-pong, would get themselves barred from church youth clubs by either brandishing a blatant Woodbine or letting slip a "bloody" in front of some cardiganned curate. Chewing gum in an Elvis half-sneer, they'd take to the streets of desolate housing estates or the hinterland near the docks, where decent folk would cross over to avoid a swaggering phalanx of Teds with brass rings decorating their fists like knuckledusters.

Saying "bloody" and even ruder words unreproached, Richie tagged along with seedy-flash louts of more powerful build and sideburns like the boot of Italy as they barracked in cinemas (except during the sexy bits, when they'd go all quiet) and, without paying, barged *en bloc* into dance halls, particularly ones where Teds – "and coloureds" – were refused admission. Once inside, they'd be studied – not always surreptitiously – by girls with ruby-red lips, tight sweaters, wide belts and pony-tails who – in their imaginations, at least – were as elfin as Audrey Hepburn in *Roman Holiday*. If pursuit of romance was either unsuccessful or not the principal mass objective of the expedition, Teds would seek more brutal sensual recreation. If you so much as glanced at them, the action could be *you*. A meek reproof by the victim had sparked off the first Teddy Boy murder on a London heath in 1954. Nevertheless, Merseyside was the setting for *These Dangerous Years* and *Violent Playground*, 1957 films supposedly reflecting the corruptness of the "new" cult, with local boy Freddie Fowell playing a gang leader.

Although runtish, Richie tried to look the part with a belt studded with washers stolen from work. "But I wasn't a fighter," he reflected. "More of a dancer, really, though that could be dangerous if you danced with someone else's bird."[6] Yet it wasn't in a ballroom where he paired off with a bird of his own, Patricia Davies, who was three years younger, fair and sufficiently *petite* not to tower over him. At the same secondary school – St Anthony of Padua's in Mossley Hill – she'd become friendly with red-head Priscilla White when both cherished ambitions to be hairdressers. "The soul of patience",[4] Elsie Graves was a Wednesday-evening guinea pig for the giggling would-be stylists as, after cooking them a tea, she allowed Pat and Cilla to "bleach her hair and do terrible things to it".[4]

When Pat was superseded by another local spinster called Geraldine, she may have consoled herself with the submission that, if you were after a man for his money, Elsie's lad wasn't much of a catch, especially after he was sacked from the ferry when, on clocking in direct from an all-night party, he was emboldened enough by booze to impart pent-up home truths to his supervisor. However, Harry was able to persuade Henry Hunt & Sons, an engineering firm specialising in gymnasium and swimming pool equipment, to take on his stepson as a trainee joiner, as it had Eddie Miles.

Richie's overalled apprenticeship began badly when he bruised his thumb with a hammer on the very first day and vertigo stranded him tremulous with terror on a high diving board during an installment job in faraway Cardiff Public Baths. But he wasn't as infinitesimal a human cog at Hunt's as he'd been with the railway. By doggedly cranking and riveting from 8am until 5.30pm day upon day for the next seven years, the road to self-advancement and that "semi in a posh part of Liverpool" would be clearer.

2 "Well, I Thought I Was The Best Drummer There Was"

Against the odds, Liverpool spawned a generous fistful of hit-parade entrants during the 1950s. Like Arthur Askey *et al*, they'd had to head south to Make It because moguls from Britain's four major record companies (centred in London), if obliged to visit Manchester, "the entertainment capital of the North", rarely made time to also negotiate the 36 miles west to sound out talent. Besides, why should Merseyside's ratio of pop artists be larger than that in any other port, or indeed anywhere at all? After all, Hull had produced only million-selling David Whitfield and Bristol pianist Russ Conway, heart-throb of BBC's *Billy Cotton Band Show*. Liverpool had had more than its fair share with Lita Roza and her chart-topping copy of Patti Page's 'How Much Is That Doggie In The Window' and Frankie Vaughan, who was to oust Dickie Valentine as Britain's most popular male singer in 1958's *NME* readers' poll.

Civic pride in these triumphs was dampened by a poor showing on the rock 'n' roll front with merely Russ Hamilton – beforehand Ronald Hulme of Everton – on *Six-Five Special* with his gentle, lisping croon.[1] Only a rocker by affinity, too, was Edna Savage, a Liverpool lass who became a 1956 one-hit-wonder on Parlophone, an EMI subsidiary, through the ministrations of her producer, George Martin, with whom some too linked her romantically. However, in 1958 she married Terry Dene, another *Six-Five Special* regular. In an enormous polkadot bow tie and hair dyed shocking pink, the best man was Wee Willie Harris, who was bruited by his

34

manager as London's – and, by implication, the entire kingdom's – very own Jerry Lee Lewis.

Liverpool had no Jerry Lee, but there were myriad aspirant Donegans, from The Hi-Hats – formed within the Mercury Cycle Club – to Crosby's James Boys, who, from intermission spots, were now main attraction at dances held at that suburb's "Jive Hive", otherwise known as St Luke's Hall. As The Two Jays, Billy Hatton and another guitarist, Joey Bower, had landed a six-week residency in a club on the Isle of Man.

Northwest of the Dingle, and then almost on the city's perimeter, Stoneycroft threw down a gauntlet in 1957 with The Texan Skiffle Group, led by Alan Caldwell, a tall youth with a wavy blond tousle and lean frame, whose parents, Violet and Ernie, supported his and his older sister Iris' activities with a zest that other mums and dads might have thought excessive. In the Caldwells' tidy Victorian house off the leafy Oakhill Park estate, the children's friends were welcome at all hours, Violet often rising from slumber to make them snacks.

She had much to boast about in Iris and Alan. The daughter had passed the Eleven Plus and, if less academically distinguished, Alan was extrovert champion of many a school sports day and football match. He'd brag that he held the "unofficial" British underwater record of 73 yards, but more verifiable was his swim one summer holiday across Lake Windermere, as much a feat of his, Ernie's and Violet's will as stamina.

The Caldwells also encouraged more glamorous endeavours, applauding the personable Iris in her choice to transfer from her city centre grammar to Broad Green School of Dancing, within walking distance of home. As their son had progressed at his own pace on the family's upright piano, he merely had to ask for a guitar when it became associated less with flamenco than with Lonnie Donegan. Like the late King George VI, Alan was cursed with a stammer, but it was noticed that this vanished whenever he sang with his group, which – to the consternation of sensitive neighbours – was allowed to rehearse in the front room. When the unit was ready for engagements, Mrs Caldwell would act as its agent, ordering a gross of business cards emblazoned with the legend "Presented By Downbeat Promotions" from a Wavertree printer.

With Violet's blessing, too, 16-year-old Alan opened the Morgue Skiffle Cellar in March 1958. With appropriate skeletons painted in luminous white on black walls, it was located in the starkly lit basement of a huge semi-derelict house – originally a home for retired nurses – in Oak Hill Park. Up to 100 customers would tap their feet twice a week to Caldwell's and other local combos, such as The Hi-Fi's and The Quarry Men, until a raid just over a year later by police acting on (not groundless) allegations that the Morgue was a place of ill repute where boys smoked and girls got pregnant.

Whatever he got up to in his spare time, Alan's day job – in a cotton mill – wasn't exactly showbusiness, but it would do while he looked for opportunities beyond youth clubs and parties to become a professional entertainer. The Group, therefore, took part in every talent showcase advertised, whether it be in village hall or at the Rialto Ballroom, right in the heart of Liverpool. Twice in three months, they turned out at Garston's Winter Gardens auditorium, where the days were won by, respectively, "rock 'n' roll comedian" Jimmy Tarbuck and Ronald Wycherley, who was making a go of it as a singer. For as little as a round of fizzy drinks, The Texan Skiffle Group could be hired for such salubrious venues as Old Swan's Stanley Abattoir Social Club.

Meanwhile, Caldwell's aptitude for athletics didn't wither, as he often elected to sprint home rather than wait for a bus, even after relatively distant bookings such as the Casbah in Hayman's Green. In spring 1958, he was picked for the Pembroke Harriers team for a cross-country event in London. After finishing, Alan couldn't go home without sampling an evening at Chas McDevitt's Skiffle Cellar in Soho, once Tommy Steele and Terry Dene's stomping ground. Still a prestigious showcase, even skifflers in the sticks considered a booking either here or, in the same square mile, the 2I's, the Gyre and Gimble and Trafalgar Square's Safari Club to be worthwhile, in case foremost pop impresario Larry Parnes or a svengali like him spotted them. The Saints, a group formed by pupils at a Norwich grammar, ran away from home and slept in doorways in order to audition there. Two members of the band – guitarists Kenny Packwood and Tony Sheridan – stayed on to back Marty Wilde, a more successful testee. As well as Wilde, Adam Faith and others who received more immediate acclaim, hit-makers from later eras of British pop – among them Spencer Davis, Gary Glitter and, all the way from Glasgow, Alex Harvey – also entertained at McDevitt's.

On the night that he was there, Dame Fortune smiled on Alan Caldwell, who, after giving an impromptu performance, was able to solicit a one-song spot – with 'Midnight Special' – for The Texan Skiffle Group on Radio Luxembourg's *Skiffle Club*, which was recorded in Manchester. Historically, they were the first such Merseyside act to broadcast in this manner, a fact not greatly appreciated at the time.

Of more pragmatic import was the Group's victory in a talent contest instigated by *The People* newspaper and holiday camp potentate Billy Butlin. With this placing them a cut above others of their kind, Iris – now earning £7 a week as a circus showgirl for a summer season in the Welsh holiday resort of Rhyl – was able to whisper in the right ears before she moved south to more lucrative work at a Butlins camp in Pwllheli. Through Iris, her brother's band secured a place low on the bill of a presentation back in Rhyl headlined by Marion Ryan. Ernie and Violet drove down to catch their golden boy's biggest moment thus far.

A mainstay in his Group's constant flux of musicians was John Byrnes, who, with a more transient guitarist, Paul Murphy (who would later assume the stage surname Rogers[2]) – a pal of Richard Starkey – had actually spent several hours in a local recording studio taping an Everly Brothers-style version of Charlie Gracie's 1957 hit 'Butterfly'. Like Alan, John wasn't a musician for the sake of his health. Indeed, Byrnes and Caldwell were all that remained of the band when it was decided to hack the word "Skiffle" from its name for a relaunch as Al Caldwell's Texans, because groups who still used instruments made from household implements had become *passé* and, worse, insufferably square, after physics professors with clipped beards conducted "experiments with skiffle" at London University; Sunday School teachers seized upon it as a medium through which to promote youthful Christianity; and Dickie Valentine covered 'Putting On The Style', Donegan's second Number One. None of them quite got the point. Into the bargain, washboard players had trouble joining the Musicians' Union, and were thus prohibited from defiling the stage at some venues.

The more "sophisticated" skiffle acts that hadn't fallen by the wayside switched to traditional jazz, but most backslid, via cautious amplification, to rock 'n' roll and an increasingly more American UK hit parade. Not alone in the practice of magnifying his volume by simply shoving a microphone through the hole in his acoustic six-string was the lead guitarist with Seaforth's Bobby Bell Rockers, who had been in existence since Bell (*né* Crawford) had seen Freddie Bell And The Bellboys in Bill Haley's *Rock Around The Clock* movie in 1956. Nonetheless, it wasn't wise to disagree when "Kingsize" Taylor – burly front man with The Dominoes, formerly The James Boys – argued that "we were the first rock group in the city, but around the same time there were two other groups – Cass And The Cassanovas and The Seniors – who also claim to be first".[3] No Russ Hamilton, either, was The Cassanovas' ambidextrous percussive aggressor, Johnny Hutchinson, who wielded reversed sticks so that the heavier ends battered his drum kit. Not to his taste was the lighter touch necessary to emphasise vocal polyphony in such as Ian And The Zodiacs – The Dominoes' rivals as north Liverpool's boss group – and Gerry And The Pacemakers, led by Gerry Marsden.

Before re-entering the lists, The Texans held exhaustive auditions which, because of the space required for electronic paraphernalia and drums, spilled into the Caldwells' hall. There but not participating was Jimmy Tarbuck, to whom one supplicant – a guitarist called George Harrison – was already familiar, having attended the same primary school. Also too young and inexperienced was a Graham Bonnet from Manchester, where the fame of the boys who'd been 'guest stars' to Marion Ryan had spread, thanks to Alan's mum's publicity machine and the local press.

With the chastening knowledge that Kingsize and his boys had just recorded ten numbers in Crosby's Lambda Studio, a glorified garage, Alan and John elected to make up lost time by plunging in with Texans drawn from a mutable pool of players shared with other groups, such as guitarist Charles O'Brien from The Hi-Fi's and the drummer with The Darktown Skiffle Group. His name was Richie Starkey.

For beer money and a laugh, Starkey and Eddie Miles had started The Eddie Clayton Skiffle Group in early 1957. As well as its more down-home connotations, "Clayton" rolled off the tongue easier than "Miles" and looked better, symmetrically. Augmented by three of Hunt's other employees – notably Roy Trafford, a singing tea-chest bass plucker – and someone with a telephone acting as their "manager", the Group moved from canteen concerts at work to a debut at Peel Street Labour Club in Toxteth and entering a skiffle contest at St Luke's Hall. Although they weren't placed, the lads weren't that dismayed because they, like most amateur skifflers, saw the group as a vocational blind alley. No one took it seriously.

No better or worse than any other tin-pot combo taking its cue from Godhead Donegan, The Eddie Clayton Skiffle Group also adhered to Bob Cort's *New Musical Express* dictum concerning "visual effect",[4] although Starkey, with his woebegone countenance, might have been hard pressed by the bit about "however worried you are, never let it show".[4] In bootlace ties and shirts of the same colour, the Clayton outfit were as one, too, with Cort's "some sort of uniform is a great help, though ordinary casual clothes are perhaps the best as long, as you all wear exactly the same".[4]

From the onset, it was decided that Richie should play drums, "because it was the only thing I could do".[5] Apart from rattling about on biscuit tins (with Cadbury's Roses the most authentic snare-drum sound), the cheapest option was a "Viceroy skiffle board" – an *NME*-advertised "tapbox" with miniature drum, washboard, cowbell and hooter that, for 39 shillings and sixpence, was "ideal for parties and playing with radio or gramophone". However, a combo of Eddie Clayton's calibre deserved at the very least a Broadway "Kat" snare-and-cymbal set costing £10 4s.

While visiting Romford, Harry Graves paid slightly less for a second-hand drum kit[6] of indeterminate make for his stepson. This was lugged onto the train and Harry sat with it throughout the journey back to Lime Street, where he dragged it over to the taxi rank. He wondered how much gratitude he could expect from Richie, who – so the tale goes – had been furious when Elsie, with the best of intentions, had arranged for him to attend an exploratory rehearsal on hearing that someone in the next street was in a "proper" band. "You can imagine how I felt," he snorted, "when this turned out to be a silver band playing old Sousa marches and all that in a local park."[7]

Richie was, however, delighted with Harry's gift, even if he'd become rather scornful of Teddy Boy rock 'n' roll recently, even giving away his collection of 78s to one of his foster cousins. Although it was finding favour more with collegians as a sign of maturity, Richie too had been infected with an apparent appreciation of traditional jazz, but then "that got boring, and I went through modern jazz – Chico Hamilton, Yusuf Lateef, people like that – but there's no great urge in any of them".[8] After a short while, he ceased striving to drop buzz-words like "Monk" and "Brubeck" into conversations, but a legacy of this phase was Starkey's purchase of 1958's 'Topsy Part Two', a 45 based on a 1930s standard and focused on a solo by virtuoso American drummer Cozy Cole, although "I've never been one to buy drum records".[8]

Cole stood on the sidelines of the *NME*'s Top 30, and – to the disgust of veteran drumming aesthetes from Jack Parnell to Buddy Rich – other jazz- and swing-band percussionists were also making records that bordered on pop, twirling their sticks gratuitously and forming contingent rock 'n' roll combos in which subtle cross-rhythms and dotted bebop crochets on the ride cymbal – *ching-a-ching-ching* – had no part. In Britain, such lapsed jazzers as Tony Crombie – who would accompany Wee Willie Harris – and Rory Blackwell were now socking a crude but powerful offbeat less like that of Haley – whose 'Rock Around The Clock' rim-shots were actually quite tricky – than those of Louis Jordan, Bill Doggett, Big

Joe Turner and other late-1940s R&B exponents, possibly so that their gold-digging could be justified because "blues is the main content of jazz",[9] according to skiffle scribe Brian Bird.

With no such pretensions, US drummers such as Preston Epps and Earl Palmer were less ashamedly jumping on the rock bandwagon. Chief among them was Sandy Nelson, a Californian who was the percussion equivalent of Duane Eddy in that his hits – like 'Teenbeat' and a revival of such as The Bob Crosby Orchestra's 'Let It Be Drums' of 1940 – were pared down to monotonous beat against a menacing guitar ostinato. He even had the nerve to refashion thus 'Big Noise From Winnetka' by Gene Krupa, who was then such a jazz legend that he was to be the subject of a 1960 biopic.

Britain struck back with Tony Meehan from Cliff Richard's backing quartet The Drifters – later The Shadows – in LP tracks like 'See You In My Drums', underlined with bass pulsation. A *protégé* of Rory Blackwell, Jimmy Nicol – a former Boosey & Hawkes drum repairer – replaced Crombie behind Wee Willie and then backed Vince Eager. Next, he was sent on tour by Eager's manager, the celebrated Larry Parnes, with his own New Orleans Rockers, who planted feet in both the trad and rock 'n' roll camps.

While Nicol's path would interweave briefly with that of Starkey's, a less shooting-star destiny awaited Burnley's Bobby Elliott, who drummed for a local mainstream jazz orchestra and splattered patterns and accents across bar-lines in a club trio that supported visiting instrumentalists like saxophonists Harold McNair and Don Rendell. Although modern jazz was "all I ever listened to and all I ever watched",[10] he capitulated to the rock 'n' roll and higher engagement fees of the town's Jerry Storm And The Falcons.

Compared to Elliott, Starkey's passion for jazz was scarcely more than a sudden flirtation that ran cold when he realised that, for all his natural sense of rhythm, life was too short to tolerate carping tutorials and "go 'rump-a-bump'"[8] for hours daily to be like Krupa – although he initially attacked his new kit with gusto, showing no signs of ever stopping. Finally admitting to himself that he – like Johnny Hutchinson – was an unadulterated rock 'n' roller, he developed his hand-and-foot co-ordination, accurate time-keeping and even the beginnings of a naïve personal style by trial and error, but "because of the noise",[11] which irritated the entire terrace, his mother – who was no Violet Caldwell – allowed him only 30 minutes of crashing about per evening upstairs in number 10's small back room "and I got really bored just sitting there banging because you can't play any tunes".[8]

In the kitchen, when he'd finished, Elsie would object to him smiting the furniture with his sticks to music from the wireless, "and that was it for me, practising. Drumming's simple. I've always believed the drummer is not there to interrupt the song."[12] Later, he'd liken it to "painting. I am the foundation, and then I put a bit of glow here and there, but it must have solid substance for me. If there's a gap, I want to be good enough to fill it. I like holes to come in."[8]

Drum solos were tedious to him, and if ever he had a pet hate amongst their perpetrators it was bandleader Buddy Rich, who was every smart-alec's notion of percussive splendour because "he does things with one hand I can't do with nine, but that's technique. Everyone I talk to says, 'What about Buddy Rich?' Well, what about him? Because he doesn't turn me on."[13] Furthermore, "I couldn't tune a drum to save my life. They're either loose or tight,"[14] and, despite Dingle Vale's "little milk bottles", Starkey would speak with quiet pride of getting by without ever being able to read a note of standard music script, let alone a drum stave. Neither could he ever manage a clean roll faster than moderato. On listening to Rich, Krupa or – later – even Elliott, "I know I'm no good on the technical things but I'm good with all the motions, swinging my head, like. That's because I love to dance, but you can't do that on the drums."[5]

He would lay himself open to misinterpretation and derogatory *bons mots* with comments such as "I like to make mistakes",[8] with regard to his chosen instrument, but with self-tuition impractical when he began, the only advice he'd be qualified to offer other budding drummers would be, "Get in a group as fast as you can.

.

You'll learn more in one day than you can hope to in six months stuck in a little room. Make your mistakes on a stage in front of an audience. You'll realise them more quickly."[15]

With the Clayton outfit often a player or two short, his errors hung in the air more flagrantly, especially when he and John Dougherty – the most consistent of its washboard players – were at rhythmic loggerheads. Moreover, as he couldn't carry heavy objects far and had to rely on buses to reach Garston's Wilson Hall and like palais on the outer marches of the group's booking circuit, he'd sometimes arrive with only half his equipment. Nevertheless, the unit was a comparative rarity in that it had a sticksman with a full kit for all to see during what amounted to a residency at Boys' Club meetings in the Dingle's Florence Institute, a Victorian monstrosity near enough for the drums to be walked there.

For all of this parochial renown, recitals elsewhere were infrequent, and Starkey's fealty to Clayton was tried by Miles' imminent departure to the marriage bed and its resultant casting aside of adolescent follies.[16] According to Wally Egmond of The Hi-Fi's, Richie was "not an exceptional drummer",[17] but there came overtures from other skiffle groups for him to join them, especially since – with his own savings and the balance donated by his grandfather – he'd bought a brand-new black Premier kit with "lapped" pigskin, rather than plastic heads. Although there was still little he could do to prevent the cymbal stands from keeling over on rickety stages, he cured the bass drum's inclination to creep forward by fitting it with heavy-duty "disappearing" spurs. On the basis of owning this customised possession, rather than how he played it, he recalled, "Well, I thought I was the best drummer there was, better than all the other drummers. Maybe I was just convincing myself."[18]

Contacted via Admiral Grove's corner newsagent's telephone, the great Richie sat in non-committally with other outfits, once drumming for three in the course of one shattering evening. A kindly conductor on the number 61 bus route to central Liverpool had eased considerably his transport problems by arranging for him to store the kit overnight at the Ribble bus depot whenever he needed, as he did in March 1959 at the Mardi Gras, a stone's throw from Myrtle Street hospital, on the occasion of his first engagement with Al Caldwell's Texans. Although the Darktown mob "turned over fast to rock 'n' roll, changing their name to The Cadillacs",[7] prospects with The Texans – soon to add the adjective "Raving" to their name – seemed rosier, particularly as they now received actual money for playing.

The Raving Texans – still with no fixed line-up yet – were tormented by an identity crisis. They mounted one evening stage decked out in Hawaiian shirts and sunglasses while, to gain a booking at the Cavern – a jazz haven in central Liverpool – they performed as The Jazzmen, their opportunism backfiring when they deviated from manager Ray McFall's purist designations about what should and shouldn't be played there. The club's clientèle put up with skiffle, but with Jerry Lee Lewis' 'Whole Lotta Shakin' Goin' On' The Texans invited enraged booing and even the hurling of chairs stagewards. For daring to rock the Cavern, McFall felt entitled to deduct 10s from the culprits' already meagre pay.

With such foolhardiness behind them, leader Caldwell reflected that his true vocation was to cut up rough with the rock 'n' roll elixir that an increasingly large following would swallow neat. As Byrnes' rhythm-guitar chopping was more than adequate, Alan – an indifferent player anyway – left his guitar at home so that he could concentrate on lead vocals, Presley-esque gyrations and pumping the piano, if one was available. He was also toying with a new group name that – like Marty Wilde And The Wildcats – differentiated between star (him) and accompanists. They could be The Hurricanes while, initially, he called himself Al Storm. The surname was a common *nom du théâtre* for, as well as Burnley's Jerry, there was Southampton's Cliff Richard lookalike Danny Storm and Tempest Storm, a notorious strip-teasing acquaintance of Elvis Presley. He'd also heard of a Billy Gray And The Stormers, who would land a season at a Butlins in Filey. By 1959, Caldwell was Jett Storm, named after the character played by Marty Wilde in his silver-screen debut. Caldwell settled ultimately for the forename Rory, a genuflection towards Rory Blackwell, who'd lately broken the world record for non-stop drumming. With the approbation of his adoring parents, who'd rename their house "Stormsville", he became Rory Storm by deed poll.

Richard Starkey pledged himself to Rory Storm And The Hurricanes in November 1959. With him at the kit, they'd come second to Kingsize Taylor And The Dominoes out of more than 100 groups during the previous month's heat of a "Search For Stars" tournament at the Empire, organised by ITV's Canadian starmaker Carroll Levis to counter the rival channel's *Bid For Fame*. In the final round, at Manchester's Hippodrome, although neither Dominoes nor Hurricanes or Bobby Elliott's new band, The Dolphins, were able to seize the prize of exposure on Levis' television series, all emerged with a more promising date schedule in which a list that had once signified a month's work became a week's. "After that, you were on your own," elucidated Cilla White. "Agents never saw themselves as more than bookers."[19] it might not have been sufficient for Richie to think seriously of resigning from Hunt's, but The Hurricanes would next appear in Liverpool in uniform black-and-white winkle-pickers (gold for Storm) and starched white handkerchiefs protruding smartly from the top pockets of bright-red stage suits for the group (light pink for the lovely Rory).

Bespoken by Duncan's, a city-centre tailor, this sharp corporate persona was assumed because the unit's turnover of personnel had abated with the recruitment of Starkey, lead guitarist Charles O'Brien – whose prowess as a boxer was a reassuring asset at less refined venues – and fellow Hi-Fi Wally Egmond on electric bass guitar. Although Salisbury's Johnny Nicholls And The Dimes had acquired one of these new-fangled instruments via a "Cunard Yank" in as early as 1956, it was only after Freddie Bell's Bellboys appeared at the Empire with one in 1957 that Kingsize Taylor stampeded his bass player, Bobby Thompson, into buying a Framus model when Hessy's imported a few. Not only were they more portable but they also radiated infinitely greater depth of sound and volume than a broomstick bass.

Rory Blackwell And His Blackjacks had been using a Fender bass in the Rock and Calypso Ballroom at Butlin's during one of Alan-Rory's fraternal visits to Pwllheli. As well as Alan ingratiating himself with the famous Blackwell, a more concrete outcome of the trip was the sensation that Egmond caused later when throbbing his new Fender for the first time at the Jive Hive.

United by artistic purpose and mutual respect, Merseyside's semi-professional outfits were civil enough to each other when queueing after an evening's engagements at Morgan's fish-and-chip shop if in Birkenhead or likewise unwinding in a graveyard-hour coffee bar – that light catering epitome of the late 1950s – such as the Zodiac just off China Town or the Jacaranda, within spitting distance of Central Station. However, easy offstage camaraderie became sly competitiveness when each individual group went back to work. Some vocalists' dedication was such that they'd cry real tears during agonised *lieder* with the aid of an onion-smeared handkerchief. They might also resin their hair with paraffin wax, which served the dual purpose of lending extra sheen and, as it ran down to soak shirts, making it look like they'd worked up a hell of a sexy sweat. Those bands that could afford a tape recorder would rig it up in the most acoustically sympathetic corner of a dance hall to capture an audible gauge whereby performances could be measured against those of the opposition.

A Rory Storm And The Hurricanes extravaganza generally felt tremendous when watching Rory's on-stage cavortings with the other four bucking and lunging about him, but as sonic vibrations *per se* you should hear it on tape afterwards! Although akin to an Irish showband in terms of band-audience interplay, The Hurricanes and Storm were also forerunners of more abandoned mid-1960s acts such as The Rolling Stones and The Pretty Things. Like the Stones, the group were coalesced by a forceful rhythm guitarist, but a given number seemed sometimes to be about to fall to bits in a flurry of meandering tempo, jarring three-part harmonies, blown riffs and bawled directives from Byrnes. More capable of musical effect rather than music, The Hurricanes could manage no more than an approximation when certain hall regulations obliged them to conclude an evening's proceedings with the National Anthem. The group were also immoderately fond of the key of G major.

For all of that, however, by 1960, the charismatic Storm was a hard act to follow. His singing voice might have been dull, but – indefatigable self-publicist as he was – his nickname of "Mr Showmanship" was no overstatement. A man of extreme strategy, he outraged heterosexual chauvinists with his gigolo wardrobe – which, from mere pink nylon, would stretch to costumes of gold lamé and sequins – and peacock antics. To illustrate Carl Perkins' 'Lend Me Your Comb', he'd sweep an outsized one through a precarious pompadour which kept falling over his eyes, but this was nothing to what he did when the group played venues attached to swimming baths, where, in the middle of a song, he was likely to push through the crowd, clamber to the top board, strip to scarlet swimming trunks and dive in.

If not conventionally handsome, he became the darling of the ladies for his grinning vibrancy, and was, therefore, not immune to the bellicose resolves of their possessive boyfriends. On mercifully few occasions, however, the Storm quintet discovered what it was like to get themselves and their equipment damaged by disgruntled yahoos in real- or imitation-leather windcheaters and jeans, their Brylcreemed ducktails in direct descent from the Teds. When he later squeezed even harder on the nerve of how far he could go, Rory's injuries were sometimes self-inflicted as he plummeted from the glass dome of New Brighton's capacious Tower Ballroom and fractured his leg or was concussed on an equally rash climb to a pillared balcony stage left at Birkenhead's Majestic.

Although Storm fronted The Hurricanes, the others didn't skulk to the rear, exchanging nervous glances. Maddened by someone's incessant whistle-blowing during one engagement,

Richie slung a stick towards the offender, striking instead a hulking local gang leader who, mistakenly, enacted a reprisal against Rory. A rowdy bunch with impressive self-confidence, The Hurricanes would sometimes swap instruments for comic relief in which notes chased haphazardly up and down fretboards amid feedback lament and free-form percussion. Both to restore order and to let Rory take a breather, Richie was bullied into 'Big Noise From Winnetka', which necessitated his commanding the stage virtually alone under his own voodoo spell for minutes on end – and he had to admit that "the audience love it. If there's a drum solo, they go mad."[20]

Sandy Nelson had also been on the recording session for The Hollywood Argyles' 'Alley Oop', which was one of the first items that Starkey sang with The Hurricanes, who, like many other Liverpool groups, had "featured vocalists" who specialised in areas not thought unsuitable for the chief show-off. Able to swoop elegantly from bass grumble to falsetto shriek in the space of a few bars, Egmond was the balladeer who stopped the show with breathtaking treatments of Peggy Lee's sultry 'Fever', The Everly Brothers' 'Let It Be Me' or Gershwin's 'Summertime', from *Porgy And Bess*.

With the humorous semi-spoken lope of 'Alley Oop',[21] Starkey was in charge of less demanding material. By *bel canto* standards, he had a horrible voice, devoid of plummy enunciation and nicety of intonation. Instead, you got slurred diction – perfect for 'Alley Oop' – and gravelly ranting as he got through a number any old how, frequently straining his disjointed range past its limits. In context, the effect of spontaneity over expertise was not unattractive, even gruffly charming, because "I'm more of a personality. It's a fun-loving attitude to life that comes across. I have a good time."[22]

It was incumbent upon Merseyside groups to exude a happy, smiling on-stage atmosphere, as well as action-packed rock 'n' roll, to defuse potential trouble amongst the customers during, say, February 1960's "Gala Rock Night" at Litherland Town Hall with

The Hurricanes, Dominoes, Bobby Bell Rockers and Ian and his Zodiacs, then constituting the upper crust of Liverpool pop. Yet, however peacefully this event passed, the Merseyside constabulary were still called out to suppress a wave of brawling and vandalism afterwards when over-excited adolescents with hormones raging wondered what to do until bedtime.

However, as long as the teenagers handed over the admission price and behaved themselves while inside, their deeds of destruction in the streets were of no concern to palais promoters, who hadn't let private dislike stop them clasping rock 'n' roll to their bosoms, either. Turning such a hard-nosed penny were the managements of Liscard's Grosvenor Ballroom, St Helen's Plaza and the Neston Institute, all of which degenerated into roughhouses on pop nights. At West Derby's Locarno, the city's first disc jockey, Mark Peters, was installed. However, after Peters devoted himself more to singing with a group, Billy Butler and Bob Wooler would surface as the city's most omnipotent masters of ceremonies, with selections from their vast record collections being borrowed by musicians eager to surprise dancers with more than the obvious Top-20 favourites.

Some, such as Kingsize Taylor, went directly to source. On the mailing lists of remote record labels like Aladdin, Chess, Imperial and Cameo Parkway, The Dominoes were able to perform selections "before anybody had heard the records. We had them sent over from the States."[3] Among precious few other native rock 'n' rollers regarded with anything approaching awe were Johnny Kidd, Vince Taylor and Ronnie Wycherley, who, as 'Billy Fury', was being groomed for fame by Larry Parnes. As for wholesome Cliff Richard, a self-respecting rocker like Richie Starkey would have "never bought one of his records in my life".[23]

Reflecting Liverpool's general cultural isolation, its groups came gradually to drink from a repertory pool singular to the region, including early Tamla-Motown and Atlantic singles, US Hot 100 smashes that failed everywhere else and songs buried on B-sides and "side two, track four" on LPs, such as Ray Charles' treatment of

'You'll Never Walk Alone' from *Carousel*. Numbers by Chuck Berry – then without major British hits – cropped up more than anyone else's, but other Merseyside cult celebrities included Dr Feelgood And The Interns, Richie Barrett, The Olympics and Chan Romero. Filling the Jive Hive and Wavertree's Holyoake Hall – where Wooler presided – well before filtering to the rest of the country were Scouse arrangements of 'Dr Feelgood', 'Money', Willie Dixon's 'My Babe', The Jive Bombers' 'Bad Boy' and other discs that, not immediately obtainable from high-street retailers, had wended their way over from a more exotic continent. "The music we liked took a different direction from the rest of the country," commented Cilla White, then completing a secretarial course at Anfield Commercial College. "We had our own versions of everything, and no one thought for a minute that they were inferior."[19]

In Rory Storm And The Hurricanes, where form overruled content, most songs were common property of scores of other groups. The traditional opener was Vince Taylor's spirited 'Brand New Cadillac' and the core of the set was drawn likewise from the Valhalla of classic rock, with Warren Smith's 'Ubangi Stomp' featuring among the more obscure choices. During Ray Charles' 'What'd I Say', Rory would, ideally, trade "heys" and "yeahs" with participating onlookers, take it down easy, build the tension to the verge of panic and, to round it off, flounce into the wings, leaving 'em wanting more.

Perhaps the Rory Storm And The Hurricanes story should have ended there, because arguably they were as good as they were ever going to get. Routining new numbers speedily and incompletely before ennui set it, Storm was averse to formal rehearsals, and so they'd venture but rarely beyond the boundaries of their stylistic definition. The consolidation rather than development of this was to be their downfall.

This, however, lay three years ahead. The first business of any pop group is simply to be liked, and none could deny that Rory and his Hurricanes were in the top division of Merseyside popularity. As a measure of their wide appeal, their fan club was situated at an address in faraway Anfield, where its secretary, Julie Farrelly, would answer letters of undying love for Rory, for whom female screams were already reverberating.

3 "I Took A Chance And I Think I've Been Lucky"

Six-Five Special's less pious successors – *Oh Boy!*, *Drumbeat*, *Boy Meets Girls*, *Wham!* and the short-lived *Dig This!* – produced a worthier strain of British rock 'n' roller by the end of the decade. You wonder how some might have evolved, had they not acquiesced to their handlers' suggestions to follow the Tommy Steele path as all-round entertainers. As well as Cliff Richard's film musicals of cheerful unreality, Vince Eager – as "Simple Simon" – would dip his toe into pantomime in Southport Floral Hall's *Mother Goose* in 1960 while Marty Wilde announced his wish to "do the real class stuff like Sinatra".[1] Even Johnny Kidd, the hardest UK rocker of them all, would soften towards country and western when his sporadic hits dried up.

Others, however, remained hostage to the beat. With his Horde Of Savages, Screaming Lord Sutch – a more enduring clown than Willie Harris – was prevented by his image from going smooth while Vince Taylor, clad in studded biker leathers, kept the faith in France. Another example was Tony Sheridan, now much changed from the absconded schoolboy in McDevitt's Skiffle Cellar. After serving Wilde and then Taylor, Tony struck out on his own, leading a trio with drummer Brian Bennett and, on bass, Brian Locking, both of whom were foreordained to join The Shadows. However, although 19-year-old Sheridan – a guitarist/singer of unusual flair – created a ripple before 1959's *Oh Boy!* cameras, an invitation to do likewise on an edition of *Boy Meets Girls* headlined by Gene Vincent was cancelled when, in his own publicist's words, Sheridan "went haywire, failing to be on time, arriving without his guitar, etc".[2] Television was therefore closed to him, and only on sufferance did Larry Parnes allow Sheridan just under ten minutes on an all-British supporting bill – including Billy Fury, Joe Brown (from the *Boy Meets Girls* house band) and Georgie Fame – to Vincent and Eddie Cochran, an Oklahoman Elvis then in the British Top 30 for the fourth time, on an around-Britain package tour, beginning on Elvis Presley's birthday, 8 January 1960.

Naturally, the host descended upon the Liverpool Empire, where, after the show, Rory Storm and John Byrnes nattered familiarly with Tony Sheridan and Larry Parnes talked with Allan Williams, proprietor of the Jacaranda. This enterprising Welshman arranged another Merseyside spectacular for the two Americans on 3 May at a 6,000-capacity sports stadium between Exchange Station and Prince's Dock. Lower on the bill, the expected smattering of Parnes' lesser creatures were interspersed with some of the city's top acts, including Cass and his Cassanovas, Gerry And The Pacemakers and, with The Hurricanes, Rory Storm, who was as much a star in Liverpool as Cochran was in the hit parade. Two more parochial outfits would also be added to that Tuesday evening's sold-out programme after Eddie died from his injuries in a road accident between the Bristol Hippodrome and London Airport on 17 April.

Bigoted old Teds threw contemptuous pennies at them, but Vincent was almost upstaged by the local boys, whether Gerry Marsden with his moving 'You'll Never Walk Alone' or Rory stunning 'em with 'What'd I Say' and Carl Perkins' insidious 'Honey Don't' with Walter and Starkey – shifty in sunglasses – anchoring its understated shuffle. When embers of excitement were being fanned too briskly, as Gene's grand entrance neared, it was stuttering Rory, rather than Gerry, whom Williams sent forth again to the microphone to douse flames of open riot with a nonplussing "S-s-s-stop it, y-y-y-you k-k-k-kids!"

A tape recording of the greatest night anyone could ever remember was, unhappily, erased, but the impact of the Liverpool groups on

Larry Parnes was sufficient for him to charge Williams with the hurried task of assembling a selection of them from which could be chosen an all-purpose backing band for use by certain Parnes signings who'd been earmarked to tour Scotland. As amplifiers buzzed into life and string-calloused fingers fluttered prelusively on fretboards, Storm *sans* Hurricanes sauntered into the afternoon auditions in Slater Street's Corinthian Social Club[3] not intending to leave until he'd had his picture taken with Billy Fury, who was to string along with his manager to provide a second opinion.

In the photograph of the pair standing on the club's threshold, Billy in daylight appeared stunted and unimposing next to Rory, an Adonis in Italian suit and hair lacquer who had somehow acquired a tan during a wet spring. It was because he looked such a pop star of a man and Fury – whose Top Ten success was not yet consolidated – didn't that Parnes threatened to call off the Scottish undertaking if Williams or Storm published a single copy of the shot. God knows what might have happened if Storm and his boys had bothered to play for Parnes that day and he'd been foolish enough to pick them. What could have prevented flamboyant Rory in Aberdeen or Inverness from shoving the cipher that The Hurricanes were backing into the wings so that he could commandeer the central mic himself?

This was mere hypothesis, however, because Rory had passed up this potential passport to a wider work spectrum, having committed himself and his band to an imminent and lengthy residency at Pwllheli's Butlin's, gained though the influence of sister Iris. Rory might have been able to pack his case with Ernie and Violet's approval, but other parents grumbled about the chances that their Hurricane sons were wasting by being silly to themselves in such a risky business as this pop music. Elsie Graves had been to see Richie perform with The Hurricanes and "thought he would eventually find a place for himself in an ordinary dance band",[4] meaning one as part-time as The Eddie Clayton Skiffle Group had been, because she didn't want him to throw away his four years' worth of apprenticeship at Hunt's. Amused by the memory, Richie would reconjure how "Elsie and Harry tried everything to persuade me to stay. 'Get your trade,' they told me, 'and you'll never be stuck for a job.' It's good advice for any lad."[5]

In the unquiet twilight of his adolescence, however, Richie's mother "talked an awful lot of rubbish. I didn't believe a word she said."[6] He was more in thrall of his Geraldine, who had so monopolised his plain charms that they had become engaged. In alliance with her parents-in-law-to-be, she prevailed upon him to be sensible and withdraw from The Hurricanes even as Storm called at Admiral Grove – as he'd also had to do at the Egmonds' in Broad Green – to affirm his own faith in the group. Its immediate future was "as good as a holiday and you get paid for it".[7] You couldn't argue with £25 pounds for a 16-hour week, could you, when eight was then considered an ample wage for a young executive slaving from nine to five every day?

"If Rory hadn't twisted his arm," opined John Byrnes, "I don't think he'd have done half the things he did."[8] Sensing that Starkey needed only courage to chuck Geraldine, Byrnes and Storm had laid on with a trowel spicy imagery of the saucy, fancy-free "birds" with whom it was feasible to fraternise at the holiday camp, even in a pre-birth pill age when a nice girl would tolerate no more than a fumble at her bra-strap while still unwed – and when Butlins' rules forbade staff from entertaining anyone with a different set of hormones in their assigned chalets. Its ballrooms – where fluorescent lighting made all look sun-tanned and fit – were hunting grounds, see, for souls aching for romance. The procurement of this was often easier for a player on the bandstand than the pimpled Average Joe mooching about with a sense of defeat in the gloom past the burning footlights. A strong enough motive for even the most ill-favoured youth to be a rock 'n' roll musician was the increased licence it gave to make eye contact with gawking young ladies fringing the front of the stage. A tryst during a beer break could be sealed with a beatific smile, a flood of libido and an "All right, then, I'll see you later".

On top of illicit perks were career opportunities at Butlin's in Pwllheli, where Georgie Fame had been enlisted into Rory Blackwell's Blackjacks in the previous year. Russ Hamilton had been a Redcoat – hearty blazered motivator of sports and social activities – at Blackpool's outpost and Cliff Richard had got his break in the Rock 'n' Roll Ballroom at Clacton, while Joe Brown had twanged guitar for Clay Nicholls And The Blue Flames at Filey before Parnes, *Boy Meets Girls* and a recording contract. If the worst came to the worst, Butlin's even had its own label, which had just issued a single by The Trebletones, its Bognor Regis band.

On resigning from Hunt's, Richard "took a chance and I think I've been lucky".[9] Starkey was one for whom Butlins was not, overall, a hellish experience, "but I hated a lot of it at the time."[10] The camps were a reflection of Billy Butlin's personality, which, before his knighthood, was that of an effervescent ex-fairground hoopla huckster. With borrowed capital, the first manifestation of his radical scheme for a walled and communal family holiday site was at bracing Skegness in 1936. From this blueprint, there grew an empire of knobbly knees contests; good-natured cheers from entire sittings of diners whenever a butter-fingered waitress let fall crockery; Olympic-sized swimming pools; noisy team games with Redcoats jollying everyone along; children lining up for ride after free ride on the deliciously terrifying Wild Mouse – and campers grousing about the food, the accommodation, the band and, of course, the meteorological whims of British Augusts.

1960's weather was indeed something to grouse about. From July to September, it was unseasonably cool in Wales, with the highest rainfall figure since before the war. This had compensations for Richie, who, more prone to burning than most, would sunbathe in dark glasses, long-sleeved shirt, jeans and improvised nose-protector. As pale as he'd been when he first exposed himself, he'd stroll back to a dwelling a good deal grubbier than those of the holidaymakers, with their new lino, bright wallpaper and chalet maids.

Starkey didn't like you taking the mickey out of him when girls were around, but when in his usual good humour, Egmond affirmed, "He was the life and soul of any party."[11] Sometimes it was unintentional. When O'Brien was teaching Starkey to swim, "He seemed to be doing fine until he realised he was in the twelve-footer.

Then he just yelled and vanished from sight. Three of us dived in and pulled him out. We had a good laugh about it afterwards."[11] On the one occasion that he went on a pony trek at Pwllheli, his nag bit him. More shocked than hurt, he chose to dismount and walk back to camp. This was not to be his only altercation with a horse.

Richie and Rory were the most reluctant of all the group to rise before midday, groaning expletives when the camp Tannoy system crackled at seven with 'Zip-A-Dee-Doo-Dah', 'Oh What A Beautiful Morning' or a tune as oppressively perky. Richie especially would be surly over breakfast if there'd been more than this ritual disturbance. "The first sign of him waking," observed Egmond, "took the form of one open eye staring 'round the chalet. Then it would be an hour before he'd stir properly."[11]

Another trait that was not always endearing was his insistence on sloping off to the Dingle – no matter how inconvenient it might be for the group – to celebrate birthdays and other anniversaries. (He could counter that Storm did likewise for the Liverpool soccer team's home matches.) Neither was he enamoured with Rory bestowing colourful stage names upon each Hurricane, just as Lord Sutch had with his Savages. As films and TV series such as *Rawhide*, *Gun Law* and *Wagon Train* were popular,[12] the Wild West was Storm's principal theme as Byrnes became "Johnny Guitar" after a 1954 Western, while saturnine O'Brien was "Ty Brien", a nod towards Ty Hardin, then famous for his title role in BBC's *Bronco*, a poor man's *Cheyenne*. Egmond metamorphosed into the less specific "Lou Walters". The group also accrued apposite accessories, such as gold cowboy boots, saloon cardsharp fancy waistcoats and the stringy desperado beards that came and went on Richie and Charles/Ty's mugs.

Not wishing to be awkward, Starkey gave in and let Rory introduce him as "Rings" – and then "Ringo" – "Starr", which he emblazoned on his bass drum in stick-on lettering. A mythical gunslinger had already lent his name to one of the younger Merseyside singers, Johnny Ringo, leader of The Colts, but Richie's new forename was for his lingering Teddy Boy habit of adorning each hand with three or four increasingly splendid rings. When

"Ringo" was juxtaposed with his run-of-the-mill last name, it sounded "a bit funny. 'Starr' was a natural. It made sense to me and I liked it. It stuck."[13]

It also better facilitated Storm's build-up to "Starr Time", a section of the show in which his drummer could now resort to more than 'Big Noise From Winnetka' and 'Alley Oop'. With vocal cords beyond remedy by the end of the season, Ringo/Richie was rewarded with scattered screams for three other selections, which included – in a lower key and with the others on the *bwap-doo-wap* responses – 'Boys', a B-side by New York's Shirelles, a female vocal group of ingenuously fragile conviction. He tried Johnny Burnette's ambulant 'You're Sixteen' less often, because Rory generally kept that one for himself.

Backing the competitors in the camp's pop-singing and jiving contests – sponsored by a tobacco firm – as well as delivering the music night after night in the Rock and Calypso Ballroom, Ringo would claim later to have been "educated at Butlin's".[13] What had once been casual was now stylised, and when they returned – rebooked for next summer – to the trivial round of Merseyside engagements Storm and The Hurricanes "couldn't have had better practice for a stage career. Those [Pwllheli] audiences really used to heckle us, and when they wanted requests it was usually for some square song that we'd hardly heard of before, so it was up to us to keep things going. We simply had to ad lib and try not to take any notice of the remarks they slung at us. And, even more important, we had to play without any sort of arrangement, most of the time."[10]

While at Butlin's, a visiting Rory Blackwell had tried to poach the much-improved Johnny Guitar for his Blackjacks, and Guitar may have regretted his folly in not taking up the offer, because the pestilence of trad jazz – springing from Bristol, where clarinettist Bernard "Acker" Bilk was king – was ravaging Britain to the detriment of rock 'n' roll. It had spread beyond the earnest obsession of the intellectual fringe and ban-the-bomb marches to a proletariat where "ACKER" was studded on the backs of leather jackets where "ELVIS" or "GENE" once were, and girls fainted to the toot-tooting of Humphrey Lyttelton. Bilk, Chris Barber and Kenny Ball each breached the Top 20. After Bilk came within an ace of a Number One with 'Stranger On The Shore', a Manchester disciple wrote to ask him if it was about Jesus.[15] As Acker's Paramount Jazz Band went in for striped brocade and bowler hats, so matching Donegal tweeds, Confederate Army regimentals and even legal gowns and barrister wigs would be the uniforms of lesser units with bland banjo players, a confusion of front-line horns and "dads" who thought that a hoarse monotone was all you needed to sing like Louis Armstrong.

In some numbers, the jazz content was frequently negligible because, if some black dotard from New Orleans had recorded a particularly definitive solo, it was considered prudent to learn it note for note for regurgitation at every public performance. The Massed Alberts (a sort of English Spike Jones and his City Slickers) and the chart-topping Temperance Seven (produced by George Martin) were only jazz marginally but still appeared on programmes like BBC's opportunist *Trad Tavern* and at jazz strongholds such as West London's 100 Club, Uncle Bonnie's Chinese Jazz Club(!) down in Brighton and, in Liverpool, the Temple, the Cavern and – with "No Weirdies, Beatniks or Teddy Boys admitted" – the Storyville (later the Iron Door), all contained within the ravines of lofty warehouses around Whitechapel.

The Liverpool Echo would advertise and review trad concerts while disregarding lowbrow rock 'n' roll. Nevertheless, possibly because queues formed round the block whenever The Temperance Seven – a pop group by any other name – were on, it made financial sense for the Iron Door and the Cavern to tentatively slip in a little out-and-out pop between the trad, even when the Cavern became "the Club Perdido" every Thursday for modern jazz. Without Ray McFall threatening to fine anyone now, Rory Storm And The Hurricanes had been one of the highlights of his club's first all-pop events, just before they left for Pwllheli.

Despite this breakthrough, the majority of such venues that counted on Merseyside remained stubbornly biased towards local trad outfits like The Joe Silman Dixielanders and Noel Walker's

Stompers, and so it was that Rory Storm's Hurricanes responded to demands from West Germany for cheap rock 'n' roll labour. It was to be a worthwhile experience, for, in as late as 1968, sending groups to the Fatherland for a three-month stretch was still considered a foolproof way of separating the men from the boys. Black Sabbath's manager, Jim Simpson, reasoned that it was "rather like training a thousand metre runner by sending him on 5,000-metre courses".[16] Nine years earlier, Acker Bilk had been well primed to capitalise on the trad boom after six weeks in a Dusseldorf bierkeller, where "you just blew and blew and blew and had 20 minutes off for a drink, and then you were back blowing again".[15]

Walking an uncomfortable line between trad and pop, Garston's Swinging Blue Jeans would discover the hard way that jazz had been old hat with West German teenagers since 1960. From Kiel's Star Palaast to Cologne's Storyville, bastions of Teutonic jazz had converted within days to rock 'n' roll bierkellers. The new policy was, however, most rampant in Hamburg, Germany's largest port, after *Oh Boy!* refugee Tony Sheridan and a motley crew of other unemployed London musicians were imported in June 1960 and christened "The Jets" by impresario Bruno Koschmider to reclaim the many patrons who had drifted away from his Kaiserkeller club, affronted by its clumsy local band's attempts to copy American pop.

Until lured away after a month by one of Koschmider's richer rivals – Peter Eckhorn, of the newly-opened Top Ten – The Jets made the Kaiserkeller thrive again by not bothering to duplicate recorded arrangements, choosing rather to pile up a sweaty intensity during indefinitely extended extrapolations of 'What'd I Say', 'Whole Lotta Shakin'' and even 'When The Saints Go Marching in'. The beauty of pieces with such loose, simple structures was that they required little instruction past the rare "No, not dum-dum-de-diddly-*dum*; try dum-dum-de-diddly-*dah*".

After fuming over the loss of The Jets, Bruno remembered an encounter with another rockin' Briton, Brian Casser, in the 2I's. Although a Londoner by upbringing, Casser was actually the "Cass" in Cass And The Cassanovas. He could be contacted by telephone – so he informed Koschmider – at the Jacaranda, where all the Liverpool groups congregated because it was near the dole office. A story goes that it was not Casser but Allan Williams who answered the ring from one of Koschmider's underlings. No, Brian and The Cassanovas are north of the border with Johnny Gentle, one of Larry Parnes' clients. Can I help at all? Perhaps we could discuss it next time Mr Koschmider and yourself come to London? Through the quick-thinking Williams, a couple of Scouse groups who weren't in either Scotland or Butlin's were sent across the North Sea to Hamburg, and in October 1960 it was Rory Storm And The Hurricanes' turn. They were to replace Derry And The Seniors – who'd been there since July – and work split shifts with The Beatles, a group traceable back to The Quarry Men. Although official stipulations had them there only until December, Bruno's advertisements stressed that they'd see the New Year in at the Kaiserkeller. Comparing the relative sizes of their respective names on its wall posters, "RORY STORM AND HIS HURRICAN [sic]", as Butlins veterans, were judged to be a bigger attraction than the small-lettered Beatles.

On this first occasion that Starkey had ever breathed foreign air, he travelled alone and had to change in Paris. During the usual scramble, he lost track of his drum kit. His attempts to explain his predicament in sign language led to the arrival of gendarmes. Fortunately, one of these understood English, but the kit was still not located until the next morning.

As he hurtled through the forests of Lower Saxony, hot-eyed with sleeplessness, tell-tale twinges of homesickness and anxiety about the mess he might now be in took their toll. Hamburg had been as torn by war as his own city, but if Ringo anticipated seeing parking lots formed from bomb sites, as you still could back home, he found instead a bustling modern metropolis – as Liverpool wouldn't be for years – fully recovered from the attentions of the RAF. The gaunt buildings on the Elbe waterfront were a link with home, and so were the cobbled streets of St Pauli, where the Kaiserkeller stood. There, instead of some dirty cellar like the

Cavern, he unloaded his equipment outside a place plusher than even the Rock and Calypso.

Whereas the Pwllheli ballroom had a touch of the Caribbean, the Kaiserkeller had a nautical theme – mock-fishermen's nets hanging from its capacious ceiling, boat-shaped dining alcoves *et al* – as befitted a port, albeit one 60 miles inland. It was but one such establishment around the Grosse Freiheit, however, a tributary of the Reeperbahn ("Rope Street"). This glum translation belied a notoriety as the neon starting point of innumerable languid evenings of perfumed wantonness, living tableaux of flesh and late-evening temptation by doorstep pimps. I am prohibited by inbred propriety from entering into distressing detail, except to state that, an erotic Butlins since the days of three-mast clippers, St Pauli's brothels and strip-tease palaces were eye-openers to anyone who assumed that humans could be sexually gratified without mechanical complexity and only with other humans.

As Tony and The Jets had guided Hamburg's first musical Merseysiders around the Salome strip club, the Roxy transvestite bar, Der Fludde, the shocking "Street of Windows" and other of the district's diversions, so the information was passed on to Rory's Hurricanes by The Seniors – who were staying on briefly in another club – and The Beatles. *Wurst* sausages, *Korn*, *Apfel Küchen* and other German foodstuffs and beverages might have been recommended, but Storm's group were more grateful when told that "*Cornflakes mit Milch*" was served in one Freiheit cafe. Like Storm, Sheridan was fond of swimming and was the original advocate of excursions to Timmendorf Beach, on the North Sea.

The prodigal Tony had no right to expect one, but Rory Storm And The Hurricanes were recipients of a testimonial from Koschmider praising their nightly entertainments. They were also paid more than both The Seniors and The Beatles; enough to lodge in the British Seamen's Mission – where lunch was something with chips and a cup of tea – along Johannis Bollwerk, rather than in the two dingy rooms with no bedding at the back of the club with which The Seniors had made do. The five Beatles still lived in some dungeons adjoining a cinema toilet.

Sardonic about the privileged Hurricanes, who were also speaking of making a recording whilst in Germany, The Beatles were particularly indifferent towards "the nasty one with his little grey streak of hair",[17] a reference to Ringo by George Harrison, the same lead guitarist who'd been too young for The Texans. There was also some open unpleasantness when Rory reneged on a promise to advance the quintet's leader, John Lennon, the cash he still needed for a guitar that he'd been drooling over in a shop window in central Hamburg. Nevertheless, the ice broke and The Beatles found the newcomers intrinsically friendlier than the rather supercilious Seniors had been. According to Pete Best, then their drummer, "That's where their friendship with Ringo began."[18]

Three Beatles – Harrison, Lennon and general factotum Paul McCartney – would be on hand when The Hurricanes recorded within a fortnight of opening at the Kaiserkeller. The sum total of all their big talk, however, was three of Wally's ballads – one take each – in Hamburg's tiny Akustik Studio, into which extraneous sounds from the main railway station would infiltrate if the door was left ajar. Financed by Storm and Allan Williams, Eymond warbled 'Fever' and Kurt Weill's 'September Song' – *à la* Johnnie Ray's 1959 treatment – while accompanied by the other Hurricanes and 'Summertime' with Richie and The Beatles. As evidenced by the ambitious Storm not actively joining in, the session was purely exploratory, a treat for the lads and a confidence boost for the bespectacled Wally.

Starr's teen appeal wasn't obvious, either, but his harmless jocularity, saucer eyes and air of bewildered wistfulness incited a protective instinct from a fair cross-section of Reeperbahn *frauleins* that they couldn't feel for Wally, even though he sang like a nightingale. After ogling the drummer all evening, one girl's bottled-up emotions bubbled over and she had to be forcibly dragged from the club, shrieking, "Ringo! Ringo!", even as she was pushed into the street.

Sending palpitations through more feminine nervous systems were The Beatles, particularly Pete, but Ringo for one would remember a time less than a year before when they'd been far outside the league of Liverpool's leading groups, who had known them by sight just as Jacaranda riff-raff. Only on noticing Harrison in its basement teaching another Beatle, Stuart Sutcliffe, the stock rock 'n' roll root notes on a new bass guitar had Starr understood that they were an actual group under Williams' wing.

All of them were ex-grammar-school pupils. Fresh from the sixth form, McCartney was wondering if his GCE "A"-level results had alighted on his Allerton doormat yet, while the older Lennon and best mate Sutcliffe had, to all intents and purposes, quit art college to go to Hamburg and Best had cancelled plans to become a trainee teacher. Stuart, Paul and John would insert the odd long word and names like Kerouac and Kierkegaard into conversations that would lapse into student vernacular and their own Goonish restricted code. They'd once been involved in a fusion of poetry and rock with *vers libre* bard Royston Ellis, who'd judged them to be "more of the bohemian ilk than other young northerners at the time, and their pleasant eccentricity made them acceptable".[14] He'd been astonished that "they didn't even know about getting high on benzedrine strips from nose inhalers",[14] a gap in their understanding that he rectified.

Partly because of their arty affectations and Lennon and McCartney's pretensions as songwriters, The Beatles were derided as unprofessional "posers" by no-nonsense musicians like Johnny Hutchinson. Nonetheless, he'd often step in on occasions when they were without a drummer, as they were when one of Best's predecessors, Tommy Moore, was very late for Larry Parnes at the Corinthian. They'd got through nine days in Scotland backing Johnny Gentle, despite mutterings from the tour manager about their slovenly turn-out. A pop fan of Cilla White's discernment complained that she "couldn't bear them. I thought they were scruffy and untidy. Their dress was horrible. They wore these terrible motorbike-type jackets. I didn't want to know."[19]

The tragedy of The Beatles was that they didn't care how awful they were. In fact, they rejoiced in it. "It seemed an incredible time before they actually started a number," averred Keith Hartley, a novice Merseyside drummer, "as if they were just messing about."[20] Sutcliffe could barely manage the simplest bass run and, as Cilla had noticed, McCartney broke strings "so often that I used to think one of us in the front row would sometime get an eye knocked out".[19] While they'd learned much from seeing Tony – nicknamed "the Teacher" – at the Top Ten, on the creaky Kaiserkeller stage you'd never know if they were going to play while perched on amplifier rims, smoking lazily, or else, infused with the fizz of readily available chemical stimulants, leap into an onslaught of endlessly inventive caperings, improvised comedy sketches and skylarks crazier (if less physical) than Rory's.

Some items might stop abruptly after a couple of confused verses, but one such as 'Whole Lotta Shakin'' could last a full half-hour, during which Paul might abandon his instrument to appeal to dancers to clap along to what they recognised as Pete's *mach schau* beat, which embraced pounding hi-hat, snare and bass drum in the same lone four-in-a-bar rhythm, chorus after chorus, amid shouts of encouragement, until the levelling guitars surged back in again and, generally, the snare reverted to the usual offbeat and the hi-hat to eight quavers a bar, while the bass drum continued to hit fours rather than its standard rock 'n' roll onbeat.

Although The Beatles had no specially designated frontman like Storm or Sheridan, the greater emphasis was on vocal selections, which ranged from slow solemnities – usually from Paul, the group's Wally – to the blood-curdling dementia of one in the throes of a fit whenever John attacked 'Money', although McCartney was just like Little Richard when he raced through 'Long Tall Sally'. At least it wasn't weak, and neither were they faking it. Far away in Liverpool, they'd endured a baptism of barracking, heckling and catcalls, but they'd gamely retaliated and so, rapidly and grotesquely, a camaraderie of turmoil accumulated between The Beatles and their antagonists so that ugly moments were bypassed as everyone tuned into their awry absurdity – especially as the five themselves conveyed the impression that they, too, were aware of it. The anarchic antithesis of the slickness that was the synchronised footwork of The

Shadows, who were now nearly as famous as Cliff Richard himself, The Beatles walked a highly strung artistic tightrope without a safety net but still stoked up a wildly enthusiastic atmosphere, even from St Pauli's small-hour *demi-monde* of prostitutes, gangsters and *Schlagers* picking fights.

Much of the Beatle attitude rubbed off on Rory Storm And The Hurricanes during the two outfits' shared workload of alternating 30- to 90-minute sets from dusk until the grey of morning. Soon, they too would see nothing amiss in cigarettes dangling from their lower lips whilst on stage, nor in serially consuming Koschmider's gratis nightly allowance of beer and salad between numbers. Ringo also altered his drumming to *mach schau* specifications while hitting solidly and defiantly behind the beat by a fraction both to invest material with stronger definition and to increase tension. It would not be too presumptuous to say that the subtleties of Best and Starr's rhythmic developments while in the Kaiserkeller were to alter pop drumming procedures forever.

Tales of what The Beatles and The Hurricanes did and said when fermenting in Hamburg are still elaborated by so-called "insiders". During that initial sojourn, the most documented incident stemmed from their joint conspiracy to render the Kaiserkeller's unstable stage irreparable via an excess of stamping and jumping so that Koschmider would be compelled to get a new one. It actually caved in during an over-lively 'Blue Suede Shoes' by Storm and The Hurricanes, who compounded their infamy by vacating the club with suspicious haste. Already unsure of the loyalty of his squad of waiter/bouncers since their supervisor, Horst Fascher, had defected to the Top Ten, it would also have been a false economy for Bruno to have ordered them to take revenge with fist and cosh against the English wrongdoers. Instead, he made an example of Rory with a hefty severance from his pay packet and an extra-legal dismissal for "breach of contract".

Storm had set no Deutschmarks aside for such an unthinkable eventuality and, rather than seek repatriation from the British Consulate, roamed St Pauli aimlessly. As he hadn't the means to continue rooming at the Seamen's Mission, he was found a bunk in Sheridan and The Jets' dormitory above the Top Ten until his reinstatement by a calmer Koschmider.

Bruno may also have feared that Eckhorn would take advantage of the situation and entice away the rest of the Kaiserkeller's British contingent, as he had Sheridan. Impervious to their employer's intimidations, The Beatles and Hurricanes' trips to the Top Ten had already gone beyond commiserating with Rory and watching the band; now they were getting up on stage and playing. Acting swiftly, Koschmider gave The Beatles a month's notice, which he shortened even more by arranging the deportation of 17-year-old Harrison for violation of the red-light curfew and two more of them on a trumped-up charge of arson. Storm and The Hurricanes were informed that they wouldn't be seeing in the New Year in Germany after all – although, if he'd so desired, Starr could have stayed on, as he was being headhunted by Sheridan, who – soon to be bereft of the other Jets, when their contract expired – was on the look-out for at least the skeleton of a backing combo (to be called, at various times, The Beat Boys and The Wreckers).

If it finished on a sour note, this first collective encounter with the Fatherland had wrought a more workmanlike Rory Storm And The Hurricanes, toughened for less demanding if more reputable tasks in England. Theirs was a common outcome of having to *mach schau* for hours on end. Through playing for three months at the Top Ten, Dave Dee And The Bostons – Wiltshire equivalent of Storm's unit – found that, "when you come home, you aren't half tight – musically tight. You don't know it's happening to you, because you get tired."[21]

Back in Liverpool, Storm and The Hurricanes reached a rapid zenith, exemplified by their being accosted in the street to sign autographs and imitation when a Bill Hart from Bootle "got a £15 drum kit. I was Ringo".[22] Moreover, Starr's cousin John Foster became "Johnny Sticks", emulating what was onomatopoeically known as Ringo's (and Pete Best's) "atom beat" in Crosby's Roy Brooks And The Dions. Part of the attraction was The Hurricanes' implied bloke-ish camaraderie of all boys together, and – with Starr and Walter in mind – the notion that you didn't have to be Charles Atlas to be in a group. With the alibi of a stage act, a mousy boy had an excuse to make himself look other-worldly as Starr did now with his rings, boots, shiny turquoise suit, gold lamé shirt and strip of hair that, silver under the spotlight, had led a few Germans to insult him unknowingly by inquiring if he dyed it.

Many British towns now appeared to have their own Rory Storm And The Hurricanes. Clacton, for instance, had a Dave Curtiss And The Tremors and Dagenham its Brian Poole And The Tremeloes. If less conveniently placed to strike at the heart of the country's pop industry, Shane Fenton And The Fentones were the toast of glum Mansfield, and tambourine-rattling Wayne Fontana And The Jets were soon to be that of Oldham, where the last chip shop closed at 10.30pm. There was also a growing preponderance of outfits – like, for instance, Bristol's Eagles (winners of a national Boys' Club talent competition) or The Hellions from Worcester – who, with no demarcated leader, were amassing substantial grass-roots followings. Although some local pretty boy might be invited on stage to be Cliff or Billy for a while, he was no longer regarded as an integral part of the group. Most broke up within months of formation, but the concept that an acephalous group could be a credible means of both instrumental and vocal expression had been established.

In Liverpool, for every group that threw in the towel – the Bobby Bell Rockers and Cass And The Cassanovas – a dozen sprang up. As well as Johnny Hutchinson's remarkable Big Three, 1961's harvest included The Hot Rods, The Konkers, The Dronetones, The Albany Four, The Katz, The Zeros, The Lonely Ones, The Quiet Five, the all-girl Cockroaches and – named after the new fortnightly journal devoted to Merseyside pop – The Merseybeats, who, in common with The Moths, The Keenbeats and others, worked the word *beat* into their titles or used insectile appelations to be more like The Beatles, who, with Gerry's Pacemakers and The Remo Four, were about to topple Storm and The Hurricanes as the area's most popular draw – although which would play at the optimum moment when any combination of them were on the same bill was still a matter for conjecture that spring. In February, Storm lorded it over The Beatles and Kingsize's Dominoes at Litherland Town Hall, but before the month was out Gerry headlined over The Hurricanes there and The Beatles did likewise at the Cassanova Club.

Rory himself had cause for more pointed nervous backward glances with the coming of further outstanding showmen such as Freddie Starr (formerly Fowell of Violent Playground fame), Lee Curtis and Faron (alias Bill Russley), a performer disposed towards knee drops and scissor kicks and whom Gerry And The Pacemakers would take to Hamburg as guest vocalist.

Consolation for private anxieties and dark nights of the ego was a full work schedule within easy reach and – in those days – only instruments, puny amplifiers (30 watts at most) and drums to transport. From *Mersey Beat*, the reader could select an evening out from a wide array of venues, from a suburban pub's functions room with The Zeros to an "Operation Big Beat" at the New Brighton Tower with Rory, Kingsize, Gerry, The Beatles and The Remo Four from 7.30am to 1am. Without an alcohol licence and below ground, the Iron Door could stay open until daybreak, as it did in March 1961 when, breaking fire regulations, 2,000 attended its twelve-hour "Rock Around The Clock" event. A more typical night's work for Rory Storm And The Hurricanes, however, was an arrival at the Jive Hive at 8.15pm for a half-hour set, then on to the Cavern to do 45 minutes before returning to the Jive Hive to play last and then home by midnight.

Their name would not be synonymous with any particular club or palais, as The Swinging Blue Jeans were to their manager's Downbeat, The Undertakers to Orrell Park Ballroom or The Delacardoes (two smart chaps in glasses) at the Green Dolphin. The Beatles were a fixture at the Cavern which would see no more Club Perdido Thursdays and was putting the remaining vestiges of its jazz dignity into booking trad acts to warm up for The Beatles. Despite its sodden, choking blackness, the Cavern had become a lunchtime haunt of those who eked out a living or fed off college grants in studio flats in crumbling Victorian townhouses to the east of the Anglican cathedral. The Beatles had fascinated a similar "existentialist" crowd in the

Kaiserkeller. To Cilla White, they were "just as scruffy as ever. They were sort of clean and scruffy, if you know what I mean. Then I started listening to their sound. They were better than I thought."[19]

Not everyone adhered to this view. For such as The Remo Four's Colin Manley, "they really weren't very good".[24] All the same, "They were loud," admitted a Swinging Blue Jean. "They had presence."[23] Sometimes they made the mistake of airing a home-made Lennon-McCartney opus, but, as a Helena Joyce moaned, "We much preferred them to belt out the old Everly Brothers numbers."[22] Nonetheless, soon the massed humanity milling about in the Cavern for The Beatles would embrace not only the beatnik set but older schoolchildren, shop assistants and office employees like Cilla, who was in a typing pool at a Stanley Street firm that manufactured insulated cable.

Cilla's reward for her incurable record buying and club going was a position as *Mersey Beat*'s peanut-waged fashion columnist. Since finding herself microphone in hand one frolicsome night at the Iron Door, she'd also become one of a handful of freelance female vocalists who performed with several different Merseybeat groups. With dance troupes like The Shimmy-Shimmy Queens and occasional suppliers of sex interest like Dot Rhone, who simply sat on a stool in the midst of The Beatles, girls like Cilla were either an aberration or a breath of fresh air in a male-dominated sphere. Like beauty queen Irene Hughes and the younger Beryl Marsden did with The Merseybeats and The Undertakers, respectively, "Swingin' Cilla" granted most of her favours to Kingsize Taylor (then her boyfriend) and The Dominoes. However, only token persuasion was needed to get her to sing with other bands with whom she and her pals hobnobbed. Among these were The Big Three, Faron's Flamingos – and Rory Storm And The Hurricanes.

In their beloved key of G ("It could be a Yale key, for all I cared"[19]), Cilla unfurled a supple – if rather nasal – richness onto the sophistications of such as 'Autumn Leaves' and 'When I Fall In Love', but she wasn't above ravers like 'Hound Dog' and 'Boys'. Wally wasn't bothered about her borrowing his 'Fever' and 'Summertime' now and then, but Ringo was damned if he was going to let her have his 'Boys'. A compromise was reached and "we did it as a duet, and even then he didn't concede anything. He had a microphone over the drums and I used to have to sing it bent over his kit."[23] Ostensibly overwhelming her with matey affection, he'd cattily dub her "Swingin' Cyril" and – a pot calling the kettle black – criticise her broad "wacker" tongue, even if it lent her the common touch with audiences, absolving himself by saying, "I'm the drummer. I don't have to talk, but you do."[19] Starr's sage, seen-it-all-before air often irritated Swingin' Cyril as much as it did many others, and yet, beneath it all, Cilla and Richie had a deep and lifelong friendship and an almost sibling pride in each other.

As Rory was keen on bringing Cilla to Hamburg's Top Ten as Gerry would Faron, Ringo was dispatched to sound her out. Rather than talk to her with her rather intimidating father within earshot, Richie tapped on the side window near her desk in Stanley Street. She'd have to ask her dad, she said, and she'd only been a few weeks here. Predictably, Mr White, as self-appointed guardian of his daughter's job (and innocence), wouldn't hear of it.

From the family home along grimy Scotland Road, Cilla's dad would walk to work down Boundary Road, which ran directly to the docks. At number 56d, a council flat, Maureen Cox, Richie's "steady", lived with her mother, Mary, while her father, Joe, was at sea much of the time as a ship's steward. With the candour of middle age, Maureen – "Mo" – would describe herself as being "thick as two short planks"[24] when she left school at the minimum age of 15 to begin as a junior hairdressing assistant at the Ashley du Pre beauty parlour, which necessitated evening classes and jolting morning rush-hour bus journeys to a stop or two before the Pier Head terminus. Whatever her way with shampoo, curlers and banal chit-chat, she was a good advertisement for the salon in that, shedding her puppy fat, she'd blossomed into a pocket Venus with an urchin cut – usually a natural brown – that emphasised the raw drama of her fashionably high cheekbones, bold blue eyes and assured if impersonal poise as she titivated some aged virago's tortured curls.

En route to one of her hairstyling lessons, she'd seen Ringo emerge from the old Ford Zodiac that he drove unqualified and asked for an autograph. From the perspective of a club stage, Mo was at first no different from any of the other pale-faced "Judies" in suede, leather or fishnet who chattered excitedly until the group was announced. On one evening, however, Johnny Guitar gave her a second glance and they "walked out" a few times. Later, at the Blue Angel, it was Ringo who started a conversation with Mo and a stout friend, offering them a lift home. The girls seemed to have some vice-like grip on each other, or maybe Mo didn't wish to show unmaidenly eagerness, for her and Richie's cinema date the following week was as a threesome. In an attempt to separate them, Starr screwed himself up to telephone Maureen at work – where personal calls were frowned upon – and, for the next assignation, the friend got the message and Ringo and Maureen got better acquainted to the extent of public tendernesses, like his lighting two cigarettes at once and passing one to her.

To some, it was inconceivable that a bird like Mo was going out with Ringo. Backstage gossip assumed that it was an attraction of opposites, the fascination that women sometimes have for the pathos of the clown. Also, celebrity – even if only parochial – can be a powerful aphrodisiac. Her sense of humour was more barbed than his but as dry and, while she was forthrightly capable of sticking up for herself, Mo was content to be an adjunct to his self-image as a renowned and much-travelled man about Liverpool, a bit of a card and more than able both to keep down his drink and to stand his round.

Richie, Mo and intimates like Cilla, Paul Rogers and Pat Davies would hold court most frequently in the Zodiac cellar (now licensed), where a jam session by personnel from The Hurricanes, The Pacemakers, The Beatles and The Big Three was still dinning long after milk floats had braved the cold of sunrise. It had been enlivened by the unveilings of Nicola, a French stripper with whom one spectator became overly and demonstratively entranced. On another night, the door was bolted hastily when a drunken rabble converged outside. With no telephone inside, staff and members – including Maureen and Ringo – quaked to the noise of gleeful ramming and savage oaths as the mob tried to break in, only tiring of their sport hours later.

During more tranquil booze-ups in the Zodiac, the Cabin, the Blue Angel and similar musicians' watering holes, bands would brag of imminent tours of outlandish countries and even record releases; but, while yet to deteriorate into a cauldron of back-stabbing, underhandedness and favouritism, Mersey Beat's *esprit de corps* was such that it wasn't uncommon for, say, Faron to vault on stage for a couple of numbers with The Dominoes or Rory Storm to stand in for a laryngitic John Lennon. Although Ringo wouldn't feel that he knew The Beatles well enough to invite them to his uproarious coming-of-age party at Admiral Grove,[25] he deputised likewise for Pete Best when the latter was poleaxed with bronchitis and on later occasions. Once, Neil Aspinall – a ledger clerk who supplemented his income by driving and unloading for The Beatles – dared to rouse Starr before noon to fill in for Best at the Cavern, "but I had no kit. I got up on stage with only cymbals and gradually Pete's kit started arriving piece by piece."[26]

If Rory Storm imagined that he was on terms of fluctuating equality with The Beatles, *Mersey Beat* editor Bill Harry was there to take him down a peg or two – literally. When tabulating the newspaper's first popularity poll, Bill – an Art School chum of Lennon's – counted "more votes for Rory Storm And The Hurricanes than The Beatles, but I put The Beatles at Number One because I'd heard that Rory was buying bundles of copies and a lot of Rory Storm entries were in the same green ink. About 20 or 30 would arrive from the same postal area at the same time, so I discounted those." Flying in the face of rancour "about you writing about The Beatles all the time" from no less than Bob Wooler, Bill placed Storm and The Hurricanes fourth, behind The Remo Four, Gerry and, of course, John and co. Looking back on 1961, *Mersey Beat* would tip The Beatles, Mark Peters and new face Karl Terry for national acclaim.

On some fronts, even Harry's darling Beatles were being overtaken. Paul Rogers had had his single '42,000 Kisses' issued, and discs by both The Seniors (with Freddie Starr) – a 45 and an album – and Scouse folk quartet The Spinners wouldn't be far behind it.

Then domiciled in England, Gene Vincent was pressing Gerry And The Pacemakers to accompany him on a tour of Israel while, grabbing the bull by the horns, Steve Bennett And The Syndicate spent much of the latter half of 1961 in a tent in rural London. Sniffing around the record companies, they failed a recording test with Pye because their diction was "too northern" but still netted lucrative engagements at US air bases in the Home Counties. Lest we forget, gone beyond altogether was Billy Fury, of lesser years than Storm and most of The Hurricanes, who was snapped consorting with royalty at Ascot.

The Beatles had lately signed with *bona fide* manager Brian Epstein. More than just a bloke with a phone, he ran North End Music Stores (NEMS), which – so its regular *Mersey Beat* box ad read – was "The Finest Record Selection In The North". As well as prodding his contacts in the business on The Beatles' behalf, he was sinking hard cash into them and, if nought else, getting them off the Liverpool-Hamburg treadmill with a booking schedule that reached as far south as Swindon.

Rory Storm was still in much the same rut, marking time with Butlin's and Germany. In 1961, the cream of south Lancashire had been represented in Hamburg by Gerry, The Seniors, Rory Storm And The Hurricanes, The Big Three – and The Beatles, who, all but Best, adopted the *pilzenkopf* ("mushroom head") hairstyle, as worn by Klaus Voorman, Peter Penner and other of their bohemian – or "exi" – admirers in Hamburg. Pidgin German left its mark in the Mersey groups' on-stage dialogue past the expected *danke schoens* and *prosts*. A frequent *wunsche* ("request") for the ladies was the langsome *lied* ("ballad") 'Besame Mucho' while the men clumped tables to Wilbert Harrison's 'Kansas Stadt'.

Conversely, the English of club staff and exis might have been riddled with Scouse slang, but there were rumblings that, if you'd heard one Mersey Beat group, you'd heard the lot. As a consequence, other UK counties had been scoured for acts that could offer more than the two-guitars-bass-drums music that was fast becoming prototypical of Liverpool. Half of the dialects of Britain resounded around the Reeperbahn in 1961, from the countrified Cockney of Kent's Bern Elliott And The Fenmen to the trill of Glasgow's Isabelle Bond to the flat vowels of Walsall's Tanya Day to the Cornish burr of Dave Lee And The Staggerlees.

Rory Storm And The Hurricanes replaced a Nottingham outfit, The Jaybirds, at the Top Ten, and, with Tony Sheridan – now the Elvis of St Pauli – shared its sleeping quarters. Although The Hurricanes accorded Tony – still without a permanent band – competent accompaniment during their stint, he'd select The Beatles for the honour of backing him on a German 45 and half of its attendant LP.

Some of the tracks – notably 'Let's Slop' – would allude to the Twist and its variations. This "most vulgar dance ever invented"[29] was as much the latest rave worldwide as trad had been in Britain alone. Its Mecca was New York's Peppermint Lounge, where, to the sound of Joey Dee And The Starliters, socialites and middle-aged trend-setters mingled with beatniks to do the Twist, in which you pretended to towel your back whilst grinding out a cigarette butt with your foot. Its Acker Bilk was Chubby Checker, but all manner of unlikely artists were recording twist singles, from Sinatra and Elvis downwards. Worse, it wouldn't go away, probably because you were too spoilt for choice with alternatives like the Fly, the Locomotion, the Slop, the Mashed Potato, the ungainly Turkey Trot, the Mickey's Monkey, the Hully Gully, the Hitch-Hiker, the back-breaking Limbo, the Bristol Stomp, the Madison and even a revival of the Charleston. Little dates a 1960s film more than the obligatory Twist sequence, and to this day the elderly will slip unconsciously into the Twist whenever the music hots up at a dinner and dance.

Dance-craze records in the charts generally indicate stagnation in pop, and Britain in 1961 was certainly heaving with that. On pop TV in those days were insipidly handsome boys next door such as Ronnie Carroll and Mark Wynter with slop ballads that your mum liked. The Mudlarks, spiritual descendants of *Melody Cruise*'s Teenagers, were voted the UK's Best Vocal Group in the *NME*. Young England responded by packing out clubs that had gone over to the depraved

Twist like Birmingham's Moat Twistacular and Ilford's Twist at the Top, which had its own Joey Dee And The Starliters in The Seniors, who would name their LP after the place.

Mersey Beat's rhetorical question "Has Trad Jazz Died On Merseyside?"[30] was answered tacitly in the volume of twist exhibition teams – The King Twisters, Mr Twist And His Twistettes, *ad nauseum* – that utilised time where a trad band once might have done. When the headliners went on, group members like Mel "King of Twist" Turner of The Bandits and – to the Judies' delight – an embarrassed Pete Best would be thrust to the front to demonstrate the dance. Classic rock was elbowed aside for renderings of 'Twist And Shout' (and just plain 'Shout') by The Isley Brothers, Dee Dee Sharp's 'Mashed Potato Time' and, from The Orlons, 'Shimmy Shimmy' and 'The Wah-Watusi'. The subject matter was less directly to do with mobility, but the beat was essentially the same in such as The Marvelettes' 'Please Mr Postman', The Contours' 'Do You Love Me' and 'I'm Gonna Knock On Your Door', sung originally in the "baby" counter-tenor of Eddie Hodges. The hipper Mersey Beat bands were also rifling the catalogues of Benny Spellman, Barbara George and other Americans unbeknownst to the ordinary Scouser or, indeed, the ordinary anyone else. Ringo Starr swore by Lee Dorsey, a black soul singer from New Orleans, to whose albums he would turn as regularly as a monk to the Bible.

The order of the day back at Pwllheli, however, was not Lee Dorsey or The Orlons but the passing joys of the British hit parade – The Marcels' mauling of 'Blue Moon', Bruce Channel's 'Hey Baby' and – when some idiot's girl wanted it – the much-covered 'Sucu Sucu'. More palatable to The Hurricanes was Ray Charles' 'Hit The Road, Jack', which was rasped out during Starr Time with Wally prominent on the skittish, gospel-esque backing responses. As Saturday was changeover day, the Rock and Calypso Ballroom was at its most untamed on the preceding night, but during Rory Storm And The Hurricanes' second Butlins stint it seemed more frenzied, the laughter shriller, the eyes brighter. Some Fridays, security officers would have to rescue Rory as he lost tufts of hair to clawing females while The Hurricanes made their escapes with mere autographs, Richie scribbling, "Best wishes from the sensational Ringo Starr."

4 "I Had To Join Them As People, As Well As A Drummer"

"RORY STORM BACK SOON!" proclaimed *Mersey Beat*'s front page, and when he was, Bill Harry was one of the first to know. "He was always plugging and plugging," he remembered. "I was in bed in my flat in Mount Street and, about four in the morning, there was this furious banging on the door. All the people in the other flats were hanging out their windows and a cop car came, shining its lights. 'What's going on?' It was Rory with some photos of himself for *Mersey Beat*." Ensuring that his birthdays, too, were public events, Storm seemed to think that everything that happened to him was worth communicating to the whole of Merseyside. Nevertheless, his talent for self-promotion was such that many were convinced that he was always about to soar to the very summit of pop. He could do just that whenever he felt like it. But why should he? He was the greatest already.

If second-billed now to Gerry, The Beatles and other acts that had once supported them, Rory and The Hurricanes made up for long absences in Germany and Pwllheli by packing in as many local engagements as the traffic would allow before they had to vanish again. In a month underscored with run-of-the-mill club dates, there'd be some prestigious presentations like a "Rock And Trad Spectacular" at Southport's tiered Floral Hall, a St Patrick's Night "Rock Gala" at Knotty Ash Village Hall or the "Cavalcade Of Rock And Twist" at the New Brighton Tower, where, wrote schoolgirl diarist Sue Evans, there were "thousands. Danced with four gorgeous Beat Types."[1] When Jerry Lee Lewis was on at the Tower or The Shadows at the Cavern, Mr Showmanship would be noticeably present, if not actually performing, as if to infer that, but for a hit record or two, he was their equal.

Sometimes, Rory would cause upset, as he did by declaring two Hurricane girlfriends as victors of a "Miss Merseybeat competition"[2] that he was judging; but, with work as far away as Italy for the taking, things were looking up again, although not as much as they were for The Beatles, now that Epstein had spruced up both their behaviour and appearance. Nowadays, they'd forsaken Hamburg leathers and *mach schau* for mohair suits and were playing to a fixed routine and not swearing or horsing around on stage half as much. In other words, Brian was reshaping them into what a respectable record-company executive in 1962 presumed a good pop group to be.

The very day before they and Epstein entered into agreement, The Beatles had played to only 18 patrons on a wintry Saturday in a palais within the military borough of Aldershot, way down in Hampshire. This booking had been arranged by Sam Leach, the most adventurous of Merseyside promoters and a great friend of Rory Storm, who, with The Hurricanes, drew via word of mouth over 200 at the same distant venue the following week. Although Leach then turned his back on Aldershot, Storm and his group continued this southern offensive on their own. Largely through Mrs Caldwell's telephone badgering, they even ventured as far east as Norwich. However, such expeditions were sporadic, for, unlike The Beatles, they hadn't the clout to get themselves attached to some big leisure corporation like Mecca or Top Rank.

A feather in their cap, however, was that 1962's Butlin's foray would be at bracing Skegness, the Lincolnshire camp that was the oldest and largest in Sir Billy's network and the setting of the latest Billy Bunter book, in which he'd been pleasingly portrayed. Earlier that year, the group had spent a sunnier spring than most Liverpudlians with their first residency in a club in Marbella where the Spanish would soon debase their culture by permitting the construction of pubs, fish-and-chip shops and further home comforts for British holidaymakers.

To keep Rory Storm And The Hurricanes on the boil back home, the news was leaked to *Mersey Beat* by his mother that Rory had, apparently, saved three – including Ringo – from drowning in the Mediterranean. However, although they'd be welcomed back with the usual warmth, a Rory Storm publicity stunt was now as commonplace as a whist drive. The Swinging Blue Jeans, The Beatles and The Big Three had all had London recording tests, and with *Mersey Beat*'s demand "London, Take A Look Up North"[3] yet unheeded, unless Storm pulled a more palpable stroke than being nabbed by a porter spray-painting "I Love Rory" on a Bootle railway station wall, he and his Hurricanes were going to miss the boat.

From other regions, some groups more electrifying than they were likewise breaking loose of parochial orbits and were even invading Liverpool clubland. The Hellions' Iron Door debut was yet to be, but frequenting it now were Bern Elliott's Fenmen, Sheffield's serpentine Dave Berry And The Cruisers, Gerry Levene And His Avengers from Birmingham (soon to have its own *Midland Beat* gazette), Blackburn's Lionel Morton Quartet and, from Manchester, The Hollies and Freddie And The Dreamers, whose spindly, four-eyed singer would fling off all his garments bar a pair of vivid "short shorts" during a Hollywood Argyles ditty of the same title.

Kent's Sounds Incorporated were constantly on the move around Britain and Europe, more often than not backing Gene Vincent, while The Eagles – after appearing in a B-feature about Bristol youth movements – had snared a weekly showcase (*Meet The Eagles*) on Radio Luxembourg. Shane Fenton And The Fentones, meanwhile, had made a higher quantum jump to a regular spot on the Light Programme's two-hour-long pop show *Saturday Club* and a modest stack of Top-30 hits on Parlophone. Their opposite numbers at Decca were to be Brian Poole And The Tremeloes (who'd been at Butlin's in Ayr in 1961 when Rory Storm's Hurricanes were at Pwllheli).

Certain Hurricanes were disturbed that the fish weren't also biting for them. Obliged too frequently to sign on at Renshaw Hall labour exchange, they may have been piqued by their leader's shameless habit lately of appearing without them for some dates as the *ad hoc* aggregation "Rory Storm And The Wild Ones". Egmond had been the first to slip his cable for a spell in The Seniors, who were about to release another 45 from their Fontana album. *Mersey Beat* gossip had it that Ringo was to join him. Instead, in January 1962, Starr threw in his lot with Tony Sheridan at the Top Ten in Hamburg after Peter Eckhorn (with Sheridan) had flown to Liverpool to be disappointed by the price that Epstein had now put on The Beatles. So that he'd have something to show for his journey, Peter tantalised Starr with £30 a week – huge for the time – and use of a flat and car.

The Top Ten would soon be losing trade irrecoverably to the Star-Club. The newer and more extensive venue's owner, Manfred Weissleder, had already out-bid Eckhorn for Horst Fascher as manager, a checkmating augmented when this compound Hercules secured The Beatles – and Sheridan – to open the place in April 1962. In anticipation (and to Eckhorn's annoyance), Sheridan named his group "The Star Combo" as he worked his notice period in tandem with Roy Young, a Little Richard type from Oxford. With a pedigree stretching back to *Six-Five Special*, Young would also desert to the Star-Club.

Ringo, however, would not be drumming before its stage backdrop of skyscrapers when Sheridan and The Beatles supported and proudly socialised with visiting US idols – including Ray Charles, Little Richard,[4] Pat Boone and the ubiquitous Vincent – who'd plug gaps in their European itineraries with nights at the Star-Club and, round-robin style, at Weissleder-controlled engagements in Stuttgart and Hanover. While Ray Charles might have thought, "That boy [Sheridan] sings with a lot of soul,"[5] Ringo had become disenchanted with Tony, who, on closer acquaintance, was given to provoking arguments, sulking and impetuously launching into songs not in the *modus operandi*, unhelpfully leaving the panicking Combo to busk behind him. Like, what key's this one in, man? Like, Z minus, man.

With more than his fill of both Hamburg and "the Teacher", Starr had gone home to his mother and Rory Storm And The Hurricanes, who had spent an expensive few months with Blackpool drummer Derek Fell whenever he wasn't required by his usual group,

The Executives. It was accepted without question that Ringo, like the equally perfidious Wally, would return to the fold. Although neither could be trusted not to stray again, it was outwardly as if nothing had happened, as they got into trim for Skegness in the Majestic, the Iron Door and other too-familiar haunts, as well as a short series of mess dances for US airmen in France. If Rory could square it with Elsie and Harry, Richie promised to see out the contract with – so Rory had assured *Mersey Beat* – "the only group to make the grade at Butlin's for three years in succession".[6]

While Starr had been away, blasé Storm had developed into even more of a ritualist. If he wasn't to be an Elvis in the wider world, he'd limit himself to remaining adored as one locally. He was now captain of the recently formed Mersey Beat soccer eleven, for whom he'd later score a hat-trick in a charity match against Liverpool FC. Moreover, he still ran for Pembroke Harriers and fronted both The Hurricanes and The Wild Ones. "He never wanted to make it nationally," his sister would insist after he didn't, "as he was happy being King of Liverpool."[7]

There didn't appear to be much future in music anyway. Fontana's patience with The Seniors was snapping, as neither of their singles had had enough airplay to near the charts, and The Big Three and the other latest contenders had got nowhere with their auditions. The studio audience on ITV's new show *Thank Your Lucky Stars* still screamed indiscriminately at male pop idols but, as much pin-ups as they were nowadays, TV and film actors like Ed Byrnes (jive-talking "Kookie" of 77 *Sunset Strip*), Sean Connery (in his first Bond movie) and even Peter Sellers (star, with Leo McKern, of 1962's *The Mouse That Roared*, a topical Cold War satire).

It had occurred to Starr that he stood more chance of a livelihood as a musician than any two-a-penny singer. Even further from the core of UK pop than Liverpool, Derek Fell had nevertheless once been a temporary Shadow. From Burnley, Bobby Elliott was now in Shane Fenton's Fentones, having distinguished himself in a short-list that included a lively London sticksman named Keith Moon. Other of Starr's percussive contemporaries had roamed beyond rock 'n' roll. Having taught himself to read the relevant dots, Jimmy Nicol had been in the ranks of David Ede And The Rabin Rock, whose upbeat muzak was an apt prelude to his next post, under the baton of light-orchestra conductor Cyril Stapleton. Nicol was also hired for a session with Cleo Laine, who was as much a *grande dame* of jazz as presenter Noele Gordon on ITV's *Lunch Box*, lightest of light entertainments, in whose studio band Pete York – beetle browed and gifted – drummed for the money he could not yet earn in various Midlands pop and jazz outfits.

While these players opted for grey facelessness outside the main spotlight, Ringo Starr pondered. As it had been just before Pwllheli in 1960, he'd reached something of a crossroads. Even in Germany, he'd tried to telephone Maureen daily, and when at home he was now foregoing carousing away many of his nights off in the Liverpool clubs, preferring instead to stay in spinning records with Mo or in front of the television. From his armchair in Admiral Grove, he became a lifelong watcher of *Coronation Street*, a soap opera as ingrained with northern working-class realism as the BBC's police series *Z-Cars*, also home produced but of grittier substance than gorblimey *Dixon Of Dock Green*.

As far as censorship would allow, these programmes emphasised what might be in store for Richard Starkey, should he choose to pack in drumming. After his grandfather's funeral in 1961, "It took a long time to get over it," sighed he. "We'd always been close, and I worshipped him."[8] Still mournful a year later, Richie would wonder whether 22 wasn't a good age to settle down. The old man had twisted the plain gold wedding ring from his hand when his grandson had been engaged to Geraldine, and "I always reckoned I'd wear it when I got married".[9]

As Harry and Elsie often reminded him, it wasn't too late for him to resume his Hunt's apprenticeship. While taking exasperated stock, he contemplated wedding Maureen and uprooting altogether for the less humdrum USA, even going as far as writing to the Chamber of Commerce in Houston, simply because it was at the heartland of the Wild West – although Texans were more likely to be in oil than bronco-bustin', these days – and was the nearest city to Centerville, birthplace of Lightnin' Hopkins, a post-war blues artist to whose grippingly personal style an enthralled Ringo had been introduced by Tony Sheridan one Hamburg afternoon around a record player.

Houston's reply was quite heartening, but the thickness and aggressive intimacy of the application forms for emigration were too offputting. Hunt's seemed to be beckoning still; but, while removed from parental pressures about a proper job, Richie in Skegness received a letter from Kingsize Taylor offering £20 per week for him to fill the drum stool soon to be vacated by Billy Hatton's friend Dave Lovelady, who had bowed to his parents' wishes that he complete his degree course in architecture. As Taylor was a bandleader of steadier stamp than Sheridan or Storm, Ringo gave tentative assent to be a Domino as soon as he was free. The personnel of The Dominoes and Hurricanes had overlapped already in the past year when the former's Bobby Thompson had stood in during Egmond's furlough with The Seniors, and so, as one professional to another, Storm was dispassionate about Richie's decision, issuing an open invitation for the drummer to re-enlist one day. Neither regarded this eventuality as improbable.

Able to suspend the question of Starr's replacement until they were back in Liverpool, Rory and The Hurricanes carried on with a season that was not passing without incident. The Wars of the Roses had not, apparently, been forgotten as two gangs of young millworkers from, respectively, Wigan and Wakefield fought each other on every possible pretext for the entire week that they were there. Several other Friday evenings were also enlivened with punch-ups. Storm was once forced to pick his way across a railway line to throw off some hard-cases riled by his narcissistic endeavours on the bandstand. On the horns of a similar dilemma, Johnny Guitar elected to take his medicine and be swung in full stage gear into a swimming pool in which an Indian elephant had lately expired and bobbed about in the chlorinated water for three days until a crane could be found to shift it. For a contravention of the Butlin edict about who could and could not enter staff chalets, Guitar and Starr were banished beyond the camp walls, except when they were needed in the ballroom, where every other request from the dance floor seemed to be for Pat Boone's 'Speedy Gonzales'.

Last but far from least, rumour has it – right or wrong – that Starr, with over a fortnight to go, decamped midweek, still owing Johnny his half of the rent for the shabby caravan they'd leased for the period of their expulsion. Possibly to thumb his nose at the authority that had willed this disgrace, Ringo was off to join The Beatles almost immediately after Lennon and McCartney had driven through a windy night to bang on the trailer's door at 10am on an August Tuesday, offering a fiver more per week than Kingsize Taylor. They'd told Brian Epstein to fire Pete Best, who "didn't even have the opportunity of discussing it with the rest of the group".[10]

Now that The Beatles had gained that elusive recording deal – with Parlophone – Pete had been of no more use to them. They'd been glad enough to recruit him in 1960, however, when Allan Williams wouldn't have let them go to Hamburg without a drummer. Back on Merseyside, Best's volcanic mother, Mona, had served them as Violet Caldwell did her boy's group. As Stormsville was the hub of The Hurricanes' operation, so the Bests' 15-room home in Hayman's Green was that of The Beatles. "She was a strong, dominant woman," Bill Harry described Mrs Best, who did much of her shy son's talking for him. "I think she was responsible for getting them their first radio gig. She was why Neil Aspinall was brought in. He was Pete's best friend and he lived with the Bests." Even after they'd clicked with Epstein, she still saw herself as patroness of the group, who, according to Bill, "didn't want her interference".

Although the imperceptible isolation of her son from the others had started during that first trip to Hamburg, Mona was victim of a more intensifying character assassinations by Harrison, McCartney and Lennon than Pete over venomous pints in a pub's murkiest corner. Stuart Sutcliffe had had no hand in this, as he'd left the group in 1961 to recommence his art studies in Hamburg.[11] The Beatles had not replaced him, favouring the simpler expedient of transferring Paul to bass.

Horst Fascher would swear that McCartney was what he called the "sunny boy"[12] of the group, although, as far as Southport promoter Bill Appleby was concerned, "Pete was definitely the big attraction and did much to establish their popularity during their early career."[13] A lot of what Best did was passive, because girls melted just beholding his athlete's physique and sultry Cliff Richard handsomeness. However, unlike Paul, he was genuinely bemused at the interest of the Judies, whose cow-eyed efforts to grab his on-stage attention had teased his dark eyes from the drums. They'd shiver with pleasure at his rare bashful grins and squeal with ecstasy when he took an even rarer lead vocal on 'Boys', Carl Perkins' 'Matchbox' and, especially, Presley's 'Wild In The Country', which exuded the breathy sentience of a man who has been sprinting.

Pete wasn't allowed to sing when The Beatles made that first radio broadcast in Manchester, but when they were mobbed afterwards he was unjustly berated by Paul's father for inadvertently stealing the limelight. Mr McCartney[14] might have preferred the group to ditch Lennon, who had the cheek to call him by his Christian name and who – as he'd once warned his son – was the proverbial bad influence. However, he acknowledged that Paul and John were the quartet's creative muscle and, like them – and young George, swimming with the tide – took exception to Best always being singled out for a front-page photo in *Mersey Beat* and on posters ("Hear Pete Best Sing Tonight!"), and when Bob Wooler whipped up an encore with "Let's hear it again for John, Paul, George—" pause "—and *Pete!*" the volume of screams rising to its loudest.

This partiality might not have mattered so much, had the softly spoken drummer not been such a being apart from the other three, a Tony Curtis among the *pilzenkopfs*, a non-partaker of benzedrine and Preludin and a swain whose intentions towards his Marks & Spencer's girlfriend were honourable. Only on the periphery of their private jokes and folklore, and as reliable as he was mature, there was no denying that, to his fellow Beatles, Best was a bit...well, you know. Anyway, he had to go.

The final nail in his coffin was a try-out for Parlophone in one of

EMI's studios down at Abbey Road in St John's Wood. As rock 'n' rollers in concert tended to accelerate and slow down *en bloc* to inconsistencies of tempo caused by the mood of the hour, it wasn't uncommon for drumming on record to be ghosted by someone more technically accomplished than a given act's regular player. In the early 1960s, among those earning Musicians' Union-regulated tea-breaks in this fashion were ex-Kenny Ball Jazzman Ron Bowden, Jimmy Nicol, Bobbie Graham, Clem Cattini of The Tornados and 32-year-old Andy White from The Vic Lewis Orchestra, whom George Martin would bring in – with no slight on Pete Best (and, next, the untried Ringo) intended – on the session for 'Love Me Do', written by McCartney and Lennon as The Beatles' debut single.

Some would recall the Lord of Parlophone denying that there was anything fundamentally wrong with Pete as a drummer and then contradicting himself a couple of years later. Locally, Best was rated highly by no less than Johnny Hutchinson, who had been advocated by Epstein as Pete's successor during the horrid conspiracy. Precursors of the late-1960s power trio, Johnny's Big Three was the most forceful outfit on Merseyside, a characteristic reflected in its members' hard-living behaviour off stage, crystallised by one of them downing a whole month's allocation of free beer at the Star-Club in the space of an evening. It was the likelihood of conflict involving fisticuffs with John Lennon that precluded Hutchinson from being the most serious candidate for the new Beatle. The real thing, Johnny wouldn't have tolerated a pretend tough guy like Lennon poking ruthless fun at him to anywhere like the degree that had driven the gentler Tommy Moore from the group in 1960.

Besides, as he'd already resisted inducements to join Johnny Kidd And The Pirates, why should Hutchinson give up The Big Three for The Beatles? Nonetheless, he consented to dep for Pete Best, who, for some reason, wouldn't fulfil two Beatles bookings that couldn't be postponed in the interregnum between his sacking and Ringo's arrival for two hours' rehearsal before his debut as an official Beatle in front of an audience of 500 at a Horticultural Society dance in Birkenhead on Saturday 18 August 1962.

Determined upon the utmost correctness, Epstein had telephoned Stormsville to inform Violet that The Beatles were prepared to wait for Ringo to finish at Skegness. Nevertheless, when not in possession of this intelligence, Rory had fulminated against The Beatles for so inconveniently purloining his drummer. However, he turned a thoughtful steering wheel while dashing back to Liverpool to find a substitute. Collecting his mother, he hastened to Hayman's Green to present sympathies to the Bests. Did Pete want to be a Hurricane? He could start right now. No, said Mona, he was too depressed. Facing the music back at Butlin's, The Hurricanes in desperation had taken on Anthony Ashdown, an actor[15] who fancied a go on the drums for one dreadful week before Norman McGarry from Johnny Sandon And The Searchers – another unit in disarray – took over. Time was when drummers were falling over themselves to work with Rory Storm.

Matters mended to an extent when The Hurricanes poached The Memphis Three's 16-year-old Gibson Kemp, who, it was hoped, would grow into the bulkier Starr's stage suit. Brian Epstein had advised Ringo that, under the circumstances, it might not be politic to press Storm or Kemp for the £15 it had cost him, as things were ticklish enough as it was. The horticultural show had been the quiet before the storm. At the Cavern on the following evening, there'd been a near riot when The Beatles had entered with their new member, with Harrison, his main champion, being punched in the face. Flanked by bodyguards, Brian ignored bawled abuse and – like Ringo – several poison pen letters from incensed Best devotees.

Later, the tyres of Epstein's brand-new Ford Zodiac were let down as further proof that, as a self-effacing Starr lamented, "they loved Pete. Why get an ugly-looking cat when you can get a good-looking one?"[16] To be fair, Ringo had shaved off his scrappy beard and, on Brian's recommendation, had had his hair resculpted at Horne Brothers to a heavy fringe that, after a decade of quiffing, wouldn't cascade naturally into a Beatle cut for nearly a year. Neil Aspinall dropped off the result at Admiral Grove, where Elsie's surprise at her son's new look was parried with, "It's no different change, really," registered by Aspinall as the first Beatle Ringoism. His mother might have liked his neater, shorter style, but when a photo of Richie was printed in *Mersey Beat* it took a while for readers to become accustomed to this changeling in The Beatles, a frog where there'd been a prince. His supplanting of Best had been represented in its pages as the amicable if sudden consequence of scarcely more than a mild disagreement between the parties, but the hostility at the Cavern demonstrated that the truth was known in the street.

Pete would remain a Beatle morally to some who heard him drum with the group, but most fans – if fickle in affections towards its individuals – found it in them to maintain overall loyalty. "It will seem difficult for a few weeks," admitted Harrison, "but I think that the majority will soon be taking Ringo for granted."[17] After an uncomfortable few minutes when the set opened at the Cavern – especially when George, with a black eye, publicly welcomed Ringo – the four were cheered by the seething crowd. Other than turn from The Beatles altogether, there was nothing for it but to accept the new situation, and by November onlookers were yelling to the now-unchallenged front line to let the underdog behind them sing a number. It was, calculated *Mersey Beat*, his "wonderfully shy personality which appeals to the fans".[13] In short, he was a Pete Best without good looks, a Beatle for girls to love more as a brother than a demon lover.

Musically, Ringo's coming made no pronounced difference. An up-and-coming Bootle vocalist, Billy Kramer didn't "think The Beatles were any better with Ringo Starr. I never doubted his ability as a drummer, but I thought they were a lot more raw and raucous with Pete."[18] Often inclined to close his eyes while playing, Ringo was hardly less reticent than Best on stage. Subordinate to even George – himself very much the junior partner – in the group's power structure, he'd been only too glad to take a back seat during the Pete Best furore. So began the typecasting of him as the one who'd "play it smoggo. I don't mind talking or smiling. It's just that I don't do it very much. I haven't got a smiling face or a talking mouth."[19]

When history was rewritten in the first authorised Beatles biography,[20] Ringo became not merely a hired hand but the chosen one, the *beau ideal*, but in 1962 there was nothing to suggest he wasn't as expendable as Pete had proved to be. The trickiest hurdle during Best's removal had been retaining the services (and the van) of Aspinall, who'd been disgusted by the group's underhandedness. After much heart-searching, he stayed on as their road manager while still lodging for a time at the Bests', with whom he would remain in regular and affectionate contact.[21] Initially, he was civil but not over-friendly towards Ringo, who was not yet one of the Beatle clan, as shown by his non-attendance on the Saturday after he joined at Lennon's dutiful wedding to a pregnant Cynthia Powell.

Ringo didn't belong then any more than Jimmy Nicol – another chosen Beatle – would years later, when "the boys were very kind but I felt like an intruder. You just can't get into a group like that. They have their own atmosphere, their own sense of humour. It's a little clique and outsiders just can't break in."[22] Just a satellite of their inward-looking firmament, Starr would draw on a cigarette and nod in agreement with whomever had spoken last as, not purposefully snubbing him, group and road manager spoke of parties he hadn't attended, venues he'd never played, people he didn't know. "It was like joining a new class at school," he'd deduce, "where everybody knew everybody but me."[23] He was also the oldest Beatle and the only one without a splash of the Irish blood that tinged the rest with variable qualities of leprechaun impishness. Neither was it practical for him – even if he'd been up to it – to add his voice to their three-part vocal harmony, which, perfected over hundreds of hours on stage, "seemed to fall into place quite naturally".[24]

While striving not to put his foot in it with some inanity, Ringo had ample opportunity to log the characteristics of each longer-serving Beatle. He felt most at ease with the selectively amiable Harrison, who, although a better guitarist than either, had been made to feel intellectually as well as chronologically inferior to the other two, whose songwriting alliance was a fount of emotional confusion for him. Unable to penetrate McCartney and Lennon's caste within a caste, George hero-worshipped the heedless John, to whom he was "like a bloody kid, hanging around all the time",[25] while George's greater familiarity with Paul since their Liverpool Institute schooldays had provoked in him an attitude similar to that of a youngest child viewing a middle sibling as an insurmountable barrier to prolonged intimacy with an admired elder brother.

To a lesser extent, Ringo would also be caught up in Harrison's wonderment at Lennon, who was a pretty raw guitarist but a driving rock 'n' roll vocalist with instinctive – if indelicate – crowd control when he brutalised himself to give "the impression of being so hard",[26] as Bob Wooler scoffed. This was at odds with his rather strait-laced, middle-class upbringing in Woolton, the village-like suburb that was more Lancashire than Liverpool. At art college, he'd been a lecture-disrupting wit, made more provocative by an illusion of perpetual mockery in the amblyopic eyes that he was too vain to protect with spectacles. While a fair if messy cartoonist, he was also a scribbler of surreal stories and nonsense verse, which Starr, in his earliest sentences to the national music press, described as "the weirdest you ever saw, but it stops him going mental".[27] Ringo also giggled politely when John outlined his invention of the group's name: "We thought of crawly things and then added the beat."[27]

However, for Johnny Hutchinson, the crawliest thing in The Beatles was McCartney, whom he vilified as "a grade-A creep",[7] while with more diplomacy Ringo would judge Paul "pleasantly insincere".[28] He had, however, a certain right to be, as he, of all The Beatles, was blessed with both the most innate musical talent and a moon-faced resemblance to Elvis. A most heterosexual young man, McCartney also got away with more romantic conquests than most, which might have led green-eyed monsters to whisper to his detractors. Those within the group would cite Paul as the most frequent originator of its intrigues and discords, but this had been mitigated by his silver-tongued willingness to picket wary landlords and entertainments secretaries on The Beatles' behalf.

Paul was the most prolific in his and John's liaison, of which 'Love Me Do' was but the tip of the iceberg. Of course, Liverpool pop composers were not unprecedented; Russ Hamilton had been one, and Mersey Beat had brought with it many more, some with the confidence to submit items to other artists, as Stuart Slater of The Mojos did to Faron's Flamingos and Lee Curtis did to Russ Conway, albeit in vain. None, however, was as formidably commercial as Lennon and McCartney were to be by 1963. A favourite of Starr's, their vibrant 'I Saw Her Standing There' was superior to many of The Beatles' non-originals. As well as inserting more of their own material into the stage set, John and Paul had started canvassing others to perform songs that they felt were unsuitable for the group. Beryl Marsden, for example, was promised 'Love Of The Loved', until Epstein insisted that it go to Cilla White, who'd be Cilla Black when she and other Liverpool performers – including Gerry And The Pacemakers, The Big Three, Billy J Kramer, and Billy Hatton's Fourmost – were signed to Brian Epstein's NEMS Enterprises management company

However profitable these acts became, The Beatles would forever be Brian's administrative and personal priority They hadn't been in complete agreement about his fastidious transformation of them into smoother pop entertainers, but outbreaks of mutiny had lessened after he'd set the ball rolling for George Martin to contract them for two singles with an option on further releases if these gave cause for hope.

As Martin's humble beginnings in a north London back street were not detectable in his refined elocution, so only the most discerning could spot the Scouser in Brian Epstein. Worlds from the Dingle, his cradle days had passed in Childwall, a district even more select than Woolton. When malevolent Nazi shadows fell over Liverpool, the Epsteins fled to rented accommodation in Southport until 1944. Out of short trousers by then, Brian was to endure the rigours of several expensive boarding schools at which undercurrents of anti-Semitism and homo-eroticism would help to make him what he was. So, too, would a curtailed term of national service and a more constructive year at the Royal Academy of Dramatic Art.

In 1961, as far as he was able, Brian was dragging the family firm into the 20th century in his capacity as a director and, more specifically, as sales manager of the city-centre branch of NEMS' record department. What must have been a potent combination of vocational boredom and frustrated artistic ambition took the 27-year-old – in his sober attire and smart haircut – to the suffocating fug of the Cavern and a desire to steer The Beatles out of it to success. Although Ringo wasn't a full Beatle yet, Brian still took it upon himself to call on Elsie and Harry – as he'd done on the guardians of John, Paul, George and Pete – to allay any reservations that they might harbour about their son's continued showbusiness career. The Graves were still wringing their hands about Hunt's but were reassured that The Beatles had at their helm such an orderly, nicely spoken gent like Mr Epstein, who was charming, open-handed, straight as a die and devoid of all the complicity of a Violet Caldwell or Peter Eckhorn.

His feelings about the new Beatle might have been as lukewarm as Neil's, but Brian had assimilated that Starr was unlikely to rock the boat for Lennon and McCartney, who began treating him as a mascot, "a faithful spaniel"[20] and sometimes a metaphorical whipping boy. "If anything goes wrong," sniggered Lennon, "we can all blame Ringo. That's what he's here for."[29] Acquiescent and exploitable, he didn't at first express indignation at John's sarcasm and Paul's condescension. More than just studiously avoiding confrontation, he attempted to ingratiate himself with them beyond simply being punctual and learning their songs.

Less endearing a trait was his nervous habit of trying to recapture the sensation of something that had raised a laugh but didn't bear him periodically repeating it. Once, to amuse his new colleagues, he sacrificed one fan's good opinion of him by churlishly dishevelling her carefully arranged blonde beehive, and, during a fierce argument with Lennon, McCartney and Epstein versus Sam Leach over payment prior to one local booking, the waiting customers nudged each other and tittered as Ringo strutted around the hall with a banner inexpertly daubed with the legend "No Pay No Play".

Happily for The Beatles, he would not be as crass when talking to those scattered newspapers who began to take an interest in them after 'Love Me Do' was released in October 1962. Nevertheless, he had a tendency to protest too much, telling interviewers the exact number of fun-packed weeks that he'd been in the group, impressing on them that he was as "offbeat"[27] as any other Beatle and – in as late as 1964 – stressing how lucky he was "to be on their wavelength. I had to be, or I wouldn't have lasted. I had to join them as people as well as a drummer."[23]

When their second 45 crept past the 'Love Me Do' high of Number 17 in the hit parade, many fears that he'd go the way of Pete Best were dispelled and he'd hear himself uttering crisp rejoinders to Paul and John's jibes. Less self-consciously, too, he'd enter into the spirit of the little comedy playlets that provided diversion during squalid time-killing in van and bandroom. By then, The Beatles had introduced their own one-song "Starr Time", which would be written-up as "one of the most popular spots of the evening".[30] For him to take on Best's sensual 'Wild In The Country' might have invited ridicule, but 'Boys', with its joyous verve, and – later – jaunty 'Honey Don't', would more than do. Although it was never implemented, there was debate about a Starr dancing display. "But only for certain audiences," mused McCartney "We all mess around on drums a bit, and we could take his place now and then."[18]

Ringo had still been a Hurricane when viewers' letters had goaded the producer of ITV's topical *Know The North* to check out The Beatles at a Southport booking. On that crucial night, morbid inquisitiveness found their drummer glooming under the Cavern's damp arches when the group with Ringo faced cumbersome television cameras for the first time. On 22 August 1962, these were lugged into the club to film The Beatles performing in uniform waistcoats. His head exploding, Pete Best made for the exit after some unfortunate remarks from a jubilant Mr McCartney.

Exacerbating Pete's misery was that "somehow I and a lot of other people up in Liverpool had a feeling they would make it – nationally, at any rate".[31] He and his mother had made it a vain point of honour to get a single out with him on it before 'Love Me Do'. He'd turned up his nose when a chance to become a

Merseybeat was put his way by Epstein. Instead, room was found for him in Lee Curtis and The All-Stars.

Pete's tenure as an All-Star began during a Monday-to-Friday residency at Birkenhead's Majestic. A solo singer in an age of groups, Lee Curtis aspired towards big-voiced ballads which, if recorded, would rely more on massed strings than electric guitars, but for now he pandered to assumed audience desires with many of the same songs that Pete had known with The Beatles. *Mersey Beat* would note "the extent to which the magnetic personality of Pete Best appeals to girls",[12] but in his heart Pete "was continuing in a group not as popular, doing the same old gigs I'd done up to August with The Beatles".[32]

Before The Beatles transcended Liverpool's scruffier jive hives, there were excruciating backstage moments that lasted forever when they and Pete affected not to recognise each other, although John supposedly once murmured a few guilt-ridden platitudes. Having shuffled past, each faction, weak with relief, would unstiffen and empty his lungs with a whoosh. Such awkward junctures were not unique on Merseyside now, as "the friendliness and comradeship between different groups seems to have lessened," observed Johnny Sandon, now parted from The Searchers. "Groups don't help each other now. If one group suffers misfortune, others are glad."[33] At the root of many other such schisms was Brian Epstein, who would divide outfits by granting, say, only the vocalist a fixed wage – as he did to Billy J Kramer and The Coasters – and reproach The Beatles for obligingly backing a vocal-harmony act called The Chants.

Conspicuous losers in this serious game of musical chairs were Rory Storm And The Hurricanes, who would just scrape into the 20 groups listed in *Mersey Beat*'s 1962 poll, a true comedown. Nevertheless, Storm had been attractive in his phlegmatic – and, possibly, tactical – forgiveness, wishing The Beatles and Starr all the best when 'Love Me Do' began its yo-yo progression up the charts. In turn, The Beatles hadn't let him down when they were among the five bands at the Tower to fuss over him on his September birthday. Brian – and Ringo – were to make more pragmatic amends later.

On a first-come-first-served basis, Epstein would not attend to the recording careers of his other charges until The Beatles had got off the ground with theirs. He ensured that *Mersey Beat* knew that they'd been genuinely and importantly airborne when they went from Speke Airport to London to tape their single almost three weeks before the Rory Storm bash.

At 7pm that day, Andy White arrived at Abbey Road for the three hours allocated to this Liverpool shower. Ringo – who hadn't been told – was already timorously aware that he lacked even the other three's lean recording experience. All that he'd notched up was the Akustik lark with Wally and 40 ragged minutes with Rory, The Hurricanes and a reel-to-reel machine in an otherwise-deserted Cavern. As White assembled his kit, Starr bit back on dismay as Martin explained, "I simply didn't know what [Ringo] was like and I wasn't prepared to take any risks."[34]

While White was then married to one of the hit-making Vernons Girls,[35] Martin was of greater celebrity to The Beatles, who were less round-eyed at his puffing oboe at Sadler's Wells than him producing the disparate likes of The Goons and Shane Fenton (whom the group had met socially, as he was currently spooning with Iris Caldwell). Martin would remain awesome for several more years, but never more so than at that first session, when he imposed drastic alterations on their rehearsed arrangement of 'Love Me Do', made them record a "professional" song ('How Do You Do It') that he'd picked from a publisher's office to be the follow-up and, finally, required them to return the following week, as he wasn't much pleased with the evening's work.

Martin was actually one of the least dogmatic of British producers, and at some point during the recording of 'Love Me Do' he waved in the dejected Ringo, seated quietly beside a white-coated console engineer, not to the drums yet but to a tambourine to be struck every third beat in the bar. He was to thump it with a maraca on the B-side of 'PS I Love You', but on several later takes of 'Love Me Do' it was he and not White behind the kit as the team edged nearer a satisfactory result.[36]

Regarding him as a mediocre musician at most, George Martin didn't appreciate that Starr was in a different rather than lower bracket to someone like White, and that, given a choice, Ringo's fills were "like a giant walking. My breaks are always slow, usually half the speed of the track."[37] One who understood was Clem Cattini, who "always admired Ringo. So many people knock his ability, but he was always ideal for The Beatles' sound."[38] As Starr had acquitted himself adequately enough on the 'Love Me Do' outing, he was trusted to execute the "intricate drumming effects"[13] that were in Martin's recipe for John and Paul's 'Please Please Me', that had surfaced as a better bet for the next single than 'How Do You Do It'.

On consulting with the high command of Lennon, McCartney and Epstein, Martin also decided that, from his selection of their Cavern crowd-pleasers, George and Ringo could be allowed one lead vocal each on the hasty album EMI wanted from The Beatles to cash in on 'Please Please Me', that topped the charts in March 1963. The drummer had "a voice I was uncertain about",[39] but, beefed up with double-tracking and hyperactive reverberation, 'Boys' – if not the most euphonious – was, along with Paul's 'I Saw Her Standing There' and John's 'Twist And Shout', the LP's most exultant encapsulation of The Beatles' early glory, not least because of its producer capturing it in one take. "Otherwise you'd never get the impact."[39]

Parlophone now had "a male Shirelles",[40] reckoned Martin, and a sure sign that The Beatles were to go places – and even match The Tornados and the precious Shadows – was sour grapes from such as Joe Meek, for whom The Beatles had "nothing new about their sound. Cliff Bennett And The Rebel Rousers have been doing the same thing for a year now, and so has Joe Brown."[41] Meek had been on the crest of a wave himself in 1962, when his production of The Tornados' 'Telstar' had been Number One in the States, where no UK pop act had ever made sustained headway nor was likely to again, if you agreed with *The New York Times'* dismissal of Billy Fury in *Play It Cool* as an Elvis duplicate without "the stamp of an original personality".[42] In the same 1963 film, Helen Shapiro – voted the *NME*'s most popular British female singer – attained the dubious accolade of peaking at Number 100 in US music trade paper *Billboard*'s "Hot 100", the highest US entry for any of her singles.

Technically, Helen had been the main attraction when The Beatles had embarked on their first national tour that spring, but audience reaction was more subdued than she'd come to expect. Possibly, this was kindled by dispiriting press articles which discussed whether she was "A Has-Been At Sixteen"[13] but The Beatles – buoyed by their 'Please Please Me' victory – were, she noticed, evoking more than passive attention from boys as well as girls for their unpolished enthusiasm and self-created musical resolution. Quite a few felt the urge to scream, probably because they were as sick as the group were of the polished patter and quasi-Shadows legwork that had been the norm since 1960.

A-twitter with excitement and childish swagger at their abrupt fame, the Liverpudlians were full of themselves on the tour coach, their conduct stopping just short of open insolence towards certain others in the cast. Not yet sure of where he stood in all of this, Ringo became – so fellow travelling minstrel Barry Booth asserted – "a law unto himself", more placid, even-tempered and in need of less hand-holding than the other Beatles. He was also readier than they to blend into the jovial, laugh-a-minute ambience of the bus as it hurtled around trunk-road England.

If not household names yet, The Beatles were now recognised in wayside cafes and cornershops and were to close the first half on the next tour, for which only Americans could possibly headline over them. Negotiations for The Four Seasons and Duane Eddy began, but two of their more perishable compatriots – Chris Montez and Tommy Roe – were sent instead and the bill underwent a merciless readjustment as crowd response dictated that The Beatles play last.

During this jaunt, one local journal mentioned Starr's "tremendous hypnotic beat".[44] Although he'd had still to be directed via nods, foot-stamping and eye contact through their more ambitious numbers, he'd got the hang of The Beatles' rhythmic *oeuvre* and had, related Cliff Bennett, "fully settled in" by the end of a reluctant Yuletide season at the Star-Club. (Ironically, the tune that

German milkmen were whistling in 1962 was a hit song from the Berlin musical *Homesick For St Pauli*.) As resentful as the others that their UK chart campaign had been disturbed, and about being away from Admiral Grove on Christmas Day, Ringo was sometimes discovered missing seconds before showtime, excusing himself with a joke when the frightening Horst Fascher, jabbing at his watch, came upon him pedantically "collecting sticks or changing cymbals, so I would tell him that, if he wasn't on stage in time, I would kick him up the arse".[11] Nevertheless, this, The Beatles' most onerous obligation to Hamburg, had hidden blessings. "By the time they came back with Ringo," even Colin Manley had to admit, "they were different altogether. They had matured, found their timing, and you could see they were going to happen in a big way."[38]

5 "I'm Happy To Go On And Play Drums – And That's All"

The rest, as they often say, is history. 1963 alone brought the conquest of Britain via hit-parade Mersey Beat, Beatlemania and *The Royal Variety Show*. The year ended with seven Beatles records in the singles Top 50 – including three on more expensive extended plays (EPs) – and the top two positions in the LP list. Lennon and McCartney had tossed spare chartbusting songs to Cilla, Billy J and The Fourmost, and their bank balance had been swelled further by the first shoal of unsolicited cover versions. Their music was also to be used for a West End beat ballet *Mods And Rockers*, and although Ringo would confess that "we didn't understand what all this stuff about Aeolian cadences was about"[1] a prosy *Sunday Times* article lauded John and Paul as "the outstanding composers of 1963".[2]

To balance circulation, The Beatles had been superimposed upon the grid of a Fleet Street that had been relentlessly overrun with "serious" news of the Profumo scandal, the nuclear test ban treaty, the Great Train Robbery, racial unrest in Alabama and, to cap it all, the West Indies beating us at cricket. Between radio reports of England's shame and East/West-black/white tension came the sinless strains of 'From Me To You', The Beatles' third 45. While they gestured with cigarettes during TV interviews and let loose the odd mild expletive like "crap" and even "bloody", "they were regarded as clean-living lads during the time they were getting established", confirmed Harold Wilson, leader of Her Majesty's opposition, "whatever may have gone on later"[3] – or before.

Innocent scamps like Just William's Outlaws, The Beatles' much-copied mid-air leap on their 'Twist And Shout' EP sleeve was the epitome of antidotal Mersey Beat, that shook theatres with healthy, good-humoured screams. There were also the asinine poems written and sent by subscribers to glossy monthly magazines dedicated solely to both The Beatles and, briefly, Gerry And The Pacemakers, then tussling with each other for chart supremacy. A Pacemakers show in Bristol was halted by Authority after repeated warnings about rushing the stage, while queues formed outside a Lincoln box office a week before Beatles tickets went on sale. A girl crushed her spectacles in her fist because her view of The Searchers was blocked, while her brother debated whether or not he liked The Merseybeats, and deb of the year Judy Huxtable was snapped clamouring for Ringo Starr's autograph like everybody else.

Scouse was now the most romantic dialect in the country, and the bigger chain stores were stocking Beatle wallpaper, 22-carat Beatle bracelets and Fab Four powder compacts. Woolworth's had moptop wigs and Sayer's had guitar-shaped cakes, "the cake for SWINGING parties". The jacket of their collarless Cardin stage suits was "the Liverpool Look for you to knit for the man in your life" as a cardigan, its pattern obtainable via an order form in *Fabulous* magazine. Learning that the manufacturers of NEMS-sanctioned Beatle boots could barely cope with demand, an enterprising Sussex company marketed "Ringo, the new Beat Boot", which also boasted elastic gusset sides and rounded toes. Less prosperously opportunist were the makers of Applejack smocks – after a Solihull sextet whose hits included Lennon and McCartney's 'Like Dreamers Do' – and shirts designed by the drummer/manager of Tottenham's Dave Clark Five immediately after their 'Glad All Over' dislodged The Beatles from a long reign at Number One in January 1964.

Girls getting used to mini-skirts would trim their newly cut fringes with nail clippers to "identify with these characters as either other girls or as sexual neuters",[4] so A Psychiatrist had it. Boys would be suspended from school for also grooming their locks to a style and length previously associated with effeminacy and crazed intellectuals – although, as Ringo pointed out, "If you took at early pictures of ourselves with long hair, we had nothing, [but] everyone – especially in America, where it was Crewcut City – they all said, 'These long-haired creeps.'"[5] After 'From Me To You' became their Top Ten debut in Australia in 1963, a prim Sydney headmistress barred not only the wearing of *pilzenkopfs* but also the carrying of Beatles pictures in satchels and membership of their fan club.

Further antagonism to the group was expressed by a Tory MP bleating that "we must offer teenagers something better".[6] He did not say what, but causing more comment in the House of Commons was the cost to rate-payers of the extra policing and stewardship compulsory at Beatle concerts. "We're rate-payers too,"[6] protested Starr.

Even middle-class fathers disparaging them in breakfast rooms knew the individual names, none better than that of Ringo, the only Beatle to adopt a *nom du théâtre* as well as the additional gimmick from which it had been born. Despite there being a French pop singer also called Ringo, the Liverpudlian's would be the Beatle name known in continental Europe long before those of John, George and Paul. "It's had a lot to do with my success and acceptance," he'd admit. "It might sound mad, but people remember it." Cornered by some foreign Beatles fans a couple of years later in Cannes, Lennon dryly signed himself "Ringo Starr" and they went away quietly

That your parents had figured out which one was which was an indication of how cosy Beatlemania became before 1963 was out. *Daily Express* correspondent Derek Taylor – later the group's press officer – could only praise them after being briefed to do a hatchet job after the quartet had agreed to play their allotted four numbers to the Queen Mother in November 1963, but "that meant they couldn't be any good",[8] according to younger pop consumer David Cook (later 1970s pop star David Essex, but then an amateur drummer). For many, The Beatles had matured too quickly and, like Tommy Steele, they'd be soft-shoe shuffling before you could blink, wouldn't they? There'd been a taste of that when they'd waved a jovial goodbye during the finale of ventriloquist's dummy Lenny the

Lion's BBC television show and – like many a British showbiz evergreen – appeared on ITV's *Blackpool Night Out*, taking part in comedy spoofs and, alongside hosts Mike and Bernie Winters, crooning 'I Do like To Be Beside The Seaside'.

More the meat of Cook and his sort were the belligerently unkempt Rolling Stones and later hairy monsters detested by adults, like The Kinks, Yardbirds and Pretty Things. Plundering Chicago and Mississippi negro ethnicism, these had sprung from the college circuit and cells of blues archivist/performers onto the new BBC chart showcase, *Top Of The Pops*. "Their scene was strictly teenage rebels," noted Ringo, "but we went from four-year-old kids to 90-year-old grandmothers. Their scene was violence. We never created violence, even in the start."[9] Yet, while you wouldn't catch them yukking it up with Mike and Bernie, the Stones had reason to be grateful to The Beatles for the endorsement that led to a Decca recording deal, as well as John and Paul's gift – as a stabilising second single – of 'I Wanna Be Your Man',[10] bestowed prior to its selection for autumn 1963's *With The Beatles* LP. They'd completed the track virtually on the spot while looking in on a vexing Stones' rehearsal in a Soho club.[9]

Lennon taught Ringo 'I Wanna Be Your Man' as his drummer's lead vocal on the album. Although Starr sang and played simultaneously on the recording, five separate sessions and an overdub of maracas were needed for an acceptable take, and even this lacked the hungry drive that the Stones had invested into their improvement on a slapdash composition – and, if it was a compliment, it was they who'd be aurally caricatured on The Barron Knights' 'Call Up The Groups' comic medley of 1964.

Sometimes he'd be overlooked, but a token Starr song towards the close of the first side on every LP or as an EP makeweight came to be as anticipated by Beatle traditionalists as the group came to be Number One every Christmas. "We weren't going to give him anything great,"[11] guffawed John, and often Lennon and McCartney gave him nothing at all beyond accompaniment on an unrevised twelve-bar rocker of yore. Both of 1964 vintage were Ringo's 'Honey

Don't'[12] for *Beatles For Sale* and 'Matchbox', another Carl Perkins opus, on the 'Long Tall Sally' EP.

"While the others created musical works of art," contended NEMS publicist Tony Barrow, "he was left in the cold and merely brought in when they wanted some percussion."[13] Although The Beatles' early Parlophone albums were conceived technologically during recorded sound's late mediaeval period, they heralded a new attitude towards a product that had regarded not been as a rounded entity but as a cynically throwaway patchwork of tracks hinged on a hit 45. Testaments to commercial pragmatism rather than quality, these were targeted – especially in the States – at fans so beglamoured by an artist's looks and personality to be rendered uncritical of frankly sub-standard, haphazardly programmed output, excused as an exhibition of "versatility" but of no true cultural value.

The first Beatles LP was padded with a brace of singles, but each that followed was to be a conscious musical progression, with an increasing ratio of tracks the equal of single A-sides, in terms of effort and imagination. Having proven themselves proportionally as sound an investment for EMI as Presley for RCA, the four would be allowed unlimited Abbey Road time and the freedom to requisition all manner of auxiliary instrumentation and, later, musicians to enhance a Lennon-McCartney stockpile that could fulfil the group's contractual commitments many times over.

With The Beatles was a tentative exercise in such experimentation, as, like unrestrained children in a toy shop, the four fiddled about with whatever weird and wonderful implement was either lying about their favoured Studio Two or staring at them from one of the complex's storeroom shelves. For Ringo, this would lead to swatting a packing case in place of snare on one number; on another, the Cuban tom-tom that The Shadows had used on 'Apache'; and to pep up 'Don't Bother Me' – George Harrison's first published solo composition – an Arabian bongo. Soon, he would feel no less odd tapping something as straightforward as a cowbell on 'I Call Your Name'[14] as rattling a *chocalho*[15] for 'She's A Woman'.

Little would seem odd by then, and in any case Ringo would be devoid of resistance to the force that had effectively finished off his old life. He was, nevertheless, aware that he was just a link in the chain but that it was to his advantage to stay malleable, as he "let the others do all the worrying. I'm happy to go on up there and play drums and that's all."[16] While he'd been awarded a small percentage of shares in Northern Songs, Lennon and McCartney's publishing company, Starr's main source of income was his quarter of Beatles Ltd, a budgetary receptacle for all net takings from concerts from which "even our accountant doesn't know how much is ours alone. Myself, I never give it much thought, money. I just always think of myself as having plenty."[17] Being the poorest Beatle was better than being the poorest Hurricane, but he'd have tenacious bouts of circular and only half-understood discussions with an affable Epstein about Beatle finance and why he didn't get as much as even George, but at least he was no longer on a hireling's wage.

Perhaps to imprint further his uncertain importance to the group, he'd even put forward a song he'd made up for consideration as an LP track, originally for Paul to sing. Shyly, he'd first demonstrated it on a piano in the BBC's Paris Theatre while The Beatles were waiting to make a broadcast, continuing "to push it on them every time we make a record".[18] Called 'Don't Pass Me By', the lyrics were his own but the tune was an unconscious plagiarism, so he was informed, of a Jerry Lee Lewis B-side. As he might have expected, it was greeted with affectionate derision, McCartney once burlesquing its chorus on air and *Saturday Club* presenter Brian Matthew dubbing Starr "the Dylan Thomas of Liverpool".[19]

While his attempt at composing for them – and his infrequent huffs and objections – remained ineffectual, Ringo felt less vulnerable a Beatle now that he was receiving as much fan mail as the rest, and there was, therefore, less occasion for NEMS publicity sheets to maximise such of his subsidiary skills as poker and billiards. Neither was he now the newest member of the crew since the appointment of ex-Cavern bouncer Malcolm "Big Mal" Evans as assistant to an overworked Aspinall, who needed all of his wits about him to cope with the tactical problems of moving the operation from A to B.

Once at B, he and Mal would buttonhole promoters, organise security, shoo unwanted company from dressing rooms and attend to the group's food, sleep and overall health requirements, both before and after they bounced onto the boards to face the ear-stinging decibels that greeted even the compere's attempts to keep order.

In the chemistry of the four interlocking public personalities, Ringo was seen as a catalyst in a grey area inhabited by glum clowns and moral agents. Admitted into a backstage sanctum, a local reporter might raise a puffy smile on glimpsing near the washbasin a bottle of Yardley's Shampoo For Men with a label on which a hand had taken the trouble to scrawl the addenda "and Ringo". The victim would also chuckle along to hearty twitting about his hospitalisations, slum background and scholastic deficiencies. "Ringo doesn't know the meaning of fear," joked John, "or any other word of more than three letters."[20] Meaning no harm, either, was a symbolic Lennon present to Starr of a pathetic stuffed dog in a glass case. "We're never serious," grinned Paul, indicating Ringo. "Just look at him. How could we be serious?"[7] On one hilariously ad-libbed *Saturday Club*, Starr himself would decline to read a cue-card because he was "the one who doesn't say anything".[21] And besides, he laughed, "I can't read."[21]

A tendency for Lennon and McCartney to butt in when Starr was about to answer an interviewer's question was often as misunderstood as their witticisms at his expense. Nowadays, they and George seemed to be forming a protective cordon around Elsie's only child, as if remorseful about earlier indifference and the ignoble reason for which their eyes had alighted on him in August 1962. More often than not, he'd pair off with Paul for joint holidays and when the group had to double up in hotel suites, but "no matter which one I'm with, it's like being with your best friend. We're like brothers. Me and whoever I'm with are really dead close."[7]

They'd make an educated guess that Pete Best hadn't his usurper's natural thespian qualities, which became plain when, striding up and down banks of hairdriers, Ringo played a salon proprietor to noteworthy effect in *The Mersey Sound*, a documentary commissioned by the production body of *Tonight*. He reverted to being The Beatles' mute Harpo in the mostly unscripted non-musical turns that they acted out beneath screams during 16 days of "The Beatles Christmas Show" at London's Astoria Cinema. This season was broken only by the kindly Epstein ordering an aeroplane to fly the Scouse majority of the cast home to spend Christmas Day with their families, with a limousine delivering Ringo to his normally sleepy street, where a crowd of children swooped from nowhere to see the smile and wave that was diffused generally as he hurried indoors.

There were mixed emotions about The Beatles in Liverpool, although it was hardly their fault that they couldn't play the city's small clubs any more. Nevertheless, because they'd once paced it, the Cavern's very stage was to be sawn up and sold at five shillings a fragment to the over-abundance of those daft enough to want one. The first coachloads of Beatle worshippers had pulled up in May 1963 and, before the high summer of Mersey Beat ran its course, "Those of us who hoped for their success now resented it," gritted one who'd once spent lunchtimes with the so-called Fab Four, "since we could no longer see them at the Cavern. What a sense of betrayal! They had been just another group of lads that everybody knew."[3]

Others front-paged by *Mersey Beat* as "hit parade Scousers"[22] were only condescending to be seen at the Empire or the Odeon now that it was commonplace for Rolls Royces to disgorge famous sight-seers – Lionel Bart, Ken Dodd, Chet Atkins, Nancy Spain – to, say, The Searchers Fan Club convention at the Iron Door in January 1964. You couldn't move, either, in the Mandolin, the Peppermint Lounge, the Sink and all the other venues that had sprung up along with the London-type boutiques now operational in the city centre.

Like Vikings of old, metropolitan record-company scouts had come for plunder. The slowest witted held the view that all pop groups are the same – "Let's sign as many as we can, see which racket catches on and hammer it hard. Make a fortune, eh? [pause] Where exactly *is* Liverpool?" With the disbandment of The Eagles indicating that there was to be no offsetting "Avon Beat", some shyster from Bristol had wanted to hedge his bets by contracting every group in Liverpool, in the hope that one might be a New Beatles who would hold sway over the rest like a baron over villeins. In the first month of 1963, the more cautious Decca made off with Billy Butler, The Big Three, Beryl Marsden – and the Lee Curtis All-Stars, who, because they had Pete Best, had been a close second to The Beatles in the 1962 *Mersey Beat* poll.

Hardly a week would go by without another Merseyside act being thus thrust forward, or so it seemed. Suddenly, someone who'd cadged cigarettes off you the previous month would be seen in the *NME* with his or her outfit posing round a fire escape or on brick-strewn wasteland. From nowhere, Jeannie And The Big Guys (formerly The Tall Boys, it says here) were in *Record Mirror*'s review column with a version of 'Boys'. It wasn't transmitted up north, but The Fourmost had been on that new *Ready, Steady, Go!* on ITV, while a *Look At Life* cinema newsreel was devoted to Billy J Kramer, Cilla opened for Gerry on his latest UK tour and The Swinging Blue Jeans were in an edition of *Z-Cars* that had been given a beat-group slant.

The Jeans had had an altercation in a BBC canteen with The Rolling Stones, whom the *NME* believed were "a London group with the Liverpool sound",[22] as were, supposedly, The Dave Clark Five, whose unseating of The Beatles was seen by some press organs as a sign that the "power" had returned more conveniently to the capital. As black rhythm and blues smashes had been automatically covered (and usually diluted) for the white market in the States, so some recording managers saved themselves a trip to Liverpool by getting groups within a closer proximity to London to steal a march on their northern counterparts by taking first grabs at the R&B motherlode, hence the Clark quintet and Brian Poole And The Tremeloes' respective vanquishing of Faron's Flamingos' 'Do You Love Me' and Bern Elliott And The Fenmen's 'Money' making the Top 20 simply because – Barrett Strong's original apart – it was the first. The Kinks, however, were unable to duplicate this feat with the two Mersey Beat-tinged singles that preceded their chart-topping 'You Really Got Me'.

As production exercises only, Joe Meek flavoured a couple of other London outfits with Liverpudlia, but while the going was good other producers would set up mobile recording units in Merseyside ballrooms to tape as many unsigned units as could be crammed onto a cheap compilation album with a title like *Group Beat '63* or *This Is Merseybeat*. Included on Decca's *At The Cavern* were Lee Curtis And The All-Stars, who were to lose Pete Best after their first two singles missed; they had no placing in 1963's *Mersey Beat* poll. By then, it had dawned on Decca that ex-Beatle Best was wasted as a sideshow. A variation on The Beatles blueprint via closer vocal harmonies and "a slightly heavier beat",[23] Pete Best's Original All-Stars were therefore budgeted for a trial single and, in collusion with Mona, pop periodical journalists sought to jot down Pete's considered replies to questions like, "Have you ever met Ringo?"[24] "Do you ever see The Beatles these days?"

To the last question, Lennon's shame-smitten mumblings to him might have given expediential leeway for Pete not to qualify to *Melody Maker* his "yes, occasionally, but we're all on the move so much, we don't have a lot of time to talk".[23] His outfit, you see, was also "going well. We're not making as much money as The Beatles, but we're working all the time, all over the country."[23] As if they were still the best of mates, he would "wish them the best of luck, and I mean it. I don't know to this day why we parted company."[23] The only tang of acidity was his wish "to clear my slurred name in Liverpool and prove to all the people who made my name mud that I have a good group".[23]

Whatever false impression readers of *Melody Maker* had of Pete's impending ascent to stardom, there was less doubt about that of Rory Storm And The Hurricanes. To his diary, even Johnny Guitar had to confide, "Group not very good these days. No new songs. Will have to improve. Not much work. Another three months in France cancelled."[25] Although still enough of a local treasure to be prominent in ITV's *Beat City* rebuttal to *The Mersey Sound*, Rory's group had become also-rans, having to their credit only a flop single with 'Doctor Feelgood' and a track on *This is Merseybeat* recorded crudely in a Rialto hallway. Their new drummer, Jimmy Tushingham, was the latest in a growing number who'd squeeze into Starr's old and fading stage suit after Gibson Kemp left for Germany and Kingsize Taylor. "They reckon that anyone who lasts more than a week is something of a phenomenon,"[26] griped Keith Hartley,[27] who, from Preston's Thunderbeats, actually served five months.

Worse than a too-rapid turnover of drummers was that Inland Revenue officials were also on Storm and The Hurricanes' trail after Ringo had had to disclose his earnings when he was in the group. Nevertheless, for old time's sake, and to salve his conscience for leaving them in the lurch, it was he who threw down a lifeline by settling the tax bill and, over a few drinks in the Blue Angel, nodded along with Brian Epstein's suggestion to pressure The Beatles' booking agent to sign them and to underwrite a 15-hour London recording session.

For Brian's only venture into disc production, he relied much on the judgement of the studio engineer as Rory and The Hurricanes ran through 'Ubangi Stomp', Bobby Darin's 'I'll Be There'[28] (then much requested in Liverpool clubs) and the two that Parlophone – in Epstein's half-nelson – would get round to releasing in late 1964. The perfectionist Brian insisted on over an hour of retakes until he was satisfied with Wally's vocal cadence in 'Since You Broke My Heart', an Everly Brothers opus from 1960. Its A-side was a mock-Latin adaptation of Leonard Bernstein's 'America' (from *West Side Story*), that had captured Storm's imagination while the group were in Spain. Through his persistence, "we shortened it, used some of our own words, and it goes like a bomb".[29] Well, it wasn't bad, and, although the bulk of its disappointing sales were in loyal Liverpool, the publicity reminding the average Joe of the group's Beatle connection put them – as it did Pete Best's new outfit – in a stronger negotiating stance for engagements that now stretched to the very edge of Swinging London – but no further.

Much was also made of the backing singers, "America", which – as well as Wally – included Ringo, Iris Caldwell and her husband Shane Fenton, with whom she was also conjoined professionally in a song-and-dance act. Confronted by the rearing monster of the group boom, Fenton had made a protracted withdrawal from the pop mainstream after declining a management offer from Epstein. Speculating in the administrative side of the music industry, among those he aided in this capacity were The Hollies, who had absorbed his old drummer Bobby Elliott into their number. Paralleling Fenton's retreat, Paul Raven (later Gary Glitter) was biding his time as *Ready, Steady, Go!*'s floor manager, because "things were getting impossible for me as a performer. The Beatles had turned the pop world on its head. I couldn't fit into a group and I wasn't from the north and I stood as much chance as a mongrel at Crufts."[30]

Cliff Richard, too, had been rendered as old as the hills by Mersey Beat, but, smiling indulgently, he plunged deeper into pantomime and evangelical Christianity, while Adam Faith swapped *pizzicato* strings for clanging guitars and walloping drums on his records. As he steeled himself for cabaret, Billy Fury was gratified to discover that, unaffected by London *sangfroid*, northern girls still screamed at him, although at the Liverpool Empire date on one of his final headlining package tours some of those screams had been for The Beatles, who'd slipped in incognito and were slipping out again when a particularly piercing female shriek of recognition caused them to be nearly killed with kindness. Their lips moving mechanically as they hastened from the *mêlée* with as much grace as they could muster, one of Ringo's favourite quips of the time might have been overheard: "Yes, I went to school with Billy Fury, but I don't remember which day."[31]

Fury then lived around the corner from Abbey Road in Cavendish Avenue. Number seven would be Paul McCartney's first official London address, after his berth with actress girlfriend Jane Asher's family in Wimpole Street became common knowledge. With the Lennons ensconced in a bedsit off the Cromwell Road and Epstein in a new block near Hyde Park – handy for West End nightclubbing – The Beatles had found it a false economy to remain a Liverpool-based organisation while attending to an increasing broadcasting and recording workload 200 miles south. His mother was already complaining in print that "I don't see much of Richie nowadays – not half as much as I'd like to",[32] but, wrenching himself from Admiral

Grove, Ringo bedded down in a small hotel near NEMS' first London office, at the top of Shaftesbury Avenue. While looking for somewhere less temporary, he became pally with property developer Roger Shines, and by early 1964 Starr and Harrison were sharing an apartment below Brian's in Whaddon House, William Mews.

Initially, Starr could "move about in London like an ordinary bloke. If you behave sensibly and plan where you go, you can be OK."[7] In sunshades, cloth cap and non-descript overcoat supplemented with hunched shoulders and a limp, he'd hazard a journey as far as Southend to catch an Everly Brothers tour (with The Rolling Stones among the package's small fry), but there was no need for any disguise when all four Beatles went to Ronnie Scott's supercool jazz cellar in Soho to hear blind multi-instrumentalist Roland Kirk. They'd long been nightbirds by then. After late-afternoon corn flakes, they weren't found wanting when scrutinised through the spy-hole of "in" clubs like the Cromwellian, the Bag O' Nails off Carnaby Street, the Speakeasy or the cloistered Scotch Of St James, a bee-line from Buckingham Palace. Ringo retained most hedonistic loyalty to the supercool Ad-Lib off Leicester Square, but he was often seen in other pop-star hangouts attractive for their strict membership controls, tariffs too highly priced for the Average Joe, lighting more flattering than that in a Butlins ballroom and no photographers admitted.

"When we first made it," he would recollect, "I lived in night clubs for three years. It used to be a non-stop party."[33] In a discotheque's deafening dark, where nobody Twisted any more, Ringo would lend truth to reports in teenage journals that "he can do all the rave dances, including a few that haven't been invented yet".[24] Partnered by a black girl attached to a US vocal group that had just come from *Ready, Steady, Go!*, he held his own as the star dance-floor attraction when necks craned to watch him do the Banana, the Monkey and other dances that no Briton was supposed to have mastered yet.

Back in the second-string Beatles' untidy sitting room, with LP covers scattered everywhere, the hi-fi would pulsate to modern US

R&B, better known as soul music. As well as those that were plugged into the lower rungs of the charts by Britain's new pirate radio stations, Ringo and George were *au fait* with eruditions like Chuck Jackson, The Marvelettes, Brenda Holloway and The Soul Sisters, the latter of whose 'I Can't Stand It' and then Holloway's 'Every Little Bit Hurts' were quickly covered by Birmingham's Spencer Davis Group (with Pete York), who were loudly admired by Ringo for sounding American. Nonetheless, he preferred Chan Romero's original 'Hippy Hippy Shake' to The Swinging Blue Jeans' more definitive treatment.

"Our music is second-hand versions of negro music," he'd theorise. "Ninety per cent of the music I like is coloured."[7] And who could quibble when he bought two copies each of such as Kim Weston's 'A Little More Love', The Miracles' 'I've Been Good To You', Little Stevie Wonder's 'Fingertips' and – more familiar to most other Britons – The Supremes' 'Where Did Our Love Go?'. When asked about the other ten per cent, he'd tell you how he "really enjoyed good country and western",[7] being particularly fond of Buck Owens and Roger Miller. In his purchase of albums by such as Woody Guthrie and early Bob Dylan, Ringo also showed a liking for that strain of modern American folk music that mixed traditional and self-composed material. On BBC's *Juke Box Jury*, his verdict on Bobby Vinton's smoochy 'There I've Said It Again' was that it was ideal, "if you're sitting in one night and not alone".[31]

While Maureen Cox would visit him as often as work would permit, she was not the only girl in Ringo's life, according to "friends" and the press gossip. She could discount a lunatic fringe exemplified by an 18-year-old Huyton girl whose parents had to place an advertisement in the local paper stating that, contrary to rumour, she was not marrying Ringo Starr.[34] However, his nights on the town with various Quant-cropped dolly-birds were supported by concrete evidence, especially as women outnumbered men five-to-one in clubs like the Scotch and the Ad-Lib. A talkative model named Vicki Hodge was remarkable for her indiscretion about a dalliance with Richie – and Yul Brynner and society photographer

David Bailey – and was still kissing and telling in *The News Of The World* years later.

In his own eyes, Richie was faithful to Mo, in that his casual romantic adventures did not adulterate his emotional allegiance to one who "knows the moment I face her what's wrong and what to do about it, and I'm happy again in a minute".[35] If he'd so desired, Richie needn't have wandered far beyond Whaddon House to take his pick of "a lot of scrubbers and exhibitionists who hang around, shout outside all day and night, ring the bell and all that. If I get out the car and refuse to sign autographs, they shout four-letter words at me and everybody near here hears it. It's not very nice."[17] The other occupiers weren't amused, either, that the environs were also a focus for Beatle-related graffiti.

One or two of these scratches made no bones about Brian's homosexuality, which sometimes reflected on Ringo. Vicky Hodge might stay for breakfast, but "I've been called a queer before, you know. You just can't win."[1] Fuelling the whispers were the William Mews Beatles' good-natured attendances at Epstein's all-male parties, despite his worries that they might guess his inclinations. They'd known from the beginning.

Mo had no worries about Richie's virility, but there were times when the wretchedness of her devotion cut keenly. In an age when a pop star would lose fans if he wasn't a bachelor and, therefore, "available", he'd been instructed "to pretend I didn't know Maureen and wasn't in love. Can you imagine what it must have been like for her reading in the papers that I didn't know anyone called Maureen Cox?"[36] That too many jealous Liverpudlian girls did had already forced his full-time girlfriend to quit her Ashley du Pré job, what with customers levelling none-too-pleasant stares and even physical threats at her. Once, as she sat waiting in his car outside a West Derby ballroom, varnished fingernails had shot through the open window and raked the side of her face to the accompaniment of screeched curses.

Unnerving though such incidents were, Mo did not yet escape to London, suspecting as she did what her parents' reactions would be to the very idea of a daughter of their living in sin. If pressed about Richie, she and he were the stock "very good friends".[37] For a change, she might say that she was his "private secretary",[37] because the highlight of many a dull day without him was arriving at Admiral Grove to ease Mrs Graves' writer's cramp as she ploughed through sackfuls of correspondence that, as well as ordinary letters, might as easily include a life-sized sketch of Richie or – because he'd said somewhere that he liked science fiction – another tea chest of paperbacks. Back from work, Harry would address the answers and, twice a week, Freda Kelly from the northern wing of the Beatles Fan Club would cart them away for stamping.

Often, admirers would call personally and *en masse*, a brigade of 200 once needed much convincing that Ringo wasn't inside before leaving his stepfather suddenly alone on the doorstep. "Mum was frightened when we first got famous," recounted her son. "She was always getting people telling her I'd been killed or had an accident. Rumours got around and the press would get on to her."[36] Nevertheless, pestering from journalists and fans was not so uncontainable that the Graves could not still be "perfectly happy living in Admiral Grove",[38] even now that Richie had the means to grant them a dotage rich in more substantial material comforts than his present of a movie camera to Harry, who "gets such pleasure out of it, putting it back in the case when he's finished and cleaning it. Me? I just leave mine lying about any old place."[33] All other Beatle parents had been uprooted to up-market housing, but for the time being Harry and Elsie would not presume as much upon Richie's good fortune. However, no one in the family could deny completely the benefits of kinship to a Beatle. With Ringo's cousin John Foster at the drums, The Escorts were one up on scrimmaging rivals envious of their Blue Angel residency and their winning of a contract with Fontana Records in the Lancashire and Cheshire Beat Contest.

Suffering now for his own and his relations' future luxuries and sinecures, Ringo had vomited with nerves just before The Beatles topped the bill of ITV's *Sunday Night At The London Palladium*, the central height of British showbusiness. Tormented with earache, he was not left in pained quietude but dressed in an oversized coat, sunglasses and low-crowned trilby and hustled to the nearest hospital for emergency treatment. Marooned on his podium that evening, Starr's knuckles whitened around his sticks and 'I Wanna Be Your Man' was sung with razor-sharp poignancy.

His humble but specific dietary predilections were frequently frustrated by platters uncovered for him on tour by well-meaning gourmet chefs. Turning queasily from caviar or onion fritter rings, his stomach would yearn for chips and overdone steak, chicken sandwiches or the lardy solace of a mixed grill. If he couldn't wash these down with either light ale or whisky and Coke, he'd order pink Mateus Rosé, the only wine he was sure about. It was a red-letter day, anyway, if the group were allowed to eat a restaurant meal in solitude.

As well as autographing table napkins while masticating a sausage, Ringo also had to put up with disobliging comments about his nose, which, if you read magazine articles without knowing what he looked like, you'd believe resembled that of Cyrano de Bergerac. "Have you ever considered plastic surgery?"[7] dared a thick-skinned *Melody Maker* reporter. In an episode of a BBC television comedy series, Eric Sykes and Hattie Jacques triggered bursts of canned laughter with a comparison of Starr and General de Gaulle's respective conks. *The Jewish Chronicle* rang NEMS to enquire if he was one of them, and an apologist in *Boyfriend* – a schoolgirl comic – defended it as "a sign of distinction, one of the things that makes him attractive".[39] As taunts about it would even be scripted in The Beatles' first movie, *A Hard Day's Night*, Ringo had little choice but to desensitise himself and get "used to anything you'd say about it. I've come to terms with my own nose. It's the talking point when people discuss me. I have a laugh, and it goes up one nostril and out the other."[7] However, his hooter was to be less unfairly eye catching after The Who, with their trowel-prowed Pete Townshend, and Dave Dee, Dozy, *Beaky*, Mick and Tich each made their *Top Of The Pops* debuts in 1965.

Even as their luck held while other groups came and went, The Beatles still expected it to run out. "It's been fun, but it won't last long," avowed Lennon. "Anyway, I'd hate to be an old Beatle."[40] To Ringo, who'd come in on point of take-off, it had happened with the spooky deliberation of a dream, but he wasn't so dazzled as to think that pop stars – contrary to definition – were immortal, or that he'd never have to wonder about Hunt's again: "A couple of Number Ones and then out 18 months later won't make you rich. You'll be back on the buses."[41]

If nothing else, he'd recoup golden memories of adulation, although he'd be the only Beatle who'd sigh for the uproarious tribal gatherings that would degrade their musicianship. "I can't take it when they just sit there and listen to you," he'd reflect from a year when they might have done, had the group still existed. "I think it gives you that 'I'm here to be appreciated', attitude which is really a drag. They don't have to keep quiet at shows. If they want to hear the music, they can buy the records and listen to them."[42]

Income from million-sellers meant that even Ringo could afford well-deserved breaks in faraway places. With Harrison and McCartney, he'd limbered up for The Beatles' 1963 tour with Roy Orbison by spending twelve days staying with German friends in Tenerife. Four months later, he was in Greece with Paul "to get my toenails tattooed".[43] Like any poor boy who'd never signed a cheque or called hotel room service from a bedside telephone before, his consumption was more conspicuous than those born into wealth: "When the money first began to pour in, I'd go and buy ten suits, a dozen shirts and three cars. I spent money like it had just been invented."[44]

Coveting Billy Fury's drummer's blue-grey pearloid kit (made by Ludwig, a US firm), Ringo shelled out for a brown one with Swiss-made Paiste cymbals.[45] In doing so, he inflicted untold injury on home trade as every other stick-wielder, from schoolboys to chart-riding professionals like Chris Curtis of The Searchers and Dave Lovelady (now in The Fourmost), started beating a Ludwig, too. Because it travelled with The Beatles, the Ludwig became the standard group drum set for most of the 1960s. Nevertheless, some such as Bobby Elliott and Bernard Dwyer (of Freddie And The

Dreamers) favoured Trixon equipment from Germany, and eventually so would Dave Clark, after his trademark Rogers kit was raffled for charity.

Dave would finish 1964 as the second most famous drummer in the world. The first, of course, was Ringo Starr.

6 "Over In The States,
I Know I Went Over Well"

The Beatles' subjugation of the rest of the world was a large-scale re-run of the hysteria they'd long known at home but with even more presentations to civic heads, louder screams every stop of the way and longer queues of handicapped unfortunates wheeled deludedly down backstage corridors for the group's curative blessing. From dismissal by an Italian radio broadcaster as "a band without a future",[1] the four were swamping foreign Top Tens five or six singles at a time. The Indonesian Minister of Culture outlawed Beatle hairdos and *A Hard Day's Night* came to Warsaw. Back home, Ringo had been proposed as president of several higher-education establishments and had been house guest at Woburn Abbey at the invitation of the Duke of Bedford's swingin' son, Rudolph. While he'd still been able to do so without too much fuss, Starr had visited Dingle Vale Secondary one open day, "and they were charging people to look at my desk"[2] – or, at least, one that might have been once been his.

A *Daily Express* cartoon had Harold Wilson and Macmillan's successor, Sir Alec Douglas-Home, soliciting The Beatles for their votes in the post-Profumo general election, thus lending credence to the homily, "I care not who makes a nation's laws as long as I can write its songs." The quartet had also been earmarked for a cameo appearance in *Coronation Street*, although this was precluded by their tight work schedule. More than just another pop group as transient and gimmicky as any other, they were now part of the national furniture, and would be honoured as such by Prime Minister Wilson.

"Our appeal," ruminated Starr, "is that we're ordinary lads",[3] which, as it had in Britain, did the corrective trick in a United States depressed with its own traumas – the Kennedy assassination, vehement opposition to the Civil Rights Amendment and the first boy soldiers blown to bits in Indochina. Into the bargain, its Top 20 was sodden with unmemorable instrumentals, drivelling ballads, a declining Presley and wholesome anthems like The Beach Boys' 'Be True To Your School'. To the chagrin of The Beach Boys, The Four Seasons and others on Capitol – The Beatles' US label – the Merseysiders were launched with one of the most far-reaching publicity blitzes hitherto known in the record industry North America was, therefore, theirs for the taking when they arrived fully mobilised in February 1964 for *The Ed Sullivan Show*, the sub-continent's *Sunday Night At The London Palladium*. Surely nothing should have topped the Palladium, but, after Sullivan and their US concert debut at the Washington Coliseum, "they could have ripped me apart," raved Starr, "and I couldn't have cared less."[4] Even after they flew out, 'I Want To Hold Your Hand' remained at Number One, while hurtling up were all their singles that in the previous year had been aired to negligible listener reaction by the more lurid disc jockeys such as Wolfman Jack and New York's Murray the K ("the fastest talker I've ever met,"[5] said Ringo). Beatles chewing gum alone netted millions of dollars within months.

As is their wont, the Americans, convinced of the incredible, exhibited an enthusiasm for it that left more reserved British Beatlemaniacs swallowing dust. Our colonial cousins were devouring the grass on which the group had trodden and the retrieved jelly-beans that had rained as votive offerings onto the stage on which the idols had played.[6] "I enjoy it at the back," said Ringo, "and when they start throwing things, it's a good place to be."[7] Girls would faint on fingering the guitar autographed by all four and owned by some pensioner in a moptop wig who'd declared himself "the oldest Beatles fan". The whingeing of their children would cause well-off parents to interrupt European holidays for a flight to Liverpool where back copies of *Mersey Beat* would fetch hugely inflated prices and the chair on which Ringo had always perched when in the Cavern band room would be kissed like the Blarney Stone.

A US "tribute" single, 'My Boyfriend Got A Beatle Haircut' by Donna Lynn, was issued by Capitol in March 1964. As sure as fate, there followed a cartoon group in *Shindig* comic called 'The Beadles' – who used imagined Scouse colloquialisms like "blimey, guv'nor" and "blighter" and addressed each other as "mate" – and hastily assembled soundalike discs were released by such as The American Beetles, The Bug Men, John And Paul, The Merseyboys, *ad nauseum*, mostly by Los Angeles session musicians who probably bitched during coffee breaks about this Limey combo everyone's talking about. Local outfits found that it paid to break up and reform as soon as they'd either grown their hair or acquired wigs and rehearsed tortuous Liverpudlian accents and slang – "wack", "gear", "fab" and so on – for on-stage continuity during a set consisting wholly of yeah-yeah-yeah Beatles-Mersey Beat imitations. Some tried passing themselves off as genuine Britons, while those in redneck areas – such as San Antonio's Sir Douglas Quintet – dared not sport a *pilzenkopf* off stage for fear of disapproval expressed in designs stronger than people simply bellowing, "Get yer 'air cut!" from a passing car.

'Lies' by New York's Knickerbockers was the most precise duplication of the salient points of The Beatles sound[9] while The Byrds' more enduring career was founded on less frenzied aspects of Mersey Beat. Modelled to breadwinning UK specifications, too, were the likes of The Ramrods[10] (who covered 'I Wanna Be Your Man'), The Standells, The Wackers, The Manchesters, The McCoys and, far behind them all, a Big Apple stage-school unit with the nerve to call themselves The Escorts – and otherwise notable only because they contained a Richard Perry whose life was to cross that of Ringo Starr in the next decade.

North to Massachusetts, The Barbarians recorded a pragmatic "Mersey Beat" 45 entitled 'Are You A Boy Or Are You A Girl', although their drummer, Victor Moulton, loathed "14-year-old girls from the Bronx who go to Mod shops and say, 'What can we get that's English to walk around in today?' and, at 11pm, they have to take off their John Lennon hats and go home."[11] Many US musicians who would loom large in the lives of certain Beatles – notably Starr – were those who'd largely defied the British onslaught. While admitting that Ringo was "instrumental in making the drums what they are today",[12] Jim Keltner – from an Oklahoman family of drummers – served Gary Lewis And The Playboys, the proudly American exception during that 1965 week when the *Billboard* Top Ten was all British. Helping to keep surf music alive in the Top 30 that year was 'New York's A Lonely Town (When You're The Only Surfer Boy)' by The Tradewinds, a "four-strong group from Providence", according to their press release, but actually Vini Poncia and Pete Anders, a multi-tracked professional team from a Big Apple songwriting factory.

For such craftsmen, jumping on bandwagons did not sate them with pride, but it nevertheless kept the wolf from the door. Donna Lynn's was not to be an isolated Beatle-related yuk-for-a-buck. When directing such a disc at an individual member, compilers were more likely to single out Ringo than John, Paul or George. John, Paul and George who? Kennedy? Revere? Washington? Who didn't know who was meant by Ringo, or thought they did? Just the title of Lorne Green's re-released 'Ringo', although an entirely unconnected dramatic monologue of the fictitious Old West pistolero, was sufficient to elevate it onto radio playlists and all the way up the Hot 100. There was, however, no doubt about who the man was in Penny Valentine's 'I Want To Kiss Ringo Goodbye',[13] which was released the week before The Beatles returned to London, or 'Ringo For President' by Australia's Rolf Harris and aimed at the States; 'Bingo Ringo' in the Deep South drawl of Huckleberry Hound; and even Beatle-Christmas crossovers in The Four Sisters' platonic 'I Want Ringo For Christmas' and 'Santa Bring Me Ringo'[14] from Christine Hunter.

"I Love Ringo" lapel badges outsold all associated merchandise, but Starr was not thus hallowed solely because he was easily identifiable. He had also stolen the show from the others in a society that was later to concede to the adoption of Cabbage Patch dolls. Promoted in like fashion, The Beatles had in Ringo something as lovably affecting, a little boy lost, a snare-drum Cinderella, the diminutive sad sack toiling on his lonely pedestal and engaging boundless sympathy for being the most inconspicuous one. As if the audience had all sat on tin-tacks, the volume of screams would climb to its loudest when Lennon moved his microphone over to the kit for Starr Time. A wave of groaned pity would filter across cinema rows during the *Hard Day's Night* scene in which Ringo received but one fan letter against the others' thick wads, with a delighted cheer issuing when a whole mailbag is belatedly produced for him alone. On his birthday, a Jeri Fannin of Xenia, Ohio, threw a celebration as an excuse to display her collection of nearly 1,000 photographs of her – and everyone's – most beloved Beatle. Perhaps George, Paul and John should have hung on to Pete Best.

In Britain, the level of applause had not risen at the Royal Command Performance when, delayed by his descent from the drum riser, Ringo had taken his curtain call a few seconds after the guitarists, "but over in the States I know I went over well. It knocked me out to see and hear the kids waving for me. I'd made it as a personality. Who wouldn't be flattered?"[15] As a consequence, he overcame many earlier inhibitions and grew more verbally self-assured as nicotine-stained digits scribbled down quotable Beatle repartee.

North Americans, you see, were accustomed to their pop stars being more devoid of independent opinion than any Larry Parnes cipher. Since the demobilisation of Elvis as a sergeant and all-round entertainer, a smooth-running, insipidly handsome youth (usually with a blow-wave and the forename Bobby) would be set in motion by his manager as a walking digest of Presley's more palatable, all-American aspects. Subliminally, through the medium of teen magazines and even in the piffle he was given to sing, the Bobby would parrot stolid middle-aged dictums – your parents' word was law, don't talk dirty, *et al* – and parade a dearth of private vices. With the gentlest humour, he'd answer enquiries about his favourite colour, preferred foodstuffs and the age at which he hoped to marry.

Having flexed their muscles with the European press, The Beatles capsized this cautious regimen through a combination of effusive zaniness, bluff unsentimentality and sarcastic one-line debates about inflammable issues and Beethoven's poems. "We were the first ones in rock 'n' roll that didn't kid the kids about drinking milk, and America was shocked," elucidated Starr. "'A scotch and Coke?' they'd ask, and we'd go, 'Yes, a scotch and Coke!' We were just honest lads, and it got us into trouble sometimes, but we didn't give in to the hypocrisy."[16] The equal of the others now, he was as instant a pundit as they, cracking back as snappily and impudently to banal, ill-informed questions – such as the classic "How did you find America?"[17] – as repetitious as a stuck record from circling media hounds. "Do you like being Beatles?" "Yes, or we'd be Rolling Stones."[18] When are you going to retire?" "In about ten minutes." "Have you any brothers?" "My brother was an only child."[7] "Did The Beatles come to America to get revenge for the Revolution?" "No, we just came for the money"[19] "Has success changed your life?" "Yep." "Don't you ever say anything but 'yep'?"' "Nope." "Why don't you sing?" "I can see you haven't heard our LPs."[20] "What about Senator Barry Goldwater?" "Not much fun, is he?"[21] "What would you be if you weren't a Beatle?" "The Beatles' manager." "What's the difference between English press conferences and those held in America?" "They're the same – people asking questions."[7]

In cold print, Ringo's remarks often seemed inane and pedestrian, but it was the poker-faced, what-are-you-laughing-at way he said 'em. In *A Hard Day's Night*, after a peppery, waxed-moustachioed rail commuter's clichéd moan about fighting a war for your sort, he humbled, "Bet you're sorry you won." In this stylised celluloid account of The Beatles' eventful preparation for a television showcase, Starr seized critical attention not with the deadpan sentences he enunciated with unprecedented clarity[23] but in non-speaking sequences that gilded his public image by bringing to light what Brian Epstein called "the little man's quaintness".[24] Less Harpo Marx than Charlie Drake, he exuded elements of that lip-trembling, doe-eyed pathos that some find endearing as a forlorn wanderer who had been badgered into thus "goin' paradin'" by "Paul's grandfather" (Wilfred Brambell[25]), a mischief-maker who'd ascertained from group banter that Ringo was its butt. Soon, Starr is seen advisedly unrecognisable in tramp's rags moping along a canal bank to George Martin's woebegone, harmonica-led orchestration of The Beatles' 'This Boy', now re-titled 'Ringo's Theme'. Among incidents *en route* are Ringo spreading his coat over a puddle *à la* Sir Walter Raleigh for a dolly-bird who, wrongly apprehending it to be shallow, promptly vanishes beneath a fathom of mud. In turn, Ringo is almost bowled over by a car tyre pushed by a grubby urchin who begins a description of his gang of four – an expanded metaphor for The Beatles.

Ringo-as-tramp's dramatic impact was not marred by the fact that he'd come "straight from the Ad-Lib out of my brain and feeling really down because I'd been drinking all night. I was incapable of saying a line, so Dick [Lester, director] had to use me somehow, and he kept making me walk 'round and look at the kid and that. So that's how that scene came off, and suddenly they say, 'Oh, you're a fantastic actor.'" Hungover as he was, "to make you laugh is not hard for me on film. I can do the funny walk, the funny looks. I can pull a few faces and limp a bit."[26]

Although Starr was designated most frequently by reviewers as the one with a likely destiny as a tragi-comedian, the group was praised collectively for its contribution to a project that ushered in a tougher, more realistic approach to pop movies. *A Hard Day's Night* was produced by Walter Shenson, a Californian whose past had included *The Mouse That Roared*, Acker Bilk's 1962 vehicle *A Band Of Thieves* and other British flicks that did not extend the boundaries of the avant garde. He did not regard Starr as "the greatest intellect in the world"[27] but nevertheless saw in him "a superb actor, an absolute natural. He can take direction from a director, which is a very difficult thing to do. You might even call it an art."[28]

Ringo's truant afternoons gawping at Hollywood hadn't been wasted in other respects, either. He'd become quite a film connoisseur by the mid 1960s, with Paul Newman – anti-hero of *Sweet Bird Of Youth* and *Hud* – as admired now as Victor Mature. Furthermore, the drummer was sufficiently intrigued by the filming process to roll up earlier than the other Beatles on the set of *A Hard*

Day's Night – if he hadn't over-indulged at the Ad-Lib – and being the most obviously thrilled at "seeing myself on that 20-foot screen, doing it and pretending".[26]

A layman's interest in still photography had been mirrored during his *Hard Day's Night* walkabout by a ludicrous attempt to take a snap of himself, but "when we were making the film, I had my own Pentax and I just kept clicking all the time".[28] As Lennon's stabs at literature had been collated into two slim best-sellers, so a tome of Starr's photos was allegedly planned for publication, initially for the USA, and he was looking forward to being "able to plug it".[28] However, all that the public saw were the two dozen or so shots captioned in *Rave* magazine's "Picture Scoop Of The Year". More were promised to *Mersey Beat*, but, shrugged Bill Harry, "I never got any of them."

Now sub-titled "Britain's leading beat paper", *Mersey Beat* was dying like a sun going nova, its final burst of energy unleashed in full-colour illustrations, articles on non-Merseyside acts and a circulation that sprawled as far south as Leicester. In March 1965, it was swallowed by *Music Echo*, in which coverage of the Liverpool scene was confined to a solitary page commensurate with faded interest – even in the city itself – in any more groups with sheepdog fringes who could play 'Twist And Shout' – although who hadn't come out when, for *A Hard Day's Night*'s northern première, The Beatles had passed in triumph through rapturous streets where chants of "We want Ringo!" outnumbered all others and a girl almost hurled herself under the group's Rolls Royce because she couldn't see him properly. They belonged to Liverpool and Liverpool let everyone know it. During the US tour that followed, a placard was hoisted in the midst of the shrieking masses in a Detroit stadium. It read, "We Are From Tue Brook.[29] We Are Proud Of You."

On the 1965 evening that The Beatles performed before nearly 6,000[30] – a new world record – at New York's Shea Stadium, Rory Storm And The Hurricanes were on at Orrell Park ballroom, with Storm as daredevil and hip-swivelling as ever. Throughout the hardship and disappointment that he had borne, Rory had not begrudged Richie his luck and had been unruffled by a gradually more tenuous contact with his old drummer. Nevertheless, Harry Graves had been there on the afternoon that centre-forward Rory and Wally scored three goals for the Mersey Beat XI against Florence Albion. One ex-member of his Hurricanes was accorded the *NME* headline, "Ringo Man Records!"[34] when his next outfit made a 1964 single, but Rory Storm's links with The Beatles had, nevertheless, not been as exploited by the press as much as they might have been.

Storm's rival bandleader Kingsize Taylor – who, but for The Beatles, would have been Starr's employer – had modestly come into his own on the Star-Club circuit of Hamburg, Kiel and Berlin, where "they are still a bit behind the times. They go for the old Little Richard gear and stuff like that."[31] Agreeing that he'd been "out of the country at the wrong time"[31], Kingsize made occasional forays to Britain, where a booking at the Iron Door sparked off a commendatory write-up in *Melody Maker*, a UK tour with Chuck Berry, a spot on *Ready, Steady, Go!* and the protraction of a prolific if generally unsuccessful recording career into 1967.

The only representative of Mersey Beat womanhood in the UK hit parade, Taylor's old flame, Cilla Black, had also been the first female to reach Number One since Helen Shapiro. On a tour with The Fourmost and Sounds Incorporated, she came to close the show after the headlining PJ Proby – "someone who is silly to himself",[4] opined Ringo – was harried from British theatres following an on-stage trouser-splitting episode. Despite her compromising casting in 1965's *Ferry Across The Mersey*, a period film whose evocative title song was Gerry And The Pacemakers Top Ten farewell, Cilla survived Mersey Beat's collapse via a lengthy and well-received season at the Palladium supported by The Fourmost, who'd portrayed the *losers* in a "battle of the bands" contest in *Ferry Across The Mersey*.

A real-life loser was now the cornerstone of The Pete Best Four (as Dave Clark was in his Five), but neither the Four's Decca 45 – a revival of Eddie Hodges' 'I'm Gonna Knock On Your Door'[32] – nor Pete's spot as mystery guest on US television's *I've Got A Secret* netted as much as his 1964 libel suit against Ringo, who'd discovered that nothing was "off the record" to some journalists. Nonetheless, it was galling for Best – who'd denied himself the amphetamines consumed by the other Beatles – when, during an interview with the soft-porn magazine *Playboy*, Starr had added a stupidly antiphonal "he took little pills to make him ill" after Lennon had explained, "Ringo used to fill in sometimes if our drummer was ill. With his periodic illness."[33] Although the case would drag on for four years, Pete would win a bitter and undivulged victory that, after legal fees, was sufficient to pay for renovations to his new house in West Derby.

A more physical dispute with Best – a punch-up in a St Pauli alley – would be recalled by Tony Sheridan during a 1964 media junket in a brave attempt to lift his new *Just A Little Bit Of...* LP off the ground. Although well placed to grow fat on Beatlemania, Sheridan had been resident in a Reeperbahn club when one of his 1961 singles with the Best Beatles was reissued to spread itself thinly enough to be registered as a million-seller without making that much of a dent in either the UK or the North American charts. Drawn from his exile by pragmatism, Tony had brushed his grey-flecked hair forward, had been "guest star" on a tour with The Searchers and Roy Orbison and had been invited to appear on British TV again. He'd also renewed his acquaintance with The Beatles, meeting them at Whaddon House after a *Hard Day's Night* shoot for "talk of the old times, laughs about some of the German raves and best wishes for the future".[35]

This hail-fellow-well-met reunion was not, however, repeated when the group and Sheridan were benighted in the same Australian hotel a few months later. It has been since chronicled that this leg of The Beatles' 1964 world tour was little more than a heavily subsidised debauch, which is why it was opportune that George and Ringo's respective parents decided not to come along for the ride. Indeed, with the intelligence that it was to be winter Down Under, Ringo had exclaimed in London, "No birds or beaches or anything? The trip's off. I'm not going!"[35] The other three had nonetheless gone on without him, after he'd been spectacularly sick in the toilet during a late-morning sitting for European publicity shots in a Putney portrait studio. Still off colour, he'd been examined by a local doctor, who diagnosed tonsillitis and pharyngitis; but it was a high temperature that necessitated an immediate removal to University College Hospital, near Covent Garden.

With the tour to commence in Copenhagen the next day, the three functioning Beatles, their manager and George Martin gathered at Abbey Road to try and resolve the quandary. Harrison was all for cancellation, as "playing without Ringo is like driving a car on three wheels".[36] Nevertheless, even he was persuaded by Epstein that their only choice was a substitute. Who? Tony Meehan? Clem Cattini? Tony Newman, from Sounds Incorporated? Andy White? What was Pete Best doing these days? "The difficulty," expounded Brian, "was finding someone who looked like a Beatle and not an outcast."[37] Martin mentioned Jimmy Nicol, who, since finishing with Cyril Stapleton, had been one of the workman-like but individually uncredited Ghost Squad on *Beatlemania*, a cheap Pye LP of *This Is Merseybeat* bent on which – at the standard Musicians' Union rate – 14 Beatle hits had been copied.

The Beatles would remember that Terry Heneberry, producer of both their 1963 radio series *Pop Go The Beatles* and The Rabin Band's forgotten *Go Man Go Show* three years earlier, had also thought highly of Nicol. From the Liverpudlians' own circle, so too did singer Tommy Quickly, after Jimmy had drummed on one of his Pye singles and with Georgie Fame, in whose Blue Flames Jimmy was presently working. Moreover, he'd also made a couple of singles with his own – and now dispersed – outfit The Shubdubs, who'd each adopted a severe moptop.

On that strange Wednesday, 24-year-old Nicol was stirred from an after-lunch nap in his Barnes living room by a ring from George Martin. No, it wasn't another session job. Well, not of the kind he might have expected. Could he be at Studio Two by three o'clock to rehearse with The Beatles? Behind Ringo's famous Ludwig kit, Jimmy ran through five items with them over two hours with curt tuition mainly from John and George and "no music script, but that didn't matter. I already knew the numbers from *Beatlemania*."[35]

Reeling with disbelief at this amazing assignment, he telephoned an understanding Georgie Fame and dashed home to pack for Denmark. On every stage, Lennon "gave me a great build-up",[39] but by the second day a banner calling for a "Ringo Quick Recovery!" (*sic*) was hauled up during The Beatles' regal progress along the canals of Amsterdam.

Despite a secrecy exemplified by the false name ("Mr Jackson") on the door of his private ward, Starr's whereabouts had been rumbled and Covent Garden exchange jammed with concerned calls. Many were from the States, where, even as they spoke, 'What's Wrong With Ringo?' – a 45 by The Bon-Bons – was being pressed. In Australia, an Adelaide radio station was carrying regular bulletins on the likelihood of him rejoining the group for opening night in the city's Centennial Hall. Over in Sydney, another presenter was whimpering that, rather than Nicol, The Beatles might have given an Aussie musician a chance. From a McCartney quip at the city's Mascot airport – "We're going to give him a gold watch, shake his hand and tell him it was nice"[40] – grew alarmist hearsay that Starr had had enough and was intending to retire, and some went on believing this, even as he countered that "the word 'retire' clicks off a little picture in my mind of a chap digging up the garden and planting seeds. Well, that's not the life for me yet."[41]

Rather than remain huddled under his bedclothes contemplating a free buss pass, Ringo had been touched by a telegram of the "miss you" variety from the other three and, not wishing to inconvenience anyone more than necessary, nor miss any of what was still great fun, he rose after not much more than a week in bed, the minimum time recommended by the doctor. Armed with a bottle of medicine "in case I get any twitches"[43] and compelling a motorcyclist to speed from Heathrow to collect the passport he'd left in his jacket pocket, he let Brian bundle him onto a flight to Sydney via San Francisco, where his transfer from Pan Am to Qantas was accomplished after the usual press conference and fan riot. A toy koala was thrust into his arms as he disembarked and the grinning Sydney media let him go after he'd itemised every piece of personal jewellery he was wearing and knocked back a goodwill glass of Australian lager. When he caught up with The Beatles in their Melbourne hotel, a vast police inspector piggy-backed him through a crowd of thousands. Pale and shaking, he ordered a stiff drink even while heading towards the lift to his suite. He may have needed another after the illuminating experience of watching the group strut their stuff that night with Nicol at the city's Festival Hall.

Afterwards, there was a party to welcome Ringo back and thank Jimmy, for whom a plane from Brisbane had been booked for the next morning. By cruel contrast to his twelve days as a Beatle when "it seemed that the whole population had turned out to meet us",[43] he'd be greeted by only his wife and infant son when he landed back in London. As well as a fair rather than markedly generous cheque, Jimmy had come out of it with an inscribed gold Eternamatic wristwatch that had been presented to him by Epstein, who had, reputedly, taken tacit umbrage at his comments to the press, such as an over-frank "I don't think he [Starr] can play in time",[44] and what was seen as rash sight-seeing, shopping sprees and, once, sitting in with singer Frances Faye and her band in a Sydney nightclub.

These excursions were partly because Nicol had never been entirely comfortable socialising with The Beatles and had sought instead the company of Sounds Incorporated,[45] The Phantoms and other of the package tour's small change who were likewise free to take the air after breakfast without being mobbed. When The Beatles and Jimmy later found themselves booked one night at the same British theatre, neither party made the effort to pop over to the other's dressing room for a chat.

Back with The Blue Flames, Nicol would be signing as many autograph books as Georgie Fame. As a further barometer of his unlooked-for fame, he was contracted to regroup The Shubdubs to take the place of The Dave Clark Five for a Blackpool summer season after Clark developed a stomach ulcer.

The Five had been the first beat group to undertake a full US tour in the wake of The Beatles, who, some would argue, they shut down fleetingly as Uncle Sam's top British act. During one 1964 week, two-thirds of *Billboard*'s Hot 100 was British in origin as more of our major pop icons (and some minor ones) made headway in the unchartered States. This was especially true of Freddie And The Dreamers and Herman's Hermits, whose respective lead vocalists looked as if they needed even more mothering than Ringo.

Top US record-business folk – songwriters like Clint Ballard Jnr and Jackie de Shannon, producers Jimmy Miller and Phil Spector[47] and manager/accountant Allen Klein – became as wasps around the jam-jar of Albion just as the island's own big-shots had lately been around Liverpool. Conversely, Jack Good, the brains behind *Six-Five Special*, *Oh Boy!* and other ground-breaking pop shows, was now inflicting similar wounds on American television. Other Britons who were penetrating North America via pop-associated styles and trends included John Peel (*né* Ravenscroft), who, because he happened to have been born near Liverpool – posh Heswall, actually – was engaged as resident "Beatle expert" by a Dallas radio network. Among less parochial celebrities were two of Ringo's London friends: designer Robin Cruikshank, with his Robin Ltd company, and photographer Terry O'Neill, who became one of Hollywood actress Faye Dunaway's husbands. "It was just like being part of an international team,"[47] said O'Neill. Another Londoner who "arrived" in the States was *haute couture* Diaghilev, Mary Quant, who, pressed by some to autograph her creations, "began to feel rather like a Beatle".[48]

One of her willowy models, Pattie Boyd, felt even more like one when, after landing a bit part in *A Hard Day's Night*, she was charmed away from her then-boyfriend by George Harrison. By 1964, she was cohabiting with the guitarist in a bungalow on his wooded estate in Esher. George's life at Whaddon House with his flatmate had been cordial enough, and they'd even composed together after a desultory fashion when "he was playing my guitar and I had the tape on, so we tried something".[49] During the filming of *A Hard Day's Night*, "the height of luxury" for Victor Spinetti (who played a neurotic television director) was to repair to their apartment "and have bread and butter and chips and watch television".[50] Outside, the marathon vigils held by tatty girls with laddered tights and someone else's love bites was tiresome, and even boys were trying to kiss the Knightsbridge Beatles as they came and went, but it was a burglary of the flat on 19 April – while the group were recording a Jack Good TV special – that had been the last straw for George and Ringo (and Brian), who decided to evacuate to dwellings less exposed to public attention.

City lights had not lost their allure for Ringo, who, unlike George and Pattie – and the Lennons, too – did not flee into Surrey. Instead, through the agency of genteel Brymon Estates, he installed himself on the opposite side of Hyde Park in a leased one-bedroom apartment on the ground floor of Montagu Square, a long Victorian block near the Swiss Embassy. He'd suffer muffled giggling from fans who'd winkled out his ex-directory telephone number but, this and worse inconveniences went with the job, and he couldn't crab about its perks. The most tangible of these was the easy money that had facilitated the purchase of a Facel Vegal so ornate that it "gets more looks than I do".[15] Because George had one, next came a silver, six-door Mercedes 600 with contoured seats, for which he'd have a chauffeur on call "because if you haven't you can't park anywhere or go out and get drunk".[51] However, it was somehow soothing to sit behind the wheel himself. "If things got me down, I'd just get out the car and drive away into the night. It sort of got me out of myself."[52] This habit would intensify after 8 October 1964, when he'd slipped furtively from Abbey Road to take – and pass – his driving test.

Both alone on a moonlit ride and switching from scotch to bourbon down at the Ad-Lib, Ringo was prone to plunging into orgies of maudlin reminiscences. You could stand him a feed in the Ritz, but he'd still be sentimental about when he used to small-talk on the pavement with The Hurricanes while chomping Morgan's newspapered fish and chips. To one who'd berate his Mercedes dealer with "but they only cost £11,000 new",[53] a gold Cadillac now could not compare to the Dingle days of his first car, "a red and white Vanguard which I bought for £75 from some guy down the road. Second gear didn't work, but I loved it."[51]

Now that he was of world renown, the past was never far away, especially when relations and family friends he hadn't realised existed turned up at stage doors, where the very security guards paid to keep riff-raff out could often be bribed to let them in. Three teenage girl "cousins" in New Zealand had – said the eldest – emigrated from Liverpool in 1963. Ringo couldn't locate where their lineage crossed with his own, but, as warlords were entertained at mediaeval banquets by jesters, he let them stay to amuse him as they span again what must have been a very likely tale to have gained them entry to a dressing room theoretically as protected as Howard Hughes' Las Vegas penthouse.

Starr and Harrison had been present in the NEMS office where, 17 years after his reported desertion of his family, Alfred Lennon had suddenly re-appeared for a short conversation with John. If less dumbfounded, Starkey *père et fils* had been "strange together"[54] when they'd been likewise re-united, but Richie's more self-esteeming sire had not had his hands as open for any bounties that might trickle from the Beatle's coffers. This was perhaps just as well, because, during a 1965 visit to his son – the last occasion they ever met – Ringo's natural father, escorting his second wife, had "got the feeling we weren't wanted. He never paid our train fare."[55]

Starkey junior would not risk discomforting his mother by being chummy with her long-lost ex-husband, especially as she was so overtly enjoying her second-hand celebrity. From the Cavern, she'd joined other Beatle relatives in a costly telephone link-up with Radio WROD in Florida, to be transmitted throughout the USA the next day. "I'd love to go to America. I believe it is a lovely place you have there,"[55] she'd enthused, as if it were the Isle of Wight.

Hardly the scoop of the century, either, was Elsie's refuting that Richie had a steady girlfriend. According to *Confidential*, Hollywood's most scurrilous showbiz gossip rag, he had plenty of unsteady ones, from Marlene Claire – captain of New York's Peppermint Lounge go-go dancers – to actress Ann Margret. He'd allegedly "bent her shell-pink ears with an hour of long-distance oogly-googling, all in a special type of Teddy Boy lingo that left little

Annie limp".[56] From the organ that assured readers that timid Cynthia Lennon had once been considered as The Beatles' lead singer, such deathless claptrap could be disregarded, as could assumptions that the sap had been rising beyond a joke when a shapely woman journalist had asked, "What subject do you not want to talk about?" "Your husband,"[15] Ringo snapped back, eyeing her with exaggerated lasciviousness. However, with countless hordes of a certain type of female admirer aspiring to an orgasm at the mere sight of a Beatle, members of the road crew were not astonished when instructed to bring the more personable up to one or other of their masters' hotel suites. In the lobby of Miami's Deauville Theater, Starr cut out middlemen and perfunctory chivalry by snatching one such girl by the arm and manoeuvring her into the nearest lift for tea and biscuits upstairs.

If in more gregarious a mood, he'd often be seen holding court in the bar area with a Southern Comfort close at hand as night drew on. He'd evidently discovered this brew's short-lived magic while in the States. When The Beatles were in Australia, a promoter at McCartney's 22nd birthday party in Sydney would witness "how absolutely rotten drunk Ringo got. At about 3am, he passed out on his feet and just slowly sank to the ground where he stood."[39]

It was a trifle unsettling for the spirited Maureen to imagine that her Richie's waking hours between one concert and the next weren't spent innocently shuffling cards, shaking a dice or slapping a table-top in time when John and Paul played their latest opus on acoustic guitars. Like his mother, Mo was still required to keep up the "just good friends" farce, even though half the world knew that they'd holidayed together with Paul and Jane in the Virgin Islands, albeit with the open-minded skipper of their hired yacht as chaperone. It was possibly a disgruntled fusion of work taking him away from her and the group taking him for granted that made him dig his heels in and refuse to leave the Admiral Grove hearth for The Beatles' first concert in France until Brian made ill-affordable time to talk him around.

Matters between Mo and Richie came to a head when he was re-admitted to University College Hospital for the extraction of tonsils that – after he'd dredged up a croaky 'Boys' in Australasia – had become so troublesome that no Starr lead vocal would be heard on some dates of their subsequent American tour. While he lay on the operating table, there was media speculation about the future of the gruesome excisions. Was it true that they'd be sent to a fan who'd requested them? Were they to be auctioned? In a Carl Giles newspaper cartoon, a girl off to keep watch outside the infirmary was commanded, "You're not bringing 'em back here!"[57] by her father.

Her patience might have been rewarded if she'd been there when George and Paul visited, bearing grapes and sympathy to their drummer's bedside. They were sent on their way with screams, but Maureen passed to and fro unnoticed by most star-struck loiterers. Legend has it that Ringo proposed matrimony during the sweet nothings of one of her visits, but some say that, surrounded by a chuckling throng, he actually went down on bended knee to her one woozy night at the Ad-Lib.

One of Starr's familiars among the Swinging London ravers was Keith Moon, now with The Who. A known prankster and exhibitionist, Moon would create mayhem from nothing, the most documented example being his disruption of a party in Chertsey by steering a Rolls Royce Silver Cloud into the host's swimming pool. However, although his antics necessitated extreme sanctions by the group, this was balanced by his principal asset: he drummed like a rhythmically integrated octopus. Much of his technique – too quick for the eye to follow – had been learned from The Pretty Things' Viv Prince, who deputised when Keith was indisposed and, in 1966, recorded a solo single entitled 'Minuet For Ringo'.

This dedication was yet another indication of how famous rather than how skilful a drummer Ringo had become. Within professional circles, he was deemed less worthy of respect than lapsed jazzmen like Bobby Elliott, The Rolling Stones' Charlie Watts ("the only drummer who leaves out more than I do"[58]) and Pete York, with his regular column in *Midland Beat* and its valuable tips from his own strict practice rota, plus learned critiques of the latest kit accessories. While esteeming Keith Moon as "the Elvin Jones of the pop world",[59]

York twitted Dave Clark – as most of the industry's intelligentsia did – for the crude percussive hooks that were clearly the selling points on any one of the Five's early hits.

There were claims that Clark didn't beat the skins on his own records, although he was a competent enough instrumentalist on the boards. Similarly, through a leak about Andy White, and on the more oblique grounds that garrulous New York session drummer Bernard Purdie had apparently been employed by Tony Sheridan when his German Beatle recordings were tidied up, allegations were made by the ignorant that Ringo didn't play on his group's discs. With Nicol in Australia, Paul might have been protesting too much by saying, "This fellow is fine, but we just can't afford to be without Ringo on a real recording session, because the kids would know that that record was the one without him."[37]

Any uniqueness in The Beatles' drum sound was partly down to George Martin's miking experiments with varying degrees of acoustic overspill and technique of swathing the tom-toms in dishcloths and even blankets to achieve the "pudding effect", as it was jargonised. "It makes me, like, thuddy," explained its prime exponent. "I've always wanted my snare to sound like a tom-tom with a snare on, never just like a snare – you know, those fast jazz snares."[60]

If the antithesis of Prince and Moon, Ringo's style – like that of Charlie Watts – was becoming outstanding for the frugality, whereby "I try and not move at all throughout a whole song, embellish or decorate it at all, keep it really, really simple".[60] Like a vicar shy of sermons, "Drum breaks still bring me out in a cold sweat. I have mental blackouts."[60]

No matter who might have been as capable of thumping The Beatles' drums, it was Ringo who bound them morally as well as within tempo. While John, Paul and George were hesitating over a marijuana cigarette rolled by Bob Dylan after they and the fêted protest-singer-in-transition were introduced in 1964, Starr had had no qualms about trying it, his blissful smile on inhaling being an indication to the other three that this narcotic was seemingly harmless. When Lennon was poised to march out of a ghastly flag-waving British Embassy reception in Washington, it was Ringo who cajoled him to "get it over with". Appearing freakish to patronising Foreign Office males with conservative suits and short-back-and-sides haircuts, the group were jostled, politely insulted and hailed like taxis; but, even after a woman had scissored off a souvenir lock of his hair, Starr seethed only inwardly when requested to present the raffle prizes to these nicely spoken if "silly people, because they hate to admit they like you, too. They think it's wrong."[61]

Just as hoity-toity, sometimes, were the mayors, beauty queens and showbiz "personalities" who were falling over themselves to have their pictures taken with these common-as-muck Scousers who were influencing the minds of millions. Despite his mystified "Vivien who?" when he'd been asked to meet her, publicity-conscious Vivien Leigh had bounded forward to pump Ringo's hand furiously before the shutters stopped clattering. It gave The Beatles deep pleasure to snub people like those many rainbow-shirted, yapping US disc-jockeys who'd dubbed themselves "the fifth Beatle". Because Noël Coward had been waspish about them, "We thought he was a spiteful old man," related Ringo, "so we behaved like spiteful little boys. You know, 'We won't see you because you didn't say nice things about us.'"[61] When classical pianist Artur Rubenstein invited them to his suite in the Sydney hotel opposite theirs, Starr sarcastically suggested the compromise of a get-together halfway across the street.

Naturally enough, the most welcome (and least transparent) of the illustrious who wanted to breathe the air around The Beatles were those who'd been central to a Merseyside adolescence, including Carl Perkins – who'd been an observer at Ringo's 'Matchbox' session – and tough-guy film stars such as Burt Lancaster, at whose Hollywood home Paul, George and Ringo had relaxed one evening, watching Peter Sellers' newest *Pink Panther* movie. Before they left, the hospitable Lancaster promised to send Ringo some Wild West six-guns, if he could get Mr Epstein to arrange an import licence. Later, Elvis Presley would give Starr holsters for them.

Brian would convince his boys that it might be bad form to back away from all of the big-names-in-good-cause galas that were now being held in their honour. You'd see Zsa Zsa Gabor, Shirley Temple and Tuesday Weld piling their paper plates high with salad. Bing Crosby and Edward G Robinson might be unbuttoning themselves in adjacent urinals to yours in the gents. On a staircase, Cassius Clay would spar playfully with Ringo. Don't look now, but isn't that Groucho Marx? That young man that no one recognises – my daughter has a pin-up of him in her school locker. Interestingly, it had struck Starr that "it's the one-shot characters who can be nasty, like the people who make one record and think they're the greatest thing ever to hit showbusiness. Deep down, they know they've got no real talent and that they've had a lucky break."[61]

Well, so had he, but every silver lining has a cloud. Waking up in a luxurious cage of claustrophobic torpor, Starr would almost expect to yawn and stretch to a standing ovation, so intrusive was the world's adoration. Where was the world? "It's great being here in New York!" Ringo had called to the crush barriers as The Beatles were herded from train to limousine in Washington's Grand Central Station. "I've heard that you've got a bridge here," he'd chortled in Sydney. "No one tells me anything. They just drag me out of bed to look at rivers and things."[61] There were photographs of him performing in every continent, but, like an insect – a beetle, perhaps – he could see only his immediate environment. He'd guess he was in Canada only by Mounties that patrolled the besieged hotel. The Earth's richness and immensity lay beyond an ocean of faces and flashbulbs, and his only bleary eyed glimpses of it would be, say, a sunrise in Indianapolis after an obliging state trooper sneaked him into a squad car for breakfast in an empty roadhouse out on the freeway.

Less pleasant a memory was someone tearing a St Christopher's medallion – an aunt's coming-of-age gift – from his neck as he struggled through a *mêlée* of New York fans. Then there was the telephoned death threat taken so seriously that a detective hunched beside the drum rostrum throughout a stadium show in Montreal (to catch the bullet, perhaps) as Starr "played low" like Pete Best, with cymbals positioned straight up, *à la* Buddy Rich. Nobody minded that his posture impaired the group's performance, because who could hear it anyway? "By 1965, we were turning into such bad musicians," groaned Ringo. "There was no groove to it."[62] For devilment, the front line would slam sickening dischords while Starr just as deliberately stamped the bass drum on the offbeat.

For the wrong reasons, tours could still be a laugh, but onlookers would wince at the hollow of Ringo's hands where one range of monstrous callouses touched the next as he fastened a life jacket. He'd scan the Atlantic for sharks while the aircraft with peeling paint that had been chartered for the group bounced through turbulence. Maybe retirement hadn't been such a ridiculous notion after all, he'd think, while sinking into an uneasy oblivion.

7 "I've Been Thinking And Wondering Where It's All Going"

After he'd asked Mr Cox formally for his daughter's hand, Richie and 18-year-old year old Maureen tied the knot on 11 February 1965. To confound the anticipated crowds, the ceremony took place midweek and minutes after the 8am opening of Caxton Hall, the registry office nearest to Montagu Square. George dared to arrive on a bicycle, looking surprisingly alert, considering that he and John had been up most of the night, polishing up two of his compositions for possible inclusion on the soundtrack of *Help!*, the next film. With the groom's stepfather, Harrison was an official witnesses, although neither Lennon nor McCartney had been informed about the ceremony until Brian Epstein telephoned the previous afternoon. "The first thing I thought," recounted Lennon, "was, 'What a sneaky thing to do,' [but] if it was a public wedding, half of America would have come across."[1] From his holiday in Tunisia, Paul brought an exquisite gift – a silver apple – for the happy couple.

Brian gave them a magnificent dinner service. If "a bit shocked"[2] when he'd heard of Ringo's intentions, he was a solicitous best man. The wedding was celebrated with a lavish breakfast in his Belgravia townhouse, and it was Brian who arranged the seaside honeymoon in the Sussex home of The Beatles' solicitor, David Jacobs.[3] By the weekend, the newlyweds were back at Montagu Square, because this secluded crescent in Hove had remained secluded for just three short hours before it was clogged with a babbling mass of well-wishers and doorstepping hacks. The latter were bought off with a press conference on the back patio, where Ringo exhibited quiet good taste in matching polkadot shirt and tie and Maureen, in a twin-set, showed off her wide gold ring with its criss-cross design and explained that her baptismal name was actually Mary.

The most depth that reportage on the event contained was speculation as to whether it would affect the popularity of the group in general and Ringo in particular. Lennon alone knew that "there might be a shuffling of fans from one Beatle to another – at least, that's what happened when news that I was married was 'revealed'."[1] George would be the next to go, but, although his Pattie had also been a salon assistant, she was used to the trappings of inherent wealth and wasn't a poor-honest-girl-from-back-home like Mo or, I suppose, Cynthia Lennon. Like Jane Asher, Pattie combined care of a Beatle with a separate career and income, and could not, therefore, be regarded with the same affectionate approval as the other wives or be the subject of a US novelty single in the vein of The Chicklettes' 'Treat Him Tender, Maureen'.

This plea was taken to heart by the new Mrs Starkey, who continued answering fan correspondence and was patient when, voluptuously weary from another time-zone, Richie would dump his luggage in the hallway and trudge straight into the bedroom for some shut-eye, leaving travel-stained clothes on the carpet. If no Fanny Craddock, she'd always prepare a full meal – Lancashire hot-pot, say, or roast beef and Yorkshire pudding – no matter how late he returned from Abbey Road sessions – which were now running over into the graveyard hours – although she "didn't hold with" trays in bed. Even in the heart of emancipated Swinging London, Mo was still a very northern woman and Richie a northern man. "I don't think women like to be equal," he confided flatly. "They like to be protected and, in turn, they like looking after men."[4]

By Christmas 1966, Maureen would have a bigger house to mind when she, Richie and Tiger – a peach-coloured poodle and wedding present – moved to St George's Hill, the same Weybridge stockbroker estate as Cliff Richard and, more recently, Tom Jones and the Lennons. Slightly dearer than John's mock-Tudor Kenwood, Sunny

Heights had actually been purchased in June, but, while it was an uninhabitable no-man's land of planks and rubble during extensive refurbishing, the Starkeys lingered at Montagu Square, which they decided to keep on, first as a *pied à terre* and then for letting. Overlooking a golf course, Sunny Heights stood in three acres, but, unlike Kenwood, it was approached not by a long drive but by three steep flights of stone steps from a four-car garage.

Ringo loved marshalling the contracted builders and master gardeners who'd dine out later on the jaw-dropping information that he talked like an ordinary bloke, just like that "randy Scouse git" in *Till Death Us Do Part*.[5] With the reckless indulgence of many a fellow from the pub who'd come into a sudden fortune, Starr treated this veritable mansion as "a toy",[6] an outlet for all manner of structural idiosyncrasies. If he liked (and he did), he'd have a go-kart track weaving in and out of the tree-lined landscaping. In a hoop-shaped alcove was his bar, The Flying Cow, replete-with mirrors, tankards, counter, fruit machine and even an antique metallic till. He even started painting a mural on a wall in the Games Room, but when he abandoned it halfway through guests were free to add to it as they wished.

This extension was dominated by a pool table. After becoming hooked on snooker in the States, he'd ordered NEMS' general manager, Alistair Taylor, to obtain the necessary equipment. US Forces' officers clubs were tried to no avail, but, hanging the expense, a table, cues and a triangle of balls wended their way over from Germany, along with two fitters. When the other Beatles disappeared to foreign climes on weeks off, the Starkeys stayed put, savouring both the initial rapture of married life and a house that no son of Elsie Graves had ever dreamed of owning until he collected his cards from Rory Storm.

Some corners of Sunny Heights were given over to gold discs and mementoes of a past that, through its unbelievable outcome, had attained a certain romantic grandeur. Appropriately, a portrait of John and Paul loomed over the main mantelpiece. Interestingly, while no vestige of a drum kit could be found anywhere ("when we don't record, I don't play"[7]), the building would be well stocked with electronic gadgets that were technological steps ahead of the Joneses, as well as the Lennons, McCartneys and Harrisons. In nooks and crannies all over the place were light machines, tape recorders, stereo record players and – even in the toilet – televisions, on which the BBC's new second channel could be seen. Screened on either of two projectors were feature films and home movies, like 20 coloured minutes centred on close-ups of Maureen's eye and another shot from the swing that had been bought for the use of children.

The Starkeys' eldest boy was born at London's Queen Charlotte's Hospital on 13 September 1965. Journalists who could count were told that he was one month premature. Boys' names are generally the most difficult, but there were still ripples of sanctimonious opprobrium when Ringo announced that the baby was to be launched into life with the name Zak. Having always dreaded the abridgement of his own to Dick, Zak was, parried Ringo, "a nice strong name, and it can't be shortened. That was something I didn't want at all."[2] In obsequious support, a few young parents in the States also gave their sons this "mad cowboy name that had been spinning 'round in my brain at the time".[8]

Zak would rue "being described as my kid" when Starr's prediction that, "by the time he's grown-up, I won't be playing rock 'n' roll drums"[9] proved false. Nevertheless, he'd received more paternal attention than most, for – heeding Elsie's advice, for once – Ringo made the most of his offspring's cradle days. As he played inexhaustibly with Zak, most of Ringo's intimates agreed that fatherhood suited him, although he'd attended personally to only one nappy-change before engaging a matronly nanny until The Beatles elected to cease public engagements in 1966.

As well as freeing him from the more nauseating aspects of child-rearing, this appointment also enabled the Starrs – like the Lennons – to accept with an easier conscience evening social engagements in London, such as attending Walthamstow Granada with George for The Walker Brothers and Roy Orbison – performing with an ankle in plaster – or the première of *Alfie*, with Cilla singing the title theme.

Sundown usually brought to Ringo an onset of high spirits, and it was sad to sink them into a sofa when they cried out to be shared with others. Therefore, there was no immediate let-up, either, in his frequenting of West End clubland, as in Weybridge "we had lots of acquaintances but few close friends because of our position, I suppose".[10] Once, he skidded across the country from a concert in Cardiff – the last in The Beatles' final UK tour – to avoid missing a Christmas party at the Scotch of St James.

An alternative to cutting a rug there or at newer watering-holes like Tiles or Sybilla's – in which George Harrison had a financial slice – was to breeze down to the Revolution in Mayfair to hear Lee Dorsey or The Ike And Tina Turner Revue. Slumming it, he might troop over to Wardour Street's Flamingo, Marquee or Crazy Elephant to mingle amongst Mods up too late to pester anyone for autographs. Instead, they'd be grooving to Zoot Money's Big Roll Band, Chris Farlowe, The Spencer Davis Group, The Graham Bond Organisation or – less often since his 1964 Number One with 'Yeah Yeah' – Georgie Fame,[11] all of whom would back visiting black Americans such as Dionne Warwick, Stevie Wonder or Rufus Thomas. If touted as "The Swinging Club Of Swinging London",[12] the Flamingo wasn't the Harlem Apollo but it was the nearest to it that Ringo was ever likely to experience, as in the States "we really can't get out. It's too much of a problem. We'd like to see The Supremes at the Copa, and I'd even like to go to Nashville, and to Harlem, especially."[13]

Sometimes he'd need little coaxing to get up and have a blow himself. On a crowded Soho stage one summer evening, he and Denny Laine of Birmingham's Moody Blues, on bass, were the bedrock of "probably one of the worst bands I've ever been in".[11]

After kicking up this sort of row or dancing 'til dawn up the Ad-Lib, Sunny Heights was more restful than the incessant background churn of traffic around Montagu Square. Nevertheless, city dwellers by instinct, the Starkeys understood that Weybridge wasn't forever. Despite Ringo's developing fascination and expertise in film, no cinema room had been constructed or even a proper screen unfurled when a bare wall would suffice. Neither did they bother with a swimming pool, maintaining that it was "not worth it when John's is just up the road".[13]

In regions further beyond the pale of London, the 1950s were only just ending, and the mildest excesses of the capital – wearing hipster flares or combing your hair in bouffant Small Faces style[14] – were a big deal. Mod clothes that no Londoner had been seen dead in since 1964 would be worn by bumpkins at every village-hall dance until they outgrew them. Now and then, certain areas would align with the capital and sometimes even supersede it. The junk shops of Aldershot, for example, prospered during a craze for Victorian military uniforms. Olde-tyme whimsy prevailed in the hit parade, too, with 1966's 'Winchester Cathedral' by The New Vaudeville Band – all vicarage fête brass and megaphoned vocals – and Whistling Jack Smith's 'I Was Kaiser Bill's Batman'. To no avail, both The Mojos and The Fourmost drew out the agony with respective quaint revivals of 'Goodbye Dolly Gray' from the Great War and George Formby's 'Aunt Maggie's Remedy'.

The Beatles had been the only representatives of Mersey Beat in 1966's *NME* poll-winners concert, their swan song on a British stage. Now that they were to stop touring, after honouring existing contracts, the group's music became even harder to reproduce in concert by using conventional beat-group instrumentation. While the backwards-running coda of the 1966 B-side 'Rain' – one of Ringo's eternal Beatles favourites – was yet to come, for 'Yesterday' from the *Help!* LP Paul would sing to solely his own guitar strumming, as there was little to be gained in taking to the road with the string quartet hired for the recording. Had it too been flung into the screams, John's flute-garnished 'You've Got To Hide Your Love Away' would have been even more like feeding a pig strawberries.

Ringo's number on this album, 'Act Naturally', however, was sufficiently uncomplicated to feature in the stage act for a while. A US country-and-western chart-topper for Buck Owens in 1963, it was to be virtually The Beatles' last recorded non-original, as no Lennon-McCartney opus had been suitable for Starr Time on *Help!*. Some of the lines of their 'If You've Got Troubles' had stuck in his throat, and

– epitomised by his distrait yell of "Rock on, anybody?" at the guitar break – this mediocre effort did not ignite in the studio and was abandoned for something in an idiom untried by the group on disc. Roger Miller's 'Husbands And Wives' was a fixture then on the Sunny Heights turntable, but it was decided that the perkier 'Act Naturally' was more Ringo. With Harrison's choicest country picking and McCartney singing the harmony part once double-tracked by Owens, 'Act Naturally' was pressed as a 45 in territories such as Australia, where it got as far as Number Three.

In Britain, Ringo's "grinchy"[15] voice had been praised in a letter to *Melody Maker* which also urged The Beatles to let him sing more. Sufficiently flattered to reward the writer with an LP ("tell him to send the bill to the *MM* and I'll pay it"[15]), Starr replied that he was "quite happy with my one little track on each album".[15] Nevertheless, there were times at Abbey Road when merely spectating until the last phase of each piece grated more than usual, and time-consuming card games with Mal, Neil and anyone else similarly redundant became unendurably yawnsome. That he was the most expendable Beatle, musically, also fed thoughts that he was being cold-shouldered like Best had been. He was not present when the other three assisted on a folkier treatment of 'You've Got To Hide Your Love Away' by The Silkie, duffle-coated university students much like they themselves might have been had they never heard rock 'n' roll. John, Paul and George were also the only Beatles heard on 'Norwegian Wood', destined for *Rubber Soul*, the LP released after *Help!*.

Starr reputedly "had it out" with the others about his growing sense of isolation. No one ever consulted him about anything or considered whether he had any opinions or aspirations, did they? Concerned that their dogsbody drummer should think they'd been ignoring him, Paul and John made amends by granting him a composing credit on 'What Goes On', an unremarkable pre-Beatle creation by Lennon that he'd "resurrected with a middle eight thrown in with Paul's help to give Ringo a song".[16] Well, with their works now covered by everyone from international stars like Matt Monro and Peter Sellers to banjo bands and barbershop quartets, John and Paul had space for generosity.

'What Goes On' was also given pride of place at the start of side two of *Rubber Soul*, and John's 'Norwegian Wood' was remade with Ringo's interjections of finger-cymbals, maracas and tambourine. Along with the Stones' 'Let's Spend The Night Together' and 'I Can't Control Myself' by The Troggs, this smokescreening of an extra-marital affair was excluded from prudish airwaves. "You can read obscene lyrics into any song," said Ringo, shaking his head sagely. "Those people are living in the past."[17]

"Those people" might have read something shocking in *Help!*, too, had they known that The Beatles had giggled their way through much of its shooting in a marijuana haze. Even more unchallenging than *A Hard Day's Night*, Ringo confessed, "It wasn't really acting. We didn't know what we were doing. We just said the lines as they were. We'd read them and then just go out and say them in front of the camera."[18] Walter Shenson had made a reportedly reluctant Ringo the central figure of the film's flimsy narrative – Oriental religious cult plus nutty professor chase after priceless ring that has ended up on his finger. Presumably because they were all new to the overseas market, some of the self-referential jokes he and the others had to utter dated back to 1963.[21] The more vitriolic reviews also gloomed that The Beatles had been overshadowed by a distinguished supporting cast that included Eleanor Bron, Roy Kinnear, Leo McKern and, once again, Victor Spinetti.

For me, Ringo's big moment in *Help!* was his flat "hullo" when George uncovers him rolled in a blanket in a car's boot. This deed also earned Harrison his one vote against Starr winning with 60 a *Melody Maker* poll asking, "Which Beatle wins the honours in *Help!?*"[20] He was worthy of the accolade if only for the cellar scene featuring him, Eleanor Bron and an unchained and full-grown tigress a yard away, with a keeper – clenching a shotgun – just out of lens range. To Ringo's relief, the movie's insurers had stipulated that a stunt-man lookalike by the name of Hans Pretscherer had to be used for the Alpine skiing sequences, but the price of this precaution was Maureen, from a distance, once mistaking Herr Pretscherer for her husband and running to embrace him.

Although both of their films were, drawled Shenson, "big-grossing because they weren't too costly to make",[21] The Beatles were adamant that, in the next one, they wouldn't be happy-go-lucky funsters any more – in fact, they wouldn't even be Beatles. After they'd dithered too long over a screenplay of lightweight comedy Western *A Talent For Loving*,[22] Shenson perceived that, "to find a good enough storyline, which has four leading men, is very difficult".[21] He hadn't visualised any Beatle appearing in a movie without the others, but by autumn 1966 Richard Lester had Lennon as "Private Gripweed" in *How I Won The War*, a curate's egg of a World War II satire. On location in Spain, John told a visiting Ringo how swiftly his enthusiasm for this acting lark had evaporated, but Ringo wasn't as sympathetic as he might have been. He'd have jumped at the chance to play Private Gripweed.

John passed idle hours off camera composing his magnum opus, 'Strawberry Fields Forever', and Ringo regrew a beard that had made headlines several months earlier, when he'd been photographed with it boarding a plane for the West Indies with Maureen and the Lennons. Bound by common ordeal and jubilation, The Beatles, their aides and most of their relations "were one big happy family", Cynthia would remember, "because we were thrown together because of circumstances but luckily enough we all got on very well together".[23] Her mother would be Montagu Square's first tenant, and decades later Paul McCartney would remember the widowed Harry Graves when sending special invitations to the première of his oratorio in Liverpool Cathedral. While an allegation that Ringo had had to ask the group's permission to marry was the brainchild of a bored journalist, Starr liked the notion "that I would do that because of our close ties".[24]

Their uniformity on stage applied when they were off duty, too, as they attended the same openings, listened to the same records and sampled the same stimulants. If George, say, had a garment that the others admired, they would acquire one like it within a week. It was no coincidence, either, that, after Ringo had led the way, Paul, George and John – and the road crew – each experimented with dundreary whiskers, pointed Imperials and similar depilatory caprices. By 1967, all were sporting raffish moustachios.[25]

No one, however, had been in complete agreement over the controversial issue of their investiture by the Queen – on Mr Wilson's vote-catching advice – as Members of the British Empire. Paul cut short his holiday in order to attend the press conference necessary to flesh out the newsflash of the forthcoming decoration, while John sauntered in 20 minutes late after Brian had had to send a car to fetch him. To John, their acceptance of it was as absurd as a demand in one of Screaming Lord Sutch's political manifestos that they should be knighted. Meanwhile, McCartney was delighted with his MBE. Not knowing what to think, Ringo smiled and waved like he was supposed to as The Beatles were driven through cheering crowds to Buckingham Palace on 26 October 1965. His strongest motive for going through with it was that the medal would be something big to show his parents, but he didn't propose ever to wear it.

For a laugh, he'd affix "MBE" after his name on a 1973 album sleeve".[26] The only other use he made of it was when The Beatles and Epstein were among those celebrities who signed a petition – published as a full-page petition in *The Times* – calling for the legalisation of marijuana. He'd been slightly put out about learning from an interviewer of the others' intentions, but had been perfectly willing to be on the list, because "even in hospitals now they can't get into it, as they're not allowed to have it for research, which is silly".[7] He would not, however, be trapped into advocating its use as a herbal handmaiden to creativity, even if he reckoned that "it gave people more scope and more things to talk about".[7]

Extremes of drug experience beyond mere reefers were implied in the self-consciously "weird" debut singles by new bands like The Move and The Pink Floyd, as well as the transition of The Pretty Things, The Small Faces and other established groups from boy-meets-girl songs to musical insights that were not as instantly comprehensible. Lysergic acid diethylamide – LSD – had been "turning on" factions within London's in crowd for almost a year before it was outlawed for recreational use in 1966. Nevertheless, the pop industry's association with acid had led The Troggs' manager to confine his clean-minded lads to provincial bookings in Britain in order to minimalise the chances of illegal drug publicity sticking to them.

Ringo didn't "turn on" in London, however, but in the eight-bedroomed Beverly Hills villa that was the nerve-centre of 1965's US tour. It was George and John's second "trip", the first having been the result of downing spiked drinks by an irresponsible middle-class swinger. For Harrison, its mental distortions had been akin to a mystical reverie, while it began Lennon's incredible journey to unknown – and upsetting – realms of inspiration. Stimulating though it was, LSD was not all it was cracked up to be for Ringo and made no appreciable difference to him beyond hallucinations and surreal sensations that lasted only until he came down. While the others spoke openly about their psychedelic escapades, he hadn't much to add. After a few more trips, he decided that he'd had enough.

Sharpening paranoia as they did, drugs – always obtainable from local narcotics dealers – did not make touring any more bearable. From stadium dug-outs, The Beatles slouched rather than rushed pell-mell towards the stage. Up there, even Paul was forcing his customary exuberance, while John roared purgative off-mic obscenities into the constant bedlam. Afterwards, withdrawn George would inscribe autographs with bad grace or refuse altogether while Ringo would carry on with his game of patience.

In the final dinning weeks of The Beatles' most public adventure, he'd been as a fish beneath stormy waves. While bemoaning the group "not playing properly but nobody hears anyway",[27] Starr made the best of the pleasanter lulls in the itinerary, such as a reunion with old St Pauli comrades backstage at Hamburg's Ernst Merck Halle. There was little else to enjoy. The four performed for three evenings in the Nippon Budokan Hall with the disquieting knowledge that, outside, there were frenzied demonstrations of protest about pop-singing *ketos* polluting this temple of martial arts. However, this was nothing to the naked malevolence at Manila International Airport, where, in official retaliation for unwittingly snubbing the Philippine president's wife, The Beatles entourage underwent an ordeal of red tape in the customs area and, reportedly, the pushing and shoving of a jeering mob. Assured of leniency or even a commendation, however, they behaved in "the roughest reception we've ever had", recalled Starr, who purportedly weathered the brunt of their aggression: "They really had it in for us."[28]

A psychological rather than physical battering awaited them in North America, where sections of the media had sensationalised a story of how Lennon had "boasted" that his Beatles were more popular than Christ. The possible in-concert slaughter of the artists by divine wrath – or someone acting on the Almighty's behalf – improved attendances but did not forestall public bonfires of Beatle records, picketing of shows by Ku Klux Klansmen or attempted peltings of the Fab Four with decayed fruit and more odious projectiles.

The Beatles downed tools as a working band at San Francisco's Candlestick Park on 29 August 1966 after a half-hour no better or worse than any other slew of stale, unheard music they'd dished out for ticket-holders that year. After 'Yesterday', Paul announced "a special request for all the wonderful back-room boys on the tour". Behind him, Ringo then piled into the rote-learnt 'I Wanna Be Your Man', and even that was fluffed as he repeated its first verse rather than remember the second. "Nice working with you, Ringo," called John just before he, Paul and George catapulted themselves into the wavering *a cappella* intro to 'Nowhere Man'.

Starr was "convinced we gave up touring at the right time. Four years of Beatlemania was enough for anyone."[29] In 1963, the pretend faints and good-humoured ecstasies had been harmless and even amusing, but now the antics of fans frightened him as, in straits of emotional blackmail, they'd dangle from ledges, gulp down poison and slash wrists to simply be noticed by a Beatle dashing past those close enough to maul him. Leo McKern would never forget the terror that chased across Ringo's countenance when a simpering, Bermuda-shorted tourist, garlanded with cameras, had waddled towards them for autographs while they were routining a *Help!* scene amid sand dunes: "At a moment of apparent security, deep in the work in hand, he'd experienced an unexpected and unlooked-for assault."[30]

Pondering an uncertain future, Ringo imagined that such intrusions would tail off "when the records start slipping, as they're bound to one day. Then I look at Elvis, who's 30, and I wonder how he keeps on. Some of the old rockers thought they were the living end at the time, then one day the public didn't want to know. I suppose the best thing to do is roll along and say, 'Well, let it happen as it does,' but I've been thinking and wondering where it's all going."[9]

Studying the charts as a stockbroker would a shares index, he'd been defensive about a recent single, 'Daytripper', not leaping as quickly to the top as previous Beatles singles. There to see the *Melody Maker* Pop 30 compiled, he masked his disappointment with "coming into the *MM* at Number Three is quite something".[31] Exacerbating the indignity of coming third to The Rolling Stones in the *NME*'s yearly chart points table, its 1966 popularity poll had The Beatles second to The Beach Boys as World Vocal Group, but "good luck to them. We haven't been doing much, and it was run at a time when they had something good out."[27] The impetus had slackened elsewhere, too. In Germany, the influential *Bravo* magazine's Golden Otto award was won in 1966 by Dave Dee, Dozy, Beaky, Mick And Tich, with The Beatles as mere runners-up.

Pop was a fickle mistress, but Ringo, if not yet a millionaire, was so amply set up now that there was small danger of him having to scratch a living again. Nowadays, he was lunching with the likes of Paul Getty. Midway through a holiday in Corsica, Maureen had more than her fill of sun, but it was no trouble for Ringo to ring Alistair Taylor to lay on a private jet to take them home.

An earlier aspiration to own a chain of hairdressing salons would be forgotten, but he'd started investing guardedly if providently in land securities recommended by Beatle financiers. His boldest step was the founding in 1966 of the Brickey Building Company Ltd, which utilised the supervisory wisdom he'd accrued during the remodelling of Sunny Heights. Most of the new firm's business was in decoration and architectural adjustments to the houses of its proprietor's showbusiness contacts – including John and George – but it also probed into property development. Nevertheless, although

Brickey "sold quite a few flats",[32] it would be credit-squeezed out of existence in less than a year by a government fighting a formidable balance-of-payments deficit. "It was impossible with Harold Wilson," snarled Richard Starkey, MBE. "We got left with five houses and two flats, what with the freeze."[33]

Starkey's grasp of political matters was hesitant. Broadly, his Dingle roots were socialist, but by 1966 his wallet might not have been. In this, he paralleled Cilla Black, but now their paths were diverging. She'd been disgusted, for example, by his and the other Beatles' advocacy of the narcotics that were already destroying Tommy Quickly and Brian Epstein. Nevertheless, their friendship would withstand this and similar ethical crises. The Graves and the Whites still dwelt in close proximity to each other, albeit in more salubrious circumstances. Through Richie and Cilla's prosperity, all had been able to retire early and leave their council terraces for a dotage on the other side of Woolton. Elsie and Harry, the last Beatle parents to move, chose a bungalow in a tucked-away cul-de-sac on Gateacre Park. While Harry would contemplate what to do between breakfast and bedtime, Elsie – pensive at the bedroom window – would peer down on her sprawling city of overlapping towns.

Liverpool still had beat groups, plucky anachronisms unknown beyond Lancashire battling through the old 'Money' and 'Hippy Hippy Shake' warhorses to those for whom Mersey Beat had become a dim recollection. In 1965, Cilla, Richie and Mr Epstein had been on a panel judging the northwest heat of the last "All-Britain Beat Contest". The outfit who came second were The Connoisseurs, who in the following year would take Vince Earl from Rory Storm And The Hurricanes. Earl had stood in Wally's shoes after that elastic-larynxed bass player had left Storm to form The Combo, a septet on the frontier of jazz and pop and notable for its sensational horn section.

It was fitting that Storm and his current Hurricanes had headlined at the creditor-beleaguered Cavern hours before bailiffs came to close it down. As incorrigible an old rocker as ever was, Rory knocked 'em dead with the same old material. He was so far behind that he was ahead of the first traces of 1968's rock 'n' roll revival, but he was too indolent to do anything about it by taking up his apotheosised former drummer's standing offer of monetary assistance whenever he was ready to record a belated follow-up to 'America'.

At the invitation of a New York record executive, The Pete Best Combo had actually been over there to tape a US-only album and for concert dates concentrated mainly in Canada. Containing saxophonists, Pete's latest campaign to recover scrapings of his stolen inheritance evoked only the sweet torment of screams by association. Back home, his career wouldn't plummet like it did almost straight away in North America simply because it had never left the runway, and Pete fastened onto the excuse that he hadn't been cut out for "the swinging scene of those times. I'm not the type that can be swayed by fashion."[34]

The life of Lee Curtis would also be clouded by not making it, but he'd got by as a singer in Germany and had been made welcome at The Beatles' after-hours party in the Ernst Merck Halle. Down at the Star-Club, The Remo Four were wowing 'em with jazz-rock these days, but not so adaptable was Kingsize Taylor, who had reached the end of the line. Largely through the bad faith of the gangsters that controlled the venues at which he worked, he'd been left destitute and had to apply for an assisted repatriation. As The Beatles jetted overhead, Kingsize heaved his guitars, amplifiers and suitcases into a second-class compartment. Miss the last train and you'll wait on the platform for ever.

8 *"They More Or Less Direct Me In The Style I Can Play"*

How I Won The War had been but one factor hinting that The Beatles were growing apart. There was also George's soul-cleansing safari to India, ostensibly to study sitar, and Paul's incidental music to the 1967 movie *The Family Way*. While it was yet to come to fruition, a film role for Ringo alone was likely, as soon as he and Brian felt sufficient heat from one of the "scripts sent in every day, but most of them are so bad".[1] As they'd been within earshot of each other for every working day since God knew when, it was refreshing, noticed Starr, "to choose when we're together instead of being forced together – and you need to break up a bit to relax, man".[2] The separateness of their individual projects, he felt – to coin a music-business cliché – Enriched The Group As A Whole. Marital fetters counted for less than Beatlehood then and, he guessed, for always. Maureen, Cynthia, Pattie and Jane were all pale blonde by 1967, but the men "have a strange hold on each other", Ringo reassured himself. "At one time, we never went out, even with our own wives and girlfriends, unless another Beatle went along, too."[3]

Not long after the armoured car had whisked them from Candlestick Park, he and Lennon's nerve-wracking pint in a roadside pub had been an exploratory brush with the outer world. Nevertheless, withdrawal from it to a private Beatle commune had been discussed. In pursuance of this subsequently abandoned scheme, the Harrisons and Starr had flown out to the Greek island of Lésvos in July 1967, although he had to leave early to be at Maureen's side in the final months of a planned second pregnancy.

During this transitional year, there'd be other such searches for both physical and spiritual utopias, most of them made possible by the day-to-day mundanities of shifting records. As the expiry date of Epstein's management contract with The Beatles crept closer, once-merry rumours darkened to a certainty that, perturbed by the unresolvable bungles he'd made while learning his craft, the group were to reduce their old mentor's cut and say in their affairs and wheel in a third party. Most fingers pointed at Allen Klein, whose reputation as "the Robin Hood of pop" stood on his recouping of disregarded millions for his clients from seemingly iron-clad record-company percentages. Through hovering over British pop as a hawk over a partridge nest, his administrative caress had come to encompass The Dave Clark Five, The Kinks and the uncut rubies – including The Animals, Herman's Hermits and Donovan – that had been processed for the charts by freelance production whizz-kid Mickie Most. The Rolling Stones had also bitten, grinned Most, after they'd "seen me driving around in the Rolls and owning a yacht, and started wondering where their money was going. Allen got them together and gave them money."[4] Klein also bet Mrs Most that he'd also be superintending The Beatles by 1967.

Klein started sniffing around them. "Allen tried to come in when Brian was there, just as a business manager, and not run our lives," Starr would recall, "and Brian would have nothing to do with him."[5] Klein wasn't the most popular among record-industry moguls, but, wasting no time with small-talk while driving hard and unrelenting bargains, one accountant with no reason to love him believed, "He revolutionised the industry. You've heard lots of terrible stories about him, most of which I concur with, but he was a tough American cookie, and he came over here and negotiated for the artists he was involved with."[6] Paul McCartney had been particularly impressed by his wheedling of an unprecedently high advance from Decca for the Stones in 1965.

Paunchy, short haired and an observer of a routine ruled by the clock, Klein had framed family photographs on his desk within the panelled top floor of a Manhattan skyscraper. For all his methodically blunt stances on the telephone and in the boardroom, he was an impassive, reflective, pipe-and-slippers sort at home and liked to distance himself from the office. Everything that painfully committed Brian wasn't, you wouldn't catch Allen nibbling afternoon scones at Sunny Heights, because he didn't "bother that much with artists, but you have to develop some sort of rapport – although it's important that you stay away. Otherwise you can really get on each other's nerves."[7] When his wooing of The Beatles moved into top gear, he – like a certain Oriental mystic they'd encountered – underwent a crash-course in their music to better butter them up. Nonetheless, the latest stock-market quotations were infinitely more engrossing. For Allen Klein, pop music was simply a commodity to be bought, sold and replaced when worn out.

In 1967, he'd been only fractionally more than a name to Ringo, who'd have been quite happy – as long as the other three were – to keep things the way they were with Mr Epstein, if only because, throughout her marriage thus far, Maureen couldn't "think of any time when we didn't do something because of the money. We never gave consideration to the cost."[7] Habit still motivated her collection of spittled books of trading stamps, but she had but to ask her husband's NEMS secretary, Barbara, if ever she wanted more than the several thousand with which Richie regularly transfused her bank account. On a self-confessed "fund-spending brainstorm" at least once a year, she'd been known to consign entire racks of newly purchased clothes to the dustbin because they hadn't looked as impressive in front of a Weybridge mirror as they had in Harrod's. With customised tailgate, Rolls Royce parts, electric windows and walnut on fascia and doors, Richie's Mini Cooper S had worked out five times more expensive than an ordinary one.

Having never had much back on Merseyside, both were immature about cash. In Greece, blithe ignorance about exchange rates led to a panicked cable to London and a Beatle hanger-on in Athens contacted to get Ringo out of a mess that almost left him without a bed for a night whose blackness would be his sole shield against the excrescent havoc that would accumulate round him. Since 1963, he'd never had to prove identity to sign a bill, and had become unused to actually paying for anything with actual bank notes. Even small change was as unnecessary to him as eyesight to a monkfish – or so he thought. Motoring home from a party in London, his petrol ran dry and, stranded without a penny, he was obliged to hitch a ride with a man from nearby Thames Ditton who, in the ensuing conversation, chilled Starr with the information that he wrote for a national daily. However, a week of trepidation slid by, not a line crept into the newspapers and he was soon able to breathe again. There hadn't been any need to be so ingratiating when, on arrival at Sunny Heights, he'd presented his dangerous but, as it turned out, honourable rescuer with an autographed copy of The Beatles' most recent gramophone record, *Sgt Pepper's Lonely Hearts Club Band*.

However much its content has been devalued by reassessment, this syncretic work was technically an improvement on the preceding LP, *Revolver*, which had contained 'Yellow Submarine', the only British Number One with Ringo as lead singer. With a suggestion or two from Donovan, a crumpled Scot who'd started as a UK "answer" to Dylan, this had been contrived by Paul and John as an ideal children's song for Starr that would simultaneously capture a flavour of nautical Liverpool,[8] with the one-shot novelty of such as 'The Runaway Train', The Singing Dogs or The Southlanders' 'I Am A Mole And I Live In A Hole' plus a topicality in its spoken prologue while referred obliquely to Dr Barbara Moore's hike from Land's End to John O'Groats. This would be cut, partly because today's news is tomorrow's guinea pig hutch liner.[9]

More and more decisions of this magnitude were being made in the studio now that ten hours – the time spent recording The Beatles' first LP – was no longer considered adequate for one track these days. "We're quite big with EMI at the moment," understated Ringo. "They don't argue if we take the time we want."[10] A brass band inserted for two bars, sea-faring sound effects and the inclusion of Pattie Harrison and Rolling Stone Mick Jagger's singing paramour Marianne Faithfull in the *omnes fortissimo* chorus were among mere touch-ups on this kitsch *meisterwerk* that, coupled with McCartney's contrasting 'Eleanor Rigby' – the 'Yesterday' of *Revolver* – nipped in the bud a cover version by fellow Parlophone act The She Trinity, fronted by Beryl Marsden. It also foreshadowed a later-1960s practice whereby a 45 was a spin-off from an already successful album, as well as being the blasting charge for 'Purple Aeroplane' – a parody by Spike Milligan – and a Maurice Chevalier mistranslation in 'Le Sous-Marin Vert'.

Joe Brown, The Beach Boys, Barbra Streisand, Richie Havens and Jeff Lynne were five of many who recorded 'With A Little Help From My Friends', the jogalong Starr Time on *Sgt Pepper*.[11] The song had started life as 'Badfinger Boogie', with "What would you do if I sang out of tune/Would you throw tomatoes at me?" its original opening couplet. Bearing in mind the jelly-babies of yore should The Beatles ever go back to the stage, Ringo said, "'I'm not singing this song,' so it was changed to 'Will you walk out on me?' [*sic*]"[12]

A segue from the album's title track,[13] 'With A Little Help From My Friends' had a sung introduction announcing Ringo in his Lonely Hearts Bandsman alter ego, "Billy Shears", because, as he explained at length, "the original concept of *Sgt Pepper* was that it was going to be a stage show – you know, we start with the clapping and people shouting and then I come on – and we were going to do it like in a theatre; we'd do it in the studio and simulate it. We didn't in the end. We did it for the first couple of tracks and then it faded into an album, but it still made it a whole concept. It was as if we did a few tracks and suddenly there was a fire and everyone ran out of the building but we carried on playing."[5]

A multi-million-seller, the LP vied with their 45 'All You Need Is Love' – issued on Starr's 27th birthday – to top the Australian singles chart, but in 1987 Ringo – unlike the other living Beatles – declined to appear in the celebratory *It Was Twenty Years Ago Today*, Granada Television's two-hour invocation of psychedelic times past that *Sgt Pepper* had unquestionably inspired. Neither had he put forward any choices of characters for the album's fabled montage cover. For Ringo, it "wasn't our best album. That was the peak for everyone else, but for me it was a bit like being a session musician."[5] But wasn't it always? A print from one of the last occasions when press photographers could enter Studio Two easily while The Beatles were there had Paul at the piano, George and John on guitars and Ringo also in hippy get-up – all beads, chiffon, crushed velvet and Afghan fluff – standing aside as if awaiting orders. "They've usually got a rough idea of how the drum goes as well as the guitar and the organ and the 40-piece orchestra," he explained. "They say, 'I'd like that bit to do that.' They more or less direct me in the style I can play."[14]

Almost invariably, he'd be the first to arrive at Abbey Road. Once, while looking for something to do until the others rolled up, he was drawn gladly into Studio One to add handclaps to a number being recorded by Solomon King, a portly American balladeer. When The Beatles got down to work at last, Starr might go home after they'd finished without having done more than cudgel up a scarcely-heeded opinion about a playback only marginally different from the first 54 takes of it that he'd heard. He'd clang tubular bells on Paul's 'When I'm 64', but for George's one *Sgt Pepper* opus, 'Within You Without You', Ringo looked on as an Indian tabla player tackled its three switches of time signature.

Starr might have been nearer the centre of events if he, too, could have come up with a convincing composition of his own. It wasn't as if he wasn't prepared to give songwriting a half-hearted go, but "They're all just ching-a-lings. There's no great tunes come out as far, as [far as] I'm concerned."[14] Through the perseverance of Klaus Voorman (at this time bass guitarist with Manfred Mann), he became slightly more dextrous a guitarist, "and with not knowing, I just jump into strange chords that no one seems to get into. Most of the stuff I write is twelve-bar, anyway."[15]

Twelve-bar songs would have been out of place during this, The Beatles' fleeting "classical" period that would straddle forms as diverse as music hall and John Cage electronic collage. However, Ringo had been permitted creative input, in a piecemeal manner. On *Revolver*, for example, his chance remark caused Lennon and McCartney to change the title of its eerie omega, 'The Void', to 'Tomorrow Never Knows'. A sound-picture of LSD's inner landscapes, its backing track included a melange of tape-loops realised by all four Beatles, Ringo's extract possibly from the wordless soundtrack of his cine-film study of Maureen's eye. Registered as joint-Lennon-McCartney-Harrison-Starkey efforts would be the avant-gardenings of 'Carnival Of Light', in a similar vein to 'Tomorrow Never Knows' but devoid of lyrics and its trace of melody, which was threaded onto a tape recorder during a "happening" at London's Roundhouse; and 'Flying',[16] an infinitely more conventional instrumental first heard on Boxing Day 1967 during *Magical Mystery Tour*, the group's television extravaganza.

Whatever hand he'd had in these pieces, Ringo's principal contribution to that year's epoch-making cache of records was by complementing McCartney and Lennon's patterns of chords and rhymes with percussive subtleties. As the corrupted snare sound on David Bowie's *Low* LP would be in 1977, so Starr's loose-skinned tom-toms and non-resonant snare – first evident on *Revolver* – were copied until then. Praise indeed had been George Martin's acknowledgement that, in *Sgt Pepper's* fragmented finale, 'A Day In The Life', the distinctive scuffed drum section was entirely Ringo's idea.

The Beatle recording of which he would be proudest, 'A Day In The Life' was the valedictory spin on pirate Radio London as it closed in August 1967, while Ringo's recorded farewell on behalf of The Beatles also penetrated the ether on the final day of operation. If *Sgt Pepper* had been this illegal station's most plugged album during that flower-power summer, the single was surely Procol Harum's 'A Whiter Shade Of Pale'. The abstract libretto and adaptation of a Bach fugue in its arrangement would not have been envisaged as pertinent to a chart hit before 1967, when – thanks in part to The Beatles' remorseless prodding of cultural nerves – pop became "relevant", a viable means of artistic expression rather than an ephemeral tangent to more egghead activity. Three of The Pink Floyd had met during a degree course at Regent Street Polytechnic from which they – like Procol Harum, Soft Machine, Cream, The Sam Gopal Dream and the like – had surfaced as darlings of London psychedelic clubs such as the Spontaneous Underground[17] and The

Night Tripper (later The UFO), where an act's appeal to a tranced-hippy clientèle, either cross-legged or "idiot dancing" with catherine wheel eyes, depended less on looks and tight trousers than on the dazzling atmosphere that thickened during incessant extrapolation of tracks from both their album debut and the unfamiliar successor being "laid down" during a studio block-booking of weeks and months. The Beatles hadn't been above sticking their noses around the door of adjacent Studio One during a Pink Floyd session or Lennon breaking into 'A Whiter Shade Of Pale' as men of the moment Procol Harum trooped into the Speakeasy one evening.

The music press had been full of how "mellow" John was now that he was in his late 20s. "It's a groove, growing older,"[18] he told them. It was also a groove to attend hippy happenings without an outbreak of Beatlemania obliging a hasty departure. Shouting, "It's John Lennon!" if he sidled past you wasn't "cool" in the capital nowadays. Without fuss, he'd absorbed a 14-hour "Technicolour Dream" at Alexandra Palace, in which the paranormal effects of LSD were emulated via the contrast of flickering strobes and ectoplasmic *son et lumière* projections on the cavernous walls and bands – not groups – played on and on and on and on. One after another, they appeared on platforms erected at either end of the exhibition centre – The Pink Floyd, The Move, Tomorrow, John's Children (with a guitarist called Marc Bolan), The Flies, you name 'em. During one of the few intermissions, the promenading audience was treated to a turn by a Japanese-American named Yoko Ono, who would conjecture that "you don't need talent to be an artist".[19]

Over in more clement San Francisco, then just as vital a pop Mecca as Merseyside had been, performance artists like her similarly bridged gaps between bands at the "be-ins", "freak-outs", "mantra-rock dances" and "love-ins" that were held in the city's parks, in its transformed ballrooms and – with Derek Taylor on its steering committee – nearby at the Monterey International Pop Music Festival, where the UK was represented by The Who and – on Paul McCartney's recommendation – The Jimi Hendrix Experience, whose Seattle-born singing guitarist had been adopted as Britain's own.

Ringo possessed Hendrix's *Are You Experienced?*, as well as albums by such as Jefferson Airplane, The Doors, Captain Beefheart And His Magic Band, Buffalo Springfield and other new US combos who captivated him briefly as "one sort of takes over from the other".[14] Finding them "nice people"[18] when they visited London, his taste was sufficiently catholic for him to also be a fan of the pre-packaged Monkees, who, aimed at pre-teens, had been thrust together to play an Anglo-American pop group of *A Hard Day's Night* Beatles vintage in a worldwide TV sitcom.

Monkees LP track 'Cuddly Toy' – later castigated for its sexism – had been penned by Harry Nilsson, a Brooklyn-born bank clerk of Scandinavian extraction. Stocky, light skinned and blond, he looked it, too. He was also prey to sudden mood swings, commensurate with the classic artistic temperament. If no Modigliani, he was a fair semi-professional songwriter and, after co-writing 'Readin' Ridin' And Racin'' – a paean to hot-rodding – for California's Superstocks, he'd placed two more of his compositions with The Ronettes, whose svengali, Phil Spector, would introduce Nilsson to Richard Perry in 1968.

Although a US Escort no more, Perry had gained more than a toehold in the record business as producer of cult celebrities like Captain Beefheart and Tiny Tim. His stylistic yardstick was George Martin's output with The Beatles, who, since *Revolver*, "represented the highest examples of recorded art from every standpoint".[20] Nilsson was fond of them, too – in fact, maybe too fond, because, "as soon as I saw what they were doing, I just backed off".[21] Nevertheless, while gaining promotion to computer-department supervisor at the bank, his brace of RCA albums – *Pandemonium Puppet Show* and *Aerial Ballet* – became, with *God Bless Tiny Tim* and Beefheart's *Safe As Milk*, the toast of the London in crowd after Derek Taylor had mailed the collected works of Nilsson to Brian Epstein with the testimonial that "he is the something The Beatles are". The group itself agreed, perhaps flattered by the *Aerial Ballet* single, a medley of Lennon-McCartney songs under the umbrella title 'You Can't Do That', one of their 1964 B-sides. Nicknaming him "the fab Harry", John took the initiative by telephoning Nilsson at the bank, while Ringo would meet him through Klaus Voorman. This began a lifelong amity between the two oldest Beatles and a man whom future fanzines would refer to as a "quasi-Beatle",[22] so much would their lives interlock.

While Nilsson's 'You Can't Do That' scudded up Australia's Top 40, Pete Anders and Vini Poncia did likewise in *Billboard*'s Hot 100 with 'There's Got To Be A Word'. Best exemplifying the passing of the old surf/British-invasion regime was their change of name from The Tradewinds to Innocence, with its hint of flower-power leanings and *à la mode* lack of preceding article.

Paradoxically, 1967 was also a boom time for schmaltz, with ex-palais crooner Engelbert Humperdinck's 'Release Me' keeping The Beatles' double A-side 'Strawberry Fields Forever'/'Penny Lane' from Number One in Britain, just as his 'The Last Waltz' would do with Traffic's 'Hole In My Shoe' a few months later. Down Under, 'All You Need Is Love' was slung from the top by Slim Whitman's 'China Doll'. Supported by smashes of the same persuasion by the likes of Tom Jones, Solomon King and Petula Clark, as well as Sinatra, this counter-revolution of "decent music" was tacitly applauded by such as the *NME*, whose alley-cat tittle-*Tatler* continued to fawn over the coups of ancient Tin Pan Alley executives while crowing, "This year, Yardbirds absent from Top 30."[23]

In view of the sub-culture's supposed bartering system of narcotics and promiscuity, you could understand the establishment attitude; but, with the hoo-hah over the famous Rolling Stones drugs bust and, later, the *Oz* corruption trial, "The news is all over everywhere," was Ringo's homespun reasoning, "so they're spreading it. They think it's great if the police raid a place, but 50 million people have read about it again, and a couple of thousand will say, 'I'll try drugs.'"[24] However, he recognised that the Summer of Love was no more the dawning of the age of Aquarius than the Twist had been. Amused, he ascribed the supplanting of flower-power in Britain by slouch-hatted, tailboard-riding Al Capone chic to "those lightweight clothes. You'd freeze to death. So flower people are putting on their overcoats again."[14]

However, via the account that everyone who was anyone had at the Indica bookshop off Piccadilly, he'd thumbed through hardbacks of mystical, religious and fashionably aerie-faerie nature – *Autobiography Of A Yogi*, *The Golden Bough*, Tolkein, *et al*. His clear expositions during interviews of karma, the transmigration of souls and the world of illusion was evidence of more than cursory poring over these tomes, which looked as well on Sunny Heights' shelves as did the fresh lick of emulsion on its walls.

Along with bouts of highbrow reading and getting the house repainted, the Starkeys' undertaking of numerous hobbies of late was symptomatic of the triumph of sedate Surrey domesticity over nightclubbing, since the arrival of Zak's brother at London's Queen Charlotte's hospital on 19 August. Maureen named him Jason, thereby thwarting her husband's desire "to give him initials – JR or something like that. My gardener said, 'You're not a man 'til you've had a little girl.' That flattened me out, and now I want a little girl."[3]

A week after Jason's delivery, Richie was not ready to tear himself away from his home to a meeting of the International Meditation Society, to which the Harrisons dragged along Paul, Jane and the Lennons. How much more gratifying than either the Ad-Lib or the latest Beatles fad was a curtained evening on St George's Hill spent oil painting, clay modelling, watching TV or cooing over the babies. The Starkeys might have been any commuting executive's family at leisure, and in a sense Ringo would become just such a person during the group's period of self-management after Mr Epstein's unexpected death, on 27 August, precipitated "a strange time for us, when it's someone you've relied on in the business, where we never got involved".[15] Come winter and he'd be rising at nine to "drive in with John and see Paul and George in town. I get home about half past seven, have my dinner, chat, do whatever you do and then go to bed."[14]

A hiccup over the costing of some landscaping by a Mr Gregory had involved legal proceedings,[25] but otherwise all of Starr's problems seemed to be little ones. As well as children, there were the mental debates before the shaving mirror over whether the dagger beard he'd been cultivating to go with his moustache gave him a touch of the corsair or was just plain silly.

Aesthetics aside, his growth as a photographer was blighted by a technological naïveté, but, gleaning what he could from trial and error, he discovered words like *field*, *gate* and *aperture*, as applied to a camera; the versatility of delayed-action shutters; and that "there's a lot you can do with a negative",[4] when he started developing and printing his own films in a newly created darkroom at Sunny Heights. Here, at least, was an area in which he was an authority, as far as McCartney, Harrison and Lennon could see, "and I had all these funny lenses".[26] Billed as its Director of Photography, he showed what these and the rest of his equipment could do in a lot of *Magical Mystery Tour*, such as "a scene with George where I put him in my living room and projected slides on him. It's nothing new – it was done back in 1926 or so – but I happened to be a camera buff, and I think it came out fine."[26]

Second to Paul, Ringo was the Beatle most active in *Magical Mystery Tour's* editing process in a cramped Soho cutting room while tossing morsels to a slavering press over scampi and chips washed down with hock in an adjacent restaurant. In *Magical Mystery Tour*, he informed them, he was the badgered nephew (in a trendy Al Capone suit) of a fat lady who joined a variegated cast of holidaymakers on a charabanc to undertake a journey of no known destination or outcome. It had been Paul's idea to make it up as they went along. Who needed a screenplay, especially one like they'd had in *Help!*? Who wanted a tenth-rate Marx Brothers? The only guide that they'd devised for this film was "one sheet of paper with a circle on it, and it was marked like a clock, only there was one o'clock, five o'clock, nine o'clock and eleven – something like that. The rest we had to fill in."[5]

He'd quell forebodings about formless eccentricity with phrases such as "aimed at the widest possible audience", "children, their grandparents, Beatle people, the lot" and "interesting things to look at, interesting things to hear".[27] On the last point, few could say that its music was a let-down, as demonstrated by a double *Magical Mystery Tour* EP – costing three times more than a single – almost topping Britain's Yuletide chart. The laboured surrealism of the film, however, wasn't quite the ticket for a nation in the hiatus between a cold-turkey teatime and mid-evening insobriety. It was not damned immediately by underground periodicals who'd been determined to like it, but elsewhere, "It just freaked everybody out," groaned Starr years later, "which was a pity. If it came out today, it would be more accepted. I always loved *Magical*."[18]

"We all did"[18] was his loyal addendum, knowing full well how uncomfortable John and George had been about it from the beginning. From an admittedly prejudiced perspective, Pete Best was even more scathing in retrospect about *Magical Mystery Tour* and "the psychedelic stuff. After that, as far as my own taste was concerned, it was waning."[28] Not the same, either, was the Cavern, now re-opened to host poetry readings and similarly arty *soirées*, although Rory Storm And The Hurricanes would still perform there on occasions. Nevertheless, soon after Ty Brien's untimely demise at the age of 26[29] and an inglorious attempt at a relaunch with two ex-Mojos and Karl Terry, Rory and Johnny Guitar finally threw in the towel. Wally Egmond's Combo – as well as Pete Best's – also packed it in around this time, so that Wally could complete his training as a psychiatric nurse.

No Mersey Beat performer of the old school had forgotten four callow lads who'd had a run of luck in 1962. Away from all this reefer-smoking music, The Beatles were probably just the same as they were – especially Ringo, who, so they'd read, remained "just a guy from Liverpool. Maybe I have changed, but only in little ways. I'm still what I was."[30] What was this transcendental meditation caper they'd cottoned on to now? To Cilla Black, "It's somebody who goes to the loo with a big pile of papers and sits there and reads them all."[31]

She could cackle, but it had been a spiritual unguent for The Beatles after Mr Epstein's lonely life had been taken by what the coroner had concluded had been "incautious self-overdoses" of the tablets, potions and draughts that had been over-prescribed to combat both his real and imagined maladies. He might not have had to rely on them, implied Starr, had both manager and group been aware of the benefits of meditation "on those tours. We got very little sleep, and some form of mental relaxation is what we missed."[32] However, it might not have cut much ice in the fleshpots of Hamburg.

On the very weekend of his passing, Brian had half-promised George that he'd join The Beatles at the International Meditation Society's initiation course at a university faculty in the Welsh seaside town of Bangor. "That's how it used to be," Starr would reminisce. "If someone wanted to do something, all we'd do was follow them."[5] Maureen was still recovering from Jason's birth, but Ringo would relay to her the enlightening nectar from the lips of the robed and ascetic Mahesh Prasad Varma, who, styling himself as "Maharishi Mahesh Yogi", had founded the British branch of the society in 1959.

Through short daily contemplations, the Maharishi had said while toying with his silver beard, the regenerative result of meditation was that all human vices would be eradicated bit by bit, until a pure state of bliss was achieved. There was also a greater alertness, increased productivity and sharper differentiation between the trivial and the important. As Starr comprehended, "People in nine-to-five jobs can use it, because it can be done anytime."[32]

Nevertheless, The Beatles had curtailed their indoctrination in Bangor so that they could assimilate their manager's death in the privacy of their own homes. A few days later, Ringo would be beside John's sombre swimming pool where his considered response to the tragedy was chronicled by a correspondent from *Disc* magazine. The Maharishi had "told us we mustn't let it get us down, [because] Brian would be able to feel our feelings in his spiritual state. If we try to spread happiness, then Brian will be happy too" – so would Ty Brien – "but the thing is not to get too selfish about it. If you get depressed about it, it is a form of self-pity, because you are only sympathising with your own loss."[32]

Out of respect to Mr Epstein's mother, The Beatles did not – as they'd intended – wear flower-power finery at the memorial service but instead turned up in dignified suits. Ringo's white shirt sleeves were fastened with the diamond cufflinks given to him on a 24th birthday spent recording a spot for *Top Of The Pops* by "a generous man. We owe so much to him. We have come a long way with Brian along the same road."[33]

Mr Epstein hadn't been sure that he wholly approved of this Varma, and in the end Ringo "couldn't believe 100 per cent in the Maharishi. He's a very high man, but he wasn't the one for me."[34] An uncle's cynical warning that "He's after your money, lad"[14] had reinforced Starr's misgivings about – for example – the guru's argument that The Beatles ought to tithe a sizeable fraction of their income into his Swiss bank account. His Grace also had pious hopes of a recording career, having already been nominal "producer" – with pride of place on its cover – of *Cosmic Consciousness*, an album by flautist Paul Horn, one of his European disciples.

Varma's advent, however, was at a juncture when Starr might well have been ripe for religion, "at a point," as he himself construed, "where I wondered what I was and what it all was."[14] A year earlier, his flippant reaction to *God* in "Think In", a *Melody Maker* word-association column, had been, "Somebody must like Him."[35] In the following year, the Starkeys' approach to Him appeared too insolently sudden to those who would assume that, in February 1968, they'd accompanied the other Beatle couples to Varma's *yoga-ashram* ("theological college") in India simply because they hadn't wanted to be excluded from another new activity. This scepticism was supported by the pair's return to Weybridge after less than a fortnight of study.

There is, however, much to suggest that the expedition was a well-meant attempt at self-improvement by Maureen and Richie, who embraced a few weeks of vegetarian meals – more baked beans and mash or egg and chips than nut roasts or samosas – "because we knew there wouldn't be any meat over in India".[2] Ringo also took off with George for a day's preparatory conference with the Maharishi in one of his Scandinavian academies.

The Harrisons and Lennons had been the advance guard when the Starkeys, Paul and Jane travelled a long, bumpy route from New Delhi to a plateau above the forested foothills of the Himalayas, where a member of the staff of 40 conducted them around not a compound of mud huts but a sunny encampment of stone cottages (each with five rooms and a four-poster bed), a swimming pool, a laundry, an open air amphitheatre, a post office and a dining hall that served a 7am breakfast of cornflakes, toast and coffee. Other seekers of nirvana at the ashram that spring ran a gamut from a Woking hairdresser to Hollywood film star Mia Farrow and Mike Love of The Beach Boys,[36] who Ringo said "goes on and on like Spike Milligan" and was the life and soul of the party. New songs poured from John, George and Paul, many of them observations of other students. Lennon's 'Dear Prudence', for instance, was dedicated to Mia Farrow's reclusive sister. For his wife, Cynthia, the stay in India was an opportunity to save their deteriorating marriage, but – like Paul and Jane's fading passion for each other – there was no help for it.

When his Grace wasn't looking, The Beatles' lofty ideals would sometimes wobble a little. A "Meditating: Do Not Disturb" notice would be pinned on a door so some could, purportedly, come up for a breath of foul air in hands of poker and firewater wine smuggled in by Mal Evans from the shanty town of Rishikesh on the opposite bank of the Ganges. Well, after all, part of the attraction of the Maharishi's creed was that you didn't have to forsake earthly possessions or – within reason – earthly pleasures. "Of course, there were lectures and things all the time, but it was very much like a holiday," summarised Ringo, who also found the place "a bit like Butlin's",[37] a comment that probably raised a derisive laugh in Stormsville when it reached *The Liverpool Echo*.

The Caldwells mightn't have been that astounded by the news that, just before lunch one morning, Mo and Richie announced their immediate departure for England to the Maharishi, who "suggested that perhaps we should go off somewhere and then come back but we wanted to come home. It was like a hundred reasons which formed into one thing." Mostly, they were homesick for the children, but – for Ringo, particularly – the prickly heat had not been mitigated by the peaceful balm of the campus, nor the spicy dinners by the supply of tins of beans and cartons of eggs he'd brought with him.

He promised to parcel George, John and Paul some more cine film as he and Maureen left by hired car for Delhi and a flight home that was largely untroubled, bar an ugly moment at Tehran Airport, where someone asked if he was "one of The Beatles. I said, 'No,' and he just walked away. I guess we're not too big in Tehran."[2]

Back at St George's Hill, the Starkeys decided to sidestep the inevitable barrage of press attention by escaping with the boys for a couple of days at a location deep in the home-counties countryside. "At the moment, I meditate every day," he'd assure waiting interrogators. "Well, I might skip the odd day if I get up late or arrive in town late or something."[38] No one doubted him for a second.

9 *"I Suppose I Seem Fairly Straight"*

If Mr and Mrs Average had been alienated by *Magical Mystery Tour*, the Maharishi and some of The Beatles' marijuana-smoking music, Ringo surfaced as the group's anchor of normality during the eye-stretching aeon between the Rishikesh escapade and 1971's disbandment amid the flying buttresses and quizzically raised judicial eyebrows of London's High Court.

Before Paul and Jane and then the Lennons and Harrisons came home in dribs and drabs from the all-too-human Varma, Ringo had been the only Beatle on the spot at NEMS' new Mayfair storm centre to excuse their latest error and plug the new single, 'Lady Madonna', on which singer Paul – via a nasal affectation – was mistaken for him by many. The lad himself had shuffled wire brushes for a rhythm track reminiscent of Humphrey Lyttelton's trad jazz instrumental 'Bad Penny Blues' from 1956. Yet, with reissues of 'Rock Around The Clock' and Buddy Holly's 'Rave On' in the UK Top 50, rock 'n' roll revival had "suddenly hit the headlines", noted Ringo. "Because this one is a rocker – a slight one, anyway – people are saying it's a rock 'n' roll record."[3] Like The Move, who'd invested their 'Fire Brigade' with an antique Duane Eddy twang, The Beatles were accused of regression as well as bandwagon jumping. "It's not a backwards step," Starr protested. "It's just another type of song from The Beatles."[3]

To his interviewers, Ringo looked very well after his foolhardy travels. More relaxed and articulate than before, he was weaning himself off booze – "just the odd bourbon or beer"[1] – with coffee and chain-smoked American Larks. The zenith of depravity nowadays was "the odd bet on a horse, but no bookie will ever get rich on my bets".[2]

Although extravagant in other matters, his wife was as circumspect about the children's "few bob pocket money each week". Said Ringo, "Once it's spent, that'll be that, though I guess I'll be like most dads, buying them something when they ask for it, then getting a row from Mum."[5] Maureen was annoyed too when Richie still dumped his clothes on the bedroom floor but gladdened by his diminished ardour for nightclubbing – "I sort of expect it to be like it used to be but it never is"[3] – and his contentment (while it lasted) with the sedate domesticity of Brookfields, their new home outside Elstead, a village near Farnham where Surrey bleeds into Hampshire. Rather than the huntin', fishin' and shootin' traditions of those born into privilege, the Elstead acres' natural lake, orchard and forest were enlivened with the new residents' practice of go-karting.

"Why should we be lonely?" was Ringo's rhetorical demand of the final edition of *Rave*. "We have each other, and we never knew anyone in Weybridge",[4] where Sunny Heights – like a few remaining Brickey Builders properties – was still unsold. With the desires of such magazines' subscribers in mind, he threw in cosy anecdotes about Tiger's new-born puppies and the harshly truncated fairy tales he related to Zak ("a bloody terror") and Jason: "There was Father Bear, Mother Bear and Baby Bear, and Mother Bear made some porridge – but a thief broke in and stole it."[5] In the short months when rural quiet and isolation from the capital were refreshing, he swore, "We couldn't live in town again – too much noise and too much going on. I suppose I get bored just like anybody else, but instead of having three hours at night I have all day to get bored in."[4]

Out-buildings around the centrally heated 16th-century manor house included stables, a garage and – exotic for even the home counties then – a sauna cottage. Within the ivy-clung walls, with their exposed rafters, the Starkeys had a cinema and a snooker room, where Ringo would "put the videotape machine on and film myself playing".[4] Owner, too, of the first privately purchased cassette recorder in Britain, his butterfly concentration now embraced all manner of soon-exhausted hobbies involving "thousands of pounds' worth of equipment. I call them my toys, because that's what they are."[6] Often, he'd lose interest while merely glancing at instructions for setting up a newly delivered gadget. When winter gloom descended, he warded off ennui with more familiar pastimes such as "a week when I'll just play records. Then I might spend a day just playing with my tape recordings."[4]

Excitedly, he'd sometimes drop everything to develop some flash of musical inspiration but, after strumming or pounding a bit, it would become too much like hard work and he'd hope the phone would ring. If not, his egg and chips would be getting cold or *M*A*S*H* just starting on television. Maybe he'd have another go tomorrow. His songwriting methodology is worth quoting at length: "I usually get a first verse and then I find it impossible to get anywhere else with the song. I can't say, 'Now I'm going to write.' I just have to be around a guitar or piano and it just comes. Usually, what I do if I'm in the mood is put the tape on, if I've got a tune, and then I play the same tune like a hundred times with different words. Then I take the tape off and get it all typed out and then I pick the lines out that I'll put together."[7] To give himself more scope, he even took guitar lessons for a while in a praiseworthy attempt to progress beyond "my famous three chords"[8] of A, D and E major.

For one incomplete 1968 ditty, 'It Don't Come Easy', he sought help with arrangement from George, who was more malcontented a victim of The Beatles' ruling composers' frequently disheartening indifference to the efforts of colleagues. For another item, 'Three Ships In The Harbour' ("which had 93 verses"[8]), Ringo called on Harry Nilsson, who had lately been gratified by a royalty-earning version of his 'One' by Three Dog Night.

Similarly lucrative was this North American vocal group's cover of Lennon and McCartney's 'It's For You', using Cilla Black's 1964 UK hit as a helpful demo. A legacy from Brian Epstein which put the lady more directly in the news was *Cilla*, a weekly 50-minute series negotiated before his death. Its huge budget could be justified by record-breaking viewing figures, bolstered by Paul McCartney's Top-Ten signature tune and guest stars of the magnitude of Tom Jones, Harry Secombe, Tony Bennett, fiery chart newcomer Julie Driscoll – and a delighted Ringo, whose invitation was at his old mate's own instigation.

On BBC1 on 6 February 1968, he became the first Beatle to sing without the others on another artist's show as unseen millions watched the inauguration of Ringo Starr's solo career, even though "without John, Paul and George I feel vulnerable, like a sultan with 300 wives who, one day, goes out to buy an ice cream for himself".[9] His pre-performance puffing of several fretful cigarettes was interrupted by a comforting telegram "from all your big brothers".

Black and Starr's scripted patter was far from 1961, when she'd had to lean over his kit to share the mic for 'Boys' at the Aintree Institute. Ringo sported a period trilby for their duet of coy 'Do You Like Me Just A Little Bit', suggested by Paul's father from his 1920s dance-band repertoire. The following week's guest, hip Donovan, had intended to simply sing his latest single, 'Jennifer Juniper', but, bragged Cilla, he'd been so taken with the Liverpudlian duo that "he wanted to do something similar".[10] In baggy black suit, shirt and white tie, Ringo's likeable disposition had also come to the fore with a solo rendition of 'Act Naturally' before he proceeded to do just that as a "ventriloquist" – with Cilla as the dummy – in a brief sketch.

Since proving himself as instant a hit in *A Hard Day's Night*, Starr (via the late Brian) had been courted by movie moguls on the look-out for new talent – or was it with cynical expediency that "they sort of stuck on me as Ringo the Film Star because I don't write or anything"[11]? Hardly a week went by in the mid to late 1960s without some pop icon fancying him or herself as a "proper" cinema attraction; Dave Clark, Manfred Mann's Paul Jones, Mick Jagger and even Cilla needed to have a go. What did the world miss when eternal Geordie Eric Burdon allegedly failed a screen test to star in a film treatment of Evelyn Waugh's *The Loved One* with Rod Steiger?

After Lennon had tested the water with *How I Won The War*, Ringo had also accepted a modest part – and his first screen kiss – in a non-Beatle film. ("Best thing around at the time, I thought."[12])

In the advisedly X-certificate Italian-French production *Candy*, he dominated the screen for a few minutes as Emmanuel, a Mexican gardener preparing for holy orders but unsuccessfully sublimating his very worldly lust. He was perceived by Starr as "a very nervous sort of fellow. I was nervous, too, as it happened, and that's how I played the part."[13]

"I'd never have got it if I hadn't been a Beatle,"[12] he admitted, but whither boxing champion Sugar Ray Robinson or Gallic *chanteur* Charles Aznavour also landing parts in *Candy*? In the title role, hitherto-unknown Swedish 17-year-old Ewa Aulin was stunned by "the chance to work with Ringo Starr"[14] during his five-day shoot in Rome, but critical accolades were to be saved for James Coburn, Marlon Brando (as an Oriental guru) and Richard Burton for their more substantial skills in this adaptation of a *risqué* novel – with long-range echoes of Voltaire's *Candide* – by Mason Hoffenberg and Terry Southern, one of Ringo's favourite writers and author of *Dr Strangelove* and the screenplay for *The Loved One*.

Certain passages – like Candy's aunt employing a clothes peg to prevent male entry to her clitoris – were deemed too indelicate for depiction on the silver screen. Even so, a projectionist was arrested for daring to show the film in one American state. Not in the book was Emmanuel's confounded attempt to undo innocent, adolescent Candy on a billiard table. With Zapata moustache and broken English ("ees a-no good"), Ringo served, in retrospect, as an untutored and more sinister model for Andrew Sachs' portrayal as a Spanish waiter in the anarchic 1970s sitcom *Fawlty Towers*.

Most press notices mentioned Starr only in passing. Neither did Starr then "see myself more as a film star than as a Beatle, or vice versa".[15] The follow-up to *Help!* that the group still owed United Artists had not yet passed beyond shallow and arrogant talk of persuading Fellini to direct and sounding out Groucho Marx, Mae West and Jimmy Durante for non-specific bit parts. Someone's brainwave of trying Tolkein's *The Lord Of The Rings* was scotched by its originator's disapproval and the argument of Ringo (pencilled in as Bilbo Baggins' confrere, Samwise Gamgee), who argued that "it will take 18 months to mount and, by that time, we will all go off the idea. What we must do is to start something on the spur of the moment, otherwise we will never get it done. We are always into other things."[15]

Among these "other things" was George's incidental music for an oddity of a movie entitled *Wonderwall*. Its soundtrack – with percussion by an Indian ensemble, The Remo Four's Roy Dyke and an uncredited Starr – was the first album to be issued via EMI by Apple, The Beatles' own record company, a division of Apple Corps, a name registered in 1963 as an eventual umbrella term for maverick artistic and scientific ventures. Also to be financed under the quartet's naïve and self-managed aegis was a Lennon-formulated plan for a school for the Beatle children. "We saw it [Apple] housing all our ideas, and we believed it would all go well," groaned Ringo when it didn't. "But we weren't businessmen, and we aren't now."[15]

Some of their pop peers had also diversified for fun and profit, off-the-cuff examples being Chris Farlowe's military memorabilia shop in Islington; Merseybeat Tony Crane's stake in a Spanish night club; Monkee Davy Jones' New York boutique; and Reg Presley's patenting of his fog-dispersal system. With what was assumed to be wealth past calculation, The Beatles could be more altruistic. According to clever newspaper advertisements, a kindly welcome awaited not just those who'd nurtured a connection with the group's inner circle but any old riff-raff who wished to solicit Apple for finance for pet projects. Impetuous cash was flung at such as a so-called "electronics wizard"; two unprofitable shops; a troupe of grasping Dutch designers trading misleadingly as "The Fool"; film-makers who wouldn't make films; poets who didn't write poems; and, remembered Ringo, a tent for "another guy to do a Punch and Judy show on a beach. They'd take the money and say, 'Well, maybe next week.'"[16] When 3 Savile Row was established as Apple's permanent address, sackfuls of mail would overload its postman; pleading voices would bother its switchboard; and supplicatory feet would ascend its steps from morn 'til night before a narrow-eyed doorman was appointed to shoo them off. Yet, to loitering pavement fixture Alex Millen, his fallible idols "did strengthen the belief that Joe Soap was important and, yes, you too could have something to say".[17]

In the white-walled, green-carpeted offices, it was a boom time for Apple's staff, too, when they'd assimilated the heedlessness of their paymasters' expenditure. A dam burst for a river of wastefulness to carry off gluttonous restaurant lunches; bottle after bottle of liquor, illicit trunk calls to other continents; and wanton purchases of trendy caprices swiftly to lie forgotten in desk drawers. With a stroke of a pen, a bold executive could award himself a Rolls Royce, a house extension and even a whole house. His secretary would conceal his thefts to better hide her own.

Out of his depth, Starr saw the organisation as another expensive toy to be disregarded, if not jettisoned altogether, when he grew tired of it. Soon he was "only involved in Apple as much as I have to be. If there's a decision to blow up the building, I'll go along and raise my hand and say, 'Aye.'"[18] Whenever he was in the mood, he'd lean forward on the hard-backed Regency chair in his office and play company director. For a while, he shrugged aside the disgusting realities of the half-eaten steak sandwich in a litter bin; the receptionist rolling a joint of best Afghan hash; the typist who counted paperclips and span out a single letter (in the house style of no exclamation marks!) all morning before "popping out" and not returning until the next day. A great light dawned. "We had, like, a thousand people that weren't needed, but they all enjoyed it. They're all getting paid for sitting around. We had a guy there just to read the tarot cards, the *I Ching*. It was craziness."[19]

Apple Records was the only department that "didn't let us down".[16] With guinea pigs like ex-Undertaker Jackie Lomax, soprano Mary Hopkin (a regular on BBC Wales' *Disc At Dawn*) and former James Brown *protégée* Doris Troy, Harrison and McCartney cut their teeth as record producers, with Mary's debut Apple single knocking The Beatles' 'Hey Jude' from the top of the British charts. She was then ousted in November 1968 by a funereal-paced 'With A Little Help From My Friends' by bellyaching Joe Cocker, an ex-East

Midlands gas fitter whose producer, Denny Cordell, had – with Keith Moon and Manfred Mann – been proposed for a freelance commission during Apple's optimistic genesis. Intrigued by Cordell's sweaty if less attractive overhaul of his *Sergeant Pepper* moment, Ringo volunteered his eager services for Cocker's subsequent album, although his contribution was scrapped.

Within Apple, Ringo had founded on 16 July 1968 his Startling Music publishing concern, initially to gather royalties should any of his pedantically wrought compositions ever warrant release. Eclipsed by the other Beatles' more tangible activities, he was, nonetheless, happy to rattle the traps for Paul and George's clients – mostly in Savile Row's new basement studio – and, after he'd got used to her, for Yoko Ono, who had now replaced McCartney as John's artistic collaborator as she had Cynthia in his bed.

Yoko had once sniffed around Ringo for his patronage for her "concept art", but he was unmoved by her wrapping Trafalgar Square statues in brown paper, her inane *Grapefruit Book*, her *Four Square* (a remake of *Bottoms* that consisted of what you think it did) and anything else she considered necessary to win his sponsorship. His bemusement with Yoko contrasted with John's jealous imaginings, after he brazened it out by escorting her to the Old Vic to catch a stage adaptation of his slim 1964 volume, *In His Own Write*. A perturbed *Beatles Monthly* passed her off as his "guest of honour", but nothing could cover up the genital display on the sleeve of *Two Virgins*, which was published in *The News Of The World* months before the eventual release date of the disc, which had been postponed while Lennon's appalled advisors tried to talk him out of it. *Two Virgins* was the first of a trilogy of Ono-Lennon albums filled with sounds not generally thought of as pop entertainment. Although they didn't "dig their records",[20] the Starkeys of all the other Beatle couples swooped most unquestioningly to Lennon's defence. Of the unclothed 'Two Virgins', Ringo commented, "It's just John being John. It's very clean."[21] Yoko became "incredible". No one else doubted it, either. "We'll be pleased when people realise that she's doing something [and] that she's not trying to be the fifth Beatle."[21]

Waiting to console Yoko just before Lennon's cremation twelve years later, Starr's muttered "it was her who started all this"[22] indicated an adjustment of his stated opinion, in as late as 1971, that her and John's amour had not taken priority over group commitments. "Ringo was a little confused," deduced Klaus Voorman, "because John's closeness to Yoko was sad to him. John and Yoko were one person, which was difficult for him to accept."[23]

When The Beatles next convened at Abbey Road, Yoko's constant and baleful adherence to John in both control room and playing area entitled Paul to bring along his current American girlfriend and then the one who succeeded her, Linda Eastman, from a family of showbusiness attorneys. Although Linda and Yoko had both attended school in the same smart New York district, they didn't have much else in common, although they'd each marry their respective English *beaux* during the same month in 1969.

Lukewarm rapport between the chief Beatles' immovable women was one of Ringo's "little niggly things that cropped up"[24] while he sat on the fence as the group muddled through a double album that, in its prosaic name alone, justified George Martin's observation that *The Beatles* was "sort of businesslike",[25] as engineers grew accustomed to two or even three Beatles missing at any given session. As the four's emotional and professional solidarity shredded, a combination of self-interest and acquiescence permitted ear-catching pieces like 'Back In The USSR' (which spurred Zak Starkey to "zoom around like an aeroplane"[26]), 'While My Guitar Gently Weeps' and jarring 'Revolution Nine' to be flanked by inconsequential filler: one-line librettos, pretty-but-nothing lieder, excerpts from raucous jamming and self-referential musical jokes like 'Glass Onion'. Ringo's chief memory of 'Birthday' was, "Anyone could shout a line...the roadies, the tea lady. If anyone had a line, it would be used."[27]

This ersatz rocker also bracketed the nearest that Starr would ever come to a recorded drum solo. Although his new wooden Drum City kit had two hanging tom-toms, neither were hit for eight petulant bars of kick-bass, snare and hi-hat bashed simultaneously on the beat, *mach schau* style.

Anything went. More catalytic familiars and guest players than ever were assembled to add icing to the cake. Mal Evans blasted trumpet on 'Helter Skelter' and Yoko was loud and clear on 'The Continuing Story Of Bungalow Bill' and 'Revolution Nine'. Because such moonlighting was frowned upon by his record company, Eric Clapton's solos on George's numbers had to be attributed to 'Eddie Clayton' – Ringo's idea – just as they'd been on *Wonderwall*. Jack Fallon – a Canadian emigrant who'd promoted Beatles bookings in the West Country during the Pete Best era – was hired to scrape country and western violin on 'Don't Pass Me By', the exhumation of which – although a personal triumph for Starr – illustrated the depth to which standards had fallen.

The track had withstood attempts to alter its title, but only several structural changes to its mediocre melody convinced McCartney, Martin and Lennon that 'Don't Pass Me By' no longer resembled the work of another. Even so, its twist-in-the-tale lyric was too nonchalantly morbid and clumsily expressed, but as no one expected little Ringo to be a genius composer that very fact would render this slight, laughable novelty – buried towards the middle of side two – endearing to Beatle diehards. "Ringo's best ever,"[28] grinned one reviewer before savaging 'Revolution Nine', which prefaced the valedictory 'Goodnight', Starr's other lead vocal on *The Beatles*.

Lennon's lullaby to his neglected son, 'Goodnight', was banked with slushy strings and The Mike Sammes Singers. Like 'Yellow Submarine', it had borne George Martin's removal of a spoken preamble – of the "toddle off to beddie-byes, kiddies!" bent – but Ringo's plaintiveness rather than John's edgy inflection better conveyed the necessary – and too apt – air of over-tiredness before the last run-out groove.

Ringo would not look back on *The Beatles* with much affection, although there'd been no discernible animosity at first. However, to engineer Ken Scott, under Paul's instructions during brass overdubs for 'Mother Nature's Son', "Everything was going really well, and then John and Ringo walked in – and, for the half hour they were there, you could have cut the atmosphere with a knife."[23] Since the advent of Yoko, and John's co-related passiveness, McCartney's attempts to motivate the other personnel had backfired, his boisterous purpose translated as barely tolerable bossiness.

An irksome lecture from *bête noir* Paul about a fluffed tom-tom fill had been the delayed-action spark that had fired Ringo to stalk out of Abbey Road mid-session. Sooner than any Beatle imagined, he'd testify in court, "Paul...is very determined. He goes on and on to see if he can get his own way. While that may be a virtue, it did mean that musical disagreements inevitably arose from time to time." Starr added that such tensions had stimulated the group's creative resources. Nevertheless, he'd had a surfeit of Paul's schoolmasterly perseverance – and the withdrawn John letting him get away with it – during the making of *The Beatles*.

Treated as but a tool for Lennon and McCartney's ebbing collective genius, "things were getting a bit rough"[30] for Ringo. After motoring the long and gradually more loathed miles from Elstead, his hackles would rise further as it became usual for the studio receptionist to see him facing her and "reading a newspaper. He used to sit there for hours, waiting for the others to turn up."[31] When a quorum of Beatles finally got to work, he'd be on the edge of agitated debates that would scale such a height of vexation and cross-purposes that console assistants would slope off for embarrassed tea breaks until the flare-up subsided to a simmering huff. Then, in his isolation chamber, Ringo's ears in the headphones would tingle after hours spent thumping out take after rejected take, his concentration split through straining to decipher the drone of murmured intrigue amid the tape spools and blinking dials. Crowned by Paul questioning his very competence as a musician, "I couldn't take it any more."[30]

That their weary drummer's resignation was more than a registered protest or one of his infrequent fits of pique became clear with his verbal notice to John and then Paul. Yet neither they nor George dared credit this extreme strategy by the standard-bearer of group stability. The matter was hushed up and they endeavoured to carry on as if nothing was wrong. Actually, Ringo's departure –

although regrettable – was by no means disastrous, as Paul, George and John managed a composite drum section for 'Back In The USSR'.

They were about to minister likewise to 'Dear Prudence' when the prodigal returned after a fortnight in the Mediterranean on Peter Sellers' yacht. Out of The Beatles' reach, he'd calmed down enough to jot down the basic structure of a new Starr original, 'Octopus' Garden', following the vessel's chef's fascinating discourse one lunchtime about life on the ocean floor. Tight coils within had unwound and, for all that had driven him from the group, it abruptly made sense to ring up and report for duty again. Half expecting a row, he was greeted with a drum-kit festooned with remorseful flowers and "welcome back" banners.

This conciliatory and even amicable mood persisted for what was left of the sessions. Because they meant one less pole of alliance for Ringo and George, Lennon's increasing absences helped, as he and Yoko hurled themselves into a ludicrous world peace mission, headline-hogging espousals of favoured minority causes and, regardless of cost, an elaborate yet slap-dash array of arty demonstrations. "John has always been freakish," explained Ringo, as much to himself as anyone. "Now that he has married Yoko, it shows more."[20]

Much of the Lennons' behaviour – especially their penchant for nudity – tarred their associates with the same brush. The riotous closure of Apple's Marylebone boutique – when all remaining merchandise was given away – touched off a *Daily Mirror* cartoon set near the queues. "Ringo got carried away, officer," says McCartney to a constable confronting a naked Starr.

While this may or may not have set Ringo hooting with hilarity, not so funny were repercussions of a narcotics squad pounce on his Montagu Square maisonette, where Yoko and John had found a temporary refuge from self-aggravated media attention. Unacceptable to the plain-clothes sergeant in charge was their plea that the cannabis his men had dug out was the lost property of some earlier tenant. While he was above shifting the blame onto his former mother-in-law, Lennon let out the raw information that Jimi Hendrix and beatnik novelist William Burroughs – a former drug addict – had both stayed there.

Stung by this unwelcome publicity, Brymon Estates Limited instigated civil proceedings against Starr to bar the Lennons and other undesirables from using the premises. Although their battle was lost before the Queen's Bench in February 1969, the affair left such a nasty taste in Ringo's mouth that he sold his freehold interest in the place.[32]

Most reports on the case pointed out that the landlords had no gripes about the Starkeys residing there. When The Beatles had publicly renounced consumption of illegal drugs, Starr was the only one who neither continued nor resumed the habit (well, not immediately), although he qualified this in saying, "Who says that booze and cigarettes aren't as much of a drug as pot?"[33] Nevertheless, in as late as 1973, he agreed without hesitation to broadcast an anti-narcotics appeal on US radio. He had his head screwed on, see, not like those other weirdos. Guilty of cocaine possession not long after the Lennons' bust, George seemed just as screwy as John on the quiet, with rumours circulating that he was to become a full-time Hare Krishna *bhakta*, bald head and all. Since Linda had moved in with him, even Paul – once the personification of narcissism – had become whiskered and scruffy.

No matter which journal still canvassed its readers on the most popular Beatle – Paul in *Jackie*, John in *Disc* – Ringo was invariably second. Seeming a beer-and-skittles sort who rejoiced in his married state, "I suppose I seem fairly straight and a family type, so people do associate more with me than, say, John."[6] When ATV bought a majority stake in Northern Songs in 1969, Ringo got shot of his holding for £80,000 but otherwise he didn't have more money than sense nowadays, because, "If I think I'm being conned, I do without."[34] Although long removed from the everyday, he was bereft of the guilt and concerned indolence of others who also had "more money than I ever dreamed of".[2] Begging letters were sifted by his secretary and "I usually give the genuine ones a hand, but the scroungers get nothing."[2] Another occupational hazard of The Man With Everything was being spoilt for choice: "My friend Ray in Liverpool has got this collection of just 40 records, and he knows them all and loves each one. I've got maybe 1,000 and I never really know which one to put on."[6]

He did not, however, hanker after the old days of Dingle poverty, as it was "so black up there. I'm not sure I could ever live there again. I haven't turned into my dad like so many of those I knew in Liverpool, [but] it's difficult if you live on the same street as those you grew up with; you think twice about putting on, say, a green suit with yellow dots."[6]

His idiosyncratic finger adornment was moderated, but, in anticipation of the decade that elegance forgot, he took to dressing in such eye-torturing garments as a *very* red shirt, a custard-yellow cravat with a jewelled pin, a white-striped green suit and knee-high fur boots. The acme of gentility, "I went up to a cousin's wedding in an old gold suit, not very startling, and some gate-crashers had a go at me."[6]

For sit-down meals on these occasions, there were no special pre-requisites (apart from his known dislike of onions) for the Starkeys, whose first try at vegetarianism had lasted just a few weeks – although Ringo didn't "really like killing anything, not even a fly".[33] Distant teenage kin jockeying to exchange self-conscious familiarities with their famous relation were often discountenanced at how like their fathers – and even grandfathers – he was. He was, nevertheless, *au fait* with recent "rock" developments across the Atlantic, but he preferred mainstream, musicianly artists like Canned Heat; Blood, Sweat And Tears; and bottleneck guitar exponent Ry Cooder, whose sticksman, Jim Keltner – from Gary Lewis And The Playboys – "really pleases me more than some incredible jazz drummer who can flit 'round them like a jet plane".[19]

He was also partial to Bob Dylan's Band's True West blend of electric folklore on *Music From Big Pink*. In perverse mood, he'd try Tiny Tim, an ineffable entertainer with a castrati warble, but the furthest-out limit of Starr's taste appeared to be the cartoon voodoo of *Doctor John The Night Tripper* – alias Los Angeles session player Mac Rebennack – with its zombie wails and throbbing murk. That Rebennack's image was not entirely contrived became evident when, on meeting him, Ringo was charmed by his "weird language, which is half English, half cajun and half rhyming madness".[23]

More a record collector than listener, "I don't play much pop, but Maureen does."[26] Nevertheless, Tamla-Motown at full blast could transport Starr – however temporarily – from the suffocating calm of Brookfields, and concerts by Frank Sinatra and Hank Snow were taken in during escapes to London. *Sotto voce*, he'd croon such sparkling "standards" in embryo as 'For Once In My Life', 'Little Green Apples' and 'What The World Needs Now Is Love'.

Ringo wasn't so square that he couldn't be reprimanded for the excessive volume of his portable record player by haughty holidaymakers sunbathing by the same hotel swimming pool. Neither was he an advocate of the Marine Offences Act that killed off the competitive pirate radio stations that had "helped to keep the scene alive. We're left now with the monopoly of the BBC and what seems like half a dozen terrible bands playing for most of the day."[1] With Radio Luxembourg's shows still hosted by leftovers from the 1950s Light Programme clique, the cautious programming by the corporation's two national pop outlets had certainly hastened *Top Of The Pops*' shallower and less subversive in content, which brushed its nadir one schmaltzy 1968 week when the only group presented was The Tremeloes (now *sans* Brian Poole), who were – with Marmalade and Love Affair – a prong of a grinning triumvirate that were hopeless pretenders to The Beatles' throne during this silver age of British beat, constipated as it was with their retinue of disposable and harmless purveyors of popular song – The Casuals (albeit veterans of Hamburg), Cupid's Inspiration, Pickettywitch, Liverpool's Arrival and all the rest of them – who faltered after maybe two Top-30 entries.

Because it exposes a point of view, even the lovey-dovey couplets contained in Marmalade's 'Lovin' Things' or The Casuals' 'Jesamine' and even 'Don't Pass Me By' might be construed as political, but, after 19th nervous breakdowns, dead-end streets and strawberry fields, composers were wringing apocalyptic drops from GIs missing presumed dead in Indo-China, slaughter at anti-war demonstrations and Ireland, bloody Ireland. The latter issue would be addressed by Ulster *colleen* Dana in a poignant version of George Harrison's 'Isn't It A Pity', written in 1969. More direct was Edwin Starr's just plain 'War'. Nonetheless, war and terrorism on the *Nine O'Clock News* was commonplace enough to horrify viewers as much as a shoot-out in a gangster movie.

When asked about Vietnam and other inflammable topics, Ringo was sufficiently hip to understand that killing people is wrong. He wouldn't join together – as Mick Jagger did – with militant anti-Vietnam War protesters outside the US Embassy, nor come up with even an irresolute anthem like Lennon's 'Revolution', but he was as active – in a detached, sweeping, pop-starrish fashion – in verbally supporting pacifism, although, "Just at the moment, we can say what we feel, but it doesn't really change anything. I can't trust politicians. They're all liars, you know. And when the younger generation get the vote, it will be very interesting to see what they decide to allow and exactly what they don't. The young people all want peace, and they'll get it if they just wait, because they're going to outlive them all."[33]

The Starkeys' own offsprings' upbringing was undramatic and as free of major traumas as the restrictions of the paterfamilias' fame would permit: "I don't want people interested in them just because they are my children."[26] Nonetheless, Zak and Jason could not help but become aware of their indulgent dad's wealth and the celebrity that he would always enjoy. Four-year-old Zak's daub of a beetle-like creature would grace the cover of 1969's Christmas flexidisc for the fan club. "Like any kid," grinned Ringo, "he wants to play with his own toys and mine as well."[6] As his father had scorned drumming lessons, Zak was restricted to just one tutorial. "Then he just told me to listen to records and play along with them."[35] Given a free choice, Zak was more likely to thunder along to The Who than The Beatles.

Like his brother after him, Zak was found a piano teacher. He'd also begun to learn recorder at the local Church of England state primary. When the family moved to London, the children would attend more exclusive seats of learning, but Starr in Elstead was reluctant to send his boys to a fee-paying boarding school. "Not unless they tell me they definitely want to go. If I can only see them as much as one hour a day, then I want that hour."[26] When he progressed from his bit part in *Candy* to co-starring with Peter Sellers in *The Magic Christian* in early 1969, he risked bringing the family to his place of work. "But this can prove to be tricky, because the kids get bored and start fiddling about with all the equipment. It can also be very embarrassing if one of them shouts out, 'Daddy!' whilst we're doing a take."[4]

Ringo's infants were not to be in evidence on the long-awaited third Beatles film, *Let It Be*. For the inter-related LP, they'd developed the "mock rock" of 'Lady Madonna' with a production criterion so shorn of gratuitous frills that it sounded *au naturel*: Cavern rawness married to advanced technology. After insisting that they'd never do so again, they were captured portraying themselves infinitely more than ever before in this documentary, in which – without premeditated *Hard Day's Night* zaniness – The Beatles rehearsed, recorded, jammed and gave an unpublicised performance under a leaden sky on Apple's flat roof, clothed against the biting wind. Public-address speakers aimed at the street below provoked the downing of measuring tapes in neighbourhood outfitters, a swelling crowd to clog the pavement and police from the station nearly half a mile away to curb the breach of the peace, MBEs or not. The most repeated off-camera joke was Ringo saying, "For the first time in years, we give a live show. Is it our fault only 500 people turn up?"[36]

Both before and during *Let It Be*, a more formal concert comeback – perhaps a full-scale tour – had been discussed with dwindling fervour. John with Yoko had set a precedent of sorts backed with the *ad hoc* AN Other on the hitherto-unscreened *Rock 'n' Roll Circus* television spectacular headlined by The Rolling Stones, who had themselves returned to the boards earlier that year with ten sensational minutes at the *NME* poll-winners bash, the same venue at which, in 1966, The Beatles had vanished from the British stage forever.

From "I can't see why we shouldn't"[37] with San Franciscan screams still ringing in his ears to "No, I don't think I ever would",[3] Ringo blew hot and cold about The Beatles' availability for bookings in 1969. In April, an Apple spokesman could not be induced to comment, whilst "Ringo and John are so obviously in disagreement"[13] over a blurted Lennon statement that the quartet "will give several public shows this year".[13] Starr would never be against performing *per se*, "but it's the whole operation of getting there that's the drag".[14] Also, he was afraid that, after tax and other deductions, "[we'd] be left with a fiver and a packet of ciggies each".[15]

Nonetheless, he'd elect as usual to go along with whatever the majority – by implication, John and George – decided. His proposition of a format "where you'd have one camera, just step in and do your bit, like the *Grand Ole Opry*"[38] went unheeded as the fly-on-the-wall wheeze took root. As Lennon, McCartney and, especially, Harrison had new songs to squeeze onto the album, Ringo's 'Octopus' Garden' fell by the wayside, too, although George and then John (on cack-handed drums) chucked in some amused ideas when he plonked it out on the Apple ivories.

This condescending levity and episodes such as an affectedly surreal exchange between John and Ringo – the film's "only true individualists"[39], wrote *The Morning Star* – were oases of borderline comedy during the frayed celluloid miles of Paul's prodding of nerves, testy George's walk-out, Yoko's screech-singing, masked bickering and all of the subtle discords discernible to anyone who has ever suffered being in a pop group, particularly one on its last legs. Like Andy Warhol's interesting-but-boring *Flesh*, with its improvised dialogue and frowsy scenarios, the tedium was nearly the idea. Viewers could, for example, sense eyes glazing over to McCartney's chatter. Nevertheless, The Beatles went the distance with *Let It Be*, largely through the introduction of a revitalising element in jovial Texan organist Billy Preston, an old acquaintance from the Star-Club who'd been taking up an invitation to drop in at Apple when Harrison "just grabbed him and brought him down to the studio".[40]

Years before they let him, the self-important Phil Spector had asserted that he wanted to produce The Beatles, and he – rather than the disinclined George Martin – was the mug drafted in to edit, spruce up and mix the "new-phase Beatles album" (as it would say on the *Let It Be* package) and its single, 'Get Back', which was peculiar to Ringo – who seemed to have forgotten The Dave Clark Five's 'Bits And Piece' – as "the only record where the drummer's the hook" and for Lennon sliding a bottleneck guitar solo "like an amateur, but it comes off".[24]

Although heard merely toiling behind his drums, dogsbody Starr's musical appetite was the least ruined by the harrowing *Let It Be* sessions. Therefore, it was he who'd sit most often beside Phil at the mixing desk whenever a second opinion was required. Past his best, the fastidious New Yorker was in poor humour after a recent car accident. So histrionically did Spector throw his weight about in Apple's basement that Ringo took loyal pity on the hectored engineers – among them an old Merseyside friend George Peckham[41] – and, pulling Spector aside, asked him to "cool it".

In the first instance, Spector's doctoring – overseen by Starr – satisfied McCartney, who, over the phone to Ringo, "didn't put it down, and then suddenly he didn't want it to go out. It was two weeks after that he wanted to cancel it."[19]

On the strength of his short cameo in *Easy Rider*, the hit movie of 1969, Spector had been recommended to the receptive Beatles by Allen Klein, whose prophecy that he'd one day represent the group seemed to be fulfilling itself. To Ringo, Allen came across as "a powerful man, and also, no matter what anyone says, he's fair".[19] Despite warnings from some of his previous clients and associates, John and George were also yielding to the Robin Hood of pop's contractual sweet-talk that he illustrated with flattering quotes from their lyrics. However, once his champion, Paul preferred to believe his lawyer-in-laws' tittle-tattle of Klein's sharp practices, high handedness and low cunning. *L'affaire Let It Be* was a handy bone of contention, and Klein – not Spector – would be the recipient of Paul's written plea – to little effect – that the *Let It Be* album be stripped of the superimposed orchestral and choral grandiloquence that contradicted the original endeavour to hark back to the Mersey Beat womb.

The Beatles' dissolution became more than foreseeable when John announced that he'd be leaving soon and yet agreed that it should not be public knowledge yet, for fear that it would unman Klein's bellicose negotiation of a more advantageous royalty deal with Capitol. Nonetheless, a hint of what lay ahead could be fathomed by journalists in Lennon's reported crack that "the circus has left town but we still own the site".[42] Those journalists uneasily in the know – such as fellow Merseysider Ray Connolly, of *The Evening Standard* – did not betray the deeper confidence, unsure of how seriously anyone could take John, who had become a laughing stock since falling in with that frightful Yoko. "John is crazy like that," chuckled Ringo. "He will say one thing one day [and] the opposite the next."[15] Only a handful of fans outside Abbey Road caught Ringo's sally as he ambled across Abbey Road car park for a session on 26 August 1969: "I'm going back to the circus."[43]

10 "I Couldn't Believe It Was Happening"

Of each Beatle's preparations for the end, Ringo's were the most pragmatic. Before *Let It Be* nestled uneasily in the album lists – among *Led Zeppelin II*, Andy Williams' *Greatest Hits*, Black Sabbath and the latest from Crosby, Stills, Nash And Young, The Who and Simon And Garfunkel – he'd struck out on his own again with *The Magic Christian*, technically his second non-Beatle film.

Terry Southern's short novel did not contain anyone called "Youngman Grand", but this rather superficial main character was, nevertheless, inserted into the script for the screen version of *The Magic Christian* at the first hint of publicity-gaining Beatle involvement. The production's press department would now be able, for instance, to instigate a *Fab 208* Ringo Competition[1] to win seats at the royal world première in December, with *Magic Christian* T-shirts awarded for the runners-up. Moreover, as well as Starr's acting, there'd be a cameo by John and Yoko and soundtrack donations by a new Apple signing, Badfinger, whose two-year chart run was stabilised with McCartney's catchy 'Come And Get It', sung five times during the picture.

While accepting that he was being "used for the name",[2] Ringo had sought the part as an admirer of Southern and as a further opportunity to discover more about what now seemed one reliable indicator of future direction, even if "I've had no special tuition but I've learned a lot from watching other people."[3] As well as *in situ* expositions by distinguished fellow thespians, he noted how lengthy periods hanging around during retakes, camera repositioning *et al* were best spent. Rather than "stand there waiting like a mummy, I relax and do things – act naturally, you might say"[3] Other than the familiar shuffle of playing cards, his hands were also occupied with newer dressing-room pastimes, notably with "my enamelling kit. I was always enamelling things or doing something with paints and coloured pens."[4]

Another lesson logged for future use by Ringo was how a product's lack of substance could be disguised with a large budget and employment of the famous. Although less prominent than Ringo, *The Magic Christian* was also blessed with – among others – Raquel Welch whipping female galley slaves and Yul Brynner in drag crooning Noël Coward's 'Mad About The Boy' to Roman Polanski. Nearer to the tale's main thrust were Sir Richard Attenborough as a rowing coach, Laurence Harvey as a Shakespearian actor, traffic warden Spike Milligan and John Cleese, a supercilious art dealer, who, respectively, are bribed to sabotage an Oxford-Cambridge boat race; outrage an audience with a striptease; swallow a parking ticket; and allow the defacing of a Rembrandt.

With others in his Monty Python gang, Cleese also left his mark on the Anglicised screenplay which was described as "an essentially genial indictment of British capitalist society".[5] Today, it surfaces as one of Sellers' lesser comedies, with Starr serving mostly as witness to his appropriation of the funniest lines as the much-altered original plot dissolves into a series of themed sketches – about folk who'll do anything for money – with predictable outcomes. To Ringo, in his lead as a Liverpudlian vagrant adopted by "Grand" (Sellers), "they were just saying, 'Be yourself'"[6] by permitting the occasional sub-*Hard Day's Night* flat truism. "To keep my ears warm" was his reply to "Why are you wearing a deerstalker?" during a scene on bleak scrubland for which he'd been kitted out in ridiculous Victorian hunting tweeds and clumsy climbing boots.

As expected, the most sympathetic reviews came from the pop weeklies – "his 'This Boy'-type pathos is particularly strong" (*NME*[7]); "first class with the facial expressions" (*Disc*[8]). Elsewhere, the general conjecture – with the artist in agreement –

was that Ringo had coped well enough with an undemanding role "as heavy as a bucket of feathers".[9] *The Daily Express* was the most vitriolic: "His sad, spaniel expressions of wide-eyed innocence suit the character and he delivers his lines competently if monotonously".[10]

Nevertheless, the project had been fun for Ringo, who had at least been among friends. As well as working alongside veterans of Beatles movies such as Patrick Cargill and Denis O'Dell, he'd welcomed George Harrison as an intrigued observer at a railway location shoot back and forth between Wargrave and Henley-on-Thames, where the Harrisons were soon to purchase the grandiose Friar Park mansion. Meanwhile, Paul and the new Mrs McCartney (plus Princess Margaret) had been present at a studio sequence in Twickenham. The Lennons' attempt to join the team for a crossing on the *QE2* to finish the movie in the States was nipped in the bud when John was denied a US visa because of his marijuana conviction. Sellers' commiserations with Lennon's plight were genuine, for, as speaker at an Oxford Union debate, the ex-Goon had been cheered for his admission that he too had dabbled with outlawed drugs.

Nervous on the first day before the cameras, Ringo had been taken aback by Peter, who "I knew quite well, but suddenly there he was going into character and I got confused."[11] Nevertheless, the bond between Starr and Sellers – previous owner of Brookfields – tightened through hedonistic joint ventures like booking Mayfair's Les Ambassadeurs for a celebrity party – a rare occurrence for Ringo in those days – that, in keeping with the film, climaxed with hundreds of dollar bills fluttering from the ceiling. There followed a fortnight together in the south of France and then Paradise Island in the Bahamas, after completing their immediate *Magic Christian* obligations in New York. In the build-up to its London première, both were forever on television talk programmes.

During BBC1's *David Frost Show*, the two sang a number from *Abbey Road*, The Beatles' latest LP. Unconvincing in embryo during *Let It Be*, 'Octopus' Garden' – Richard Starkey's second published solo composition – had passed muster when the group convened for what was tacitly assumed (by John and Paul, anyway) to be the vinyl finale. A simpler companion reverie to 'Yellow Submarine' and with a country and western tinge, 'Octopus' Garden' stood as tall as most of McCartney's sugary *Abbey Road* offerings and was easier on the ear than, say, Lennon's stark 'I Want You (She's So Heavy)'. It wasn't, however, a masterpiece of song. Against nearly 200 for George's 'Something' (the album's attendant single), it spawned not one cover version known to me. Nevertheless, the requisite breezy, infantine effect was fully realised via Paul and George's emollient backing harmonies and Ringo's sound-effect idea of a blowing through a straw into a close-miked tumbler of water.

More indicative of John, George and Paul's disinclination than their producer's artistic regard for the budding Schubert was Ringo's good-natured appearance as token Beatle among The Hollies, Pan's People, Cilla Black and other guests on *With A Little Help From My Friends*, a Christmas Eve tribute to George Martin on ITV. Obeying Musicians' Union dictates, he re-recorded the lead vocal to mime 'Octopus' Garden', gripping a trident with a few children at his feet.

Flickering into decorated living rooms at an optimum yearly moment of homecomings and Timex commercials, Ringo's reputation as the straightest Beatle had been further strengthened by recent family events as "normal" as susceptible fans might have imagined them. At Queen Charlotte's as usual, Maureen's third pregnancy had on 17 November produced Lee Parkin, the daughter that she and Richie had so desired, her second name being a restoration of a Starkey family name. Home for the baby was a six-bedroom spread along leafy Compton Avenue on the exclusive Glentree estate in Highgate, rather than rural Elstead, which was "too far away"[4] for her father to commute to Apple in his new six-door black Mercedes. As with Sunny Heights, Ringo endured a long wait for a buyer, eventually letting Brookfields go for £100,000 to Steve Stills from Crosby, Stills, Nash And Young, who declared that he intended to have the libretto of 'Within You Without You' carved in stone for display in the garden. Although "it wasn't until after The Beatles folded that I started to do a lot of session work",[1] Starr was listed by Stills – omnipresent at Apple Studios then – among the illustrious assistants on his debut solo LP, listed on the sleeve as "Richie".

Big names who saw the New Year in at Ringo's Highgate housewarming included next door neighbours Maurice Gibb of The Bee Gees and his first wife, singer and media personality Lulu. Sharing the same profession, it would have been odd if the Gibbs and Starr hadn't collaborated informally in the privacy of their respective home studios. With Lulu's brother, Billy Lawrie, Ringo knocked together 'Rock And Roller', which surfaced as a 1973 single when Billy trod briefly in his elder sister's footsteps. One evening, Maurice "sang" on 'Modulating Maurice', a track from an album's worth of woofing and tweeting that Ringo had concocted on one of these new-fangled monophonic synthesisers. "They take control of you, those machines," he confessed. I turn all the dials and press buttons and get excited and put a few mics out and put it through amplifiers into my Revox. We found this riff on the machine and I was playing with it, and [Gibb] started humming words and read the dials, like [the] modulator and envelope shaper, things like that."[12] Another item featured drums with "lots of echo, and it just sounds strange. I love it. Some of the tracks are just incredible."[12] Though pre-empted somewhat by George's *Electronic Sounds*, the self-explanatory solo album that followed *Wonderwall*, Starr's more calculated twiddles were earmarked for consumption by a dwindling public still uncritical of any goods branded "Beatle", until "I got involved with John Tavener, who was doing *The Whale*, which was more far out."[12]

During pop's fleeting "classical" period, when *Sergeant Pepper* and its syncretic ilk had ushered in concept albums, rock operas such as The Who's *Tommy* and other questionable "works", CBS promoted American minimalist composers such as Steve Reich and Terry Riley as if they were rock stars, while Britain's Island label saw similar potential in French electronics boffin Pierre Henri and "Samurai of Sound" Stomu Yamash'ta, a percussion virtuoso awarded a classical Grammy for an album of pieces by Henze and

Maxwell Davies. In tall, long-haired John Tavener, perhaps Ringo of all people had stumbled on some sort of English equivalent.

Tavener had attended Highgate School before gaining a scholarship at the Royal Academy of Music, where he ditched his keyboard studies to concentrate solely on composition. Pop passed him by because, he said, "It hasn't got much to do with what I'm doing."[13] At the Royal Albert Hall Proms in 1968, his first major works, *The Whale* and the BBC-commissioned *The Alium* were applauded rabidly, thus establishing Tavener as a behemoth of what Ringo called "underground classical music"[12] when, via the local grapevine, he listened to a cassette of a BBC broadcast of *The Whale*. Contacted at his parents' Wembley address, a bemused Tavener – only vaguely aware of The Beatles' stature – was invited to Compton Avenue, where in his enthusiasm Ringo had set up a meeting at Savile Row with Lennon and Ron Kass, manager of Apple Records, with the intention of discussing a record deal.

More than even the *Wonderwall* soundtrack, *The Whale* was an intellectual challenge rather than entertainment to the common consumer. Juxtaposing the Jonah story with laudable anxiety about ills perpetrated against sea mammals by humans, Tavener's frame of reference embraced the pioneering tonalities of the post-serialists – unorthodox tone clusters, free choral babbling and a sound painting of Jonah being vomited onto the shore. Not Gilbert and Sullivan, either, was 'Melodrama And Pantomime' with its explosions and megaphone shrieking, although another movement, 'The Storm', was surprisingly subdued, an unlikely link with 'Octopus' Garden' and its "we would be warm below the storm/in our little hideaway beneath the waves".

Sales of *The Whale*, its creator's "serious" credibility and guaranteed Radio 3 exposure were just enough to make a second Tavener album – of three shorter and more theatrical pieces – a worthwhile exercise. Its main track, 'Celtic Requiem (Requiem For Jenny Jones)', had been scored for the London Sinfonietta in 1968. Tavener's observations of "a very strong connection between children and death"[14] were underlined musically with a preoccupation with E flat, as Riley's 'In C' was with its implied key. Nevertheless, recurrent children's play rhymes (by Little Missenden Primary School pupils) were suspended over instrumental ensembles and a soprano tackling a mainly Irish and Latin libretto. Also taped at St John the Evangelist Church, a cavernous Islington edifice, were 'Nomine Jesu' and 'Coplas', both more stubbornly chromatic and of more obviously Christian bent than 'Celtic Requiem'.

Discounting drivel like *Electronic Sounds* and the Lennons' self-centred soul-baring, Ringo's discovery was responsible for Apple's most adventurous releases. Tavener's commercial downfall, however, was less to do with his music than with Derek Taylor's retrospective confession, "We didn't promote it. We really couldn't."[15]

At just over £30,000, Ringo's was but the smallest individual Beatle overdraft now harrying the company ledgers. Overnight, glib unconcern deferred to pointed questions – "as business men, not Beatles,"[16] verified Ringo – regarding the whereabouts of the colour television and fitted carpet that vanished from the Lennons' room and questions such as, Which typist phones Canberra every afternoon? Why had so-and-so given himself a rise of £60 a week? Why is he seen only on pay day?

After Allen Klein proved his worth by procuring the promised higher royalty rate for The Beatles, John had persuaded Ringo and George to support the official appointment of the New Jersey go-getter to steer the ship back on course. Even Paul – who didn't want to trust Allen – had to applaud the cessation of all of the embezzlements and fiddles. Suddenly, it was beans on toast in the office kitchen instead of Beluga caviar from Fortnum & Mason.

Something of a pop personality in his own right these days, Allen was not above granting interviews to relevant organs. "I intend to make [Apple] financially successful and tailored to The Beatles' own specifications," he vowed to *Melody Maker*, "but when you get a lot of energy wasted, it doesn't make for an efficient organisation."[17] As old retainers were cast adrift, sinecures discontinued and a clocking-in system installed, Starr concurred with Klein: "We used to keep everyone on until our new business manager came along and showed us the real facts of what they were all doing. A lot of them got sacked because they weren't doing their jobs, and that's fair. They would usually hate you for it, but that doesn't bother me."[18]

Even the enterprise's only true money-spinner, Apple Records, was subject to cuts as unviable releases were cancelled and contracts unrenewed. "If you have a big tree with a thousand million roses," pontificated Ringo, "prune it down and you'll get maybe ten fantastic roses. That's what's happening."[19] Starr and Harrison, components of the most fantastic rose of all, teased both journalists and themselves with talk of a follow-up to *Abbey Road*: "There's nothing wrong with The Beatles," chirped Ringo in as late as March 1970. "When we've got something to do, we'll do it. We're all in touch."[20] A return to the stage was "unlikely, but you can never tell with us",[21] he winked. Ere 1969 was out, however, he hedged his bets with a planned solo LP, which – unlike *Two Virgins, Electronic Sounds et al* – was to be marketed as if it was a *bona fide* group record.

When John Citizen read the "shock" announcement in December that the LP *Ringo Starrdust* was to be recorded for issue in 1970, three tracks were actually already in the can, while the rest would be cut in time for rush-release in March. While the concept of collecting every disc that The Beatles ever made was not yet economically unsound, buyers still scanned the provisional track listing with trepidation – 'Whispering Grass', 'Love Is A Many Splendoured Thing' and 'Autumn Leaves'. "The only good thing to come out of the break-up was the opportunity to buy four Beatles albums a year," reckoned a future member of post-punk act Squeeze, "and then I heard Ringo's first album. I left it at a party one night."[22] Many other home fans would also be listening to successive Starr records *before* purchase.

"I really dug all that old music," Ringo explained, "because that was the first I ever heard, and I thought, 'My mum'll be pleased if I sing all those songs.'"[23] Apparently, the notion had been fermenting for a couple of years and, with the group in abeyance, time hung heavy. Like the man who paid to conduct the London Symphony Orchestra at the Albert Hall for just one night, Ringo had the wherewithal to fulfil a dream.

While *Ringo Starrdust* was as self-indulgent in its way as mucking around with a synthesiser, at least a Beatle was taking on "decent" music instead of any John-and-Yoko crap. EMI retailers' attention could also be directed to its George Martin production and Starr's hire of arrangers of the calibre of Quincy Jones, Count Basie's Chico O'Farrell, Johnny Dankworth and some of his own musical cronies, such as Klaus Voorman and Maurice Gibb. Because he'd impressed Ringo with his orchestrations on the *God Bless Tiny Tim* album, Richard Perry was chosen to frame a version of Doris Day's 'Sentimental Journey', which he invested with a new American device called a Vocoder.

To stress the selling point of nostalgia, the cover and full-page advertisements would show a dapper Ringo in front of a mock-up of the mean junction on which the towering Empress pub stood. Some of his Liverpool relations would gaze from the windows. In its bar, all of the aged standards on the record had once poured from ale-choked mouths and flushed, happy faces. Indeed, the promotional shot – directed by Neil Aspinall – would be of Ringo backed by The Talk Of The Town Orchestra crooning 'Sentimental Journey', which had been seen to make greater sense as the album's title than *Ringo Starrdust*.

'Autumn Leaves' and a version of 'I'll Be Seeing You' were also rejected. You wonder what they were like when assessing the numbers that did survive. The immaculate scoring was exemplified by the few bars of fluid saxophone busking that leaped from the horn riffing on O'Farrell's 'Night And Day', the glissando swoops of Voorman's violins in Ted Daffan's 'I'm A Fool To Care' or Elmer Bernstein's witty 'Have I Told You Lately That I Love You?' *leitmotifs*.

"He sings better than you'd expect him to,"[24] wrote a

particularly snowblinded reviewer. Unchanged to the pressing plant went a misjudged note on the coda of 'Bye Bye Blackbird' and some brief but dubious scatting in Fats Waller's 'Blue Turning Grey Over You'. *Sentimental Journey* certainly contained material tried by the likes of Crosby, Sinatra and Matt Monro, but none were so deluded to think Starr a quality vocalist any more than Johnnie Ray – an entertainer, incidentally, whom I am perverse enough to admire. Who cares if *Sentimental Journey* isn't real singing? Admittedly, on more than one outing, it could have been a faceless anyone, but otherwise, as Ringo would assure you himself, "Once my voice comes over on the radio or record, you know it's me."[24]

Those touchy about the original 78s of the LP selections may not acquiesce, but, although I'd never have bought corny *Sentimental Journey* myself, I felt that Ringo's humble vocal endowment, with its hit-or-miss pitching and untutored phrasing, compounded a mesmerically hideous charm common to certain singers who superimpose a disjointed range and eccentric delivery onto a given song's melodic and lyrical grid. Others in this idiosyncratic oligarchy are asthmatic Keith Relf, laconic Dave Berry and Reg Presley, with his Long John Silver burr. Nonetheless, the hoisting of *Sentimental Journey* high up Top 40s throughout the world testified less to this virtue than to the value of showing the title clip on such as *The Ed Sullivan Show* and a media jaunt made by Ringo in the flesh. "The great thing was that it got me moving," said the artiste, "not very fast, but just moving. It was like the first shovel of coal in the furnace that makes the train inch forward."[25]

Although it was announced that there were "absolutely no plans"[26] for its release, 'It Don't Come Easy' was typical of many Starr compositions that studio onlookers like Richard Perry would "hear grow until it becomes a real song".[27] Under George Harrison's supervision, three versions of 'It Don't Come Easy' were recorded during the graveyard hours on 18 January at Apple with help from a movable feast of musicians that included Stills, Eric Clapton – and Voorman, with whom Ringo would become associated "like Bill and Ben"[11] as a competent rhythm section on numerous records for a cabal of musicians, mostly expatriate Americans on the make.

Ringo would plead that they "only want me because of the way I play",[11] but, as most had endured an age of anonymous studio drudgery, perhaps they'd also ascertained that breathing the air around The Beatles was a springboard, if to not fame, then to a stronger negotiating stance for more extortionate session fees. Some had arrived with Delaney And Bonnie And Friends, an amalgam from Los Angeles' 'Blue-Eyed Soul School' to whom Eric Clapton had rendered practical endorsement with finance for a European tour and a place in their ranks as lead guitarist. Harrison, too, was roped in after he and the Starkeys attended the troupe's London concert in December.

If not indulging himself on the boards, Ringo was overwhelmed by the Friends' ebullience and flattered to be requested to help out on this demo or that backing track. Phonetically pliant as he was, keeping such company affected his vocabulary. Suddenly, a "guy" – not a bloke – "balled" a "chick", instead of a bird. You didn't go to the toilet any more but to the "john". He was loud, too, in praise of the Friends' drummer, Jim Gordon, and his successor, Jim Keltner, who, on a par with Hal Blaine, now, echoed Starr's eternal opinion that "drummers don't need to be so tricky. The best ones for me are the ones with less technique to show off."[28]

Ringo didn't always practise what he preached. On a take for a Doris Troy session, "I forgot what I was doing and made a lot of noise just to cover up. [I] never forgave myself."[28] Such aberrations aside, he earned an accolade when rattling the traps on an eponymous LP by multi-instrumentalist Leon Russell, whose perpetual on-stage top hat and star-studded LP credits were symptomatic of in-crowd acknowledgment that he was the epitome of the smug sexism and "funky" rhythmic jitter of the interchangeable Delaney And Bonnie "super sidemen", who, crowed their saxophonist, "went on to back all the players that really do have a lot of influence".[29] You didn't need to hear a self-

absorbed Friend's "laid-back" solo album to know what it was like
– maybe four songs on each side, all delivered in a nonchalantly
"raunchy" caw and bloated with hip restricted code and dragged-
out fades, it would dwell on balling chicks, "toking" and being on
the road with a rock 'n' roll band. Yet Ringo was willing to play
with them. "I'll play with anyone, but I like to know at least one
person there."[11]

After over six hours spent labouring with Harrison and The
Grease Band's bass guitarist for *Leon Russell*, Ringo "amazed the
shit out of me"[30]. Russell was especially impressed that his versatile
Beatle assistant was up to "that New Orleans syncopation"[30] on
'Shoot-Out At The Plantation', shrill 'Pisces Apple Lady' (about a
Savile Row employee with whom Leon had "got it together") and
'Delta Lady', a retread of a single by Joe Cocker, who – with Russell
and other former Friends – would form the cumbersome Mad Dogs
And Englishmen.

Considerably more prestigious than aiding Russell was Ringo's
part in albums recorded in London by BB King and the late Howlin'
Wolf. Since the blues boom of *circa* 1968, many revered black
practitioners in the evenings of their lives had been advised to gear
their music for a wider forum by reprising their classics with some of
the renowned white musicians that they had inspired. Although Wolf
had been disappointed with the US outfit used on *Electric Wolf*, his
first album of this persuasion, the deferential humour and glad co-
operation of producer Glyn Johns' British volunteers for 1970's
London Sessions was more satisfactory – although, with Starr,
Voorman and Clapton, "Monday's session wasn't too successful at
all," growled Wolf, "but yesterday we managed to get four sides cut,
and it was really great."[29]

After initial awe in their wizened presences, Ringo concluded
that working for Wolf and, later, BB King (alongside personnel that
also included Charlie Watts, Alexis Korner and Dr John) was "no
more important to me than sessions with John or George".[11] He was
also among stalwarts reeled in by Harrison for his *All Things Must
Pass*. According to Ringo, "he paid his dues"[19] on this triple album,

the first evidence that George had broken cover as a true solo artist. The album absorbed an immortalisation of its participants' arrogance in 'Apple Jam' – a whole two sides of meandering extemporisations that Ringo "didn't play much"[19] – and a less tedious majority of George's accumulated songs, including 'Behind That Locked Door', which addressed itself to hopes and apprehensions about Bob Dylan's first major engagement since his motorcycle mishap. Dutifully, the Harrisons, Starkeys and Lennons turned out for this set (with The Band) at the Isle of Wight Pop Festival in September 1969.

Later that month, because he'd just left Middlesex Hospital after three days' observation for an intestinal complaint, it wasn't Ringo but session drummer Alan White who'd been asked along when a new Lennon composition, 'Cold Turkey', was previewed by a hastily rehearsed Plastic Ono Band at a Canadian event similar to Dylan's comeback. If uxoriously shy-making at times, Lennon's outpourings were leaner and tastier meat than Harrison's, and Starr had not been tardy in offering his services for a studio remake of 'Cold Turkey', John's second hit 45 without The Beatles. With Maureen, Ringo had also deputised for John and Yoko – recovering from a road accident – at the Chelsea Town Hall press launch of its predecessor, 'Give Peace A Chance'. In return, while no fellow Beatle had metaphorically held Ringo's hand for the unveiling of *Candy*, the Lennons had been there on for *The Magic Christian* charity première, albeit bearing a placard daubed with the slogan of another cause they'd been incited to support.

As far as Starr was concerned, McCartney's absence on these occasions was of his own choosing, rather than ostracism by the other Beatles. He and Linda had been invited to the New Year celebration at Compton Avenue, and the Starkeys had joined them as spectators on the opening night of Mary Hopkin's season at the Savoy. It seemed to be all smiles professionally, too, with Ringo's rataplans still detectable on Hopkin records and Paul arranging Hoagy Carmichael's 'Stardust' for *Sentimental Journey*.

Starr was to inform his solicitor that *Sentimental Journey* was one bone of contention to which McCartney alluded, late one afternoon at Cavendish Avenue, during a tongue-lashing of such violence that Ringo could no longer imagine that The Beatles would regroup. "We'd gone as far as we could with each other."[31] As well as the lines drawn over Klein, there loomed a market collision detrimental to the sales of all if, as scheduled, *Sentimental Journey*, *Let It Be* and Paul's eponymous solo LP all reached the shops in the same spring month. Separate letters from each of his colleagues supplicating Paul to postpone *McCartney* were awaiting delivery, and Ringo, brusquely scribbling autographs while hurrying down Apple's steps to his waiting Mercedes, "didn't think it fair that some office lad should take something like that 'round".[11] At Paul's place, he identified himself on the intercom and was welcomed for what began as a friendly chat until underlying tension came to a head when Paul "told me to get out of his house. He went crazy. He just shouted and pointed at me. I couldn't believe it was happening."[11]

Outside that banged front door, Ringo strove to detach himself from this unprecedented upset: "It's only like a brother. You mustn't pretend that brothers don't fight, because they fight worse than anybody."[11] *En route* to an immediate conference with George and John, he decided on the line of least resistance: *Sentimental Journey* would be brought forward, "which makes me seem like a good guy, but I wasn't really, because I needed to put it out before or else Paul's album would have slayed me. And it did."[24] Half a million sales for *Sentimental Journey* seems quite healthy, but you can understand why Ringo might have eaten his heart out when McCartney garnered two million in US advance orders alone.

That June, Starr elected to strike while the iron was lukewarm with a long-mooted album of country and western, then the squarest, most right-wing genre in pop. Nevertheless, it had started to remove itself from earlier association with lowbrow redneck antagonism towards commies, niggers, queers and hippies – even if, in 1970, a Houston radio station had been twice fire-bombed by some good ol' boys who begged to differ with its radical, anti-draft slant.

Taking their cue from the popularity of spaghetti westerns and Nashville's spellbinding gaudiness, multitudinous licensed premises of the early 1970s had been transformed into parodies of Dodge City saloons. Barging through the swinging half doors of an Edinburgh pub or Auckland bar, you'd bump into Calamity Jane lookalikes and stetsoned quaffers of Southern Comfort. Belying daytime guises as janitors or computer programmers, conversations would be peppered with Deep South slang – "mess of grits" for "plate of food" – picked up from Merle Haggard albums. On a nicotine-clouded stage, the band would crank out 'Okie From Muskogee', 'Crystal Chandelier' or 'Polk Salad Annie'. If these mightn't have made the charts, they were at least as well known as many that had.

Another sound fiscal argument for Starr's intention was that, lately, The Byrds, Neil Young and – as Ringo had observed first hand, at a London showcase – ex-Monkee Mike Nesmith had all "gone country", while Keith Richards and Gram Parsons (of Byrds offshoot The Flying Burrito Brothers) had discussed possible fusions of country and classic rock for an audience still biased against one or the other. Furthermore, both Jerry Lee Lewis and Charlie Rich had managed recent comebacks in the *Billboard* Country And Western chart.

The first choice as Ringo's producer was Bob Johnston, who'd been at the console for Dylan's austere *John Wesley Harding* and its *Nashville Skyline* follow-up. Johnston satisfied busy Starr that the album could be completed as quickly as one Beatles track, without fussy overdubs and retakes. Bob was also amenable to cutting it in England, "but he wanted a lot of bread, so I decided not to do it with him".[19] Instead, Ringo gave the job to the steel guitarist on the Dylan records, Pete Drake, a 39-year-old virtuoso equally at ease improvising the orthodox "Nashville sound" for entertainers as diverse as Elvis, Perry Como, The Monkees – and George Harrison, who'd had him flown to London's Trident Studios for *All Things Must Pass*. Ringo remembered, "I had to fetch him from the office one day, and he was in my car and I had all these country tapes, and we got talking about country music."[19]

Drake advocated Nashville's Music City complex as the most fitting setting to cut the kinda tunes folk like a-tappin' their shoe leather to. They could begin next week. Starr had started an opus, 'Band Of Steel', which namechecked Hank Williams and lesser country legends in much the same manner as Cowboy Copas' 'Hillbilly Heaven'. It was not, however, among those selected from more than a hundred new copyrights grubbed – possibly over-hastily – from demo tapes in offices clotted round 16th Avenue, the Tin Pan Alley of Nashville. As Buck Owens sang in 'Songwriters Lament', there were "songwriters under every rock". Ringo "was with a few guys with guitars, and we were picking out the songs I liked".[19] To be published by Startling Music, those shortlisted were mostly lachrymose ballads, often just a few degrees from schmaltz, with titles such as 'Silent Homecoming', 'Loser's Lounge' and 'Love Don't Last Long'. All bar 1968's 'Wine, Women And Loud Happy Songs' had been written in 1970, mostly by either Sorrells Pickard or Chuck Howard, guitarists on the sessions.

This pair also belonged to the pool of city musicians whose close knowledge of each other's capabilities grew from playing together as accompanists at the Grand Ole Opry and on countless daily record dates. Some of these craftsmen were recording artists in their own right. Drake himself had won a gold disc for a 1963 single, 'Forever', and was planning *The Steel Beatle*, an instrumental LP of Lennon-McCartney numbers. Just as distinguished were Buddy Harman – the bass player on Roy Orbison's biggest hits – and guitarist Jerry Reed, composer of Presley's 'Guitar Man', the 1968 smash that convinced many that the King had returned to form. Other Presley associates enlisted by Drake for Starr were the celebrated Jordanaires vocal quartet, engineer Scotty Moore – more familiar as a guitarist – and, regarded with sentimental reverence by Ringo, drummer DJ Fontana.

With brisk finesse, 20 tracks – for trimming down to a strong but soothing single album – were ready within three days, although for much of the first morning Ringo "was really nervous, and Pete would say through the glass, 'Hoss, if you don't get loose, I'm going to come in there and stomp on your toes.'"[20] So lacking in conviction – and accurate pitching – was he at first that a Jordanaire was instructed to sing along in unison over the headphones. Even so, suspect high notes – such as that which concluded 'Without Her' – remained and had to be veiled in reverberation.

The mood, nevertheless, relaxed sufficiently to bring forth perhaps the most adept singing of Starr's career. Soon, he was joining in whenever someone kicked off a bout of informal jamming while warming up for the next track. All inhibitions gone, he even strummed one-chord acoustic guitar and ranted perfunctory lyrics for a 25-minute work-out. Ebbing zeal for issuing this as one side of a future LP still resulted in an excerpt appearing as 'Coochy Coo' on an Italian A-side – and a US flip-side beneath the album's title song, 'Beaucoups Of Blues', which, in a swirl of fiddles and Drake's metallic careen, crept into the lower half of the Hot 100.

Among brighter choices for a fanfare 45 were the episodic 'Love Don't Last Long'; 'Fastest-Growing Heartache In The West', a rootin'-tootin' narrative about a corrupted Beverly Hills housewife and her tired hillbilly husband; or 'I Wouldn't Have You', a virtual duet with Jeannie Kendal. As well as sustaining the ambiguous atmosphere of enjoyable melancholy, 'I'd Be Talking All The Time' had Ringo as a homespun prairie Plato, while he was cast as the prodigal, guitar-pickin' scion of a wealthy family for '15-Dollar Draw'. Even better suited to his hangdog voice, 'Woman Of The Night' was the *cri du coeur* of some poor, uncomplaining fool in love with a tearsheet.

A flawed but altogether reasonable record of its kind, *Beaucoups Of Blues* deserved more than a wretched struggle to Number 65 in the States and no chart placing whatsoever at home, where more vivid memories lingered of the pig in a poke that was *Sentimental Journey*.

What else could he do? A Beatle fan – if not member – for life, Ringo "was not interested in being in a new band. I was bigger than any band I could have joined."[21] Bolstering all of his objections in principle, an album of drum solos was out of the question, because abler technicians such as Jon Hiseman – another *Leon Russell* helpmate – or Ginger Baker could wipe the floor with Ringo Starr. Besides, Cozy Powell, fresh from The Jeff Beck Group, was about to fill what he'd perceived as a market void for a Sandy Nelson of the 1970s.

As for films, Ringo vacillated between a desire for "a serious role that calls for some real acting to show I can do it"[16] and "to be a character actor sort of like Peter Sellers. I wouldn't mind doing a musical. When I'm 45, it would be kidding myself to try to be a pop star, but you can make films when you're 50."[32] Founded in wishful thinking, too, was a Hollywood Western, and his acquisition of a script "for a science-fiction film which I'm trying to get together", although he could not divulge its title. "There's a big part for me, the biggest I've done. Apart from that, I've no other film waiting at the moment."[33]

As his small-screen guest spots increased, the quality of Ringo's performances so improved that he was accepted in comedy circles as both a joker and a fair "feed" (a straight man who reacts to phoney insults). During a *Magic Christian* publicity blitz in the US, he'd made cameo headway with a sketch on the cult comedy series *Laugh In*. "Sometimes they don't catch me," was his doleful riposte to Joanne Worley's remark about how wonderful it must be for him when girl fans chased him.

During this trip, Ringo's presence was announced from the stage at one of Elvis Presley's cabaret pageants at the International Hotel in Las Vegas. "There wasn't a lot of the old stuff," moaned Apple executive Peter Brown. "He left us old rockers wanting more."[34] When Brown and the Starkeys wormed their way backstage to pay respects afterwards, so began weeks of speculation that Ringo, Elvis and Raquel Welch were to team up for an imminent TV spectacular, but, sighed Starr, "It was just dragging on too long, what with the preparations and the talks and Elvis having other commitments. I told Elvis I couldn't wait – it was holding me up – and he could see my point."[35] With Ringo as proud guest of honour at the Cannes showing of *Woodstock*, Presley's private abhorrence of this and other movies' glorifying of hippy sub-culture (of which he saw The Beatles as a part) was probably at the root of his dilatoriness.

In the wake of *Sentimental Journey*, Ringo had already been approached to entertain diners for a season in Las Vegas *à la* Elvis. His deep thought before declining – "I wouldn't mind, but it would mean putting an act together"[36] – demonstrated the appeal of mainstream showbusiness. The Fourmost, The Swinging Blue Jeans, Billy J Kramer and lesser lights of dear, dead Mersey Beat were attempting to tread that path, too. Even tongue-tied Rory Storm had hung up his rock 'n' roll shoes and was commuting as a disc jockey between engagements in Benidorm, Amsterdam and the Silver Blades ice rink back in Liverpool. At another extreme, 1970's Television Personality Of The Year, Cilla Black, was starring in the extravaganza *Way Out In Piccadilly* with Frankie Howerd. Up in the West End, too, Starr and Lennon had been there on the night that Gerry Marsden had gladly taken over the male lead from Joe Brown in *Charlie Girl*, which ran and ran.

After a fashion, Paul McCartney – with his sketchy "granny music" and irrepressible spirit when in the limelight – awaited a destiny as a showbiz evergreen. By late 1970, he'd set irreversible wheels in motion for the official dissolution of The Beatles. "Suddenly your brain gets twisted and you do strange things," lamented Ringo. "I just kept thinking, 'What's he doing it to me for?', but then I realised he's got to do it to get what he wants, so I don't put him down for that. [But] you'd get lawyers coming 'round day and night, millions of affidavits, too many problems that I didn't want to do because I just wanted to play. We got a bit catcalling, which really wasn't right, but we had to go through it."[11]

While clouds of litigation gathered, all four parties were "tight, nervous, everyone watching everyone else",[37] noticed the forgiving Cynthia Lennon, who, with her new spouse, was "at home" one day for well-wishers that included her increasingly distant Beatle pals and ex-husband. "Everyone was wondering," recalled Ringo, "and I was the one who wondered longest."[38]

At a Hollywood press binge for *The Magic Christian*, Ringo had sidestepped questions about The Beatles, as he'd deemed them irrelevant to the function's purpose, and also because he didn't want the painful truth to hang as a vibration in the air. A year later, when the case was declared in Paul's favour and Apple's finances placed under the Official Receiver's scrutiny, Ringo Starr could no more not believe it was happening: "I felt so absolutely lost. I went into hiding to escape the pressures. You just sit around the house like everyone else does. You go to London or you go shopping or to see a film or watch telly."[21]

11 "I Love It When They Let Me Go Off On My Own"

Even when weakened by the after-effects of pneumonia in 1972, Elsie Graves continued to sort out and pass on the hundreds of letters that still arrived for Richie, who still spent Christmases in Liverpool, among those who loved him best. Long resigned to how he made his living, Elsie was overjoyed to fuss over her famous son and his family for a few uninterrupted days. Paying duty calls on elderly relations and his mother's intimates, he seemed the same as ever on the surface.

Many of his old stomping grounds, however, were much changed. The Rialto was now a warehouse, the Locarno a sports club and the Mardi Gras flattened to create space for a multi-storey car park. Although Ringo and others had put their eminence at proprietor Roy Adams' disposal, this only drew out the ultimate agony when the sinking of an underground railway shaft would necessitate the demolition of the Cavern, too. Since its 1966 facelift, the club had kept a ritual weekly "Beatle Hour" of records spun in regretful affection for the departed "Four Lads Who Shook The World", as a plaque in Mathew Street would read after the English Tourist Board latched onto its cradling of The Beatles when pop's history became as lucrative as its present.

A pop memorabilia auction had been held in New York in as early as October 1970, with Pete Townshend's broken guitar and a Cadillac that had once transported The Beatles its dearest lots. Already, there was a sense not so much of nostalgia as impending hangover after the Swinging '60s. On the cards were "British

Invasion" reunion tours of the States, which gave a welcome cash transfusion to many old acts, among them The Searchers and Billy J Kramer. Although *a* Big Three would cut a 1973 album, Ian And The Zodiacs had thrown in the towel after turning down 'Even The Bad Times Are Good', which later cracked the UK Top Five when picked up by The Tremeloes.

Other unlucky Mersey Beat brethren had returned to secure anonymity via application form or beseeching telephone call. Like demobbed servicemen, they'd often find their old jobs waiting for them. Some would reappear at the parochial venues from whence they came, but real or imagined horrors about this unmarried mother or that outraged Mr Big from Germany obliged certain ex-beat group musicians to renege on their past and jump at shadows.

Dame Fortune granted a few another bite at the showbusiness cherry. Billy Fury's former pianist, Lancastrian Peter Skellern, made it in his own right with 1972's 'You're A Lady', although Ringo qualified that its homely brass-band backing "was more of a hook than he was".[1] Closer to home, Tony Waddington and Wayne Bickerton, former "Lennon-McCartney" of The Pete Best Combo, created the chartbusting Rubettes from session players in 1974. Best himself had gone "into a different kind of lifestyle"[2] as a civil servant.

Another denied the acclaim he may have merited was Rory Storm, who died in his Stormsville bedroom in September 1972 after an injudicious quantity of whiskey washed down tablets prescribed for a respiratory infection. A lay verdict on Violet Caldwell's suicide the next morning was that her golden boy's demise was too grievous to be borne, coming as it did so soon after that of her husband in May.

A couple of the national tabloids that headlined the tragedy carried a quote from Shane Fenton – now back in the Top Ten as Alvin Stardust – comparing his brother-in-law favourably with Rod Stewart. Ringo had also been tapped for his feelings about his old boss, with whom he'd long lost touch. No, he wouldn't be at either the cemetery or the wake, because "I wasn't there when he was born, either."[3] Pressured newshounds who'd never heard of Storm seized on another big-name link in Cilla Black, who had just sacrificed a day's break from a Blackpool variety season to tape – with Starr and George Harrison in attendance – 'When Every Song Is Sung', a Harrison song meant originally for Shirley Bassey.

Because his debut on *Cilla* had gone down so well, Ringo had been chosen for a spot in the second series. Shot on location at a Scandinavian ski resort, it was not a particularly enjoyable chore, marred as it was by a Professor Thorolf Rafto selling a chance conversation with the ex-Beatle as an exclusive to a Norwegian newspaper and another report of a tipsy Starr's facetiousness in refusing to cough up even a symbolic coin to a World Refugee charity until the English football results were obtained for him.

Now that the protective bubble of Beatlehood had burst, there'd be further evidence that Ringo wasn't Mr Normal after all – but probably he never had been in the first place. He'd still imply that a typical evening *chez* Starkey was spent slumped in front of the colour TV, and he switched on the old Fab Four charm when required, as he did when doggy eyes, a grin and autographs settled the matter when police pulled him over for suspected drunken driving. When in his cups, he would dismiss his chauffeur and try to win bets with Maureen over how quickly he could race the Mercedes to some fashionable London niterie – usually Tramps in Jermyn Street – where whirring Nikons would herald their skidding arrival. On one such dash, Starr took a bend too speedily. A tree ricocheted him back onto the road.

Richie's private sweetness remained apparent to Cilla when, unknown to her, the Starkeys had, by coincidence, booked a bungalow in the same hotel grounds in Antibes. He jumped out from out behind a rock, roaring like a lion as Cilla, her husband and their push-chaired son were taking the air one morning. This good-natured ambush precipitated a pleasant holiday for the two families. The only sour note was struck during the Starkeys' farewell dinner for the Blacks. After Ringo had turned his nose up at more exotic fare on the menu, the French waiter uncovered his order of fried egg and – so the chef had understood – crisps. No one at the table could prevent Starr, his rage sharpened with Dom Perignon, from berating the hotel manager, whose kitchen had "ruined my friends' last evening here".[5]

Once bitten, he emphasised to the galley cook that with every meal was to be served "*pommes frites* to you, not chips, because those are crisps in your language"[5] when the Blacks and Harrisons were among guests on SS *Marala*, the luxury yacht – with original masterpieces on its walls – that Ringo had hired for the duration of 1971's Cannes film festival. As 'Octopus' Garden' had been born at sea, so he and George pieced together an opus entitled 'Photograph' with, recalled Cilla, "everyone on board chipping in with bits for it".[5] Some months afterwards, Ringo proffered a newer opus, 'Back Off Boogaloo', when Cilla was shortlisting material for her next single. She preferred 'Photograph', but her plea for a demo had already been met with Ringo saying, "No, it's too bloody good for you. I'm having it myself."[5]

He could be as less affectionately rude to entertainers he didn't know, too, especially the latest teen idols, such as The Osmonds, Jackson Five, Bay City Rollers and "that lumberjack",[1] David Cassidy. Although Rollermania was rampant among schoolgirls for several months, none of these callow newcomers shaped up remotely as either new Beatles or new Elvi,[6] but they did not warrant Starr's disparagement of them as "no-talent bands or talent that's been forced".[1] Under pressure, he'd admit to listening to The Jackson Five for their precocious youngest member, Michael – "the only kid I really like in that respect. Usually, a kid in a show gets all the sympathy applause: 'He's only two foot eight and he got up there and sang that song.' It's a load of rubbish."[1]

Starr's uncharitable surliness and increased alcohol intake were detectable in the immediate aftermath of The Beatles. He had taken the group's messy finish the hardest and, for longer than the other former members, "would not rule out that one day we might play together again. Just say the feeling is based on my natural optimism."[7] In the event, however, he would hope that "no single

Beatle could ever again dominate the others".[7] With McCartney the fly in the ointment, a rumour spread that Ringo, John and George were to try again with Klaus Voorman, as The Ladders.

When both were guests at Mick Jagger's San Tropez wedding in May 1971, Ringo had nattered awkwardly with Paul, whom he hadn't seen since the McCartneys had left London for their Scottish home from home shortly after the unpleasantness at Cavendish Avenue. A fortnight later, Ringo received a copy of his old chum's second post-Beatles LP. As skimpy as *McCartney*, *Ram* was worthy for only "a couple of lines, that's all", in Starr's opinion. "It's like he's not admitting that he can write great tunes. I just feel he's let me down."[8]

Blunter still was John's view that his estranged colleague's efforts were "rubbish".[9] From watching helplessly as the two pilloried each other in the press and even record grooves, Starr's allegiance to the Lennon camp was strengthened by McCartney's social and professional boat-burning and John's need of a drummer with whom he'd "played together so long that it fits"[9] to keep unostentatious pace on the two "his and hers" Plastic Ono Band albums that resulted from the Lennons' course of primal-scream therapy under American psychologist Dr Arthur Janov. "There's no real toe-tappers on it,"[8] was Starr's understatement on John's bald personal exorcisms and regurgitant confessions – 'Mother', 'Isolation' and so forth – as well as the spurning of former ideals and heroes (notably in 'God') and self-projection as 'Working-Class Hero', a track without percussion that was banned from BBC airwaves for its use of the f-word. It was "an all-time great" to loyal Ringo, who could "sit with some people and they swear and you think, 'Christ, stop it!', and you can sit with people who swear because it's a word, and that's how it was on the album."[8]

However gravely cathartic the released result, the sessions were more fun than *Abbey Road* and closer to the spirit of Mersey Beat than *Let It Be* had ever been, as Voorman and Starr reacted instinctively whenever guitarist Lennon warmed up, as always, with ancient rockers half remembered from the Cavern. Surfacing on later bootlegs were Lennon's knockabout reclamations of 'Honey Don't' and 'Matchbox' from Ringo.

Whatever avant-garde changes her improvisations rang, not even the slowest-witted fan hoped for ersatz Beatle magic from Yoko. With a musical past not accordant with that of her accompanists, Yoko's looser jamming on her *Plastic Ono Band* outing and its *Fly* follow-up were less governed by common time and rote-learnt chord patterns. Just as pre-ordained were the wordless orgiastic moans and nanny-goat vibrato as "OK Yoni" – so *Private Eye* lampooned her – ululated free-form like a front-line jazz horn over Ringo's patient beat.

If inwardly baffled by her, Ringo – like hundreds of other celebrities asked – contributed to Yoko's hastily organised "Water Event" at New York State's Everson Museum of Art, set to run for three weeks from 9 October 1971, her spouse's birthday. Starr's green plastic bag filled with the correct liquid was found a place among the steam engines, test-tubes, blotting paper, fish tanks, *et al* – not to mention the toilet customised to emit 'Working Class Hero' when flushed – and other banal exhibits that filled three halls. For Ringo and every other guest who didn't know much about art, the occasion climaxed at John's post-preview party, at which – with Phil Spector its heart and soul on a makeshift podium – the *omnes fortissimo* choruses of olde-tyme rock 'n' roll were mixed up with Beatles hits (including a 'Yellow Submarine' with Starr befuddled over the words) and *in absentia* "tributes" to Harrison and McCartney.

After an ITV chat show a month earlier, John had slipped across the Atlantic and, in the teeth of attempts to deport him for his drug conviction, was to reside in the States for as long as he lived. Among purported vocational tangents during his final months in England was writing and producing 'Four Nights In Moscow' for consideration as Ringo's maiden solo 45. However, Starr shied away from appearing as beholden to Lennon as he had been as a Beatle, arguing, "What I have to combat is the original image of me as the downtrodden drummer. You don't know how hard it is to fight that."[10]

Association with a non-melodic instrument to the rear of the stage prejudices the acceptance of pop drummers as serious composers – and even serious musicians – by those who imagine that any fool can bash drums. An off-the-cuff case is that of Yardbird Jim McCarty, who, despite co-writing his group's most enduring songs and his subsequent formation of Renaissance and lesser-known but equally adventurous outfits, suffered from years of categorisation as an incorrigible R&B swatter before recognition in the 1980s as a colossus of new age music, with pieces as innovative in their way as any in the Yardbirds/Renaissance canon. Other talents from behind the kit who were up against similar undervaluation include Thunderclap Newman's Speedy Keene, David Essex and – on the tail end of Mersey Beat – comedian Russ Abbott.

Rather than 'Four Nights In Moscow' (if it ever existed), Ringo Starr chose to blow the dust off 'It Don't Come Easy', which was his greatest work as a commercial songwriter – but perhaps I'm only saying that because it had once gone down well as a request in a grim metropolitan palais when I was singer with a quintet called Turnpike in the early 1970s. With only the vaguest clue about the verses, I had to make most of them up as I went along. Any meaning in Ringo's hard-won but sloganised lyrics had less importance than the cumulative effect of this sub-Spector production's prelusive fizz of cymbal; Harrison's clanging guitar arpeggios; the fat gusto of the horn section; Mal Evans' tambourine beefing up Voorman and Starr's moderato punch; gospel-esque backing harmonies; and the lugubrious carriage of a tune that the milkman could lilt on his round.

Helped on its way by *I-never-knew-he-had-it-in-him*-style reviews, 'It Don't Come Easy' deservedly outsold then-current offerings by George, John and Paul. While more intrinsic virtues swept it into Top Fives across the planet, those for whom The Beatles' regrouping was seen then as sure as the sunrise focused instead on the topical B-side, 'Early 1970', which would have gone in one ear and out the other had it not been possible to guess the identity of the distant comrades to whom its main subject – an instrumentalist of limited ability – alludes, one with "a brand-new wife", another "with his mama by his side, she's Japanese" and a third who's "always in town playing for you with me".

Ringo had been at so desperate a loss after *Abbey Road* that, to his own six-string tinkering on 'Early 1970', he'd wondered whether Paul, John and George were still going to "play with me". However, million-selling 'It Don't Come Easy' and its afterglow of instant self-esteem was buoyed with the inauguration of the first fan club devoted to Starr alone and his placing as Top Drummer in *NME*'s 1971 popularity poll, in which The Beatles had been superseded as Top Group by Creedence Clearwater Revival. (Just prior to his hit, he'd been at a lowly 13 place in *Beat Instrumental*'s tabulation.)

On 1 August that year, the *NME*'s Top Drummer had belied previous insistences that "personally, I don't want to play in public again"[11] by smacking the skins alongside Jim Keltner in George Harrison's spectacular at Madison Square Garden in aid of Bangladesh, prostrated as it was by disease and famine in the wake of a cyclone and an invading Moslem army. With *All Things Must Pass* its principal source of repertoire, George had drawn together the ex-Delaney And Bonnie minions, a small choir and – on acoustic guitars – three members of Badfinger to accompany more illustrious peers. Of these, only Starr and Billy Preston were punctual attendees at a rehearsal studio near Carnegie Hall. With two sold-out houses to entertain, as well as consumers of the event's movie and triple-album spin-offs, Harrison knocked together a disciplined presentation embracing nothing that hadn't been a smash for someone in the band or wasn't sufficiently well known for a spatter of clapping to swell and subside over its unannounced introduction. "We weren't out to just entertain each other," concurred Ringo. "It's no good just standing there with your guitar, freaking yourself out."[1]

On the night, Ringo "was crazy with nerves beforehand, [but] I enjoyed myself immensely. It was nice, anyway, because we had a lot of good pals around."[9] A sort of bloated 1970s equivalent of a "scream-circuit" package, it was held together by an adaptable combo common to a cache of "featured popular vocalists". These included Harrison himself; Preston, who supplemented his Apple hit 'That's The Way God Planned It' with some fancy footwork; and Ringo, who was loved for a distracted, breathless 'It Don't Come Easy'. He also rattled an apprehensive tambourine in the trio behind Bob Dylan, whom George had talked into a 20-minute spot before the big finish. As Dylan had been in hibernation since the Isle of Wight, George spoke for everyone when he said, "It was great to have him in it at all."[12]

Overlooked in the next morning's newspapers was the fact that it had also been Ringo Starr's first true stage show since Candlestick Park. Nevertheless, the barrage of cheering, stamping and whistling after 'It Don't Come Easy' had dissipated lingering twinges of disappointment about The Beatles' break-up. From the purposeless time-killing that followed *Beaucoups Of Blues*, he had made an indelible mark as a non-Beatle – as opposed to ex-Beatle – and now there were even handsomer dividends inherent in the work put his way these days.

That "it gave Ringo an opportunity"[12] had been one incentive for Allen Klein's underwriting of *Blindman*, an Italian-made spaghetti western that xeroxed the salient points of those that had recently hoisted Clint Eastwood, Lee Van Cleef and Charles Bronson to international acclaim. Indeed, like Eastwood's *A Fistful Of Dollars*, its plot was an Occidental rewrite of a Japanese picture.[13] Two a-penny then, cowboy films were also much in vogue for pop stars wishing to extend themselves. Bob Dylan's economic acting abilities, for example, would be realised with an apposite role as "Alias" in Sam Peckinpah's *Pat Garrett And Billy The Kid*, for which he also penned incidental music. Ringo, too, had donned spurs, "because it was so far from anything I'd ever done",[1] despite elements of *déjà vu* compounded in his part of a Mexican named "Candy" whose dastardly deeds embraced the ravishing of a pulchritudinous blonde played by a Swedish actress.

Although he disliked unnecessary sex and violence in the cinema himself, Klein thought it prudent to stress the more gory aspects of *Blindman* on posters. But, however much it reflected plebeian taste, the new picture would wait years before a rigorously scissored general release in Britain. One day, Ringo would see the censor's point. "It was over the edge," he later admitted. "There's a scene where all these women are running through the desert, trying to escape from us Mexican bandits, and we're just sitting on our horses picking them off."[14]

Resplendent in sombrero and dyed jet-black beard, Starr as Candy was proudly "evil from start to finish"[14] as psychotic brother of a chief bandido who kidnaps the intended brides of 50 Texan miners from a wagon train guided by The Good Guy. The word "guided" is crucial here, for the gringo in question was sightlessly feeling his route by relief map. However, his responsibility for many Boot Hill burials – including Candy's – would be testament that blindness was no barrier to his gunfighting expertise.

This risible plot was mitigated by the sands, cacti, stony hills and seas of dry mesquite grass around Almeria, the Spanish location of *Blindman*, just as it had been for *The Good, The Bad And The Ugly* and the two *Dollars* movies. Authentic, too, were the unwashed, olive faces of beggars hovering outside the town's Grand Hotel, where Ringo – muttering his lines over and over again – was joined by Klein and Mal Evans, both of whom would serve as extras when shooting began.

His watch and all but one of Starr's trademark rings were locked in the hotel safe so that the pallid circles of skin round his wrist and fingers could tan. Another headache for director Ferdinando Baldi was the homely Scouse intonation that simmered just beneath Latinate Candy's broken English, even if he was otherwise "real slimy"[15] or, at least, the film's investors wanted badly to believe he was. However, Ringo's performance – even when dubbed for the première in Rome on 15 November 1971 – actuated not vicarious loathing but mirth from paying customers, although "playing a cowboy" had made the butt of their humour "a hero to my children for the first time".[16]

He'd decided to "start every scene fairly straight and end up as an out-and-out madman".[1] His dementia might have verged on genuine at times, for – as well as the prickly heat and Baldi bragging later of keeping "the great Ringo waiting five hours for only one shot"[14] – he'd grown heartily fed up – and saddle-sore – with riding a horse so herculean that aid was required each time he mounted. Into the bargain, the main title song he'd written and produced (with Voorman) had been turned down. Instead of booming from the silver screen, it would B-side 'Back Off Boogaloo', tardy successor to 'It Don't Come Easy'.

Starr's most menacing creation, 'Blindman' ("best film part I've ever had"[17]), smouldered from a monochordal narrative verse, gathering tension via a bass-drum thud and a two-note synthesiser motif simulating a tuned guiro-castanet effect, the chorus springing from a sudden tacet. If not a precursor, neither was it dissimilar to 'Baby's On Fire', a minimalist "standard" by Brian Eno, then the thinking man's glam rocker. Certainly, it was more of an intellectual experience than straightforward 'Back Off Boogaloo', with Ringo's voice almost drowned in a unison chorus that went on and on and on. "Play me a pop song that isn't,"[3] he retorted when taken to task over how repetitious it was.

Supposedly a put-down of Paul McCartney, 'Back Off Boogaloo' was no profound insight into the human condition. On one Sunday, Starr had woken up with the melody in his head as he hunched over a guitar downstairs. "It just all came out, all the verses part, and then I was watching the football on the telly in the afternoon and [commentator] Jimmy Hill said, 'That was a tasty goal' about someone, and I said, 'Tasty! What a nice word!' and rushed over again, and that's how I got the middle."[18]

Quasi-military drum tattoos that punctuated its arrangement were also a feature of 'Amazing Grace' by the Scottish regimental band, which kept 'Back Off Boogaloo' from topping the UK charts in spring 1972, just as T Rex's 'Hot Love' had with McCartney's 'Another Day' a year before. Both of T Rex's next two Number Ones – 'Get It On' and 'Telegram Sam' – and 'Back Off Boogaloo' were characterised by a hard rock chug and pseudo-cryptic lyrics, so much so that T Rex devotees – and the group's self-glorifying leader, Marc Bolan – would make waspish and spurious allegations that Bolan had ghosted 'Back Off Boogaloo' for Ringo.

T Rex's grip on singles charts in most territories – with North America a glaring exception – evinced a swing back to the flash and cheap thrills of the big beat era as Bolan, Slade, Alice Cooper and The Sweet paved the way for the theatrical glam-rock excesses of Gary Glitter, David Bowie, androgynous Eno's old group Roxy Music and Suzy Quatro, clad in biker leathers while reviving 'I Wanna Be Your Man' with no lyrical revision. Woodstock Nation denim and cheesecloth was chic no more. In the ascendant were sequins, lurex and mascara'd gentlemen dressed like ladies.

Glam rock was not denigrated by Ringo to the same degree as The Osmonds and their bland kind. Nevertheless, Slade – who were the Black Country's as The Beatles were Liverpool's – were another "no-talent band, but they have created an image and a way of life for a lot of people. But I can't see them lasting."[1] In his lordly view, too, "Bowie is a step beyond what Marc is doing, and then you've got Alice somewhere in between."[1]

From a chequered past as a child actor, fashion model and underground celebrity, Bolan's dogged quest for renown and his garrulous conceit when he achieved it had infuriated older contemporaries. When he boasted of being now on an artistic par with Lennon – which he might have been – after visiting pop's Grand Old Man in New York, his host warned him, via the press, to watch his step. When Bolan implied that the squealing "T Rexstasy" that attended his recitals was one in the eye for The Rolling Stones, Jagger sneered that he was "not interested in going back to small English towns and turning on ten-year-olds"[10] – or, presumably those under ten, like Zak and Jason Starkey, who were – so their Dad comprehended – as spellbound by T Rex as he had been by Little Richard. An admirer of Marc's stagecraft – "he knows how to sway the atmosphere and that's a great skill"[1] – Ringo telephoned his Kensington flat with "this idea. See what you think, yes or no."[19]

The ensuing meeting between the down-to-earth Scouser and foppish Marc was one of these Momentous Encounters when, reported Bolan, "It's always the people I least expect to get close to that I end up friends with."[20] Before Marc's magnificent certainty about everything he said and did grated, Ringo was presented with a splendid Les Paul electric guitar from one to whom he became "almost a father. He has been through it all before, and there's so much he has taught me."[20]

As well as his unlikely counsellor snapping Bolan for the sleeve of T Rex's *The Slider* album, another concrete cause for gratitude emanated from Starr's desire to venture beyond merely acting in films, as "the easiest thing is being in them. It's harder when you start producing and getting them together."[18] His first – and most abiding – essay as a director was to be *Born To Boogie*, a full-colour cinema picture about T Rex, financed by Apple. An artist of Marc Bolan's calibre deserved nothing less.

Its centrepiece was a T Rex bash on "the day pop came back",[21] 18 March 1972, when tidal waves of screams hurled rampaging girls towards the stage at the Empire Pool, Wembley. There in 1966, with the cadence of 'I'm Down' yet reverberating, Ringo had had to bolt pell-mell to a ticking limousine which fans quick off the mark had chased as far as Harrow Road. Six years on, he was in the orchestra pit presiding over operations, oblivious to the commotion. It must have been a strange sensation to be completely ignored by crazed females to whom he was just some bloke nearer than they were to darling Marc. Afterwards, the *mêlée* outside was so uncontrolled that a camera was demolished and Mal Evans had to heave Bolan bodily to an armoured getaway car.

At least one lens had been focused constantly on the crowd during the show. In the cold light of a Twickenham Studios' cutting room, an intrigued Starr found that, rather than just screaming, "everyone in that audience was getting something different. That's why we used all those close-ups. There's one guy and his chick and they're just sitting very still watching it. Then there's the chicks who are going completely insane."[18]

On further examination, "I wanted to do some more. You see, my theory about filming concerts is that you can't create the atmosphere that's in the hall. We got [Bolan] to write a few things and set up a couple more days' shooting."[18] Set mostly at a small airfield and Tittenhurst Park – the Lennons' vacated 80-acre estate in Berkshire – the additional footage was reminiscent of *Magical Mystery Tour*, with contrasting scenes threaded together with a deadpan catchphrase – Ringo's suggestion – taken from Wanda Jackson's energetic 'Let's Have A Party' from 1958. Just as arbitrary was the random casting, which included Ringo himself (as the Dormouse to Bolan's Mad Hatter in one sequence), a bearded nun, a dwarf that gnaws offside mirrors from cars and Elton John, who, prior to his chart debut in 1971, had been Reg Dwight, pub pianist and jobbing tunesmith.

The *Born To Boogie* music – T Rex's hits and showstoppers – plus the infectious Wembley excitement could not be overwhelmed by any superfluous visual silliness, and Ringo was to be commended for his long weeks of daily scrutiny – 9.30am until late evening – of each reel, frame by frame, even though "I don't want no editor's trip where it's all fast cuts, because I get bored. I like to use a large proportion of straight shots."[18] Marc, at his elbow, and the studio technicians were astounded by his learned recommendations about rhythm, pacing and camera angles. He also cut an impressive movie-mogul figure during the publicity jaunt, which took in children's television and – for what it was worth – a trip to the States, where 'Get It On' had clawed up the Hot 100 in time for the world première on 14 December 1972.

Ben Hur it wasn't, but Starr had cause to be elated by critical compliments – even back-handed ones, like the sniffy *Morning Star*'s "directed(?) by Ringo, this is the best teeny-bopper entertainment since The Beatles succumbed to insecticide".[22] Excited after an EMI executive told Marc that his daughter had tried and failed to get into her local ABC to see *Born To Boogie*, Starr and Bolan "drove down there together just to look at the queues forming up outside the cinema".[23]

Yet, as if it were one of his hobbies, Ringo's passion for film direction had cooled, not with its creative labour but with the mind-stultifying legal and budgetary mechanics of post-production clearance and distribution. Like a gymkhana pony refusing a fence, he now balked at the project he'd first put to Marc of a TV series documenting the day-to-day lives of famed personalities.

Always stimulated by the celebrity of others, Starr had banked on the co-operation of such as footballer George Best, Marc, Cilla and Elizabeth Taylor, for whose 40th birthday the Starkeys had jetted to Budapest – the location of her current movie, *Bluebeard* – to celebrate. The editing block at Twickenham was no fun whatsoever compared to being a desired guest at so many glittering occasions. As well as Liz's knees-up, vibrantly gregarious Ringo would be photographed sharing a joke with Mick Jagger, Barbra Streisand, Princess Grace of Monaco – you name 'em – at Cote D'Azur launches of new record companies, gala award ceremonies and on/off shindigs like David Bowie's lavish "retirement" do at the Café Royal in July 1973. Through George Harrison, Starr's self-endowed leisure also facilitated a spectator's enthusiasm for Formula One racing. The VIP treatment that was automatically theirs at these buzzing panoramas found both ex-Beatles on celluloid toasting Jackie Stewart – winner of 1970's Monte Carlo Grand Prix – in Polanski's *Weekend Of A Champion*.

Ringo's companions in revelry were of a world more cultivated than that of a Scotch of St James raver *circa* 1965, but his renewed zest for the social whirl was so voracious that he'd hide rings around his eyes from the previous *soirée* with the mirror sunglasses that became standard party accoutrement during that period.

A soulmate during these roisterings was Keith Moon, Zak's hero and another *Born To Boogie* starlet, just as Starr would be a minor commentator in *The Kids Are Alright*, a 1979 film portrait of The Who. Seven years earlier, in 1972, he was most effective as perverted, spivvy "Uncle Ernie" in Lou Reizner's soundtrack of a stage presentation of *Tommy* at London's Rainbow Theatre. When commitment to a new film, *That'll Be The Day*, prevented Ringo's participation in the actual show, an obvious substitute was 25-year-old Moon, his new drinking partner (with brandy the favoured tipple).

In a lucid moment, Keith had confessed that his role as The Who's newsmaker was purely for publicity. However, that he maintained his maniac persona throughout his short life infers a less sound motivation. Perpetuated by the easy money that had fallen into his lap since gatecrashing the group in 1963, his tomfoolery – like parading around West End clubs in Nazi attire – would often deteriorate into a nonsensical, attention-grabbing frenzy of explosives in hotel bedrooms; breaking into an aeroplane pilot's cabin while airborne to rap his drumsticks on the control panel; slashing his wrists at the drop of a hat; and applying a cigarette lighter to his £150 pay-packet for a day's film work. Since accidentally killing his chauffeur in 1970, Moon had become even more lost, afflicted with worsening black-outs – both on stage and off – through punishing up to four decanters of spirits within an hour of waking "just to get things moving".[24] On his final tour with The Who in 1977, his fee would be a paltry £40 after deductions for depredations he'd inflicted *en route*.

The older Ringo tended to laugh at Moon's larks rather than be drawn into them. Although only a passing role was provided for him in *That'll Be The Day*, Keith made a disproportionate impression off camera by hiring a helicopter to touch down on the roof of the Isle of Wight hotel allocated to the cast so that he could emerge from this conveyance in full Red Baron flying rig. "It's the only way to travel, man."[17]

On one night, back at the hotel's ballroom stage, there was an extraordinary assembly of "Ringo on lead guitar, me on bass", recalled David Essex, along with "Graham Bond on drums, Harry Nilsson on tambourine and Honky Tonk(?) on drums – and we had

Billy Fury as singer. You never heard such a noise in your life, because we were all playing about with instruments we don't normally play, just for the fun of it."[17] By 4am, enough guests had complained about the row that police materialised in their midst and the music terminated. Less ruinous of others' sleep was the night on which the funfair scenes were shot. "Ringo and I were in T-shirts, pretending to have a good time when all the time it was pouring rain" – Essex again – "[but] that was great, because we had the run of the fair all night. Years ago, I used to work on a funfair, and I had to teach Ringo how to balance as we went 'round, collecting money from the punters."[17]

Pleasurable, too, was the extravagant party that Moon threw on completing his part as drummer in Bickerstaffe Happy Holiday Camp's Blue Grotto's resident rock 'n' roll combo for 1959's *Stormy Tempest And The Typhoons*. Ray Connolly's screenplay had plagiarised Rory Storm's group at Butlins in more than name. In silver jacket and hair stiff with lacquer, Tempest was played by Billy Fury, a touching instance of typecasting for the ailing rock-a-balladeer, soon to undergo a second heart operation.

With his days on the Mersey ferry holding him in good stead (especially when required to carry a tray of glasses), Ringo-as-Grotto-barman's scripted comments on Tempest's band included a description of their off-duty carnal pastimes and – considering his real-life career, post-Hurricanes – an ironic "but there's no future in being a Typhoon. I mean, where does it get you?" From director Claude Whatham, he'd been given *carte blanche* "to ramble on all I wanted, because people write lines for you that you'd never say. So I did my own dialogue. I love it when they let me go off on my own."[25] This may invoke howls of derision, but I think that Ringo's second lead in this poignant evocation of provincial England in the late 1950s stands as his most powerful artistic statement. Through improvising around his own character and personal history, his role as Mike Menarry blew away like dust his previous and future efforts in records and films. Any argument that *A Hard Day's Night*, 'It Don't Come Easy' *et al* created the opportunity to do so is irrelevant.

The promotional spiel that it was "a strong dramatic part laced with humour"[1] was justified. As Sinatra had begged for his Oscar-winning part in *From Here To Eternity*, because he "might have been"[26] Joe di Maggio, so Ringo Starr was Mike Menarry – or, at least, aspects of him were. "My part as Mike is total flashback," he observed, "since he's very much me as I was in the late 1950s."[17] A Liverpudlian Ted, Ringo/Mike dons "my own actual velvet-collared jacket. Everyone reeled back from the smell of mothballs when I put it on. I wear a pair of socks I used to wear in those days, too."[17]

The unlettered Menarry's sole reading matter is comics. He is otherwise preoccupied with getting off with birds – "a quick tickle to see if they go, then it's 'round the back and getting me end away" – but unbothered and philosophical about any repulsions. Less brazenly, but just as unashamedly, he fiddles the Grotto customers' change. When boasts of prowess in any given field is disproved, he blames anything but himself. For his two left feet in a Grotto jiving contest, "it was the band, you know. No one can dance to that noise." The "sodding cue" loses him a round of snooker.

Shabbily likeable though he is, Mike/Ringo does not immediately impress his chalet mate, Jim MacLaine, David Essex's big-screen debut. Jim is a good-looking Somerset youth who, although earmarked for university, had left a sheltered life on impulse on the morning of his "A"-levels to the dismayed confusion of his mother, with her middle-class values. At Bickerstaffe, the would-be rakish Mike's unwitting machinations lead MacLaine to lose his virginity in a haze of cheap perfume, Australian wine and grubby bedsheets. "From then on," sniggered Ringo, "he'll have anything. He doesn't care. I introduce him to the naughty side of life."[1]

Mike next finds his doubtful friend a job as his assistant operator on the dodgems with a travelling fair, inducting him into the routine procedure of how to "work and sweat and work and fiddle". However competent a tutor he is, Mike inadvertently cheats one rider too many, and after a bloody reprisal by the aggrieved party's motorbike gang is left with a limp for the sequel, *Sooner Or Later* –

retitled *Stardust* by autumn 1973 and with Adam Faith assuming the role of Menarry – now road manager and confidant of MacLaine as he becomes a 1960s pop star. Ringo felt that his continuance as Menarry would be to condone a storyline too close for comfort to that of The Beatles. More specifically piquant for him than the tough realism of behind-the-scenes drugs and sex was the fact that a mainstay of Jim's group, The Stray Cats, is underhandedly replaced just as they crack the charts.

Although Faith delivered a portrayal of Menarry as convincing in its way as Starr's, Essex would always speak fondly of his previous co-star, who'd "really knocked me out. One of the biggest thrills of my life was working with Ringo,"[27] two of whose "sculptures" – a milk and a Coca Cola bottle – would be among ornaments in David's 16th-century Essex home. Their mutual appreciation of Dr John's Creole psychedelia and the research for *That'll Be The Day* combined to inspire Essex's first Top-Ten strike, 1973's 'Rock On', which aligned itself to 1950s rock by namechecking "Jimmy Dean" in its hook.

Further signs of disassociation with contemporary pop was that same year's *American Graffiti*, with its recreation of 1962 in a small Midwestern town. Rock 'n' roll revival acts abounded, like Sha Na Na and Shakin' Stevens And The Sunsets, and forgotten Mod classics would shortly be attempted during The Sex Pistols' exploratory stumblings. These regressive trends and the snowballing of specialist fanzines chronicling them encouraged many hearts to pound in anticipation while squeezing between jumble-sale hags blocking passage to a pile of scratched 45s and brittle 78s on white-elephant stalls. Such expeditions for overlooked artefacts from earlier musical eras helped to hold a ghastly present at arm's length.

In this respect, Ringo's sterling acting – if it *was* acting – in *That'll Be The Day* could not efface his compromising elitist connections – however remote – with such as *All Things Must Pass*, the overblown *Tommy* rehash, Leon Russell's triple *Live* album and disc jockey John Peel's chortling that Starr's was "one 'superstar' family that still makes it"[28] on 'Back Off Boogaloo'. Ringo's future actions would take no account of adverse reactions towards the distancing of the rock star – forever, in the States – from a home audience that would soon be ripe for the shouting and banging of punk, a movement that by original definition precluded stardom. Other territories, especially North America, would stay amenable to Ringo Starr's output for a while longer, and – commercially, anyway – the best was yet to come. But otherwise, his tide was already ebbing.

12 "I Can't Wait To Go, Half The Time"

For a while, he didn't trouble to wash off the Teddy Boy tattoo – or, rather, the transfer – on his right ear. He may have also kept the Cupid and heart that had likewise adorned Mike Menarry's buttocks – as seen in a chalet scene – but these were not revealed on the chat-shows he undertook at the time. As well as pushing *That'll Be The Day* and drumming behind Jimmy Tarbuck and Tim Rice's 'impromptu' 'Singing The Blues' on ITV, he used the exposure to promote steel, glass and plastic furniture purchasable from "Ringo Or Robin Limited", who were exhibiting at Liberty's department store, off Regent Street, during the last fortnight in September 1971.

Among keen patrons of Starr's collaboration with Robin Cruikshank was Prime Minister Edward Heath, who received a specially designed mirror – on which was inlaid his own image over a postcard English landscape – for Christmas 1973. With Cruikshank in charge of the technological donkeywork, Ringo's mechanical turn was given its head with the likes of a coffee stand fashioned from Rolls Royce radiator grilles, circular fireplaces and flower-shaped tables. Like vintage champagne, these goods were available for any citizen to buy. From the shop in Rathbone Street, near Oxford Circus, you could spend your loose change on, say, a £600 sofa or – a snip at £40 – a smallish mirror with either a Bambi or Apple logo.

While art deco was still fun for him, Ringo had a particularly glowing newspaper review of the firm's latest creations blown up and displayed in Apple's front windows, but – his dilettante's attention flitting elsewhere – the business would be up for sale by 1976. Nevertheless, there was a time when a livewire ex-Beatle stuck to office hours, during which "we have a lot of hassles and we have a lot of fun. It depends who comes to see us."[1] In this less hectic phase of his celebrity, however, many plans progressed no further than discussion. He formed Wobble Music Ltd and the Reckongrade production company, but for what purpose was anyone's guess. He also spoke of financing a film with one of the Smothers Brothers – a kind of US Mike and Bernie Winters – and "one with a guy about models, which I think is a saleable thing".[1] Dating from this time, *Adventure: Ring Of Fire* was a documentary – with incidental music by George Harrison – about Lorne and Lawrence Blair's expedition to the Indonesian archipelago. This would be screened at last in summer 1988 – albeit in seven parts on BBC television – with Ringo as Executive Director.

Even with excellent notices for *That'll Be The Day*, Starr never got around to acting in another movie halfway as appealing, sticking instead to mainly minor roles that required little preparation. There was, however, mention of a silent movie, which "would be great, [because] I wouldn't have any lines to learn. It's the words that get in the way all the time, in many films."[2] Neither would he have minded "a costume drama – that's the ultimate fantasy. Something like *The Three Musketeers* or *The Knights Of The Round Table*, where I could wear a suit of armour and do a bit of swordfighting."[2]

At one point, he approved Michael Pertwee's screenplay for *The Biggest Dog In The World* and his choice of producer in Walter Shenson, from The Beatles' days, but eventually Ringo let this children's comedy slip from his grasp, possibly because it would follow too soon after *That'll Be The Day*. Furthermore, as well as his finding memorising lines and the demanding schedules with their early mornings onerous, "There's all the steps they have to take after you agree to do it. I have said yes to a few things, but they're still out there looking for the money I find it very hard to make the sort of commitment you need in movies. It's such a long-time situation."[3]

Just prior to *That'll Be The Day*, Ringo's marking time between more challenging projects had been typified by his part in *200*

Motels, the only major film by Frank Zappa, leader of The Mothers Of Invention, whom Ringo had considered "a real weirdo but, once you get to know him, he isn't. He's probably one of the straightest men I've ever met."[3] Via a rapid turnover of personnel and changes in his stylistic determination, Zappa's records were attracting – for better or worse – a wider audience in their drift from incisive aural junk-sculptures towards lavatorial "humor".

This strain was lamentably palpable in *200 Motels*, which, while praised for its spectacular and pioneering visual effects, was stamped by *The New York Times* as being "a subjective *A Hard Day's Night* in desperate need of the early Beatles".[4] Actually, it was as close to *Magical Mystery Tour* as The Mothers' *We're Only In It For The Money* had been a cursory send-up of *Sgt Pepper*, from its parodic sleeve to the 'Day In The Life' piano omega. *200 Motels* also absorbed traces of *Candy*, to which Mother Howard Kaylan actually makes delicate and pointed reference when discussing pornographic literature.[5]

Perhaps *200 Motels* might have been more like *A Hard Day's Night* had one of its principal hirelings, Wilfred Brambell, stayed the course. Instead, Paul's ex-"grandfather" despaired of ever understanding – let alone learning – his part as The World's Oldest Bass Guitarist in a script riddled with "balling chicks"-type slang for Zappa's sluggish "fantasy opera" of his Mothers' sleazy adventures when their tour reaches Centerville – not Lightnin' Hopkins' birthplace but a mock-up of a surreal US town inhabited by "just plain folks".

Busy behind the cameras, Zappa elected to appear only in musical segments with The Mothers and a put-upon Royal Philharmonic Orchestra. Therefore, as well as playing a character called "Larry the Dwarf", Ringo – in straggly black wig and dagger beard – doubled as an ill-at-ease Zappa, who composed songs around his recorded eavesdropping on the discord and intrigues that make pop groups what they are. One inducement to burden himself with these peculiar roles was the fact that Keith Moon was in it too, as a nun, as well as The Mothers' own august percussionists, Jimmy Carl Black and latter-day Mojo Aynsley Dunbar. By one of Zappa's chance operations, involving the first person to enter a particular room, Ringo's current chauffeur and former Apple errand-boy, Martin Lickert, was given a rewrite of Brambell's part.

As the fragile storyline was lost to in-jokes, cartoon sequences and Frank's ructions with his co-director, it hardly mattered that Ringo made no effort "to other be" as either Zappa or Larry. Too much for the common movie-goer, 200 Motels faded swiftly from general circulation to be shown occasionally only in film clubs and "alternative" cinemas, where it was watched as a duty by those who'd wished for time to stop in the late 1960s.

By 1973, whatever was left of hippy conviviality at Apple had contracted into a unity of darting suspicion when – uncool though it was – turgid examination of Allen Klein's handling of Messrs Harrison, Lennon and Starr's divergent affairs could not be postponed, especially with the expiry date of the contract approaching. The mustering of legal forces to compile evidence of an increasingly distant manager's transgressions was motivated by a new willingness to credit provocative but not completely fictional tales by their friends and various of Klein's incensed former associates of his shifty and senselessly blunt stance in negotiation.

For all the fear that spread from him like cigar smoke, Klein was not as greedy as he might have been. Compared to some of his peers, who were entitled to half of everything that their clients earned regardless, the Robin Hood of pop took only a fifth of that which he'd actually secured for his artists. As John, Ringo and George became more adept at dealing directly with third parties, so the counter-suing Klein was dyed a villain of the darkest hue by October 1974, when he lost the case and Apple's complex finances were unfrozen. With its original ideal of bucking the bourgeois system long forgotten, "All Apple does is collecting," said Ringo. "We have no artists. We have nothing to push, but it looks after the films. It owns The Beatles' name, so, in fact, collects The Beatles' royalties."[6] These would now pour along defined streams towards the deltas of each separate ex-Beatle's business executor – that is, John's Yoko, George's Denis O'Brien and Paul's Eastmans.

Ringo's counterpart was Hilary Gerrard, a former Apple executive who'd also act as personal retainer on the mighty rough road that lay ahead. To those outsiders who twigged that he was Ringo's manager and not merely some companion, Gerrard's name would for years be as synonymous with that of his flamboyant charge as Colonel Parker's with Elvis.

Missing the team activities and glamour of The Beatles, Gerrard's man was still making the most of his fresh lease of life since 'It Don't Come Easy' by seldom turning down a worthwhile opportunity to promote himself, whether discoursing about his favourite records on Radio 1's *My Top Twelve* or dressing up as a pope with twirled moustachios in *Lisztomania*, directed by the outrageous Ken Russell, fresh from immortalising wretched *Tommy* on celluloid. One of Starr's favourite directors, his film biography of the prolific Hungarian composer was as true to life as a comic strip. Playing a Scouse "Urban IV" with the same disregard for authenticity as he had "Frank Zappa", Ringo's big moment was imploring Liszt – The Who's Roger Daltrey – to focus his talent towards exorcising the devils from Richard Wagner (Paul Nicholas, straight from *Stardust* and *Tommy*).

After acting and directing, Starr had had a stab at producing, too, when it was agreed that he should be head of Apple Films, as he was the only ex-Beatle then to make strides in that direction. Initially, he ruled in fact as well as name from a plush office (with bar alcove) near Horse Guards Parade. Visitors could deduce what the division would be up to next from macabre props dotted among the spindly potted trees and smaller ornaments in the executive suite, as well as the plaque on its door reading "HQ Dr Baron Frankenstein, Brain Specialist". Ringo was going to make a horror movie.

He'd seen himself in the title role of *Count Downe* – or, as it was renamed, *Son Of Dracula* – but pragmatism prevailed and, like Zappa, he plumped for a smaller part to concentrate better on administration and supervision. To direct, he'd appointed Freddie Francis, whose *curriculum vitae* bulged with good, honest British trash like *Dr Terror's House Of Horrors*, *The Evil Of Frankenstein* and – also starring Peter Cushing – 1965's *The Skull*. For Ringo's updating of the Dracula legend – the impending ascent of his lovestruck son (who yearns to go straight) onto the throne of the netherworld – Francis recommended such genre shellbacks as Suzanna Leigh and Dennis Price while, at his employer's insistence, fitting in last-minute cameos for show-offs like Keith Moon. He didn't put his foot down, either, when the old-pals act extended to Nilsson, for whom Ringo was "now a very dear, close friend and I love him".[7] With no theatrical experience but in the public eye then with the million-selling single 'Without You', Nilsson consented to be Count Downe in what was now "like a non-musical, non-horror, non-comedy comedy," quipped Starr, "or it's a horror-horror, musical-musical, comedy-comedy."[8]

It wasn't all smiles, however, when shooting began in late 1972 within the foggy, slip-slapping wharfs and gilded bridges of London's docklands. The novice producer was soon beset with "such a headache. Everyone shouts at you. I didn't know that, if you didn't get the crew home and in their beds by midnight, you couldn't work them the next day, because, you see, I'm a musician, and if we start working and it starts to cook, we'll keep it rolling for three days, if necessary."[9]

As well as learning the hard way about union dictates, Ringo had become disagreeably aware that the plot *per se* was too feeble to go the distance as a full-blown epic. Like other scenes featuring the Wolfman, Frankenstein and other stock characters, his own – in robes and long white beard as 200-year-old Merlin the Magician – was not altogether relevant to the basic yarn but was necessary to both regain wandering audience attention and justify the printing of the words "Ringo Starr" in large letters on the lobby placard inside the Atlanta cinema, where – like *Gone With The Wind* 35 years earlier – *Son Of Dracula* was premièred in May 1974.

Too early for the gothic craze that afflicted a faction among post-punk British adolescents, Ringo's effort was seen only in the States, to the chagrin of a less fervent home following; for many, the exclusion provided an absolute cure for Beatlemania. Yet, for the lucky Yanks, even personal appearances by Starr and Nilsson when the film opened elsewhere could not prevent its relegation to "all the little villages because, if we put it on in a town, it got slated".[10] The soundtrack, too, could not be rescued from deletion by wringing monetary drops from the presence within its grooves of Ringo, George Harrison (on cowbell) and guitarist Peter Frampton from Humble Pie, whose album *Wind Of Change* – with Billy Preston and Starr on some tracks – was the small beginning to solo success in North America later in the decade.

Frampton and Starr had also been present at Soho's Trident Studios for the recording of *Son Of Schmilsson*, which, by apparent coincidence, had Nilsson-as-Dracula on its front cover (and with a dummy in his mouth on the rear). This LP, like its bigger-selling predecessor, *Nilsson Schmilsson* – containing 'Without You' – was produced by Richard Perry, whose long residence in California and frequent working trips to England had not tempered his East Coast twang. From overseeing Captain Beefheart, Tiny Tim, the blues singer Taj Mahal and Theodore Bikel (later a *200 Motels* star), the emergence of Perry as the most fashionable record producer of the next decade began with 1972's *No Secrets* and its attendant 'You're So Vain' hit for Carly Simon. With his very name a selling point, Perry then moved closer to middle-of-the-road pop with customers like Johnny Mathis, Barbra Streisand, mushy Percy Faith and, purring Mister Wonderful, Andy Williams. A conspicuous feather in his cap was a London album with Ella Fitzgerald.

In truth, although grandiloquent in style, Perry was nowhere as inventive as Joe Meek, George Martin or even Phil Spector, but he'd acquired the knack of injecting just enough of prevailing fads into an easy-listening artist's music to avoid turning off older fans. Hence we were blessed with Mathis' adaptation of 'My Sweet Lord' and Faith's 'Sun King' for the supper clubs and Streisand recording at Keith Richards' French villa. There was even a period in 1974 when it was cool to dig Williams' *Solitaire* album, because he'd been backed by musicians hip enough to be listed on its back cover.

Among these was Klaus Voorman, whom Perry had also called upon for *Nilsson Schmilsson*, and it was through that elegant Teuton

that George Harrison became sufficiently intrigued to look in on an
Ella Fitzgerald session and Ringo to actually drum on *Son Of
Schmilsson* and, just prior to this, on a solo 45 by Righteous Brother
Bobby Hatfield, after Perry – damn his impudence – had considered
Starr "good enough to play sessions for me".[11]

Basking in his 15 minutes of fame, Perry took the Other Two
Beatles' flattering surveillance in his stride, while acknowledging the
group's influence in his "knowing what they did and why it was great
and applying it to other situations".[12] The concord when taping one
Nilsson track was such that, relaxing in Tramp afterwards, Perry was
emboldened to offer Starr his console favours, if or when he was
ready to commence another album. However, although fascinated by
Richard's visionary notion for selecting "a certain song and create
visual for it, instead of the other way 'round, as it is traditionally
done",[12] a sceptical Starr decided to put his first "proper" post-
Beatles album on ice.

Above the tour-album-tour sandwiches incumbent upon poorer
pop aristocrats, Starr would wait until he felt like making a new
record while picking and choosing the studio dates that were earning
him legion (if usually pseudonymous) LP credits. At Trident,
Olympic and Apple, he did his bit for such as Grammy-winning
songwriter Jim Webb, as well as this or that "super sideman" for
whom it had become convenient to migrate to Europe to fulfil a
rewarding workload. For saxophonist Bobby Keyes, his
augmentation of The Rolling Stones had been a springboard to his
own boring, boring album, in which "a lot of the tracks just came
about from jamming",[13] with stellar assistance from pals that
included the Tweedledum and Tweedledee of such occasions.
Harrison and Starr also applied their touch to 1973's *Brother* by Lon
and Derrek Van Eaton, Apple's last signing. On their 'Sweet Music',
Ringo tapped out that changeless 4/4 next to another drummer, Jim
Gordon, whose drug-related problems had led to the recent
cashiering of him by Traffic. He ended up in an asylum for the
criminally insane for matricide, an incarceration attributed to the
chemicals that were common currency when, from Delaney And

Bonnie's Friends, he'd muscled in among that superstar elite that exchanged smirks with ol' George across the mixing desk at Trident.

Starr did not always assume that records could only be made with the same smug oligarchy, for in 1972 he tried again with John Tavener. Although in the throes of composing an opera based on the life of St Theresa, the clever young man put his mind to "a bit for some pop record they're producing – just something for the middle, different from the rest. Ringo just said, 'You write whatever you want to write.'"[14] It must have been rather too "different", however, because, if Tavener ever finished it, his musical bridge has not been heard to this day in connection with any disc by Starr, who in the following spring finally got around to commissioning a thrilled Richard Perry to go ahead with *Ringo*, which would stand forever as the artist's best-selling solo album and Perry's apotheosis as a producer, "one which I may never top".[15]

This dark self-judgement might have been wavered had Ringo adhered to "this great plan of doing a world album: you know, two tracks in Nashville, a couple in London, some in Peru or wherever".[3] Instead, a compliance with Perry's request for him and Nilsson to compere a Grammy-awards presentation in Nashville enabled the finalising of details and a decision to cut corners by block-booking Los Angeles' Sunset Sound Studio for five exploratory days when Starr was to be in the city anyway for a meeting about the Klein business with Harrison and Lennon. It was also the involvement of these two during a second week of *Ringo* sessions that marked the closest that The Beatles would ever come to an artistic reunion before the 'Free As A Bird' single in 1995.

On the five tracks – including a 'Photograph' with strings, choir and Bobby Keyes sax solo – that were dispatched during the initial sojourn, some were propelled by guitar sections too singular to have been played by anyone else but George. For Perry, the overall outcome had been most pleasing, "right from opening night. We had to keep the tape going because, as soon as we'd start the playback, they'd go into a jam which didn't sound like a jam [but] a new song, which was totally different from what we were playing."[12] "We" embraced a mutable pool of familiar cohorts, from the Van Eaton siblings to Marc Bolan to pianist Nicky Hopkins on the rebound (like Starr) from Harrison's *Living In The Material World*. Yet, of all the negotiable names that would be annotated on the *Ringo* back cover, none was more so than all four former Beatles.

Staying on in Los Angeles to promote his wife's new double LP, *Approximately Infinite Universe*, John socialised with Starr and Perry, stringing along with them to a screening of the prurient *Last Tango In Paris*. He also listened hard to *Ringo* thus far and was prompted to submit a song himself. Grown from a weak hook but two tough riffs, 'I'm The Greatest' was a semi-autobiographical opus made to measure for Starr, mentioning specifically his birthplace, his part in "the greatest show on Earth", his age and his "kids". The Lennons' so far unrequited longing for children was casting a shadow over their marriage, and this may have contributed to the bite inherent in John's demo that was missing on *Ringo*'s slicker retread, with its over-larded applause.

'I'm The Greatest' had been lacking only a middle eight, which Ringo, Lennon and Perry were puzzling out on the studio's concert grand when Harrison telephoned to invite himself along. If John was still huffy about the specific exclusion of Yoko – and, indirectly, himself – from the Bangladesh extravaganza, he and George were inclined not to bicker in their old drummer's presence and, therefore, "You could really tell that they were excited!" gushed Perry. "There was such a fantastic energy coming out of the room!! It was really sensational!!!"[12]

Not sending him into quite the same verbal paroxysms as this coup were less pronounced instances of ex-Beatle creativity during the *Ringo* sessions. With The Band, George backed Ringo on 'Sunshine Life For Me', a hootenanny hoe-down that had been composed and then shelved when the Harrisons and Donovan were holidaying in Ireland in 1969. Its sub-title, 'Sail Away, Raymond' pertained to a creature of Klein's. With Mal Evans, George also penned 'You And Me (Babe)', which, although tuneful and riven with a deft fretboard obligato, was a vehicle through which Starr could close the album with a monologue that thanked everyone – famous and obscure – who'd taken part.

His juxtaposition in this of the words "John", "Lennon", "Paul" and "McCartney" could only have been deliberate, although neither had played on the same tracks. More objective about Apple's legal turmoils as well as John's public insults, Paul had been amenable to pitching in on 'I'm The Greatest', but he was refused a US visa owing to a recent fine for possessing narcotics, which had been seized during a European tour with Wings, a new group built around himself, ex-Moody Blue Denny Laine and Linda – now his occasional songwriting collaborator – on keyboards. This setback did not, however, stop Paul from contributing his mimicking of a saxophone *à la* The Fourmost on Johnny Burnette's ambulant 'You're Sixteen', his pursed-lips roughness mitigating Nilsson's too-pat multitracked backing responses. Paul's digits were also employed in the latter's compilation – also at Abbey Road – of a backing track for a new number, 'Six O'Clock', for editing as necessary by Perry, who was taking a breather from Sunset Sound to help supervise a McCartney television special in London.

Notable for its snotty synthesiser ostinato, 'Six O'Clock' could have been made up by McCartney in his sleep. It was certainly commensurate with the wispy lyrics and syrupy jingles that comprised *Red Rose Speedway*, Wings' 1973 album. However, its intrinsic value mattered less than its use – with Starr's added drums and vocals – in a campaign that would colour *Ringo* as a bastardised Beatles collection, supplemented too by Voorman's *Sgt Pepper*-ish lithograph on its sleeve and the teasing insertion of the odd Lennon-McCartney song title into its lyrics. Whether they conjured up magic or mere music wasn't the issue; that the Fab Four were theoretically together on the same lump of plastic was sufficient to feed hope that soon everything would be OK again, just like it was before John went funny in 1968, and that The Beatles would regroup officially to tour and record the chart-toppers that John and Paul – all friends now – would be churning out once more.

In 1973, whether these four mortals as individuals sold records or not did not yet depend upon commercial viability As Paul demonstrated, an ex-Beatle was guaranteed at least a minor hit, even with sub-standard produce. In the States, both he and George had clambered as far as Number One, and, after the climb of 'Photograph' up the same Hot 100 that autumn, Ringo's turn came too – just – when, on knocking off Eddie Kendricks' 'Keep On Truckin', he ruled pop for one glorious week.

The lead voice apart, 'Photograph' would not have been out of place on one of its co-writer's discs. Like a lot of Harrison items, something about it was infuriatingly familiar, its very introit invoking both 'Let's Spend The Night Together' and The Lemon Pipers' 'Green Tambourine'. Nevertheless, its fetching aftertaste of "beautiful sadness" – broadly, a yearning for an absent loved one – made it a much-requested radio spin for a nation still awaiting the return of many of its sons from Vietnam following the January cease-fire. Similarly, long after tumbling from its domestic high of Number Four, 'Photograph' lingered as a home thought from abroad on Radio 2's *Two-Way Family Favourites* as Britain scoffed its Sunday roasts.

Although 'Photograph' was half George's, this single represented Ringo's peak as a composer in hard financial terms, especially as its B-side, 'Down And Out', was all his own work. This leftover from 1972 was unsuitable for *Ringo*, living only in its stabbing horns, Gary Brooker's piano and producer Harrison's bottleneck solo. If its lyrics were almost as perfunctory, 'Step Lightly' – another attributed to Richard Starkey alone – reconciled more easily with the album's pervading climate. With clarinets and the syncopated clattering of Starr's own feet lending it a 1930s dance-band feel, it was selected as the second track on side two, just where 'When I'm 64' – in the same vein – had been on *Sgt Pepper*.

Just as savoury an ingredient in the *Ringo* cauldron as its Beatles affiliations was Starr's songwriting liaison with Vini Poncia, a bond that proved to be more lucrative than that of Poncia and Peter Anders with The Tradewinds and Innocence. Since 'There's Got To Be A Word', the duo's entry into Richard Perry's trendy orbit had resulted in an LP under their own names and Vini's production of

Melissa Manchester and other of Richard's clients. Ranking, I suppose, as Perry's lieutenant on *Ringo*, Poncia was fumbling one evening for a key to suit Starr's larynx for one number "and I had lots of bits of songs and I played some to him, and then he had a few bits and we found we could write together. That's how we got together, and we've been together ever since."[16]

The first harvest of the Poncia-Starkey team reaped the catchy 'Oh My My', with a fake party atmosphere infectious enough to warrant its release as a US-only Ringo 45 and a hit to boot. Had its "get you into bed" line been altered, that honour might have gone to 'Devil Woman', which, with its standardised title, had a guitar lacerating it with clichéd heavy metal fuzz. It was, however, peculiar for Starr, hitting a different rhythm to that of the less heavy-handed Jim Keltner, who was otherwise heard on another four tracks, mainly clumping along in unison with Ringo in a like manner to the percussion artillery in Gary Glitter's Glitter Band.

Starr's reliance on Keltner – increasing in years to come – invites speculation both about Starr's self-picture as a musician and his preferred studio methodology. As Sly Stone and, I suspect, Dave Clark did, he and his producer – head to head in the control booth – appear to have sometimes employed the disciplined Keltner for the backing track, with Ringo layering his own more idiosyncratic drumming only after the beat had already been invested. Ringo's technical input was also guided by instinct. Engineer Stephen Lipson recalled that, because Starr liked the look of a certain microphone, "We tried it on the drums. He was happy. They sounded like Ringo Starr."[17]

One of the strengths of *Ringo* was that no participant was expected to suppress his individuality. Harrison's vocal harmony on 'Photograph' and Lennon's on 'I'm The Greatest', for example, were not "depersonalised" in the mix. Neither was Bolan's pulsating 'Telegram Sam' guitar buried in the descending piano inversions and booting saxophones on a version of Randy Newman's 'Have You Seen My Baby?'.[18]

Tending to drive his T Rex underlings hard in the studio, Bolan was not conditioned to Perry and Starr's laid-back attitude. This expression was taken almost too literally on some of Ringo's vocal takes, when onlookers made bets on "which side of my face I'd fall on after a whole fifth of bourbon".[19] Through interpolations like a vignette from 'What Shall We Do With The Drunken Sailor?' on the fade-out of 'You're Sixteen', ordinary fans might also have ascertained their hero's giggling intemperance. Even so, his singing was more consistently and clinically accurate than it had been on *Beaucoups Of Blues*.

In an industry where sales figures – especially North American ones – are arbiters of success, the proof of the pudding was the rise of *Ringo* to the top of *Billboard*'s album tabulation. In its singles chart, triumph chased triumph when, with 'Photograph' still in the Top Ten, 'You're Sixteen' likewise lasted seven days at Number One, until dragged down by Barbra Streisand, of all people. 'You're Sixteen' was not a Starkey original, but only McCartney had also hit the jackpot twice. To Lennon, who hadn't managed it at all, it appeared that the Beatle least likely was "doing better than any of us".[20] However, if signs were not yet perceptible, Ringo was about to fritter it away to all but the very dregs.

He'd anticipated the profits from *Ringo* and its offshoots by purchasing Tittenhurst Park within a fortnight of the Lennons' putting it on the market in September 1973. A compromise between remote Elstead and metropolitan Highgate, the Starkeys' new spread off Ascot's main thoroughfare to London was the opposite side of "Hollywood-on-Thames" to the Harrisons in olde-worlde Henley. Nearer neighbours who were also Starr's *nouveau-riche* equals in the hierarchy of pop included Rod Stewart in Bray, Jimmy Page of Windsor and Rick Wakeman in Camberley To a man, they were now inhabiting a world as exclusive as that of Berkshire's other landed gentry, and as far removed from whatever back-street terrace or middle-class semi-detached they came. Sunny afternoon idylls were blighted mildly by the whoosh of an occasional Concorde from Heathrow miles away, but otherwise only cascading pylons towards the horizon reminded them of the 20th century

Ringo's 26-room white Tudor mansion and some of the outhouses were buildings of historical importance that he was obliged by law to maintain and to permit National Trust inspectors "reasonable access". Alien to an Elizabethan squire, however, were many allowable alterations, such as the sauna, the swimming pool and – behind stained-glass windows – the inevitable snooker den. John had recorded his second solo LP, *Imagine*, in the eight-track studio that had supplanted all but the pipe organ in what had once been a private chapel. Renamed "Startling Studio" by its new owner, it was made available for public hire via the Reading area's classified telephone directory; nuisance calls from Beatle fans were rewarded only with an answerphone or manager/engineer Mike O'Donnell lifting the receiver. Nor was Ringo ever seen more than rarely among the seed trays of Tittenhurst Nurseries' market garden.

As the family settled into the new home, a strange question occurred to Maureen: would she lose the place if she and Richie split up? If in the midst of even more material comforts now, their partnership – of two old friends who used to be lovers – was not proportionally blissful.

A man suddenly preoccupied with success is likely to be an inattentive husband, but the road to the Starkeys' divorce could not be ascribed to such a tidy cause. Prior to *Ringo*, each had holidayed separately, with Ringo seizing the chance to get foxed without disgusted reprimands from her. Roaring drunk on champagne *en route* to the Bahamas, he, Marc Bolan and Bolan's missus had guffawed so hysterically and often at the in-flight comedy film that an irate fellow passenger batted their heads with his paperback and summoned the chief steward. The ensuing altercation had turned into a real-life farce.

Back at Tittenhurst Park, not so funny was George Harrison's after-dinner outburst before other guests that he was deeply in love with Mrs Starkey. As he and Pattie had also drifted into open estrangement, he had not intended so much to bewilder Maureen as to offend Pattie, who tore from the table to lock herself in the bathroom. Although Ringo's immediate reaction had been token anger, this tense evening had not concluded with any showdown, and he was astonished at how easily he could make light of it the next day and, worse, how slightly his pride smarted at the thought of Maureen reciprocating George's affection.

Any bad blood between Harrison and himself was soon diluted, and he'd always drum on George's records whenever he was asked and was available. Together, the two also considered buying up and relaunching Apple, until it made more sense for Harrison to found his own Dark Horse record label. Its releases included a rescued Apple project, *The Shankar Family And Friends*, on which Starr and other Western rock 'n' rollers blended with the Indian orchestra – bamboo flutes, sarods *et al* – that Ravi Shankar had assembled to support George on an unhappy 1974 tour of North America.

His pressured preparations for this trek had meant that Harrison could pluck not one stinking note on Starr's *Goodnight Vienna*,[21] the album calculated to snap at the heels of *Ringo*. Paul was fresh out of songs for Ringo, too, busy as Wings were with what many would regard as their leader's *pièce de résistance*, *Band On The Run*. History would repeat itself when Paul's LP – released just after Ringo's – would wither its sales potential.

The commercial inconvenience of George and Paul's desertions was cushioned by John, whose attendance on the *Goodnight Vienna* sessions in Los Angeles would be more insidious than it had been on *Ringo*. He had time to spare, because he'd left Yoko to hurl himself into a 15-month "lost weekend" in California in the company of Keith Moon, Mal Evans, and Nilsson, hard drinkers suffering from a premature male menopause, marital difficulties or both. With his own marriage floating into a choppy sea, Starr flopped onto the next stool for three-in-the-morning bar-hopping and late-afternoon mutual grogginess by the pool. Staying the phantoms of middle age, the *côterie* – bar Mal – jointly rented a well-appointed beach villa on Stone Canyon Road in smart Santa Monica beneath the cedared sweep of the Hollywood hills.

With Keith as likely to fling a bottle at the television screen as rise from an armchair to switch it off, more than a formality – until he moved next door to a nervous Steve McQueen – was the proviso that they meet costs of all repairs to the premises and its contents, which included the gold discs of more regular tenants like Carole King and portraits of John F Kennedy. From his frames, the late president gazed reproachfully at rooms littered with junk-food debris, empty crates of liquor, overflowing ashtrays and drunken layabouts. Now the house that had once belonged to his family was liberty hall for its present occupiers' circle of friends of friends, as well as redundant super sidemen, members of Rick Nelson's Stone Canyon Band and more fabled and fleeting callers, like Alice Cooper, ex-Monkee Mickey Dolenz, Phil Spector and ace guitarist Joe Walsh,[22] a New Yorker who had lately joined The Eagles.[23] Fanning dull embers for Beatle watchers, McCartney and – more frequently, from a Beverly Hills *pied à terre* – Harrison popped by, too.

Hollywood breeds many insecurities, but the cardinal sin is to show them. Visible desperation is too nasty a reminder of the impermanence of stardom and wealth. With artificial adrenaline pumping, the gang and their hysterically chattering hangers-on would saunter into topless clubs; gatecrash parties, race by moonlight to the Malibu surf; and kerb-crawl in phallic Lincoln Continentals with deafening sound systems. It wasn't uncommon for any one of them to stir with a hangover in a strange bed, unable to recollect the circumstances that led him there. Lennon, with his immigration woes, was afraid to fly off on whimsical side trips to London, where his boozy boys would lark about in Apple, Tramp and pubs like the Pheasantry in King's Road, where their roistering was tolerated.

If futile and public, their escapades were mostly harmless and stories of what they got up to have been improved with age. Revelling in his wickedness, Ringo was photographed with a cigarette inserted up his nose in Sunset Strip's Playboy Club, but that was nothing to his jumping three red traffic lights and a subsequent court order to attend a two-nights-a-week course on the US highway code. Then there was Lennon's ejection – with a sanitary towel fixed to his forehead – from west Los Angeles' Troubadour, where he and Nilsson had been heckling The Smothers Brothers. Less widely reported was an excessively worshipful and inebriated audience with Jerry Lee Lewis. For John's birthday celebration, Ringo secured Cherry Vanilla – a singing actress much given to exposing her bust – to recite Shakespeare in her New York whine, while on 7 July 1974 Moon had splashed out on a skywritten "Happy Birthday, Ringo!" across Tinseltown's rind of smog. A more practical gift to the Starkeys was the $7,000 drum set Keith had no clear memory of buying a visiting Zak, for whom Moon was the god of percussion, "the very best in the world".[24] If prompted, he'd concede, "My old man's a good timekeeper, but I've never thought of him as a great drummer."[24]

Zak's old man indulged himself with a kit of greater antiquity, handmade in 1926 and unusual for its steel-bottomed tom-toms. No recent hedonistic extreme had been "more satisfactory than playing. It still feels magic to create something with somebody in the studio."[25] In the same interview, he referred to "a pretty weird group" of himself, Carly Simon and Dr John on a track on *Playing Possum*, Richard Perry's latest production for Carly. For Ringo, more typical artistic tangents were albums by Nilsson and Moon, as well as *Harry And Ringo's Night Out*, a jettisoned 1974 film.

There was nothing too interesting or original on either Nilsson's *Pussycats* – produced by Lennon – or his swift follow-up, *God's Greatest Hits*, renamed *Duit Où Mon Dei* to placate his record company. The first had come simply because he and John "were sitting around with nothing to do, so we said, 'Let's do an album.' We picked songs off the top of our heads and just did them."[7] With Ringo, Klaus, Bobby Keyes and Moon – all the usual shower – he and Lennon wrapped up *Pussycats* in New York after Los Angeles sessions had collapsed.

Both Sides Of The Moon was a more mischievous fiasco. From out of the woodwork, Keith had drawn the likes of Dick Dale ("King Of The Surf Guitar") and Spencer Davis – a quieter member of the Hollywood Raj – to help out, but although their names looked well on the album's cover nothing could save Moon – who didn't compose – from desecrating his own heritage with laughable remakes from the repertoire of The Who and selections from that of his previous group, Wembley's Beachcombers, who'd gone in for surf music. Even purposefully amusing items like 'Solid Gold' – with Ringo as an announcer in a crossover routine – palled on replay, as recorded comedy often does.

The laggard of the pack, Mal Evans had needed little cajoling to arrange a horn section for Moon's version of a Lennon B-side. Having gained nothing from deserting his family to trail along with his former masters, 40-year-old Mal's slaughter by gun-toting police after a fracas in his flat with some mean-minded tart he'd picked up was said by some to have been a sort of suicide.

Marc Bolan was to perish in a car crash in 1977. The Grim Reaper was coming for Keith Moon, too, and many who knew "the Madman" – as best friend Starr knew him – were not entirely surprised at his body's final rebellion in 1978, after a lifetime of violation. By coincidence, the stretcher carried him from Ringo's old Montagu Square flat, which no later tenant had troubled to strip of its psychedelic decor.

As he hadn't bothered with Rory Storm, why should Starr stir himself to attend Bolan, Moon and other old mates' funerals, when "I totally believe your soul has gone by the time you get in the limo"[26]? Not as enigmatic as it might have been was his dejected aside, "I can't wait to go half the time."[26] Although Moon's mindless bravado was peculiar to himself, faintly disturbing to Ringo in retrospect was Nilsson's remark, "Pete [Townshend] protects Keith. I always think John would defend Ringo in the same way."[7]

Mastering his inner chaos, albeit temporarily, Starr pulled back from the abyss. As the madness subsided, he'd realised, "I just got caught up in that strange belief that, if you're creative, you've got to be brain-damaged."[27] With Nilsson's first shipwreck as a sea mark, Starr steered *Goodnight Vienna* using *Ringo* as his map. A spliced-up medley of Lennon's title song and its reprise was a minor US Top-40 entry as a single. To preserve a rough-and-ready edge, each kicked off with tempo announcements, and the second version closed the album like some cocktail-lounge combo with an accordion winding up for the intermission. Banked by a riff reminiscent of 'Money', 'Goodnight Vienna' was more complete an opus than 'I'm The Greatest', particularly in lyrical touches like "I felt like an Arab that was dancing through Zion".

The affable Lennon also stuck around to play guitar on 'All By Myself', one of three *Goodnight Vienna* efforts by the Starr-Poncia team. Its "fool" bassman grumblings were quite compelling, but 'All By Myself' – plus 'Oo-Wee' and the plodding 'Call Me' – sounded like the merely competent output of a couple of blokes who fancied themselves as songwriters. The album's backbone, therefore, was what Ringo called the "foreign tracks" by such as Nilsson, whose 'Easy For Me' – mixed feelings about a dowdy spinster – discharged the same drawn-curtain menace as that wrought by Jacques Brel. It was more the stuff of Scott Walker – the fiercely emotional Belgian composer's foremost interpreter and a proverbial "pop singer who can really sing" – than a painstaking croaker like Ringo Starr, who was ideal for the less wracked 'Snookeroo'.

Engaged in some tedious household task, I was vexed at hearing myself humming 'Snookeroo', which, although soothing, was the work of Elton John, one of myriad artists I love to hate. In the 'I'm The Greatest' tradition, 'Snookeroo' was tailored by Elton's wordsmith, Bernie Taupin, as an authorised overview of a squandered youth in Liverpool. As well as one of Starr's school reports featuring in advertisements for *Goodnight Vienna*, the old days were addressed more obliquely on the record's front cover, which reproduced the cinema poster for 1951's *The Day The Earth Stood Still*, with Ringo's mug pasted over that of Michael Rennie in space-suited salutation.

The ancient ditty 'Skokiaan' was the source of 'No No Song' by folky Hoyt Axton, a Jamaican-flavoured litany that warned – probably sardonically – of the horrors of whiskey, cocaine and so forth against the paradise of total abstinence. Unreleased as a British 45 for fear of Radio 1 programmers getting the wrong (or right) end of the stick, 'No No Song' came within an ace of duplicating the feat of 'You're Sixteen' in the States.

Recommended by Lennon, an overhaul of the evergreen 'Only You' was less of a US hit, but a hit all the same, and as unsuitable for Starr as 'Easy For Me'. Wisely, he did not try to compete with the soaringly lovesick lead tenor on The Platters' original. Instead, Ringo's inability to attack higher registers without sounding querulous was supposed to convey the impression that his devotion was too intense for satisfactory melodic articulation. It was a joke, all the same.

Roger Miller's creaky 'Husbands And Wives' was comical not for Ringo's singing but for a mawkishness comparable to anything on *Beaucoups Of Blues* and its tune's too-close affinity to Miller's 'Little Green Apples'. Quirkier but more credible, 'Occapella' from the Lee Dorsey catalogue held the ear with a sparkling arrangement that nodded towards Dr John, and was flexible enough to switch smoothly from verses jittery with timbales to a wordless choral passage that might have been lifted by time machine from some mellow new age compact disc.

Highlights like 'Occapella' and 'Goodnight Vienna' itself balanced 'Call Me', 'Only You' and other *faux pas* on an album that was as likeable, after its fashion, as *Ringo*. During 1974's Yuletide sell-in, its crawl to a *Billboard* Number Eight, while abiding just a week in the UK Top 30, signified less a deterioration in quality than its dimmer "Beatle reunion" aura, plus a generally smaller quota of famous guests. Furthermore, Richard Perry's star was on the wane, as his much-touted 1974 LP for Martha Reeves – a former Tamla-Motown *grande dame* – failed to live up to market expectations.

Goodnight Vienna might have fared better if Starr had realised that a few half-page adverts in the music press and a round of interviews in same were no longer sufficient to incite readers to consume his latest record. You had to howl it a bit louder in apocryphal 1974, when the "high-energy" entertainments of roving minstrels like Led Zeppelin, Peter Frampton[28] and Grand Funk

Railroad packed out US stadiums and European outdoor festivals. Despite its potential value in stabilising his wobbling winning streak, "Touring right now is not my cup of tea. I just don't need it right now."[29] After doing his minimal duty by the new album, he couldn't wait to "get back to the drinking and partying".[29]

13 "Wherever I Go, It's A Swinging Place, Man"

After *Goodnight Vienna* and 'Only You' slipped from modest apogees in their respective charts, Ringo never had another solo hit in Britain. Any ex-Beatle's television slots were always special, but home viewers began to care less about them as personalities. More intriguing nowadays was the flowchart of titbits – true and untrue – that splattered vivid and often scandalous hues onto their private lives. Second to John – now a permanent US resident – Ringo, say, plugging his album on Radio 1's *Rockspeak*, was regarded as a phantom from the recent past who'd returned to haunt moth-eaten Mods and Rockers saddled with mortgages and a daughter at art college who couldn't stop talking about some group called The Sex Pistols. Her cousin in the police cadets could reel off the personnel on the latest Return To Forever, Billy Cobham and Weather Report jazz-funk albums. For Top Drummer in *Melody Maker*'s 1975 poll, he'd probably favoured technique over instinct by voting for either Cobham, Bill Bruford, Phil Collins of Genesis or Alan White, who, after *The Plastic Ono Band*, had replaced Bruford in Yes.

What was a minor sales territory like the United Kingdom to Ringo, now that Mammon had spirited him away to the New World? If on an irreversible slide elsewhere as a mere pop star, he was lionised almost as if he was an Artist in the States, with its "different atmosphere to anywhere else in the world. And I love television over there."[1] His sojourn in Santa Monica had caked his speech with words like "gotten", "sidewalk", "candy" (for "sweets"), "pants" (for "trousers") and "elevator", and it became his habit to celebrate Thanksgiving – for the secession of the American colonies from his native land.

US tax laws were slightly less harsh than Britain's, but more of a magnet for Starr was its scope for playing the field. To one of many "friends" who sold his story to the *paparazzi*, Ringo "had been labelled for so long the least significant member of The Beatles that he was desperate to assert himself, if only by pulling beautiful girls".[2] His infidelities in California climaxed when a romance with Nancy Andrews – a Hollywood maid-of-all-work – took a serious turn. As much part of the furniture at Stone Canyon Road as Nilsson's Irish girlfriend and May Pang, Lennon's Chinese secretary and extra-marital paramour, Nancy – a wasp-waisted brunette eight years Ringo's junior – was worth more than a second glance. Since graduating, she'd travailed on the periphery of showbusiness as a model, publicity agent and pursuant of other occupations that relied similarly on keeping up appearances and creating a favourable impression.

More Linda than Yoko, she would put her talents – some of them previously unrealised – at Ringo's disposal during her six years, on and off, as his "constant companion". Whilst proving no stranger to many of the commercial and economic machinations of his calling, Nancy's photographs were published on his album sleeves and press hand-outs, and the Andrews-Starr composition 'Las Brisas' was recorded on Ringo's *Rotogravure*, the album that appeared after *Goodnight Vienna*.

At first, Ringo's new love was known only to the Santa Monica set. When Maureen saw him on his infrequent flying visits to England, she explained away his worn-out moodiness as a combination of jetlag, vocational pressures and Los Angeles' ordeal of conviviality. While wishing that he'd unwind a little and actuate an unstrained conversation with her, she kept in her heart the hope that their present separation was but a temporary setback. As her advocate would tell the judge, "She doesn't want divorce. She is fond of her husband and would like nothing better than to make a go of it."[3] Sometimes, Maureen would blame her own shortcomings, but he seemed more abstractedly tolerant of – or indifferent to – her accumulation of eye-stretching bills on his Apple account for costly objects she couldn't see without wanting to possess them. Neither she nor Richie were lovestruck and irresponsible Cavern dwellers any more, but still she was not beyond extreme strategies, if not to rekindle the flame of their lustful courtship then to remind him of what it had been like.

She may have also feigned aloofness to retain composure, but Maureen's frank nature could not allow her to stay silent about stray mutterings that she'd read in gossip columns. Recalling his cheery promiscuity as a London bachelor in 1963, she wasn't so naïve to presume that her "sodding great Andy Capp"[3] of a husband hadn't been tempted into a fling or two while in another hemisphere for all those months. What was she complaining about? He'd provided her with everything she could possibly want, hadn't he? Anyway, he still loved her, didn't he, in hand-squeezing farewells and in the respect accorded the mother of his offspring? After all, he reasoned, "Someone has to look after them."[4]

The mist of resigned despair shrouding Tittenhurst Park thickened with the tightening of Richie's attachment to this Nancy Andrews. More quizzical than angry, the eclipsed Maureen implored him to help her grasp what it all meant, so he "gave me the names of two or three solicitors".[3] He'd admit adultery, and she could name Nancy as co-respondent, if she so wished. Maureen would have preferred him to have shouted back or grope for some excuse for his conduct, some avenue for forgiveness, but he reckoned that "it comes to the point when it doesn't work. You try all these different rooms, and 'Let's do it for the children' and all that, and in the end you have to say, 'It's not working anyway. Why am I doing this? Why is she into that? She's probably into that because I'm into this' – and then it's the breakdown." Like his father before him, "I'm northern, so once it's broken, I cut it off as fast as I can. It's just an attitude I have. Once it's gone, it's gone."[5]

He endured her incessant circular arguments and cliff-hanging silences for a decent interval before leaving – eyes bloodshot with emotional fatigue – for Heathrow and the next flight to California and Nancy. Prior to the hearing for the decree nisi on 17 July 1975, Ringo flaunted his shame across two continents by squiring his girlfriend at the West End première of *Tommy* while treating her to her first Grand Tour of Europe. Maureen saw their photograph with his bow-tied tuxedo and her tanned cleavage in the newspaper.

With pale, drawn cheeks and clasped hands, Maureen gave evidence on that comfortless summer morning in the London Divorce Court, where each bewigged forehead prickled with sweat. The extent to which the humidity might have affected the sitting's financial ordinances was not immediately obvious. Ringo's ex-wife did not face the prospect of earning a crust again, as long as she wasn't too frivolous with a generous award of a yearly lump sum, with increments and a side-serving of assorted sinecures and life policies. On top was Starr's continued support of her parents and Maureen's custody of the children, who would move to the mansion he'd bought her[6] in London's Little Venice, overlooking the canal.

For a while, Ringo was unable to fully exercise his right of access *"pour des raisons fiscales"*,[7] as *Paris-Match* had it, that permitted tax exiles only 90 days per annum in the United Kingdom. The ravages of the Inland Revenue had already driven Maurice Gibb to the Isle of Man, The Rolling Stones to France and Tony Sheridan to apply for Irish nationality. However, it was the loosening of family ties as much as his desire to shield those monies not annexed by Maureen that unleashed the gypsy in Ringo's soul, and he "went wandering".[8] With a mountain of keepsakes and memorabilia in storage, and Nancy gripping his arm proprietorially, he roamed the Côte D'Azur and around Los Angeles from hotel to rootless hotel, where he'd be conducted to the best seat in the restaurant and the switchboard or room service would relay complimentary tickets and social invitations, offering flattery without friendship to one whose every workshy action was worth half a page in *The Sun* or *The Los Angeles Times*. At the reception desk, his thick Scouse articulations would draw muffled titters from those to whom opulence had always been second nature.

While an onyx cigarette-holder protruded from his lips and gold and precious stones festooned his neck, chest, wrists, fingers and ears, depilatory whims also became more vital a subject of discussion than his artistic substance. "To see what it looked like and to make sure I didn't have boils or anything on my scalp",[9] he upset his mother – already dismayed about the divorce – by shaving every hair from his head, including his eyebrows. To please her, he let it thicken to a kind of tonsured stubble. In 1991, after a decade with a full beard and moustache, he would grin at a lucky tabloid photographer while dashing through Heathrow with a face planed of all but what he called a "third eyebrow"[10] beneath his lower lip. It looked comical, but credulous Beatle followers would lap it up as the prerogative of glamour.

"You wonder about getting up," he sighed, "and there is nothing special to do, so you delay it. Finally, you do get out of bed, and you just try to fill the day."[11] Fleeing from boredom, if he wasn't on an aeroplane he'd be in the departure lounge waiting for the next one. With the ease of a daily commuter on the 8.23 to Waterloo, he'd jet from Monaco to Amsterdam for dinner with The Three Degrees – the Prince of Wales' favourite vocal group – and Rod Steiger; from Amsterdam to Johannesburg to watch some tennis match; from Johannesburg to New York just to buy shoes from Ebony; from New York to Las Vegas for a calamitous evening of blackjack or roulette; from Vegas to London for Wimbledon; and from Heathrow back to Monaco for some rich gadfly's wedding. There he'd queue for the buffet with such as Rudolf Nureyev, Christina Onassis and the principality's own Princess Caroline. When he described himself as "a jet-setter – wherever I go, it's a swinging place, man",[12] it was a statement rather than a boast.

The most swinging place of all was Monte Carlo, where, instead of breaking the bank, he gambled for small stakes in Loews, a casino recommended by Peter Sellers. With London less than two hours along the air corridor, he began to regard the resort as a base when, putting a brake on a life of suitcases, he purchased a penthouse suite in one of its "neo-brutalist" modern blocks. To Loews' manager, Paul

Maser, "He's still a little outrageous sometimes – like, he turned up here with his hair in a ponytail – but, overall, he seems to be exactly like someone who is now sitting back, enjoying the fruits of success."[2]

As travel had brought him weariness without stimulation and souvenirs without wisdom, so a pampered but empty semi-retirement led him to sometimes shun the sun, the beautiful people and evening meals in restaurants frequented by expatriate gentlefolk nearing middle age. Instead, he'd have a quiet night in, wallowing in episode after episode of *Coronation Street* and other videoed and soapy links with all that he'd left behind.

Bathed in tedium, he might put down his schooner of white wine, apple cider or brandy – depending on the hour – to mess about on piano or guitar and maybe sort out a *chanson* for the next album. More often than not, days would trudge by without a glimmer of a tune or lyric, or else everything that he attempted would sound the same. Nancy would think so, too, and intimate that a change of scene might make a world of difference – or half a world, anyway, if he took her to his bungalow, rented from Nilsson, high in the hills above Los Angeles. At an address that included the rather iconoclastic street name Haslem Terrace, Richie and Nancy would extend a gladder welcome to callers whose drawling ebullience was more comfortable than the stilted "Franglais" of the Monaco socialites they hardly knew.

Although the Starkey children would spend school holidays there, it was also open house for "all the old faces"[13] from the dissipated *Pussycats* era. "Once the bars close," he calculated, "they'll all drive up here," to be greeted with Starr's expansive "'Hi, man! Yeah, come on in!' If I'm really wrecked, I say, 'You know where everything is. I'm off.' You can actually leave your guests and they don't mind if you're there or not. So that's LA for you. It is a great town, because of the passing strangers."[13] In Ringo's "matured" contemporary abode, visitors would be armchaired with a drink before the open grate, or – if wishing to stretch their legs after a car ride – they would peruse walls lined with framed photographs, platinum discs and other relics of their host's distinguished past. In a playroom, their host had assembled a drum kit for anyone who fancied flailing around.

He would have no need ever again to rattle the traps – or sing, for that matter – because, by 1976, his nine-year EMI/Capitol contract would have run its course. The easiest option was to do as Lennon would and take "a year off, with no obligations to anybody. He's his own man for twelve months, and he's never been that."[14] Nevertheless, the company submitted to Ringo – via Hilary Gerrard – a tantalising bid (albeit one much less than those by other labels) for Starr to re-sign, as he was still hottish property in the States, even if only as good as his latest record elsewhere. On the scorched streets of Monte Carlo – and, by implication, the rest of Europe – "people notice him and point him out," observed Paul Maser, "but they don't go rushing up to him for autographs like they used to. Let's face it, he's hardly a sexy young pop star any more, is he?"[2]

Indeed he wasn't. Although he sported earrings and wore his hair as short as it could be, the newly radical *NME* categorised Starr and those of similar 1960s vintage as pop dinosaurs. If the Pistols dismissed The Beatles as "Scouse gits"[15] and later fired Glen Matlock for liking them, a lot the older outfit's public postures – particularly Lennon's – both before and after Beatlemania had been wilder than those of any punk group. Among salaams to them within the new regime were revivals of 'Help!', 'I Wanna Be Your Man' and 'Twist And Shout' by, respectively, The Damned, The Rezillos and Siouxsie And The Banshees. Chasing punk was a hyped fad for "power pop" (punk minus the loutish affectations), of which the Great White Hope was the winsome Pleasers, blue-grey-suited propagators of "Thamesbeat" who shook their moptops and went "oooooo" as well. Rick Buckler, drummer with The Jam, and The Damned's Rat Scabies acknowledged Ringo's influence, while Roag Best – rehearsing with his Watt Four in the Hayman's Green basement – was given a few pointers by his big brother.

One day, Pete would make the best of a bad job by appearing with a reconstituted Combo at the "Beatle conventions" that were now becoming annual fixtures in cities throughout the free world.

Further entertainment at these functions came courtesy of guest speakers, archive films, weird-and-wonderful exhibitions and sets by bands who, even more intensely than The Pleasers, had cloned The Beatles' image, complete with big-nosed sticksmen, unsmiling lead guitarists *et al*, plus handles like "Walrus", "Cavern" (whose Paul Garrigan was rated "best Beatle drummer since Ringo"[16]), "Abbey Road" and mild sensations of Merseybeatle '90 at Liverpool's Adelphi Hotel, the Soviet Union's own "Beatles Club", managed by Allan Williams. After a record-breaking season at the Everyman Theatre, *John, Paul, George, Ringo – And Bert* – a stylised musical play about the Beatles saga by William Russell, a teacher at Dingle Vale secondary school – moved to London's Lyric. Perhaps its most poignant moment was "Pete Best" dirging 'With A Little Help From My Friends', sacked and alone beneath the proscenium. From the slicker *Beatlemania*, also up the West End, The Bootleg Beatles – the most accurate imitators of all – were formed from the cast.

Because EMI/Capitol still owned the genuine article's master tapes, it was able after 1976 to run riot with posthumous million-selling double albums, such as the up-tempo *Rock 'n' Roll Music*, which in the States spawned a smash 45 in 'Got To Get You Into My Life', culled from *Revolver*. In the interests of expediency, the compilers had ignored offers of help and even injunctions from Lennon and Starr, who were powerlessly sour-faced about its running order, reversion to the pre-1967 royalty rate and the "craphouse"[17] packaging, which, scowled Ringo, "made us look cheap, and we were never cheap".[17]

As a prelude to the campaign, the old firm had recycled "greatest hits" collections by those ex-Beatles about to fly the nest. A few weeks after John's *Shaved Fish* and a year before *The Best Of George Harrison*, Starr's *Blast From Your Past*, with its muzzy sleeve portrait, almost missed being shipped to Christmas shops owing to delays at the pressing plant and the artist's own intervention when its five tracks per side were being selected. As well as giving short weight, this predictable ragbag – the last Apple album – offered little stimulus for the hunter of Beatle rarities.

Giving Ringo more than just a financial return was the chart-swamping aftermath when all 20 of "the finest pieces of plastic around that no one has done anything beyond yet"[13] were reissued on the same spring day in 1976, almost a quarter of a century after 'Love Me Do'.[18] Perusing the UK Top 40, a *Time* correspondent enquired rhetorically, "Has a successor to The Beatles finally been found? Not at all – it is The Beatles themselves."[19] Just before The Sex Pistols shaped up as if they might, Ringo pleaded doubtfully for "a band that gets up there and wipes us out".[13]

A perennial alternative, of course, was for The Beatles themselves to deliver the *coup de grâce*. Not a week passed without some twit or other asking Ringo when the group were going to reform. Now and then, there'd be reports of his tentative agreement to recitals on closed-circuit television for $50 million, or as a surprise on the Rolling Thunder Tour that – with Bob Dylan and a pot-pourri of guest performers – was traversing North America with an itinerary publicised only locally. However, only one Beatle – Ringo – put in an appearance when Dylan and The Band headlined a benefit night in Houston for imprisoned boxer Rubin "Hurricane" Carter. In 1985, rumour would be rife among the multitudes at Wembley for Live Aid that their segment of the international spectacular would culminate with a spot by Julian Lennon and his father's three old comrades. Of that "get-together stuff",[20] Starr regretted that "it doesn't matter how many times we deny it, it'll still go on. Even if there's only one of us left, they'll say he's getting it together with himself."[20]

The four were tempted to call the bluff of Lorne Michaels, producer of *Saturday Night Live* (a TV satire transmitted from New York), who said that he'd squeeze them onto the show if they'd accept the prescribed Musicians' Union fee of $3,200. He didn't mind, apparently, if John, Paul and George wanted to "pay Ringo less".[21] In this playful slight, Michaels showed his ignorance of Starr's higher average of US singles chart placings than the rest, prior to the comparative failure of the 'Goodnight Vienna' medley.

When found guilty in September 1976 of "subconscious plagiarism" in the most notorious civil action of the decade, George was sagging on the ropes as Paul basked in rave notices for his *Wings Over America* concert album and Ringo teetered on the edge of the *Billboard* Top 30 with 'A Dose Of Rock 'n' Roll', harbinger of his *Rotogravure*. With Marc Bolan informing him that "a girl asked him about that new artist, Ringo Starr",[17] he was puffed up enough to demand that Dutch fanzine *Beatles Unlimited* retitle itself *Starr Unlimited* for the edition for which he had deigned to be interviewed, "because we're not The Beatles any more. We're trying to get away from that."[22]

Ringo's pride before the fall might have been aggravated when his visit to Amsterdam in March 1976 was front-paged by *De Telegraaf*. He was merely sight-seeing, he told Holland's most popular newspaper, but only an incurious press would not have got wind of more portentous reasons for a former Beatle's descent into their midst. When he later purchased a stately 19th-century house, it transpired that he'd been shown around properties along the canals. In the gabled Hilton Hotel's Presidential Suite, he'd also been honoured with a party bountiful with topless go-go dancers, a lake of Bols (Dutch gin, that he didn't like) and Manke Nelis, a crippled accordionist bribed in from the *straat* outside.

Footing the bill was Ahmet Ertegun, goateed supremo of Atlantic Records, with whose destiny Starr would be bound until 1981, although Ertegun, as its embodiment, was "not going to control my artistic life. I can give them the records and they can sell them, if they can."[2] As its snatch of The Rolling Stones when they fled Decca in 1971 attested, Atlantic – and its Stax subsidiary – had long been a receptacle, as Ringo knew well, for "a lot of good acts",[22] from The Coasters and The Drifters back in the 1950s to a bevy of chart-busting black soul singers, among them Wilson Pickett, with whom Starr had a fast friendship. Moreover, the guitarist with Stax house band Booker T And The MGs was Steve Cropper, who'd been one of those twanging the wires on both *Ringo* and *Goodnight Vienna*. Therefore, Ringo, at his lawyer's urging, let Germany's Polydor pick the bones of the less important "rest of the world", while Atlantic took charge of selling him throughout North America.

It was to be quite a job, and Starr's easy-going shiftlessness didn't help. "I never work on anything," he confessed. "Dedication is such a weird word, after Albert Schweitzer and people like that. No one dedicates themselves to anything now."[13] Knowing him of old, Tony Barrow – now a senior executive at Polydor – would complain, "We had many offers for TV specials and whatever for him, but he was always totally unavailable to do them."[2] In the studio, too, "Ringo just seemed content to let the producer lay down some backing tracks for him and then he would pop in from Monte Carlo and just stick on his vocals."[2]

In fairness, his drum fills were heard on all bar one track on *Rotogravure*, even if these were anchored as usual by Jim Keltner. However, a break from precedent was the replacement of "busy"[14] Richard Perry with Arif Mardin, a Turk like Ertegun, who – in elevating him to Atlantic's vice presidency – gave practical recognition of the combined musical and supervisory skills that Mardin had perfected through his studies at the Schools of both Economics and Music in London and New York, as well as his dexterity as a bebop pianist as much at ease with the mainstream euphoria of Duke Ellington as the textural complexities of Dizzy Gillespie. It was through arranger Quincy Jones – then in Gillespie's employ – that Mardin came to Atlantic as a producer on emigrating from Istanbul in 1958 at the age of 26.

He saw himself as "a catalyst to bring the administrative situation together – all the musicians, the atmosphere, the happiness in the studio – and then to get the sound and edit and splice".[23] As such, the calm and flexible Arif was much praised by clients as diverse as Wilson Pickett, Dusty Springfield, King Curtis, Aretha Franklin and Petula Clark. Trusting his artists instincts, he was rewarded with a Grammy in 1975 for guiding the talents of The Average White Band – brassy Hibernian soul – and The Bee Gees, who, on *Main Course*, had been in transition from 1960s teen idols to paladins of the disco fever that by 1976 was sashaying towards its John Travolta zenith.

Main Course struck Ringo as "too squeaky – it's like brown music, not black music",[20] but he agreed to meet Mardin in London "to see if we could sit together for an hour".[13] There grew a practised but rather detached professional relationship between the parvenu who "didn't know an E flat from an F demented"[14] and the wine-sniffing jazz connoisseur. While understanding – as Ertegun did – that Starr's economic potential outweighed any artistic merits, Mardin still enjoyed The Beatles enough for 'Glass Onion' to be the title theme of one of his own rather specialist instrumental albums.

At Los Angeles' Cherokee Studios and, later, in Atlantic's own New York complex, sessions ran smoothly, with rarely more than a few takes for each track. Ringo needed time to adjust to Mardin hardly ever expressing either distaste or excitement verbally. By gazing up at the glass-fronted control room, Starr learned to gauge his producer's reaction: "If I see Arif dancing, then I know we're getting a take, but if he's just looking around the room, someone must have played wrong."[13]

Ringo liked "a party atmosphere if we're working well. We all sit around and drink and really have a good time."[14] There might, therefore, have been plenty of scope for squiffy errors within the small army of famous friends that had rallied around to – hopefully – recreate that *Ringo* miracle, for "there isn't a player I know or have heard of who I don't feel I could call and they'd come and play for me".[14]

Satisfying every musical and lyrical qualification required of an evergreen like 'Yesterday' or his own 'Something', George Harrison's 'When Every Song Is Sung' had had a chequered career since Cilla Black's abortive recording in 1972. Retitled 'I'll Still Love You', it was then attempted by Mary Hopkin and, in 1974, by Cilla again, who felt that "even then it didn't have the magic it deserved".[24] Mainly via George's thrillingly ponderous obligato, with its shades of Jeff Beck, some "magic" crept into Ringo's shot at this "big ballady thing I've always loved",[14] but not enough to prevent its burial on side two, among makeweight bagatelles like 'Spooky Weirdness' – a concluding collage of funny noises and electronically doctored utterances – and, driven by a guttural bass throb, 'This Be Called A Song', which, if Hilary Gerrard's favourite *Rotogravure* number, remains a shallow lunge at pseudo-reggae selected from out-takes of Eric Clapton's *No Reason To Cry* LP.

Like Clapton, John Lennon flew to California "just to play on his song".[14] His self-satisfied donation, 'Cookin' (In The Kitchen Of Love)', was premonitory, as he was to extend considerably his "year off", since his position as Yoko's reclusive house-husband in New York's snooty Dakota block had been complicated by the arrival of Sean. Not a note would be heard commercially from John for the next four years. "He's really into that now, cooking,"[14] noticed Ringo during conversations whenever those on the Lennon number took five.

Leaving behind their own cosy domesticity on a Sussex farm, the McCartneys were in the throes of the Wings Over America tour, which, on reaching Los Angeles, was thrown into confusion by an incapacitating hand injury sustained by the group's guitarist. Time hung heavy, so Linda and Paul dropped into Cherokee Studios, where several tankards of cider oiled the wheels of their reunion with Ringo. As Mardin didn't need Ringo for a while, the three continued reminiscing in a nearby restaurant. During a further carouse after dessert, the McCartneys capitulated to Starr's persuasion "and we wandered round to the studio, and they decided they were ready to sing",[25] backing him on 'Pure Gold', a slop-ballad with plinking piano triplets and a limpid sweetening of violins that he had already received from Paul's assembly line.

Starr and Poncia had some mush of their own in 'Lady Gaye',[26] which – avoiding the George Harrison mistake – was an authorised rewrite of 'Gaye', a UK Top-Ten entry for Kidderminster schoolteacher Clifford T Ward in 1973. In their Americanised clutches, 'Gaye' surfaced as "more universal, so it's about a lady who's vaguely a hooker".[22] As token country and western morosity, their 'Cryin" – nothing to do with Roy Orbison – was more elegantly resigned, a feathery bank of strings stripped away in favour of a lonely and lachrymose pedal steel guitar, played by "Sneaky" Pete Kleinow, who had likewise serviced The Bee Gees.

The only other Starr composition thought worthy of his

Rotogravure was 'Las Brisas', which was a memento of a furlough in Acapulco with Nancy. By straying from formula, the couple – now engaged – hadn't struck gold, exactly, but this was the album's most arresting outing. Its instrumental core was 'Legend Of Xanadu' trumpets, Ringo's own maracas and the cantering propulsion of Los Galleros, a mariachi combo recruited from a Mexican eaterie in downtown Los Angeles. Completing this pastiche was the artist's Costa Del Dingle emoting of his holiday romance.

Nancy had impinged further on his act by duetting with her intended on 'By Your Side', but this – along with another Lee Dorsey cover ('I Can Hear You Calling'), an obscure Dylan song ('I Didn't Want To Do It') recommended by Harrison and other items[27] recorded over the three weeks in Cherokee Studios – still moulder unreleased in, presumably, Atlantic's vaults. Perhaps the same fate ought to have befallen the album's singles, especially 'A Dose Of Rock 'n' Roll', which was not anything of the sort but a laid-back, loping concession to disco that borrowed indirectly from the lyrical thrust of 'A Shot Of Rhythm And Blues'. Of the same inspirational vintage and as over-vocalised was a rehash of Bruce Channel's 'Hey Baby', Ringo's US Hot 100 swan song, while just as much of a *moderato* muchness as 'Pure Gold' was 'You Don't Know Me At All', which, aided by a promo film shot on the Reeperbahn, entered chart listings all over Europe.

That all of these A-sides were "foreign" tracks confirmed much of Tony Barrow's assessment of Starr, as well as the present aridity of the ex-Beatle's songwriting well. His principal creative input to the album was in its title – from a line in a Judy Garland movie[28] that he'd caught on television – and cover. Because "the tracks were like pictures",[22] this contained a liberal smattering of Ringo's snapshots of his children, Lennon, McCartney and so on: "All these people are eating and I'll just be drinking."[22] The concept had come to him when this was precisely the scenario at one New York session.

Other personal touches were the assignment of publishing for some *Rotogravure* compositions to his own new set-up, Zwiebel, German for his detested "onion". Further mention of gastronomic preference was evidenced in his "no garlic, thank you" remark on the fade of 'Cookin'' and the inclusion on the back cover of a photograph of the front door at 3 Savile Row, which, since The Beatles had vacated the premises, had been defaced by felt-tip and blade with an *imbroglio* of fans' graffiti. By so doing, Starr stole a march on Lennon, who might have "had it on his – and, as he's not got a record coming out, I thought I'd get in fast."[9]

Ringo may have been unconscious of the irony of the release date of *Rotogravure* – 17 September 1976 – coinciding with the final closure of the Cavern. He was, however, cognisant that his own undertakings weren't what they used to be, either – although he might have once imagined that he couldn't go wrong with George, John and Paul all on his latest album, which, if not first rate, was at least superficially enjoyable. As always, the record industry was voracious for new faces to exploit and discard for a fickle public, and the danger of Ringo being left behind in this soul-rotting race was perceptible even in the States, now, where *Rotogravure* clawed to Number 28, a true comedown by previous standards.

To achieve this, he and Gerrard had hired Los Angeles publicity firm Brains Unlimited to organise his most intense media expedition since The Beatles, covering the USA, Japan and Europe. Patiently sipping Mumm Cordon Rouge – he knew better than to mix drinks – Ringo would give unblinking copy, but his handlers would exchange frequent fretful glances at his commendably frank appraisal of his singing ("the range of a fly, but a large fly"[13]) and how he approached it ("you try it drunk, you go back sober and do it for real – some takes you use when you're drunk"[13]). Mention at the Paris stop of Cliff Richard's contemporaneous LP, *I'm Nearly Famous*, drew the self-denigrating remark, "I used to be."[29]

However, he had high hopes of those he'd signed to his Ring O'Records, inaugurated on 4 April 1976 and destined to peter out just like Ringo Or Robin Limited and the rest of his entrepreneurial sideshows. Depressingly familiar was one Polydor helmsman's observation that he was "using it like a toy",[17] as epitomised by the label's greater specialisation in transitory singles because "they reminded him of his youth".[30] Typical of these were the one-shot likes of 'Cokey Cokey', coupled with 'Away In A Manger' – also with a reggae arrangement – by "Colonel" (alias a Douglas Bogie). Contrary to sound legal advice, Starr chose to settle contracts with a simple handshake rather than chain anyone – himself included – to small-print mumbo-jumbo.

Apple in microcosm, Ring O' had to lease its output to a parent company – Polydor, and then Mercury – until that unreached day when it could afford to declare its independence, without any middlemen claiming a slice. To help the venture on its way, the renowned proprietor's endorsement of its artists and hints that he might add himself to its roster ensured airplay – if not sales – of products that reflected Ringo's musical preferences rather than their inherent marketability, as demonstrated in his reissue of Tavener's *The Whale* to forecasted approbation by "quality" journals but few takers from among the great unwashed.

These days, Ringo also tapped his feet to a conservative assortment of old and new: Led Zeppelin ("they're the tops!"[9]), Clapton, 10cc, Bryan Ferry and – rebutting his earlier dim view – Slade. He was delighted to see that his beloved country and western was now tickling the fancy of a younger audience, thanks to the unhurried emergence of a new tradition of performers who swept a new broom while upholding the genre's down-home lores and veneration for its elder statesmen. Presaging the kd langs and Dwight Yoakhams of the 1980s were Guthrie Thomas, gauche Kinky Friedman and his Texas Jew-Boys and Gary Stewart, who impressed Ringo as "simply amazing, and he'll come through like a teenage Jerry Lee Lewis".[9] He didn't, but he may have given cause for Ringo and label manager Barry Anthony to rub their chins while talent-spotting for Ring O'.

Initially, Starr had sought an established star – a friend, if given the choice – to be the company's flagship act in order to mitigate insolvencies encountered while launching unknowns. However, after failing to outbid RCA when Harry Nilsson was up for grabs, he looked around for "a new one to make him that big".[31]

Unfortunately for Ring O', nobody on its books amounted to much, in spite of what was on paper the fullest distribution network and promotional support around. Mostly too appropriate to the blander end of the mid-1970s pop spectrum, Johnny Warman (no, I've never heard of him, either), Stormer (the label's very own 10cc), Suzanne (its Olivia Newton-John, but blonder), Bobby Keyes (that man again) and all the rest of them were deserved flops, or else were drowned in the riptide of punk.

"Works" were very much the order of the day, then. With 1973's *Tubular Bells* rather than *The Whale* as precedent, Yes, Jethro Tull and Hawkwind were three prominent outfits who cut florid albums with an overall unity teeming with interlocking themes, links and *leitmotifs*. Even Dave Dee – several worlds from 'Legend Of Xanadu' – sang on one (*Few And Far Between* by Jean Musy, an intensely bearded Frenchman), while Steve Winwood had a bigger say in the overblown *Go* by Stomu Yamash'ta. Glutted with EMI producer Parsons' famous associates, The Alan Parsons Project boarded the "works" bandwagon in 1976.

Ring O' responded with *Startling Music* by David Hentschel, a console engineer and keyboard player who'd been engaged by McCartney, Carly Simon, Jim Webb, Elton John and Rick Wakeman, amongst others, before advancement to plum production jobs for the progressive likes of The Nice and Genesis. Through Sussex-born Hentschel's own co-producer, John Gilbert, and via Neil Aspinall, a demo tape of his arrangement of Richard Strauss' *Also Sprach Zarathustra* was identified as the *2001* tune by a "knocked out"[9] Ringo, who suggested a retread of "the most successful thing I've done since The Beatles, which we thought would give it a certain familiarity".[9] When could David bring his machinery down to the Ascot studio? Already there for his use was a state-of-the-art ARP 2500 synthesiser.

In its track-for-track interpretation of the entire *Ringo* album for this instrument, plus slight help from session guitarist Ronnie Caryl and Genesis drummer Phil Collins, Hentschel's technological feat was – despite jazzy and pompously "symphonic" interludes – as lightweight, after its fashion, as James Last. During what was to him but a production assignment, Hentschel found Starr "just like a normal bloke", who, if a little over-fond of a wee dram, did not exercise any executive control whenever he dropped in to review progress – and provide finger clicks for 'Step Lightly'. Nevertheless, despite this blessing and Hentschel's spate of radio and newspaper interviews, *Startling Music* was soon lost to the archives of oblivion.

Next came Graham Bonnet, who, undaunted by his audition with Alan Caldwell's Texans, had bided his time before achieving qualified fame as half of Marbles in 1968 with a version of a Bee Gees song, 'Only One Woman', at Number Five in the UK. Four years of scrimmaging later, he'd landed both the title role in Lou Reizner's stage production of *Tommy* and the managerial acumen of comedian Bill Oddie. Although a gritty vocalist, Bonnet's parameters as a composer were limited to royalty-earning B-sides during his stint as a Ring O' recording artist. After another of his Bee Gees covers and a Hall And Oates opus both bit the dust, the label soldiered on with Bonnet's ambitious disinterments of 'Rock Island Line', 'Danny' – a then-unissued Presley film song[33] – and Dylan's 'It's All Over Now, Baby Blue'. However, as the similarly placed Joe Cocker – and, indeed, Suzanne, with her retread of hoary old 'You Really Got A Hold On Me' – could have told him, a mere Great Voice wasn't enough – although, after a spell fronting Deep Purple splinter group Rainbow, Bonnet finally cracked the charts under his own name in 1981.

Carl Groszman, an Australian singing guitarist of Cat Stevens' stamp, didn't get very far with Ring O', either. Having written 'Down The Dustpipe' – a hit for Status Quo – within a year of his arrival in England in 1969, Groszman had ticked over for a while with such as 'A Dose Of Rock 'n' Roll' for Ringo, who vouchsafed the pressing of his debut 45, 'Face Of A Permanent Stranger'.

This promising young songwriter was also allowed to tape "an album which got wasted. I mean, it didn't surface"[22] after Ringo "wound up going to all these meetings. I was getting nutsy [*sic*] and there was nothing happening. Artists always try to run a record company like it isn't a business."[31] On top of mind-stultifying meetings to decide about the next meeting, Ringo and Anthony were disquieted about Polydor's lack of faith in Ring O' and its related unhelpfulness in securing releases in continental Europe. Starr's company, therefore, laid low until the Polydor deal expired in August 1978.

Cutting back, Ring O' re-emerged on a smaller scale as Able Label Productions, which – while keeping a grip on creative initiative – leased its product to bigger organisations via new director Terry Condon from freshly-painted Mayfair offices not a few hundred yards from where Ringo used to run Apple Films. Before Ring O' also became an albatross, he approved the retention of Warman, Suzanne, Groszman and Stormer and the massing of manipulative force behind records by newcomers like a highly rated singer (another one) in Scotland's Rab Noakes, as well as Colonel-type novelties such as Dirk And Stig,[33] whose 'Ging Gang Goolie' – the Boy Scouts campfire singalong – had been Able Label's first release as Noakes' 'Restless' was its last.

Fed up with trying in vain to tease hits from often dispirited and malcontented artists, Starr terminated the operation in December 1978. "If you don't sell records, then it costs you money," he observed. "You have to look at it straight and say, 'What's going on?', and you either turn it around or you do as I did yet again [and say] that it is time for it to end."[2]

14 "If I Don't Get You, The Next One Will"

It was some kind of back-handed compliment when Ringo heard that up-and-coming film actors John Belushi and Dan Akroyd with Joe Walsh and other members of The Eagles had unwound on an after-hours club stage in Chicago with a long extrapolation of 'With A Little Help From My Friends', rather than 'It Don't Come Easy' or 'Photograph'. Ringo was, however, probably unconscious of bobsleigh rides through 'Boys' and 'I Wanna Be Your Man' by The Milkshakes, who in the early 1980s presided over a Medway town's group scene that was as self-contained in its quieter way as Mersey Beat.

Whether in Chatham, Alice Springs or Centerville, the muzak dribbling from supermarket Tannoys was more likely to be 'Yellow Submarine' than 'Back Off Boogaloo' or even 'Octopus' Garden'. Tune into an easy-listening radio station and The Beatles orchestral medley you'd hear would be all Lennon and McCartney, who could have "made it" with any competent drummer and second guitarist.

Nevertheless, Ringo Starr had proved himself no slouch without them. Now that the halcyon days of *That'll Be The Day* and *Ringo* were gone, who could blame him for doing nothing in particular? It was no sin to make a fortune by providing harmless entertainment, was it? A disadvantaged back-street lad who climbed to the top of the heap, who could begrudge him a secluded but cosseted retirement in his mid 30s? Look at Lennon. With Harrison his heir apparent as the Howard Hughes of pop, he was sighted less often than the Loch Ness Monster nowadays.

What Starr could not articulate was that he adored being in the limelight, seldom missing opportunities to be the focal point of eyes grateful to him for just existing. How would he have felt if politely brief clapping rather than a howling, foot-stomping ovation had greeted him when he mounted his drum podium for just the finale of The Last Waltz, The Band's farewell to the road after 16 years, that had begun in hick Canadian dance halls just as The Beatles had in the jive hives of Merseyside? At San Francisco's 5,000-capacity Winterland auditorium on Thanksgiving Day 1976, it was a Pacific coast "answer" to the Bangladesh concert in its array of the famous and semi-famous – Muddy Waters, Van Morrison, Dr John, Emmylou Harris and Bob Dylan to name a few – individually bowling on to sing a couple of numbers with the departing Band and joining in the *omnes fortissimo* 'I Shall Be Released' from *Music From Big Pink* and – kicked off by Ringo – the dinning instrumental work-outs that followed.

A few months earlier, at the Los Angeles Forum, Ringo could not restrain himself either from sauntering on when Wings were called back for an encore to present Denny Laine – not "obvious"[1] Paul – with a bouquet after "just going to the concert like anybody else".[2] Words are cheap, but after similar wistful attendances at the metropolis' Roxy Theater for Bob Marley And The Wailers and in Den Haag with Vini Poncia for The Hollies – chin-wagging with their Allan Clarke afterwards – he "got 'round to thinking that I want to do it. I'd like to go out with a circus – not elephants, but a circus. Dylan's [Rolling Thunder] and Bangladesh [were] that way"[3] A year later, he was still dithering: "It'll be like a revue, not like Paul and Wings, but Ringo and other people. More theatrical."[1]

With such innovations as graphic equalisers, programmable desks and even synthesised drums to do battle against adverse acoustics, Ringo wasn't alone in feeling that touring with a backing group was attractive enough to erase flashbacks of how dreadful it had been in the distorted epoch when vocal balance had been achieved by simply moving back and forth on the microphone. Riding a so-called Mod revival, The Who – with Kenney Jones on drums – were on the boards again, and so soon would be diffident Steve Winwood, bankrupt Gary Glitter and others from quiet fastnesses where the only manifestations of the squalid holocaust over the hills in London, New York and Hollywood were gold discs lining balustraded stairwells.

As the 1980s loomed, his spirit might have been willing, but he lacked financial motive. It was less grief to get smaller kicks with short, one-off events like The Last Waltz and a Labour Day telethon in aid of medical research in 1979 from Las Vegas, where – at the request of Bill Wyman's agent/girlfriend – he beat the drums on 'Twist And Shout', 'Jumpin' Jack Flash' and, appropriate to the occasion, 'Money' in an all-star assemblage called "Superjam" and, with Bill, lent an hour answering telephoned pledges.

To a less charitable end, he'd present a white horse to Julian Lennon at that fledgling pop star's 19th birthday celebration amid the gold-diggers and brattish swells in London's faddish Stringfellow's night club. All that he had to do to upstage founders of such feasts was to simply go to them. Glam-rock latecomers Queen[4] began 1976 with 'Bohemian Rhapsody' at Number One and EMI International's dazzling party in their honour at the Cunard Hotel. Petals from the very flower of UK pop in the 1970s were there – Bowie, Rod Stewart, Bryan Ferry – sipping posed cocktails that looked like melted crayons, when a buzz filtered through the 300-odd guests that Ringo Starr had arrived. This wasn't television or a picture in *Jackie*; that impossible yardstick of teenage escapism and aspiration – a Beatle – was actually within, asserting his old power in abundance in his involuntary lure for the younger conquistadors and their acolytes who buzzed around him like bees around a jam jar.

Ignored at his side was Lynsey de Paul, to whom he had given a fishing rod, because she was always angling for compliments. Some of these were deserved, for, although her five-year chart run was about to end with a British Song For Europe entry, singing in public was secondary to Lynsey's songwriting skills. 1972 had been her red-letter year, with a Top Five debut ('Sugar Me') and The Fortunes showing class in the US Hot 100 with her 'Storm In A Teacup'.

Her confidence boosted by this syndication, Lynsey crossed to

Los Angeles to better ply her wares before more prestigious customers than this lucky Birmingham combo. A tangent of this expedition was her romance with actor James Coburn, and it was on her return to London after breaking with him that she embarked on a more light-hearted affair with Ringo for several months. Possibly, this was an antidote to the vulnerable de Paul's protracted and harrowing legal wrangling with her ex-manager. As well as the new boyfriend's masculine charms, she was also beneficiary of his tambourine-bashing and image in the publicity photo for 'Don't You Remember When', a ballad she produced for aging "Forces' Sweetheart" Dame Vera Lynn. If not a hit, it was an excuse for another EMI beanfeast at the Dorchester, in Park Lane, where its composer had no complaints about any shortage of compliments. When Starr's 90 days in the United Kingdom were up, so, more or less, was their amour, Lynsey penning 'If I Don't Get You (The Next One Will)' as its requiem.

Over in California, Nancy might have supposed that the main purpose of her fiancé's 90 days a year in England was to make a fuss of his children. She was, therefore, taken aback by reports of his supposed satyric exploits in UK tabloids[5] and reported airy comments such as "there are girls in my life because I still have all the normal urges".[6] Nevertheless, although there were frank exchanges in their Los Angeles bungalow, she held onto the belief that her ex-Beatle was worth keeping and that his intentions remained honourable. She tried, therefore, not to hear any more of his other attachments and clung onto her dignity as his official lover by devoting herself, as always, to the enhancement of his neglected career.

It may have pleased her to think that it was the ante-start agonies of the sensitive artist that impeded his knuckling down to another album. He seemed to be holding it at arm's length by accepting more record dates for friends. Although not confining himself as much to the established, it was a reversion to that trough between *Beaucoups Of Blues* and *Ringo*: nothing too strenuous – "a couple of days, only three or four tracks, because I don't want to get stuck in to do the whole album, because I don't even want to do my own album".[7]

While he grappled with his depressed muse, a Starkey original, 'Band Of Steel' – the one from the *Beaucoups Of Blues* period – was resurrected by Guthrie Thomas on his *Lies And Alibis* LP. Its inclusion – with the composer on drums and, with Thomas and Steve Cropper, lead vocals – was more to stoke up airtime from curiosity-seeking disc jockeys beyond Guthrie's usual orbit than its worth as a song. The stylised blue yodels on its fade-out hinted that 'Band Of Steel' – an all-purpose country and western item stuffed with negative symbolism – might have been just end-of-session badinage.[8] If it was, far funnier were earlier send-ups of the form, such as The Rolling Stones' 'Dear Doctor', 'Rameses II Is Dead (My Love)' from The Fugs and – a few months after *Lies And Alibis* – 1977's 'Men's Room LA', an attempt by to see if God could take a joke by Kinky Friedman, who was blessed with Ringo as "The Voice Of Jesus" on its spoken passage, which was personalised with references to Liverpool and France.

With Friedman on Dylan's Rolling Thunder wayfaring was The Alpha Band, who – via Friedman's owlish guitarist Joseph "T-Bone" Burnett – got Ringo to play on a brace of tracks (including Dylan's 'You Angel You') on their US-only *Spark In The Dark* album as a change from their own jazzier drummer. Often flanked by cronies like Jim Keltner and Dr John, Starr was roused to serve likewise Manhattan Transfer – who, with Bette Midler, spearheaded an injection of archly kitsch cabaret into pop – and Keltner's own Attitudes, a loose convention of "funky cats" who performed for their own delectation in venues local to Los Angeles, until Jim's pal George Harrison underwrote and issued their two albums and a pestilence of singles on his Dark Horse, a label only marginally more lucrative than Ring O'.

The most interesting – and disappointing – of these diversions was Adam Faith's cluttered Los Angeles production of *Puttin' On The Style*, an album on which, at Paul McCartney's suggestion, Lonnie Donegan remade some of his skiffle smashes – as Howlin' Wolf had his blues set-works – with a host of famous lifelong fans like Ringo, Elton John, Faith's *protégé* Leo Sayer and Queen's guitarist, Brian May, sitting in with Donegan's regular band. With only one barely remembered US hit, Lonnie might bring much of the aura of a fresh sensation to that majority of young Americans who'd never heard of him.

Everyone had heard of Ringo Starr, but this appeared to be to his cost now, as shown by the album that he'd eventually finished – *Ringo The Fourth* – faring worse than even the Lennons and Harrison's *avant-garde* abominations of the 1960s. As some English history primers start with the Battle of Hastings, so when numbering his new solo LP Starr excluded the two released during the Dark Ages of The Beatles. Significantly, this was also his first effort since the group's sundering that was bereft of any aid from John, Paul or George – although, even without this omission, I doubt that *Ringo The Fourth* could have risen much higher than its dismal Number 162 in the States. As Starr's name on the sleeve of Attitude's *Good News* and Harrison's on Splinter's *Two-Man Band* could not forestall tumbles into the bargain bin, so it was understood that having an ex-Beatle on board – even on another ex-Beatle's record – was no longer a licence to print banknotes in that watershed year of 1977.

Most of Starr's old retainers – including Keltner – were also missing from *Ringo The Fourth*. Instead, he left it to Mardin to pick and choose from the slickest supporting musicians on Atlantic's files, as well as layer an icing of contemporary celebrities such as Bette Midler, Luther Vandross, Jim Gilstrap and Melissa Manchester, whose latest 45, 'Monkey See Monkey Do', was a much-demanded radio spin.

Belying this ominous preamble, *Ringo The Fourth* was in theory Starr's most courageous musical statement, in that the bulk of its ten tracks were from the Starkey-Poncia songbook, even if two were cast-offs from *Rotogravure*. However, other than 'Gypsies In Flight' as the country-and-western weepie, most were gorged with an over-generous helping of a *moderato* soul style – smoother than Stax or Motown – that was then just ceasing to waft from trend-setting Philadelphia as the likes of Gilstrap, The Stylistics, The Three Degrees and MFSB neared their sell-by date and such as Vandross, Chic and Tavares took up the slack – a word well chosen, because still exhaling from late-night stereos were routine "Philly soul" duplications, all synthesised string backwash, clipped *chukka-wukka* guitars and prominent backing chorale lowing an over-stretched coda as the main vocalist's hopes of imminent sexual congress increased. For good measure, there might be bursts of beefy horn riffing or a key change whenever you started to doze off.

Left off *Ringo The Fourth* but a B-side common to both of its US singles, 'Just A Dream' – original in its unoriginality – utilised this yawnsome formula as well as a lyrical juxtaposition of unconscious reverie and agonised waking reality, as pre-empted in Roy Orbison's 'In Dreams' from 1963. On the album, neither 'Simple Love Song' nor the McCartney-esque 'It's No Secret' are about anything much, 'Out In The Streets' – in which he was less dockland Ted than Bowery switchblade-wielder – being Ringo's most specific self-projection. He was, however, more attractive as a rueful pipe-and-slippers survivor of school and adolescent trauma in 'Gave It All Up'. Its narrative underlined with street-corner mouth-organ, this was the collection's most poignant stroke, if marred by a weedy chorus and sub-Philly production.

Rather than scourings from the archives of his youth or specially commissioned songs, Mardin and Starr consumed needle time with reworkings of 1970s items that walked a tightrope between *bona fide* songs and fine-quality disco fodder. Because Ringo's version of La Seine's 'Tango All Night' had permeated the dance floor in as recently as 1976, the *Ringo The Fourth* single on which Atlantic pinned its hopes was 'Drowning In The Sea Of Love', composed for Joe Simon in 1971 by Gamble and Huff, the very Lennon-McCartney of Philly soul.

Of slightly greater antiquity was 'Sneakin' Sally Thru' The Alley', a Lee Dorsey effort from the previous year that had been revived by Robert Palmer, Yorkshire's highbrow soul connoisseur, then on the verge of a Frampton-sized US triumph. Its clichéd re-arrangement for Ringo's album absorbed the processed handclaps, flatulent clavinet and "twanging-plank" bass lines that would plague pop for the next decade.

As Palmer gained a toehold in the US charts in 1975, so – more gingerly – did Gold Rush with 'Can She Do It Like She Dances'. With a hookline of ascending semitones as lewd as the verses, Ringo coped well with its feverish lechery, but essentially he wasn't cut out to sing most of the material on *Ringo The Fourth* because, however much he attempted to hack it as a fervid blue-eyed soulman without affectation, he was no Cliff Bennett or Steve Winwood. Although he tried hard, the voice was raucous rather than passionate when he extemporised. While it might have been enchantingly ludicrous for, say, *Sentimental Journey*, Ringo's ingrained Scouse pronunciation – "I love you so mooch", "our uffur [affair] is over" – was often just ludicrous on *Ringo The Fourth*.

His accent may have stuck out like a sore thumb to his all-American session crew, but only its Californian gloss made it conspicuous back in Liverpool, where some still saw him not as a gilded ghost but as a scrawny drummer from Rory Storm's Hurricanes who'd hit the jackpot and had stayed lucky. By his own admission, "I don't know why it happens to me half the time."[3] All they knew was that, if he hadn't joined The Beatles, he'd probably be in a job where he had to metaphorically touch his cap, as they did.

By keeping his nose clean, Pete Best had worked his way up to deputy manager at Garston Job Centre. On leave, he'd bank extra brass by answering questions about the old days and beating his drums at Beatle-associated events and – less often but more lucratively – on US television. His autobiography was on the cards, too, but whatever this earned him would he peanuts against the millions he missed. Some childish Beatle fanzines mocked his resentment, calling him "Mr Sour Grapes" and suchlike for being the spectre at their revels, an impurity who must have deserved their heroes' cowardly purging as well as "heartache, grief, financial embarrassment – you name it. Now and then, something comes up – a bill or something – or, when it snows, you'd like to disappear off to the Bahamas. Then you think, 'If I'd been a Beatle, I wouldn't have had any worries.'"[9]

One day, Pete would regard himself as more fortunate than poor John – and Ringo, too. With a happy marriage and two lovely daughters, he was certainly better off than Tommy Moore, who, since The Beatles, had been more contented with his lot, a job with the Liverpool Corporation while playing in a jazz band some evenings. An apoplectic fit would take him at the age of 47.

Nothing could alter the less professional affinity of another long estranged from The Beatles, but all that Ringo's natural father – a Bolton window-cleaner, these days – had to show for it now was a signed photograph of the group. He'd stopped sending unacknowledged presents to his grandchildren, but could only be proud of his son: "He's done well, the lad, and good luck to him. He owes me nothing."[10]

The eldest of Richie's brood, was proving a bit of a handful. With his dad's gallivanting absences and "Count Dracula hours"[11] setting no good example, Zak's truancies and disruption of classes were causing anxiety at his private academy in Maida Vale. With an open invitation to bolt to "Uncle" Keith Moon's West End apartment, what chance had the unhappy youth had? "See, during my puberty, Moonie was always there with me," he explained, "while my old man was far away in Monte Carlo or somewhere." Although he took after his dad facially and in his manner of speaking, "Being Ringo's son is a total pain," he'd grimace. "I'm always written about as Ringo's son, always classed with him in every single thing I try to do."[12]

Like all but the most serious-minded teenagers of the late 1970s, Zak had been excited by punk and, while still modelling himself on Keith Moon, was a fan of The Ruts, a sub-Pistols bunch from north London. From merely looking the part (earring, zippered bondage trousers, black leather bomber jacket), Zak became the youngest member of The Next, who, from weekend rehearsals, risked engagements at parties and then alternating with El Seven and The K9s, as well as a group formed around the sons of late Yardbird Keith Relf and other local outfits at South Hill Park Community Centre, the rougher Bridge House and like venues within spitting distance of Tittenhurst Park, where Zak would occupy a lodge cottage on leaving school. Eventually, Sarah Menikides – a girlfriend five years his senior – would live there too.

As well as his prowess as a percussionist, Zak's supplementary importance to The Next was his procurement of free time at Startling Studio, despite his insisting, "I don't want any help from my dad. I want to prove that I can do it by myself. He hasn't done a thing to help me, and I don't want him to."[13] Source of much envenomed discussion was Ringo's wariness about his boy drumming for a living. Dad did not "envy him the challenge".[14] Besides, The Next might not be able to use the studio for much longer, because Ringo had just put the manor up for sale through Chancellors, an Ascot estate agency.

Windsor and Maidenhead Council's concern about its state of repair – a lot of dampness, apparently – brought forth contemptuous offers of less than half of its six-figure asking price, and thus it was taken off the market, even though its peripatetic owner flitted between California and Monte Carlo most of the year and was actively looking at properties elsewhere in Europe. As Amsterdam was fast becoming one of the music industry's storm centres, two floors of Mr Starkey's house there had been converted to white-furnitured offices to deal with the fingers he'd poked into various pies.

He'd also looked over likely looking buildings in Hamburg of fond memory. After so doing, he couldn't push off without looking in at the Star-Club, now, could he? An erotic cinema was on its old site, for it had relocated – as a discotheque featuring occasional live acts – to the Grossneumarkt, further from the disreputable heart of the Reeperbahn, which, now under government licence, was not as open-minded about human frailty as it had been. While there were many new auditoriums, such as the Fabrik (once a factory), some old haunts still bore their original names, if nothing else. The Top Ten had long gone, as had Peter Eckhorn and Manfred Weissleder, but the Kaiserkeller was still in business as a transvestite bar.

Although he'd kept in touch with acquaintances from that distant chapter, Ringo couldn't help but visualise them in some fixed attitude, doing what they did then. Sure enough, when he and George looked in at a Star-Club anniversary show, there was Tony Sheridan – who'd been rumoured to have been killed while entertaining US troops in Vietnam – slaying 'em on stage. Backed by former Presley sidemen, he brushed aside the millennia since 1962 like matchsticks. On sale in the foyer was his new so-so LP, *World's Apart*, produced by Klaus Voorman, who had also made a prodigal's return to Germany.

Nature hadn't been particularly kind to grey-haired, grizzled Tony, but ex-bouncer Horst Fascher was in rampant good health. The proprietorship of the place and marriage to Bill "Faron" Russley's daughter obviously agreed with him. For Horst, Starr and Harrison ambled on to shake hands with "the Teacher", but, if bubbly before the flashbulbs, Ringo left soon afterwards, harassed by the general onslaught of the German media – that had buttonholed him the second he'd stepped off the 'plane – and by Sheridan's manager harping on about The Beatles doing a concert for the Vietnamese boat people.

There seemed fat chance of anything of the sort as George went on to the next stop on the promotion campaign for his newest album and Ringo tooled back to Monte Carlo. Unlike the other two, he was still close enough to John to persuade that home-keeping mister to donate a drawing to another Big Apple Beatlefest raffle (for UNICEF), even though "we don't live in each other's pockets any more. After Paul was busted for carrying pot in Tokyo, I didn't even have his phone number."[14] Putting the kybosh on that leg of Wings' world tour, the detainee's week pondering his folly in a Nippon gaol elicited a sympathetic telegram from Harrison and "flowers and a packet of candy"[14] from Starr.

As any creative reunion appeared more and more untenable, the group's hardcore fanatics fragmented into separate camps, subscribing to, say, Wings' Fun Club, the Harrison Alliance or – through a *Record Collector* small ad – the Ringo Starr Fan Club, instigated by an enthusiast from Chesham, Berkshire. Whether scorned, admired or just tolerated in this new phase of Beatlemania, Ringo was still perturbed that "being an ex-Beatle or being Ringo Starr sometimes doesn't allow you to be yourself when you walk into a room full of people, but I am pleased that I was what I was, and I am happy that I am me."[2]

Others weren't as happy with him as they used to be. To Klaus

Voorman, excluded from *Ringo The Fourth*, "He's changed. He's not as reliable and he's not so nice."[15] Other musicians hadn't a bad word to say about Starr, but "they only see me on a nice day".[3] One who did was *Beatlefan*'s London correspondent, Andrew Matheson, who, at the Queen gathering, found him "chatty, funny and natural".[16] Waiting outside for a taxi after his new-found friend had departed, our man Matheson's favourable opinion was enhanced when Ringo's limousine glided back from the Dorchester to give him a lift home.

However, there was no mistaking the steel underneath the happy-go-lucky exterior whenever he had matters to discuss at Atlantic's Los Angeles headquarters. "I wouldn't say he's rude," estimated one employee, Kristen Gunderson. "Let's say you're not left in any doubt what he wants. If it's to do with his recordings, then he wants it dealt with first. He's no different in that respect to every other artist; it's just that, in Ringo's case, you don't quite expect it."[17]

More than anyone, Elsie Starkey understood that "he doesn't want to be thought of as a clown any more. He's more serious than most people realise, and he can be forceful when he needs to be. More than anything, he wants to become successful as an actor."[18] A US go-between, Alan Pariser, was on the look-out for such an opportunity, but the route to any role as strong as that of Mike Menarry was fraught with potholes such as the *NME*'s not-unfounded jibe that, other than his records, Starr had spent most of the years since 1970 in "duff movies and heavy-duty ligging".[19]

He couldn't resist the proverbial "something to tell his grandchildren about" of a not especially ample part in Mae West's final movie, *Sextette*, no matter how disappointing the reviews that caused its fade with indecent haste from general circulation after a midnight première in Atlanta in July 1978. In this bawdy farce, Miss West – wisecracking in her sexy serpentine husk – was in character as Marlo Manners, a Hollywood screen goddess who'd just plighted her troth to her sixth husband.

Ringo played Laslo Karozny, a temperamental European film director who'd also been so manacled to her. At first, as with Peter Sellers and *The Magic Christian*, Starr "felt completely out of things"[20] in the presence of a celluloid legend who'd "never needed Panavision and stereophonic sound to woo the world. I did it in black-and-white on a screen the size of a postage stamp. Honey, that's talent."[21] However, comforted perhaps by the knowledge that she was a Beatles fan,[22] "by the second day, I would have stayed for as long as she wanted me. She's old enough to be my grandmother, so it's sort of embarrassing to say, but she's bloody attractive. And Mae's no Garbo. Mae doesn't want to be left alone."[20] Doddering she might have been, but she turned out for the post-production blow-out to receive the plaudits of male co-stars, which also included Tony Curtis and George Hamilton. Also on hand were bit-part players like Alice Cooper and – as a camp dress designer – Keith Moon. As well as being a mediocre epitaph for Mae West, *Sextette* was also Keith Moon's last film.

More certain an indicator of future direction for Ringo than *Sextette* was his effortless lead in *Scouse The Mouse*, a concept album of a children's story by distinguished old stager Donald Pleasence, under the musical direction of Roger Brown. As a poor consolation to Starr's UK following, chagrined at so much US-only product, this soon-deleted record of late 1977 and its affiliated illustrated book[23] and painting-competition entry form was exclusive to Britain and the Commonwealth. However, although an ITV animation of *Scouse The Mouse* was proposed, the powers that be procrastinated until the advent of the grander Roland Rat brought the curtain down on Pleasence's rodent.

Rat would be to Scouse what a Sherman tank is to a Mini. Like Tony Hancock, he'd abide none of the doe-eyed winsomeness that some – including Scouse's investors – deemed touching. If crass and insensitive, Rat was further favoured by a more colourful supporting cast and funnier plots than that which launched – and finished – *Scouse*, a mouse's progress from pet shop to cage in a Liverpool household, where he learns English from the television. Inspired by a vocal group called The Jollys, he learns to compose, sing and dance. Aflame with ambition, he escapes and, after various adventures, sails on the QE2 into New York harbour, intending to take the land of opportunity by storm.

Hmmm. With Ringo at the taping in Soho's Berwick Street Studios were members of narrator Pleasence's family and a motley assortment of stars that included Barbara Dickson (from *John, Paul, George Ringo – And Bert*), Adam Faith (the other Mike Menarry) and, just blown in from the Windy City, comedienne Ruby Wax. It was produced by Hugh Murphy, who was about to shine with an international hit in Gerry Rafferty's 'Baker Street' – but not with 'The Taster', (Alan) Clayson And The Argonauts' debut single.

In our yokel innocence, we were too unsure of ourselves for open mutiny when, during the session with Mr Murphy, our keyboard player's triplets were ghosted by one of Rafferty's men, Tommy Eyre, who was also among those musicians that Murphy called up for *Scouse The Mouse*, a most polished album in its crossfading of sound effects, songs and dialogue. If swallowing chaff behind later efforts in the same mould by Roland Rat, The Mister Men and Rupert Bear (under Paul McCartney's aegis), Murphy's raw material was tolerable and pertinent to imagined visuals – particularly 'Caterwaul' (a "cats' choir" waltz), Faith's gorblimey 'America (A Mouse's Dream)' and 'Scousey' by Lucy Pleasence, whose clear soprano was worthy of a Maddy Prior or Jane Relf.

Within Ringo's lion's share of eight numbers, 'Scouse's Dream', 'I Know A Place' (a duet with Polly Pleasence) and the hootenanny 'Running Free' stuck out, but the ace in the pack – although it's not saying much – was the nautical lament, 'SOS'.[24] Far less objectionable than *Ringo The Fourth*, this album for infants was a suitable vehicle for Starr's unforced urbanity, always a handy resort when the going got rough, which it would with growing frequency

Adapted from 'A Mouse Like Me', the *Scouse The Mouse* finale, A Man Like Me' (watered-down Kurt Weill), concluded *Bad Boy*, Starr's seventh solo LP. As he couldn't get a hit to save his life now, Ahmet Ertegun had let him go to Portrait, a CBS tributary. It was, therefore, a matter of pride for Ringo and Portrait to ensure that *Bad Boy* left more of a wound in the US charts than *Ringo The Fourth* had. Who needed Mardin and his layers of treated sound when aiming for home-made passion with Vini Poncia at the helm in studios in far-flung Canada and the Bahamas?

That was the theory, anyway, and *Bad Boy* certainly clambered fractionally higher in *Billboard*'s tabulation than its predecessor, thanks largely to a leg-up from a US television special, chat-show spots and – for the inventive Beatle rumour-monger – the enigmatic and pseudonymous listing of auxiliary musicians on its sleeve.[25] Balancing these manoeuvres were the paucity of critics who went ape over *Bad Boy* and, crucially, that mighty watchdog of pop propriety *Rolling Stone*, kicking Starr when he was down with "not even passable cocktail music. Ringo isn't likeable any more, and that truly is depressing."[26]

This was a harsh dismissal because, pin-pointed in the crash of exasperated cymbals that jerked you from 'A Man Like Me', *Bad Boy* was a more idiosyncratic if warmer work than either of Mardin's squeaky-clean Atlantic albums. Nevertheless, now a stale songwriting team, Vini and Ringo had virtually shed their creative load on *Ringo The Fourth*, for only two more Poncia-Starr compositions were ever released, both on *Bad Boy*. 'Who Needs A Heart' was its punchy opener, and lame 'Old Time Relovin'' was just one degree removed from country and western by its staccato organ obligato and jammed *accelerando* coda. As insignificant an opus was the *Bad Boy* UK single 'Tonight', offered to Ringo by author John Pidgeon and Ian McLagan,[27] a beau of Keith Moon's widow and a jobbing musician since leaving Rod Stewart's Faces.

A sense of simply going through the motions once more was evident in Ringo's strained and often uninvolved singing on merely workmanlike overhauls of 'Monkey See Monkey Do', Gallagher And Lyle's 'Heart On My Sleeve' and 'Hard Times', a wittily observed piece that had been suggested by George Harrison, who'd played on Peter Skellern's 1975 album of which it was the title track. Older items rehashed on *Bad Boy* included a Benny Spellman single from 1962 ('Lipstick Traces On A Cigarette') and 1957's 'Bad Boy'[28] by The Jive Bombers, covered lately by both Mink De Ville and Sha Na Na, as was 'Heart On My Sleeve' by Bryan Ferry. Likewise,

Manhattan Transfer's 'Where Did Our Love Go?' may have nudged Ringo's revival of this revival of The Supremes' 1964 smash, which was infused on *Bad Boy* with that strutting boogie rhythm synonymous with Canned Heat but programmed on an aberrant sequencer. Now that he was free from the constraints of sustaining a chain of chart entries, Ringo would be sating himself with many more too-premeditated reconstructions of the ancient hits of others after *Bad Boy*. Although he'd never succumb to drum machines, with their robotic exactitudes, the latest studio gimmick would intrude upon guts and – especially if the original versions of the likes of 'Where Did Our Love Go?' had emotional significance for the listener – leave a queer aftertaste.

So, too, would *Ringo*, the TV tie-in, which was a vehicle for him to mime to pre-recordings of his best-loved songs with and without The Beatles and – implying by association that they were just as eternal – excerpts from *Bad Boy*. These were hung on an approximation[29] of Mark Twain's *The Prince And The Pauper*. Set in Hollywood rather than Tudor London, it begins with George Harrison's cameo explanation about two identical babies born at the same moment. One grows up as Ringo Starr, idol of a world shortly to watch him perform in a satellite-linked concert. He swaps places with his doppelgänger, "Ognir Rats" (get it?), a pitiable sandwich-boarded pedlar of sightseers' maps of Beverly Hills. Seen along the way as both changelings get into various scrapes are such as Vincent Price, Angie Dickinson and *Star Wars'* Carrie Fisher (as Ognir's girlfriend). Nonetheless – you guessed it – all ends well in the nick of time, with Rats taken on as highly waged road manager to the proper Ringo, who wows 'em – as evidenced by heavily overdubbed screams – in the bounced broadcast.

Despite this element of wishful thinking, *Ringo* was a splendid if dear means of publicising *Bad Boy* and Starr's back-catalogue, and – with Ringo playing both himself and Rats – as an elaborate general audition for any suitable film roles going, because "no one is going to offer Ringo Starr a top role these days just because I used to be in The Beatles. I've got to be able to do the job. That's much more demanding, but much better, too. I could end up with egg on my face but, succeed or fail, it's all down to me standing on my own two feet as an actor."[14] It could have been *Ringo* that brought him his first solo top billing – "I'm the hero, you know, the king of the castle"[20] – in a family movie in preparation since 1977 called *Caveman*. "When you need a small, suave, funny, awkward, unprepossessing leading man," elucidated its director, Carl Gottlieb, "there aren't a lot to choose from: Dustin Hoffman, Dudley Moore, Robin Williams – and who else is there who's also a star? There's Ringo."[30]

As an afterthought, *Ringo* was shown elsewhere five years after North America. In the lonely Sunday hour after the God-slot, it induced a glaze over many British eyes maddened already with the prospect of an evening sabotaged by snooker. Back in 1978, even in the States the impact of *Ringo* had abated quickly, and people who read of his personal desolations over the next year felt sorry for him, but not sorry enough to buy his records, not even the albums that had now been made available on budget labels.

When seated by the fireside on one November evening in Haslem Terrace, Starr had been alarmed by sparks belching suddenly from the chimney, where a stray shard of flame had already ignited the roof and the attic, where he'd stowed cherished memorabilia, from gold discs to his first pair of drumsticks and the shoes he'd worn for that official maiden booking with The Beatles at Port Sunlight. On dashing to investigate, he rang the fire brigade before singeing his hair in the process of grabbing what he could from the spreading inferno. No one was hurt, and half an hour's hosing by six engines saved most of the bungalow and Ringo's costly musical equipment, but little remained of the blackened attic's contents.

To journalists, who'd had no inhibitions about quizzing him as the building still smouldered, he'd wailed, "Money could never replace those things."[31] A more deliberate blaze had long ago incinerated further links with Ringo's past when Iris Caldwell threw most of her deceased brother's remaining possessions onto a bonfire instead of putting them under the hammer at the auctions of pop artefacts that were so beyond a joke as to concern Christie's and other top salerooms. However, Iris' drastic clear-out had uncovered a 1962 tape of a Rory Storm And The Hurricanes engagement, with Ringo, at the Jive Hive, and there was talk of finding someone to hire a studio to clean up its atrocious sound quality for release as a tardy 1979 supplement to a double LP, out two years earlier, that had improved digitally a similarly hand-held recording on Kingsize Taylor's tape machine of a night during The Beatles' last season at the Star-Club.

If documentary rather than recreational, The Beatles' *Live At The Star-Club, 1962* was more engrossing to most people than anything current by Ringo Starr. Nevertheless, as Elvis Presley had demonstrated in as recently as 1977, a death in pop could still revive a flagging chart career, and certain record-business moguls wondered what Starr tracks they'd be entitled to rush-release if he didn't survive an emergency operation on 13 April 1979 in a Monte Carlo hospital. Five feet of blocked intestine had to be removed by laser surgery after he'd been carried in doubled up with the tell-tale abdominal pangs of his old ailment, peritonitis. As it had been when he was six, "Everything twisted up inside me."[32] However, although he'd told the convalescing Ringo that "another minute or two and it would have been curtains",[32] a surgeon was able to inform both well-wishers and a press corps itching to relay obituaries that the patient was "a courageous man and responded well to treatment. A lot of sick people tend to be miserable after an operation, but Mr Starkey was very cheerful and able to swap jokes and banter with the nurses. The doctors are very pleased, but work is out of the question for the time being."[32]

Although still green about the gills, Ringo was sufficiently recovered to pass a medical examination for United Artists' insurers on the postponed *Caveman*. As a legacy of McCartney's arrest in Tokyo, Starr and his luggage would be searched thoroughly by customs officials desirous of a dope-free Mexico, but, assuming that he was cleared, the initial shoot was scheduled for February 1980 in the rocky sierra surrounding Puerta Vallarta, near Durango. He was to play "Atouk", chief of a rebel tribe, in this prehistoric comedy with no highbrow pretensions. Neither were there qualms about authenticity as Atouk tames dinosaurs who were extinct aeons before humankind commenced its deplorable sovereignty of the planet. While *Caveman* swiped gently at 1966's *One Million Years BC* in the Raquel Welch coquettishness of shapely Barbara Bach (as "Lana") and, in a more overall sense, the apemen section of *2001: A Space Odyssey*, it was closer in spirit to earlier stabs by Buster Keaton, Charlie Chaplin and Laurel and Hardy at the Neanderthal sub-genre of film in its slapstick simplicity and jokes about dung. Apart from a 15-word language created by the community's Chinese wise man (*ca-ca* for "excrement", *zug-zug* for "copulation" – you get the drift?), the dialogue consisted mostly of grunts and moans accompanied by much gesticulation, body talk and face-pulling. It definitely beat having to learn lines. As a sop for Beatle freaks, the tale begins in one zillion BC on 9 October, John Lennon's birthday.

For the first few reels, Ringo appeared in the same guise he had striven to hurl aside since *Help!*, as a Chaplin-esque underdog – although one more lively and engaging than before – but he was in no mood to care about that. In his eagerness, he'd have cheerfully dusted off his *A Hard Day's Night* character.

Treated like dirt by the other tribesmen, who use their womenfolk as fishing poles, Atouk becomes a vagabond who, while gathering about him his own warriors, trains himself to walk upright, discovers fire (and barbecued chicken) and, in the film's most diverting sequence, makes music with his band, one of them thrusting a dotard's hand rhythmically into the flames so that he screams in time. After defeating hefty tribal bully Tonda (American footballer John Matuszak), he wins Lana, the object of his desire, but, chuckled Barbara Bach, "I'm the bitch. In the end, the girl next door wins out. I get thrown in the dinosaur dung."[30]

How frightfully funny. Gottlieb's credentials as co-scriptwriter of 1975 blockbuster *Jaws* and saturation advance publicity guaranteed *Caveman* a fair critical appraisal in a society that had taken Benny Hill's saucy inanities to its heart. Indeed, US press comment is worth quoting at length. Against the *Chicago Tribune*'s "not so much a bad movie as it is a tedious one with a slight script",[33] there was "nicely whimsical"[34] from *The New York Times*, "enchanting"[35] (*Village Voice*) and "infantile but also playful and appealingly good-natured"[36](*Newsday*). Although hardly Marlon Brando as Don Vito, Ringo didn't come out of it too badly, either. *The Washington Post* might have turned its nose up with "going 'round pointing and saying 'ca-ca' is not what one would have expected from a legendary Beatle",[37] but to sweeter-natured reviewers he was "better here than he's been in anything since The Beatles' films",[37] "a delight"[31] and – possibly a double-edged accolade – "as puppy-dog charming as ever".[33]

With all of the attributes of a box-office smash but none that actually grabbed the public, *Caveman* was soon booming out in half-empty Midwestern drive-ins, and on its second night in London's West End it drew all of six customers in one cinema. Some even stuck it out to the National Anthem.

However its shortcomings affected Starr professionally, his participation in *Caveman* was also one of far-reaching private import – at least, as private as one whose every waking hour was chronicled was allowed. Tongues wagged about Ringo and leading lady Shelley Long in the teeth of his stock assurance that they were "very good friends but that's as far as it goes",[14] but of infinitely more substance were rumours about him and Barbara Bach, which provoked "confirmed reports" that they were to wed as soon as her divorce to Italian industrialist Augusto Gregorini was finalised. There was no reason not to believe that this "B-Movie Queen Might Turn A Beatle Into Prince Charming",[30] as, holding hands, they seemed never to be off US television throughout the spring of 1981 while plugging *Caveman*. Next broke the distressing news that the pair were co-habiting a leased house off Sunset Strip, while a Los Angeles estate agent was under instructions to go up to $2 million for a more permanent dwelling spacious enough to contain her two and his three offspring as well. Contradicting the gossip, Barbara – like Ringo – could not "imagine why I would ever get married again. The way I am now, if I want to be with someone, I'll be with that person, but I see no reason to carry his name as well."[30]

Lana and Atouk's on-camera flirtations (prior to the

unpleasantness with the dung) had, he admitted, "just spilled over nicely into real life".[38] Their social circles in Hollywood had overlapped before *Caveman*. "It wasn't love at first sight," reflected Barbara; "it began to grow within days of meeting each other."[38] In Durango, she'd been touched when he chose to sport with local children between takes, and he'd admired her stoicism as John Matuszak hurled her time and again into the Maguey River when one scene had to be re-shot until Gottlieb was satisfied.

Underneath a brash outer shell, Ringo came across as "so interesting, a very nice guy",[30] and she was quite happy when he escorted her both to a St Valentine's dance held during the last week of filming and on a trip to the Mexican Grand Prix. His wooing of her was consummated "when Ringo invited me to his home in Monte Carlo to watch the Monaco Grand Prix. I didn't hesitate [for] a second. It seemed totally natural."[38] On his part, Starr was as besotted and full of jaunty vitality as a middle-aged man could be with a stunning starlet eleven years his junior: "I haven't been this happy in years. I'm ecstatic."[39]

All of this was mortifying for both Nancy Andrews and Barbara's boyfriend, cinematographer Roberto Quezada, who gallantly withdrew. Nancy, however, was not prepared to be so acquiescent. Via the US legal system, Richie would pay. Although his alien status was among pleas for the quashing of her case against him (a kind of updated breach of promise), a precedent had been set by showbusiness attorney Marvin Mitchelson, whose eloquence had won Michelle Triola a sizeable chunk of her ex-lover Lee Marvin's assets and established the right in California for unmarried partners to sue for property division. Securing Mitchelson to speak for her, too, Nancy sought "palimony" of several million dollars' share of communal property and a percentage of Ringo's earnings for her toil on his behalf to the erosion of her own vocational prospects. However, bar the shouting, she was reduced to just a memory in Ringo's mind, as he only had eyes for his new love, now.

Her surname having been shortened from Goldbach when she left her all-girls convent school on Long Island at 16 to become a model,

Barbara's high cheekbones, hazel eyes and avalanche of silver-blonde hair betrayed more of her mingled Austrian, Irish and Romanian ancestry, although she and sister Margerie were raised in Queens, New York's predominantly Jewish suburb. While she "never felt I was a fantastic beauty",[30] she had been in a younger but comparable league to Twiggy, Celia Hammond and Pattie Boyd on the catwalks and before the shutters, after a cover picture in *17* led to assignments in Europe. Through a casual encounter along a Roman via, Barbara was featuring in Italian TV commercials when she was noticed by director Franco Rossi, who gave her a part in a film treatment of Homer's *Odyssey*, despite her amateur standing as an actress.

Although she could have pursued this opening, Barbara had committed herself to Gregorini and subsequently the rearing of Francesca – born in 1969 – and Gianni ("Johnny"), whose emergence four years later had been complicated by the umbilical cord coiling around his neck and briefly but crucially cutting off his oxygen supply. A sufferer from cerebral palsy, Johnny was, nevertheless, fortunate in that his rich father paid for the best therapy that money could buy and a corrective operation in the States.

With the children still babies, Barbara was an active campaigner for reform in staid Italian legislation on abortion and divorce until, with the souring of her relationship with Augusto, she moved to Los Angeles to dip her toe back into movies with pot-boiling parts in minor chillers such as *The Island Of The Fish Men*, *The Humanoid* (as evil Lady Agatha) and a remake of 1945's *The Unseen* (where she met Quezada), as well as professionally humiliating and very American satires like *Mad Magazine Presents "Up The Academy"*, in which "I could have been a stuffed doll".[38]

Despite submitting eventually to a nude photo spread in *Playboy*, "I did not want to be known as a sex symbol. I had different films offered to me where I was to play attractive, sexy people, but I was not interested."[38] Without realising what it would entail, she auditioned for television's *Charlie's Angels*, but was bypassed for looking "too European, too sophisticated. I'm afraid I didn't take them seriously enough when they asked questions like, 'What brought you to Hollywood?' I'd often wondered myself. Somehow, I sensed that the problem was not whether I could act but whether I could be fluffy enough."[38]

In 1977, she compromised between thespian aspiration and natural radiance with the role for which she will be best remembered: Major Anya Amasova in *The Spy Who Loved Me*. This tenth James Bond excursion was a rewriting of an old plot, with Anya – an added character – as Roger Moore's Russian opponent and bedmate. Barbara's reluctant voluptuousness here was vindicated in the following year, when she starred with Edward Fox and Robert Shaw as a severely uniformed Yugoslav resistance fighter in *Force Ten From Navarone*, the sequel of sorts to Alistair Maclean's *Guns Of Navarone*.

At the opposite extreme to this taut espionage drama was *Caveman* and blossoming romance with Ringo Starr, ex-Beatle, who seemed an odd choice to her family, because he was so different from her previous sweethearts. Also, Barbara was not a pop consumer. If pressed, Ray Charles and Aretha Franklin were about her limit. As for Ringo and The Beatles, "I don't think I could have named five of their songs a year ago. I was never really into music, though I am now, up to my ears. I'm surrounded by it, because Richard is making another album."[30] The one-line lyric of a new Starkey composition, 'Can't Fight Lightning', was dedicated to Barbara. On the hitherto-unissued recording, she and Francesca had shaken maracas.

15 "I Knew I'd Had This Problem For Years"

Whereas Paul McCartney was accorded 41 lines in the *Who's Who* social register, Ringo Starr was squeezed between Kay Starr and Steppenwolf in *Whatever Happened To...?*, a publication purporting to be "the great rock and pop nostalgia book".[1] As Paul gave a speech of thanks for another Ivor Novello statuette, 40-year-old Ringo was almost artistically inoperative, as "by 1980 I could not write any more and I was just that personality person. I would be at all the parties with my bow tie on. If you listen to the records, you can hear them going downhill."[2] While *McCartney II* and its 'Coming Up' single were each Number One virtually everywhere, the Lennons were almost ready to return to the fray with a new album, *Double Fantasy*, and a willingness to impart to the weightier journals pearls of beatific precepts and wisdom that they'd accumulated during their five years away.

When prodded whether he had a message for the 1980s, Ringo's reply was as nihilistic as any punk rocker: "Message? I'm not a post office."[3] His Chesham fan club advertised no more in *Record Collector*, but, just as much "Mr Showbusiness" as McCartney, he was the ex-Beatle most likely to host award celebrations, accept plaques on behalf of the group[4] and be amusing on chat shows when prompted to retell one of the old, old stories. "Nobody ever asks about Rory Storm or The Eddie Clayton Skiffle Group," he lamented. "They were good bands, too."[5] Like other 1960s has-beens, he'd also answer perfunctory and unnoted enquiries about whatever current record his interviewer would or wouldn't ever hear. Then everyone would clap and the case would close again on Ringo Starr.

He'd let go, stopped trying to prove himself. Unlike Paul, "I don't want to put a band together and play every night. I just don't want the hassle."[3] Instead, he went on more holidays than the Duchess of York. What was escapism for most was the world in which he lived. When in Paris, no waiter's eyebrows would rise if he ordered sausages and chips to go with a minor Beaujolais in Montparnasse restaurants where only such as Bardot, Dali, Fellini, Warhol, Hemingway and Jackie Kennedy could afford to clatter fork on plate.

Borabora, in the Tahitian archipelago, was so remote a tropical paradise that it could only be reached by boat. Yet, on its beach, his lilo would be adjacent to that of, say, Charlton Heston or Raquel Welch.

In common with the dolphins he might have sighted there, Starr seemed to be devoting his life to the pursuit of pleasure, much of which was derived from staying in the public eye. "Most of the time," he'd pronounced, "I do things because I want to do them, which isn't necessarily right, but I like to have a good time."[6] The 20th anniversary of 'Love Me Do', for example, would be an excuse to drum and sing an ill-advised medley of 'Honey Don't' and 'Blue Suede Shoes' with the house band – and Barbara cavorting in the foreground – on Michael Parkinson's Australian chat show.

It wasn't as if he needed the cash, but he became the first – and only – former Beatle to palm some for endorsing merchandise on television, when he extolled the virtues of a make of leisurewear in a series of seven Japanese commercials. He also appeared in dubbed sketches, composed four short ditties (all entitled 'Simple Life') and – relaxing on a sofa – ruminated generally about Renown T-shirts, slacks, *et al*. Yen had also beckoned aesthete David Bowie into the spheres of Oriental advertisements, but he'd pulled back after just recording a soundtrack to one for a brand of sake (rice wine).

Although not the Sir Henry Irving he may have presupposed himself to be, Bowie had also been more circumspect about his availability for dramatic projects than Starr. A pretext for Ringo's trip to two of his favourite European capitals were his respective

discussions about his next movie with X-certificate writer Harold
Robbins at Amsterdam's Amstrel Hotel and then on to Vienna and
Robert Altham, producer of 1975's Academy Award-winning film
Nashville. As vibrantly purposeless was the noise made about Ringo
playing a "way-out psychiatrist"[7] in an aborted comedy – but,
although films seemed a rosier basis for optimism nowadays, "I do
want to make one rock 'n' roll album a year. Once a rock 'n' roller,
always a rock 'n' roller."[7]

If 1978's *Bad Boy* was classified thus, Ringo was rather behind
schedule when, on 15 September 1980, he spent Thanksgiving with the
Lennons in New York's Plaza and picked John's brains for feasible
numbers for a new LP because "he knows me better than anybody else
in the world, better than the other two, so he really becomes involved
– playing, singing, doing everything he can."[8] For self-designated
Beatle patriarch John, "It was like a brother relationship," May Pang
would recollect sadly. "It's so hard to explain, but it was just that he
had great love for all of them – for George, for Ringo...and for Paul."[9]

As well as tossing his former drummer demos of four new songs
– including 'Life Begins At 40' and 'Nobody Told Me' – and
promising to be there when recording began in January, John
sounded out Ringo about Portrait's efficiency as distributors, as he
was wondering about issuing the one after *Double Fantasy* on his
own label. Starr seemed rather disgruntled with Portrait then. With
Bad Boy a disheartening speculation, the label had insinuated that
he'd be better off with someone else. Furious, too, that CBS had
denied him both adequate funding and use of the company jet for
promotion of the record, Ringo had been hawking his talents around
other labels before coming to roost on Boardwalk – a subsidiary of
Neal Bogart's Casablanca corporation – in the States and RCA for
other territories. His maiden album under the new regime would
bear the title *Stop And Smell The Roses*, having exhausted several
others such as *Stop!*, *Ringostein*, *Can't Fight Lightning* and *Private
Property*. The latter was also the name of the lesser of two
McCartney contributions, as Ringo had fallen back on his "famous-
cast-of-thousands" approach.

Paul had decided to cling onto 'Take It Away', considering that "it would suit me better, the way it went into the chorus. I didn't think it was very Ringo."[10] However, less a Wings cast-off than 'Private Property' and its synthesised brass,[11] 'Attention' was typical of many McCartney creations to which Ringo's first reaction – like mine to Elton John's 'Snookeroo' – had been, "No, not this time. Then I've been in the hotel lift and his song comes out of my mouth as a whistle, and I think, 'Sod him. He writes bloody catchy tunes.'"[12]

'Attention' hinged on a clever-but-simple two-note tiff honked by saxophonist Howie Casey, who, since leading The Seniors, had become a denizen of the London session scene and had been hired by Paul to augment Wings in the studio and on tour. In the Superbear complex in the Nice mountains, Paul also produced 'Can't Fight Lightning' – left off the album in the eleventh hour – and a countrified Starr treatment of Carl Perkins' jogalong 'Sure To Fall', once a McCartney lead vocal with The Quarry Men. He was also loud and clear, now, in the vocal unison sections – with Casey's wife, Linda McCartney and Barbara Bach – and in his backchat with double-tracked Ringo over Lloyd Green's steel-guitar solo.

The album would touch on Western swing, too, in George Harrison's supervision in Paris of a vicariously delightful version of Jo Stafford's 'You Belong To Me'. Expressive of Harrison's own re-creations of childhood preferences on his recent *Somewhere In England* collection, Ringo sang the 1952 million-seller more or less straight. He also made a credible job of George's solemn gambol 'Wrack My Brain', deservedly the LP's only single. Another Harrison piece for *Stop And Smell The Roses* had been 'All Those Years Ago', but Starr couldn't pitch its higher notes. When a hit 45 for George in 1981, it had been re-invented as a requiem to John Lennon, who hadn't been able to manage the subsequently cancelled January sessions after all.

"John who?" her shaving husband in the bathroom had spluttered when Kathy Best had shouted the news from the wireless that creepy December morning on Merseyside. Meanwhile, the drummer that Lennon had rescued from having to get up to go to work was far from the differing greynesses of Liverpool and New York when he was told by Barbara's Francesca. He knew which John had just been slain on the sidewalk outside the Dakota by a former hospital security guard – henceforth referred to by Ringo as "the arsehole"[6] – who was mad about The Beatles in the most clinical sense.

In Maida Vale, it was dawn when Maureen and Cynthia Lennon – who chanced to be sleeping there – were woken by his call from the Bahamas. Next, Richie, as fearful as George and Paul of a copycat shooting, summoned the tightest security net for his and Barbara's immediate flight to New York via Miami to offer condolences to Yoko. The hundreds of air miles across the Atlantic seaboard was the only opportunity for continuous thought, the final sanctuary in which he could catch and hold happier images of the intimate that horror had swallowed so mercilessly.

From the aircraft, the couple were shepherded by five minders to a purring Cadillac. Through its one-way windows, they glanced at chalked headlines on newspaper stands and electronically transmitted images of Lennon on TV sets in electrical goods shops pocking the stop-starting drive from Kennedy Airport to the city centre. Suntanned amidst the cold, they were self-contained spectators with no stake in the tragedy until, with no parking space in the Dakota forecourt, shock impinged itself on them as they hastened past clutching hands (some flapping autograph books), winced at the pitiless *whoomph* of flashbulbs and stepped over the self-same paving stones that had been wet with Lennon's blood. Although he apprehended the massed grief behind that corridor of police barricades, Ringo "was not very happy with the vigil. Those people showed very little respect for either John or Yoko. It was disgusting."[13]

Once inside, the compulsory journey appeared even more foolhardy when the widow insisted at first on speaking to only Ringo. Barbara could wait in another room. Biting back on his anger, Ringo persuaded Yoko gently that, as she and John had been – sorry, still were – one, so it was with him and Barbara now. After defusing what might have developed into an untimely flare-up, Ringo played for a while with Sean, the Lennons' son, bringing a smile to the five-year-old's face before leaving – but, commented one of her friends, "Yoko was not forgiven. Oh, Ringo was nice. He always was nice."[14]

"When we came out," Starr explained later, "I didn't need to hear people telling me how much they loved The Beatles, because I wasn't there to see a Beatle. I was there to see my friend."[15] That it had been a rite by which the "Beatle generation" – if rendered wrinkled, balding and old by the speed of events – was saved by the sacrifice of its leader in his prime was one analogy that may have appalled him, but, while between planes in Miami, he'd perceived some fatuous truth in a youth's comment, "'At least the rumours that you're getting together will stop now.' But, of course, they probably never will. There's already this crap going down about us doing a memorial album for John."[6]

Actually, it was only a single, 'All Those Years Ago', on which Ringo and Wings had backed George, but otherwise the surviving Beatles and fellow travellers – like Tony Sheridan, who hadn't spoken to Lennon since 1964 – behaved much the same as any outsider who kept, at Yoko's request, the worldwide ten-minute silence for John on the Sunday after the shooting. Ringo "just stayed at home and I thought, 'John's dead.' That was probably the best way to pay my respects: by keeping quiet."[15] To this day, he has forbidden himself to record the songs that John had given him at the Plaza and from any media comment far beyond suppositions as uninformative of deeper feelings as any in the rash of "tribute" discs that were being composed while the corpse was still warm. According to Starr, Lennon had transcended to some meritocratic pop heaven "up there with Jimi Hendrix and Elvis and all the rest of them".[15] For years, eyes would stretch when he began interviews by tweely addressing an unseen Lennon, before assuring others present that "he's watching over us, you know".[6]

Whether these performances were designed to be funny or not, dreadfully serious were the fangs of Alsatians tugging at leashes gripped by a squad of sentries on 24-hour surveillance around the Starkey residence in Los Angeles. Like some Mafia don, their employer was edgy when approached by even the mildest of strangers. Visitors would not he admitted, therefore, unless they'd telephoned well beforehand with the precise hour of arrival. "Suddenly I felt I could be a target for the next madman."[16]

Without premeditation, death had already come close at dusk one spring evening in 1980 when Ringo and Barbara were motoring to a Surrey party from the Dorchester. At 60 miles an hour, Ringo swerved to avoid a collision with a lorry on the dual carriageway of a Kingston bypass made slippery by a downpour. After ramming two lamp-posts while riding out a 50-yard somersaulting skid, he ignored a leg injury and pulled his passenger clear before calmly limping back to the upside-down 1973 Mercedes 350 SL for his cigarettes. As he tended to a shaken Barbara, curtains were drawn back in nearby windows and someone dialled for the police and an ambulance. Surrounded by flashing blue lights and rain-coated watchfulness, Ringo comforted Barbara while a grim-faced constable jotted down facts and elected not to charge him. His "We had a crash; it's cool"[17] was the most-quoted remark, after he and Barbara – with her cuts, bruises and hurt back – were rushed to Roehampton Hospital, where they were discharged before the rest of the world woke up.

If made temporarily wary of powerful automobiles, Starr still found the emotional detachment to purchase the same model a month later. By then, a crusher had pummelled the wreck to a cube for plinth display as a Ringo Or Robin-type conversation piece in Tittenhurst Park. Ringo also decreed that splinters of the windscreen be mounted in a heart-shaped broach each for himself and Barbara, whose resolve to stay together had hardened *en route* to the casualty ward.

Their courtship had been assumed to be stormy by those who perused one tabloid hack's scoop of the two's violent quarrel outside Tramp as they clambered into a taxi. As the vehicle sped their fist-shaking ravings off into the neon night, the scribbling newshound saw no reason why the incident could not be portrayed as a common occurrence. Nevertheless, any gleeful hopes of pursuing the couple's turbulent separation were thwarted when, three weeks after the Kingston accident, Barbara announced to her father that she intended to marry the boy.

Originally, they'd planned to plight their troth in Malibu, sending a video of the service to the groom's parents, who, while they could manage the occasional outing to Ascot for his and the grandchildren's birthdays, didn't fancy venturing overseas from Woolton. Possibly, it was John's slaughter in gun-totin' North America that caused Richie's switch of location to Marylebone Registry Office on 27 April 1981. By coincidence, not only had registrar Joseph Jevons officiated at the McCartneys' nuptials in the same town hall but the bride in the ceremony preceding the Starkeys' that windy afternoon was the daughter of former Apple engineer George Peckham, whose own espousal Ringo had attended.

These fascinating snippets – and, indeed, the wedding itself – was less interesting to *The Daily Express* than "The Reunion"[20] that it splashed across its front page the next day. The photograph that Terry O'Neill had flown from New York to take was later syndicated throughout the globe for a tidy sum. The three surviving Beatles were shown together in public for the first time since John's passing. The second set of faces that drew the viewer were those of their American wives, especially the new Mrs Starkey, who, mixing metaphors, "had always believed in Prince Charming if ever he came riding up on his charger".[18]

In her joy, she was as flushed as the roses that decorated her plunging ivory silk wedding dress. Designed by David and Elizabeth Emanuel, who'd likewise served the Princess of Wales, Barbara's get-up clashed with that of Ringo, all black with Teddy Boy bootlace tie and sunglasses unnecessary beneath the leaden skies outside, where his and Paul's exits to non-descript taxis were hailed by screams from an 800-strong crush of fans, who'd divined what was going on. More averse than his former colleagues to adulation, George – with Olivia Harrison – contrived to shuffle out almost unnoticed.

At the wedding party for the first Mrs Harrison and Eric Clapton in 1979, George, Ringo and Paul had pitched in with an *ad hoc* combo – that embraced various Rolling Stones, Denny Laine, the reunited Cream and Jeff Beck – on a makeshift stage to hammer out mostly classic rock and the peppier *Sgt Pepper* songs. While queueing for a go on the drums with Ginger Baker, Jim Capaldi, classical-turned-pop percussionist Ray Cooper and Zak of The Next, Starr was struck with the notion of doing "one like that again with just the four of us [Beatles], once Sean is five and John starts playing again, [because] it didn't seem strange at all. We were having a booze-up and a laugh. It felt pretty good to me."[19]

Of course, a few twitches of a trigger had put paid to that; but, at the Starkeys' wedding reception at Rags, a Mayfair club, a car-rental firm had deposited amplifiers, two guitars and a bass should any among those present feel an urge to entertain in what was described by Roger Shine – one of the witnesses on the certificate – as "a knees-up Mother Brown and lots of dancing, with people playing spoons and overturned champagne buckets".[20] Although Ray Cooper rattled the cutlery, others stuck to conventional instruments, with Nilsson and McCartney taking turns at the piano while Harrison and Starr plucked guitars. The strains of 'Strawberry Fields Forever' were, allegedly, heard as a homage to poor John. Other than the five-pointed, solid-silver star given as a keepsake to each of the 70 guests, it was a very down-home affair, with a high percentage of relations and old chums from Liverpool, a wedding cake – star-shaped, naturally – and, with 20-odd youngsters up past their bedtimes, all over by midnight. The happy couple had left already in a white Rolls for a decoy honeymoon "in California". Actually, it was spent in London, the last place any prying reporter would expect to find them.

For the 161 days per annum that the Department of Immigration permitted Ringo to reside in the States, the family could make itself comfortable in a rented mock-Georgian dwelling in Beverly Hills with obligatory swimming pool and orange grove. Although the refinement of the owner's Picassos was mitigated by Starkey touches, such as the strands of twinkling Christmas lights around the front door in April, the USA was less than a second home, now, as Ringo's first "American period" had terminated effectively with Lennon's murder. For several years, there'd be but flying visits on business, for TV promotions and social duties such as a pal's New York wedding in May 1962. With an attempt on President Reagan's life by another "arsehole" that year, "What chance do other people have? I always loved living in England."[21]

He would regain little lost native popularity and he'd miss the Californian sunshine, but the weeks arranging the wedding had made him understand how homesick he'd become during his six years of globe-trotting. Back at Tittenhurst Park, he could develop tolerance towards the local council's officiousness in refusing him permission to modernise "antiquated"[21] Startling Studios with video facilities. They also turned down his cheeky application for a grant of a few hundred quid to improve the riding stables, now that, with Barbara's enthusiasm for equestrianism, he was over his antipathy to horses, galloping his acres on "Dolly Parton", a beast more his size than the *Blindman* stallion.

Spoken of as if an old nag out to grass himself, the fellow was never seen to do a stroke of work. As in the "happy ending" of a Victorian novel, with all the villains bested and the inheritance claimed, he'd settled down to a prosperous lassitude where nothing much was calculated to happen, year in, year out. Beneath an untroubled sky, "Squire" Richard and his lady would stroll around the grounds with their dogs – a labrador, a spaniel and an alsatian – and children, of which they'd decided enough was enough. For balance, there was the occasional hiccough, such as the eye that bled when the alsatian bowled him over. It was serious enough for Ringo's transference from Heatherwood Hospital, on Ascot's main roundabout, to the optical unit at King Edward VII's in Windsor, but in his usual shades he was able to keep a tea engagement later that afternoon, where the day's misfortune provided something to chat about.

Too arcane a subject in some southern parlours were tidings specific to Merseyside. However, like several other British cities, the festering unrest in its most depressed districts had exploded during 1981's humid July. From Toxteth and the Dingle, the reek of burning had seeped as far as central Liverpool, where, for two nights, shops were looted with supermarket trolleys and torched with petrol bombs. Alarm bells and sirens executed a discordant threnody as the

Rialto Ballroom – where all the groups used to play – crumbled in a haze of smoke and powdered plaster.

Ringo had remained *au fait* with south Lancashire affairs through his study of the *Liverpool Echo* and other local journals that were mailed to him at Tittenhurst Park. Although he thought it "good that students are actually into the music that much, rather than the Great War",[23] he wouldn't go as far as Paul in patronising the University's Institute of Popular Music, although he would be – along with Virgin magnate Richard Branson – in a consortium bidding for the cable television music franchise in Merseyside.

In its battle against recession, the area had fallen back on its potential for sight-seers through its then-near-invincible football team – and its cradling of The Beatles. As well as twice-daily guided tours to such golgothas as Admiral Grove and conferring Beatle-connotated nomenclatures on the shops and watering holes newly operational around redeveloped Mathew Street, Liverpool further stressed its pride in the group by naming four streets on a Wimpey Homes estate[24] of raw red brick after each of them – Ringo Starr Drive, Paul McCartney Way and so forth – despite one sniffy councillor's earlier objections that, in the light of Allan Williams' published memoirs[25] of "what went on in Hamburg and their use of filthy language", "The Beatles should in no way be linked with the civic name of Liverpool."[26]

Although it dominated national news bulletins for a day, there wouldn't even be a "Billy Fury Mews" when – like he knew it would – a heart attack finished Ringo's fleeting classmate in 1983. As he might have wished, Fury passed away with a single in the Top 50, although unable either to begin his comeback tour of Britain or complete *The Only One*, his farewell album. His fans' sorrow was either exorcised or exacerbated by a special edition of *Unforgettable*, a Channel 4 nostalgia romp, on which he was seen running through his best-loved songs for the people who loved them – and him – most of all.

Unlike Fury, Cilla Black had no need to dwell on past glories. Genial hostess of ITV's *Surprise! Surprise!* and, next, *Blind Date*, her shrill giggle would also infiltrate 1980s situation comedy. The highest-paid woman on television, her generation's Tessie O'Shea, a defiant wearer of genuine fur coats and now an evangelical Tory, she said that she planned to retire at 50 to her Buckinghamshire manor.

Pete Best had no such expectations, but he was employed gainfully during one break from the Job Centre in publicising *The Complete Silver Beatles*, a 1982 release of the group's Decca test 20 years earlier. This had been purchasable for years as a bootleg, which, defying all copyright laws, was a commodity abhorrent to Ringo – although John had built up quite a collection.

Perhaps Pete's maligned sense of humour was more acute than Ringo, John, Paul and George had realised, as, during this jaunt, he autographed one of Ringo's gold discs that was up for auction at a Los Angeles Beatles convention. On similar occasions, both the Starkey and Harrison family's Liverpool lavatories were displayed and sold as solemnly as Duchamp ready-mades. Like a splinter from the True Cross, one of Ringo's ties fetched the highest bid at a Methodist fête in Wolverhampton.

Money matters of greater portent were on the agenda whenever the living ex-Beatles and Mrs Lennon met to discuss the dividing of the empire and, later, long-running litigation against EMI/Capitol over royalties. At one such council in Starr's usual roof-garden suite at the Dorchester, one of Yoko's gofers observed that "nothing was accomplished",[14] but, when she wasn't around, the three who'd travelled a longer road with John loosened up with selective reminiscences about the struggle back in Liverpool and Hamburg, when the Earth was young.

Time would never heal totally, and there'd always be traces of sibling rivalry, but none of them were feigning indifference about the other two's activities any more. Liverpool City Council would have to wait forever "for sentiment to work the oracle [*sic*] that showbiz millionaire entrepreneurs have tried in vain", as they refused to reform without Lennon "in an effort to launch Merseyside as a major tourist centre".[26] That would be up to others. Nonetheless, the outlines between Paul, George and Ringo's recording endeavours had merged a little more since the jolt of 'All Those Years Ago'. McCartney was also back in the harness with George Martin, and it was at the latter's newish Air Studios on the Caribbean isle of Montserrat that Ringo – with Barbara – had eluded a few days of an English winter on a working holiday, at Paul's behest, to drum in tandem with *Ringo The Fourth* veteran Steve Gadd on 'Take It Away', which, ratifying McCartney's earlier judgement, would be the hit spin-off from the follow-up to *McCartney II*, *Tug Of War*.

After a companionable French holiday with the McCartney brood, the Starkeys were there in fancy dress for the rock 'n' roll dance championship during one of the annual "Buddy Holly Weeks" that had taken place since Paul's acquisition of the bespectacled Texan's publishing rights. For the laugh, too, Barbara, Ringo and Zak turned up at a complex in northwest London to be in the 'Take It Away' video before an invited audience, who were thrilled with the post-shoot jam session, which included requests for ancient Cavern standbys like 'Searchin'' and 'Lucille'.

The video's director, John Mackenzie, was also the grey eminence behind *The Long Good Friday*, a gangster flick whose greyer eminence was George Harrison, executive producer of HandMade Films. As with Alfred Hitchcock, the sharp-eyed might espy George playing bit parts in these. With Ringo behind the kit, for instance, George was one of The Singing Rebels band during a concert sequence in *Water*, starring his Thames Valley neighbour Michael Caine.

If he was only too pleased to assist Harrison and McCartney, who could blame Starr – once the most engaging and arguably, if briefly, commercially viable ex-Beatle – for eating his heart out with Paul still an international chart assailant and George – with music of less prevalent significance – a paladin of British cinema? With no such negotiable strings to his bow, what was Ringo nowadays?

His wilderness years were by no means over, but *Stop And Smell The Roses* had sidled to the outskirts of the US Hot 100 on the back of 'Wrack My Brain' – his first Top-40 entry since 1976 – and the associated aftershock of Lennon, who was presumably one of the "three brothers" thanked by Ringo on the album jacket. He needed every marketing device he could procure, what with the chaotic effect on Boardwalk of the death of Bogart – Starr's principal champion on its board – and one influential journal voting *Stop And Smell The Roses* the "worst record of 1981".[26]

With pioneering essays in the brutish *braggadocio* of rap behind counters in that year, Ringo's album wasn't truly as awful as all that, but, as *The Toronto Star* pointed out, "There's lots of sludge, stuff no one except, perhaps, an ex-Beatle could get away with."[27] The weirdest outpouring of all was when – like the late Gene Vincent, The Hollies, The Nashville Teens, The Dave Clark Five's Mike Smith and other shameless stars *in extremis* – he revamped one of his old hits. There'd been no half measures with 'Back Off Boogaloo', either. As producer Nilsson had with 'You Can't Do That' in 1968, Starr squeezed in vignettes of Beatles numbers, as well as the circular riff of 'It Don't Come Easy'.

Quotes from hits by Rod Stewart, Otis Redding and David Bowie[28] broke up the monotony of Nilsson's song for Ringo, 'Drumming Is My Madness',[29] which would not have been out of place on *Both Sides Of The Moon* in the ambulant, blaring broadness of the instrumentation behind its nonchalant, slightly camp vocal that also pervaded Nilsson and Starr's 'Stop And Take The Time To Smell The Roses', with Ringo's burlesque spoken passages.

'Brandy' and 'Waking Up' were two duller Starr-Nilsson items that suffered the same fate as 'Can't Fight Lightning'. Not even taped by Ringo was 'How Long Can Disco On?', the only other known handiwork of this half-serious collaboration. A weedy joke underpinned with downbeat reggae, it had already fed 1980's *Flash Harry*, on which Nilsson had taken a leaf from Ringo's book by mobilising illustrious contemporaries, among them Lennon, Little Feat's Lowell George and lyricist Van Dyke Parks, who was also called upon to arrange 'Back Off Boogaloo '81'.

A side-effect of Ringo's pattering tom-toms on 'Heart Of Mine', for Bob Dylan's *Shot Of Love* album, was a concurrence with another present, latter-day Rolling Stone, guitarist Ron Wood.[30] From their tinkerings between takes came 'Dead Giveaway', which lifted the ear only with Wood's over-dubbed saxophones and Eddie Cochran-ish bass twang. More sweat had been invested by Steve Stills – the last of five *Stop And Smell The Roses* producers – and co-writer Mike Stergis into gentle 'Nice Way', which, other than Starr's singing, might have been a Crosby, Stills And Nash out-take.

Apart from a short article about Ringo's return to recording in the *NME*, his patchy album was all but ignored in a Britain where Adam Ant was 'Prince Charming', if not king. Not reaching a particularly wide audience, either, were its promotional films, *Wrack My Brain* and *The Cooler*, a musical psycho-drama that was screened in the Short Subject category of 1982's Cannes Festival. As it was underwritten by his MPL Communications, it was to be expected that McCartney's three *Stop And Smell The Roses* concerns would be at its heart. Beginning to fill for Starr the void left by John, Paul himself appeared in various guises throughout the clip, which – borrowing a little from an episode in BBC2's Monty Python offshoot comedy *Ripping Yarns* – had Ringo as an inmate in a prison camp guarded entirely by women (one of them Linda McCartney). His perpetual machinations to escape – punished by spells in the said "cooler" – are tempered by deteriorating sanity and resultant ambivalent feelings towards the commandant, played – as was proper – by Barbara.

Despite the polish of Godley and Creme, then the apex of pop video direction, *The Cooler* "wasn't suitable" to Walter Shenson at Universal, who passed on the most tenable scheme for its general distribution – a pairing with his *A Hard Day's Night*. He considered the film to be "too depressing and surrealistic. We want to preserve the innocence of *A Hard Day's Night* as much as Paul."[31] That it starred Ringo mattered less than the much more bankable McCartney being "only seen in it briefly".[31]

Wrack My Brain was shown and the LP plugged on some of the US television spots – *Good Morning America*, *The Johnny Carson Show*, et al – that Starr's handlers had been able to negotiate in spite of his "taking less and less interest in recording or promoting them".[32] Nevertheless, on a parallel channel, Pete Best with *The*

Complete Silver Beatles in *Whatever Became Of...* put up a more sedate if less morbidly breath-taking dispatch than Ringo, who was the worse for liquor on *The John Davidson Show*. Prior to similar routine interviews, he'd often knocked back more than he should have, but had always got a grip on himself. He'd never been as far gone as he was then, when "those nights when you drink more than you remembered had become almost every night".[32]

His entourage watched him anxiously if indulgently from the wings, but to the coolly professional studio cameraman it was fantastic television as the fuddled subject with the pale, puffy complexion repeated his perplexed and then outraged host's questions as well as his own answers and fiddled around with a Polaroid on his lap. Starr's usual mannerisms were exaggerated as he raised his voice almost to a shout and then dropped it to near inaudibility. It was necessary to splice together two segments of the pre-recorded programme as Davidson stormed off and, recalled a contrite Ringo, "They had to convince him to come back – but I was in the dressing room, having a few more cognacs."[23]

Footballer *manqué* George Best would likewise make a clown of himself before millions. Less publicised, however, was PJ Proby who, incoherently outstaying his welcome on an early evening magazine programme on UK provincial television, had staggered from the Plymouth studio to busk on a carelessly strummed guitar in the foyer of the nearby Drake Cinema. Similarly chewed upon and spat out by the Swinging '60s, the likes of Tommy Quickly, Wayne Fontana, Keith Richards and The Bonzo Dog Band's Viv Stanshall were bobbing like corks on seas as shoreless. Heroin, tranquillisers, scotch, beer – whatever the drug of choice, it was but a temporary analgesic, an alleviation of the pangs of despair.

To Tony Barrow, Starr's addiction – once a private matter – had intensified because he felt himself to be "a second-class Beatle".[33] Whatever the cause, he confessed, "I knew I'd had this problem for years,"[34] and, although not a Latin scholar, Ringo ineffectually, started practising Seneca's maxim *pars sanitatis velle sanari fruit*[35] by replacing spirits – even his customary afternoon Remy Martin brandy – with the less toxic wine. With no ill effects, this had accompanied lunch and dinner for Barbara when in Italy, where she "didn't drink to get drunk".[21] However, by emptying 16 bottles a day, her second husband would be resigned to a self-imposed house arrest, as going anywhere else "meant I'd have to be in the car for 40 minutes without being able to have a single drink".[21] Barbara held no steadying sway over him as she "fell into the trap because of me. She used to go to bed at ten at night and get up at eight in the morning until we met. Then her career went the same as mine."[34]

A part in *Dallas* was dangled in front of him, but, while he had no objection to being in a TV soap opera almost beyond parody, he'd wait until 1983, when a US mini-series of Judith Krantz's novel *Princess Daisy* had him and Barbara as a jet-setting couple denying themselves no expensive whim. It didn't require much acting, although Ringo – ever the professional – had to force himself to eat caviar in one scene, washing out his mouth between each take.

Since *Princess Daisy*, Barbara has been seen but rarely on either the small or silver screen, as "no work has been offered to me that is worth two to three months' separation from my family".[27] Nevertheless, over a drink – and another and another – in an Ascot pub, a chat with Harry Nilsson led an eavesdropper to spread the spurious tale that he and the Starkeys were to finance a movie entitled *Road To Australia* with a screenplay by Norman Panama, who'd written the Bing Crosby/Bob Hope/Dorothy Lamour *Road* comedy films in the 40s. Ringo would be Hope, with Barbara providing romantic interest in the Lamour role.

She'd tell you, "We've always thought of work as an extension of marriage,"[17] but as the 1980s slipped into gear theirs had degenerated into an open state of warfare. It was simpler for her to go with him than go against him, but the mean slanging-match outside Tramp wasn't an isolated occurrence after all, as threats and quarrels frothed and fumed. Next came shabby paragraphs in gossip columns stating that the Starr fairytale had gone wrong. There were more subjective worries, too, that one or other of them would attempt suicide out of spiteful bravado. At home, Richard and

Barbara would "sit around for hours and talk about what we were going to do – and, of course, I'd get so bleeding drunk I couldn't move. The result was nothing happened."[34]

Ringo made no long-term plans. How could he? All the same, only new diversions would save his marriage, and possibly his life, so he cast about vainly to find some; but, from Nilsson to Elizabeth Taylor – pictured portly and plastered on the cover of Kenneth Anger's *Hollywood Babylon* exposé[36] – Ringo kept the company of only those united by a taste for liquor. "If you were straight, I wouldn't have you in my house. And, in the end, I couldn't even get a record deal. I wasn't hungry any more."[3]

16 "Please, God, I Have To Stop Living This Way"

With a New Year's Eve engagement at the Fulham Greyhound the ceiling of its ambition, The Next had thrown in the towel by 1981. From its ashes arose Monopacific. Zak Starkey would protest, "I'm every bit as hard up as the rest of the band."[1] Poor lad, his moneybags of a father had given him only a hi-hat cymbal for Christmas. When Startling Studios were booked, Monopacific battled with their equipment in a disused lodge on Tittenhurst estate, but whenever Zak was staying with his mother – who'd given him a jumper – "I have to get a train from the station"[1] the same as everybody else.

It was a tough old life but, unlike Julian Lennon and other acquaintances he could – and did – mention, Zak preferred the quainter hostelries of Ascot among old friends, because "even if I get successful, I don't want to live like my old man. I'm not into all that. I want to be respected for my drumming with the rest of the guys than earn a million pounds."[1]

The ease with which nightclubbing Julian secured a recording contract was a howling example of a surname opening doors, and Zak deserves respect for his musicianly self-image for attempting to actively earn a living and for not kowtowing to those music industry bigwigs who "talk to me just because of who my dad is".[1] Nevertheless, it was through his connections with Keith Moon – whose picture adorned the wall of the Tittenhurst lodge – that Monopacific acquired a manager in the late outrager's personal assistant, Peter Butler, and the attention of The Who's John Entwistle, Roger Daltrey and Pete Townshend, the latter of whom considered young Starkey's to be "the most accurate emulation of Keith's style",[1] qualifying this with, "Luckily, Zak also has a style of his own, but many have been moved when listening to his explosive solos to say, 'My God! It's him!'"[1] Obviously, Zak's shadowing of Moon hadn't been wasted, for at the few venues Monopacific played before going the way of The Next his performance – if gratuitously busy – still maintained a precise backbeat, as his sire would have expected.

While assisting on Ringo's new LP, *Old Wave*, at Startling Studios, Entwistle found time to produce Zak's next ensemble, Nightfly, who, smiled Starkey Snr, were "heavy and hard, but I'm not allowed to call it 'heavy metal'".[2] It was a step up, professionally, in that Zak was now hitting in time for battle-hardened ex-members of Bad Company, Status Quo and Whitesnake. Largely through Entwistle, he was employed for what he did rather than what he was on many lucrative sessions, notably for Denny Laine's *Lonely Road* and – its title track a nod to Zak's mentor – Daltrey's *Under A Raging Moon*. In conjunction with ageing keyboard *wunderkind* Eddie Hardin – who, in 1967, replaced Steve Winwood in The Spencer Davis Group[3] – Zak recorded his debut album, their *Musical Version Of Wind In The Willows*. For all Zak's desires to be accepted on his own merits, pragmatism ruled, and he'd acceded to his father's trick of giving the record more than an even break by garnering a shoal of whatever well-known names could be trawled to sing on it, with Donovan, Entwistle and Joe Fagin[4] being the biggest that could be legitimately printed on the sleeve. There were mutterings about staging this work in a London theatre in 1986, but the album's sales had been too discouraging.

To his exasperation, Zak's music made less of a splash than press muckraking about his relationship with Ringo, in which, essentially, he reacted as most temperamental adolescents – especially eldest sons – might, under the circumstances. Allowing himself one grand gesture of defiance against a nosy world, he kept his registry-office hitching to Sarah Menikides on 22 January 1985 a secret to even his parents – even though, in all conscience, neither disapproved of either Sarah, their cohabitation or of young marriage. Once over his deceived surprise, Ringo characteristically wished them all the best by throwing a small celebratory party for family and friends at Tittenhurst Park.

He'd do the same when Zak came of old-fashioned age – 21, not 18. By then, Starr had become the first Beatle grandfather, as Sarah, after an induced labour, had given birth to seven-pound Tatia Jayne that same September a week year earlier in a private ward at Heatherwood, near enough for twice-daily visits by one whom the baby would be taught to call "Grandad", a diminutive that had been good enough for his own immediate forebears. Zak would prove equal to his new responsibility, as would an elated Ringo to his less stressful one, whereby "you can have all the pleasures, give all the chocolates, then go home when the baby gets sick".[5]

"Grandma" Maureen's rapture was compounded by her imminent wedlock to another affluent man with a beard. Taller and much younger than her first husband, Isaac Tigrett had made his loot via the founding of the worldwide Hard Rock Cafe chain, which he sold in 1988 for an eight-figure amount. While Starr was pleased for Maureen – and himself, because he'd no longer be liable for alimony – there had been a *soupçon* of recent discord. Tigrett had bought one of Starr's drums to put on display with other pop artefacts in his New York branch after it had found its way to an auction. However, since the Haslem Terrace fire, Ringo's fevered replenishing of Beatle memorabilia led to a telephoned plea to Maureen to restore the drum to his possession. He'd love to have it back. Upset by her disinclination to pull strings on his behalf, he straightaway got onto Harry Nilsson, then in the Big Apple, to go around to the diner and, if need be, prise the desired object from its hanger. His bosom buddy was so fraught that Nilsson set off on the (ultimately failed) mission immediately.

When Maureen and Ringo spoke next, he seemed resigned to – even amused by – her intransigence over the drum, as their atrophied affinity continued to mellow into a remote cordiality epitomised by

RINGO STARR

his congratulations when she presented Isaac with a daughter –
Augusta – in 1988. With the Tigretts abiding mostly in Dallas
nowadays, and with Barbara's children spending part of their time
with Gregorini, the offspring of the extended family were never in
the same place at the same time; Richie and Barbara's children, for
example, didn't meet until just before the wedding. Nevertheless, at
Tittenhurst Park, all subdivisions of kindred dwelt in harmony,
accepting that there were perks to domestic complexities. However,
Zak's emotions might have been mixed at Ringo's obliging and
solicitous pointers when Johnny – charmed by the sound of his big
stepbrother's thrashings – wanted to play the drums too. Perhaps
Ringo had already gauged that Johnny had no aptitude for rhythm,
and that his enthusiasm would falter when he became taken with
another boyhood craze. As it turned out, Johnny would follow his
natural father's footsteps, after graduating from a US university with
a degree in Business Studies.

The most wayward adolescence was endured by Jason, who
rounded it off by falling foul of the law for possessing cannabis. If
Ringo dared lecture his second son on any aspect of this
misdemeanour, apart from the stupidity of getting caught, he had as
brittle a leg to stand on as he had when Zak shacked up with Sarah.
His boozing was getting out of control, and the only ace up his sleeve
was his narration for US radio of a heroin caution for "today's kids"
which, to synthesised accompaniment in waltz time, excused his past
psychedelic escapades with "but that was then" and invoked 'Yellow
Submarine', 'Blue Meanies' ("more of them than ever before") and
Lennon, who'd known the drug well. His views on the subject were
further clarified when he gave John Cleese, Bill Oddie and Michael
Palin – radical balusters of British comedy – percussive assistance
and the run of his home studio to produce the satirical 'Naughty
Atom Bomb' for the *It's A Live-In World* LP, which – with such as
Paul McCartney, Paul's cousin Kate Robbins, The Thompson Twins
and Zak lending a hand, too – would benefit London's Phoenix
House drug rehabilitation centre.

From the starting line of The Concerts For Bangladesh, pop by the

1980s pop had cranked into top gear while hurtling along the road to respectability and, after Live Aid gained The Boomtown Rats' Bob Geldof a knighthood, Ringo – who'd received an MBE for less – was seen, like everyone else of late, to be involved in quite a few good causes. These ranged from passive attendance with Olivia Harrison and Barbara at a Fashion Aid event (associated with live Aid) at the Albert Hall to tagging onto a queue[6] of the famous – plus those who'd like to be and some who were no longer – at London's Sarm Studio, where he sang – without the affectation of many of the others – one line over a craftily sampled backing collage of jungle noises in one of the more scintillating charity singles of the 1980s, 'Spirit Of The Rain Forest', proceeds of which went towards protecting same. Both Ringo and Zak would demonstrate solidarity on the matter of racism by taping at Ascot an unobtrusive contribution to the post-Live Aid *Sun City*, a recording project that would aid anti-apartheid movements in South Africa and the Americas.

The recording was masterminded by guitarist Steve Van Zandt, who used to back New Jersey's Bruce Springsteen, whose bit in 'Sun City' was more pronounced than Starr's. Bruce was renowned for his Yogi Bear vibrato and an energetic stage act – that Ringo proclaimed "unbelievable"[7] – sharing similarities of style with Nils Lofgren, another of the ex-Beatle's East Coast songwriting acquaintances.[8] Lofgren's best-known opus was 'Shine Silently', co-written with Alice Cooper's guitarist Dick Wagner and covered – with a riveting *a cappella* introit – by The Hollies.

Lofgren's friend Springsteen was abetted by his E-Street Band, whose animated saxophonist, Clarence Clemons, had once been in James Brown's more disciplined Famous Flames and was also in the horn section for the 'Sun City' bash. However, he was not introduced to Ringo (by Springsteen's drummer Max Weinberg) until later. This cordial encounter – like Starr's with Lofgren – was to have a more than incidental bearing on the future professional activities of all three, not least of which would be Starr's singing on 'Bein' Angry' – a track from Nils' 1989 *Silver Lining* album – and appearing with Springsteen and Clemons in a later Lofgren video.

Another of Ringo's more philanthropic cameos had already produced a remunerative side-effect – or so it seemed when it began. Bill Wyman had been among those persuaded by multiple sclerosis sufferer and ex-Small Face Ronnie Lane to make up a supergroup at a London gala in aid of ARMS (Action for Multiple Sclerosis). Shouldering much of Lane's load, Wyman organised further ARMS concerts, which spawned a more fixed set-up, with guest players around a nucleus of Wyman, Charlie Watts and singing guitarist Andy Fairweather-Low concentrating on olde-tyme rock 'n' roll as Willie And The Poor Boys. In a half-hour-long video of the same title focused on a show at Fulham Town Hall, Starr was brought in to sweep up afterwards as a janitor-cum-middle-aged Teddy Boy

Bill was, as much as Charlie, Ringo's opposite number in The Rolling Stones, and it was these two who cemented a Beatle-Stone business liaison when American architect and property speculator John Portman and London hotelier Alan Lubin were scouting around for financial support to open a posh restaurant in the Peachtree Center, an Atlanta commercial development. Through his brother Len, Lubin cultivated an association with Starr, who was counted in, and – like Wyman – put forward his own eminence for the partnership's use.

So it was that he and Bill boarded a chartered flight from Heathrow to Atlanta with a prattle of Radio 1 disc jockeys and competition winners for the official opening of "the Brasserie" on 5 October 1986. Although doomed to closure within two years, the place got off to a flying start, with the bulk of US media folk homing in on Ringo, who required police protection. Bill's was a relatively calm corner of the proceedings, despite the Stones being between world tours, as well as his semi-public intrigue with an under-age girl. This publicity binge concluded with a self-conscious and oddly matched jam session, with the Englishmen presiding over front-line rollicking by Jerry Lee Lewis, Stax soulman Isaac Hayes and Jermaine Jackson, whose more acclaimed brother Michael had sung with Paul McCartney on two hit singles.

Concrete proof that Wyman's appetite for feeding his peers was not dampened by the failure of the Brasserie was his Kensington eaterie "Sticky Fingers" – after a Stones album – which, so some bored journalists made out, was in direct competition with Lennon's, which served dishes like "Penny Lane pâté" and "Rubber Sole and chips" over in Covent Garden, next to Stringfellows. Joining owner Cynthia and her son Julian for a meal, a chat and a comparison of catering procedures one evening were Maureen Tigrett and her daughter, Lee. Maureen and Cynthia's younger selves would have just about recognised the well-dressed divorcees nibbling at Lennon's.

No matter how far their wanderings had taken them, all Merseysiders looked homeward when hearing of the Hillsborough disaster, in which 95 ordinary people were crushed to death in a swollen stadium during a Liverpool soccer team away match in 1988. On the following Saturday, the entire city observed a two-minute silence for their lost neighbours. Nowhere was it more absolute than in the Anfield ground, where tears ran down the cheeks of elderly supporters. For some, Gerry And The Pacemakers' 'You'll Never Walk Alone' – the Kop Choir anthem – was the only pop record they'd ever bought. Three years earlier, Gerry had led The Crowd – another all-star aggregation that included Zak Starkey – to Number One with a cash-raising remake of this plaintive showstopper for victims of the *Herald Of Free Enterprise* shipwreck.

With Paul McCartney and members of Frankie Goes To Hollywood, The Christians and other newer Scouse bands among those joining him, Marsden was back on top following Hillsborough when his 'Ferry 'Cross The Mersey' was likewise used in aid of a Liverpool FC relief fund, which had been already buoyed with a vast whip-round from local factories. Ringo also dipped into his purse and, with Cilla Black, recorded a comforting message on *The Sun*'s prompt emergency hotline "to help those families try to rebuild their lives".

It was Cilla who tipped off a "very angry"[9] Ringo when their names – and photographic images – were taken in vain in an ingenious advertising campaign by Security Omega Express, the crux of which was the correlation between success and Richard Starkey, Priscilla White, Harry Webb and other entertainers' rechristenings.

"He personally and The Beatles," gritted a Starr aide, "are always getting ripped off."[9] Who knew, for instance, where income generated from Beatle records issued lately in the Soviet Union went? How about Ringo's blue suede shoes appreciating by several thousand per cent, or his 1966 Mini Cooper – including its Richard Starkey log book – fetching a fortune for some Londoner 20 years later? A five-carat diamond ring stolen from Starr in Paris changed hands several times at an increasingly inflated price before finding its way back to its rightful owner when gendarmerie swooped on a shop in the city's St Quen district.

Sometimes it appeared that the ex-Beatles were being cheated by each other, too, during the perpetual unscrambling of Apple lucre. This was demonstrated by Starr, Harrison and Mrs Lennon's lawsuit against McCartney over a deal whereby the last six albums he'd delivered to Capitol had rewarded him with what was interpreted as an increased royalty increment for Beatles output.

While he couldn't be reproached for more personal animosity towards McCartney, Pete Best had now found it in him to "harbour no bitterness over what happened". Via the same Sotheby's sale that flogged off a pair of Starr's drumsticks, he'd disencumbered himself of much accumulated booty from his Beatle days, but "I'm keeping my drums and the clothes we wore when we first started out and the gifts we gave each other, like bracelets and little trinkets, because they still have a very great sentimental value." With brother Roag supplementing his drumming, the forgiving Pete would dust off his kit and, with an eponymous group, play a set – which would even embrace a Beatles B-side – in a John Lennon Memorial Concert at Liverpool Philharmonic with other Mersey Beat musicians belying their daytime occupations as pen-pushers, charge-hands and captains of industry.

Neither Best's combo, The Undertakers, Earl Preston and his TTs nor any other of the old hands up there on that night of nights would be invited to perform at a televised and international tribute from Liverpool's Pier Head, sanctioned and partly compered by Yoko, who, since her husband's slaying, had not retreated from public life.

George Harrison would have nothing to do with her Liverpool extravaganza, but while they declined to show up in person Ringo and Paul each sent a filmed piece, with Ringo's "Hi Liverpool!" and supergroup rendering of 'I Call Your Name' – a minor Beatles track from 1964 – bridging a gap between Philadelphian duo Hall And Oates and Welsh guitarist Dave Edmunds' John Lennon Tribute Band.

After his own manner, Starr had tampered with The Beatles legend as much as Yoko when, in 1983, the man who'd shied away from *Stardust* because it was too near the knuckle had been inveigled into a 26-part series entitled *Ringo's Yellow Submarine: A Voyage Through Beatles Magic* by a US radio syndication network whose vice president, Willard Lochridge, had crowed of him being "the DJ, working intimately with ABC on the content and presentation".[10] As disappointing to fans as Ringo's undignified decision to participate, his pre-recorded and scripted commentaries – plus a culminant live phone-in from Tittenhurst Park – were peppered unthinkingly with tiny factual errors[11] as he endorsed the group's function as a commodity that could be recycled indefinitely.

Perhaps I've misread his motives. His surrender of no fresh anecdotes or weighing of experience might have been quite deliberate. Maybe they'll be revealed if he authorises a biography or, more unlikely, writes one himself. Certainly, the *Beatle Magic* nonsense was no bone to be picked, any more than the resolved Capitol wrangles with Paul whenever the three survivors of one of the most singular human experiences of that Coca Cola century met – as they did more frequently than ever, these days – for hotel-bar or dinner-table evenings that bred coded hilarity, matey abuse and retrospection about days gone by. "Sure, we keep in touch," confirmed Ringo. "With Paul, it's a good month and then a bad month, just like a family. I see George more often, because we live closer to each other."[12]

As George and Ringo were each sorrowfully aware, it was no longer so easy for new albums by old heroes to be passed without comment by record-label quality controllers. Neither ex-Beatle was sufficiently "current" in either output or "attitude", with Ringo expressing doubts about the advent of compact discs, which were "a bit too clean for me. I'm from the old school. I like a bit of dirt on the record."[13] His favourite modern group were New York's archaic but exhilarating Cramps, who specialised in psychobilly – a collision of rockabilly and psychedelia – and were as dirty as they come.

George had employed a drum machine to toughen his 1982 album *Gone Troppo*, but at heart he too was "from the old school", so much so that, sickened, he told the whole fair-weather music business to get knotted by announcing – wrongly, as it happened – that *Gone Troppo* was to be his vinyl farewell. In that year, Starr – with *Old Wave* mastered – was in no position to make such unrepining calculations.

However, prior to Ringo's leaving, the label's A&R department had harkened to Joe Walsh's hunch that Ringo still had "a good rock 'n' roll album in him".[14] Brought in to draw it out of him, Walsh "beefed up"[14] *Old Wave* by spicing certain numbers with his over-amplified guitar clichés, developing likely fragments of song computed in his old friend's oft-sozzled mind and persuading him to invest in harder drumheads, which certainly lent the kit a tarter drive – but, with the project's very title (and sleeve photograph, of a teenage Richard Starkey) indicating how seemingly out of touch Starr was, Boardwalk might have feared a tarring with the same brush.

A subtext to Boardwalk and British RCA's dumping of Ringo Starr – the only ex-Beatle to be thus cast adrift – was Walsh's "allowing me to have one party – and then he tried to stop it, but it was too late then. He had to wait until the next day."[15]

With a composing credit granted to all participants, 'Everybody's In A Hurry But Me' was the too-apt title to one of three excerpts from instrumental rambles onto which Starr and the harassed Walsh superimposed whatever lyrics could be strung together. Much superfluous blowing on more substantial songs – and, on the fade-out of 'Alibi', some half-baked scat singing – also padded out the album, but the meeting of its deadline was rendered irrelevant by RCA and Boardwalk's action after hearing the result, an extremity that was validated when Ringo was then unable to kindle any worthwhile interest in *Old Wave* from any other British or US companies, who all seemed to have too vivid a recollection of *Stop And Smell The Roses*. He was, therefore, at more of a loose end than usual when his name cropped up as Paul McCartney and his production staff planned *Give My Regards To Broad Street*, MPL's first feature-length flick.

A romantic undercurrent of this much-criticised and egocentric caper was Ringo – drummer in Paul's band – and "this gorgeous girl reporter from a music paper" (Barbara) who "get friendlier and friendlier as the movie progresses. Falling in love with your own wife isn't as easy as it looks."[16] The main story was a hybrid of an atypical day in the life of MPL and aspects of *The Wizard Of Oz* and *Magical Mystery Tour*. Ringo wanted originally to be its villain, but Paul had him down merely as rather cantankerous, sniggering, "which we all know is different to his usual sweet-natured self"[17] – or it used to be.

Although (or because) it was "more like family than work",[16] on locations as varied as a Victorian graveyard and a reconstruction of New Brighton's Tower Ballroom – destroyed by fire in 1970 – Ringo insisted on pauses, however inconvenient, so that he wouldn't miss the goings-on in *Coronation Street*. Possibly afflicted with an unquiet conscience about his *Yellow Submarine faux pas* of the previous year, he was also pernickety about what songs he'd drum on when Paul got to grips with the soundtrack, with a large helping of refashioned Beatles items, on which Starr would not let himself be accommodated. However, Paul didn't need Ringo like Ringo needed Paul.

Beyond film set and console, McCartney's social attachment to Starr was strong enough for each to sit together at an Everly Brothers reunion show in London. Worship of pop's greybeards would extend beyond such acts of faith and garrulous praise. The 60th birthdays of both Chuck Berry and Fats Domino would each be sanctified on purchasable video with famous younger helpmates in sight giving them a contemporary seal of approval – and buttressing their own standings with credible influences. An array of British stars – including Screaming Lord Sutch, Brian May and The Kinks' Dave Davies – would pay homage to a truculent Jerry Lee Lewis during one of the Killer's recitals at Hammersmith Odeon, and a link-up with The Art Of Noise had delivered Duane Eddy back to the UK Top 20 in 1986. Backed by George Harrison, Jeff Lynne and others who'd grown to manhood to his twanging, Eddy was also able to cut a new album, which – for those who hadn't listened to him since the early 1960s – was much how they might have imagined him to sound as his pension beckoned.

On 21 October 1985, it was *Carl Perkins And Friends: A Rockabilly Special*, commissioned for Channel 4 at Limehouse Studios in London's West India docks. Its genesis lay in *Homecoming*, Perkins' album of earlier that year with three other chicken-necked campaigners – Jerry Lee Lewis, Roy Orbison and Johnny Cash – at the now much-modernised Sun Studio in Memphis, where opinionated console sage Sam Phillips had primed four country boys for greener pastures *circa* 1955. Pre-empting George Harrison's Traveling Wilburys, many *Homecoming* tracks were communal efforts, with verses and middle eights apportioned more or less equally between all four vocalists, in rough-hewn harmony on the choruses. Among auxiliary musicians on the LP's eight-minute party number, 'Big Train (From Memphis)', was Dave Edmunds, whose adolescent imagination had been fired by rockabilly.

Fifty-three-year-old Carl had been a contributor – as had George Harrison – to Edmunds' production of the soundtrack for *Porky's Revenge*, a US teen-exploitation movie, and it was Edmunds and his regular band who'd be stage fixtures in the *Rockabilly Special* and Harrison the foremost Friend. Ringo, too, was another to whom Carl sent a "video letter" with a reply slip and stamped, self-addressed envelope. On jumping at the chance, Ringo secured seats in the studio audience for Hilary Gerrard, Barbara (with a camera), Jason and Lee, so that they could see him breathe the air around one of his old idols. Paul McCartney declined to appear, but other delighted invitees – such as Eric Clapton, Rozanne Cash (daughter of Johnny), two of The Stray Cats and *Double Fantasy* guitarist Earl Slick – also squeezed names onto the guest list.

The rest of the 250 tickets were snatched by Teddy Boys who

queued, freezing and iron-bladdered, in their garish regalia until admitted to a homely auditorium, where grey-haired Carl would be close enough for everyone to watch his fingers create that terse resonance that was rockabilly guitar-picking at its most refined. Unswerving in their fidelity since the 1950s, the older Teds would push past ex-Beatles to besiege Perkins for autographs. What was it to them that this was the first time George Harrison's light baritone had been aired in front of a British audience since 1966?

Before the fond smiles of backstage staff, George and Ringo had bear-hugged each other, united forever by common ordeal and jubilation, as well as the unbearable excitement of the task that lay immediately ahead. It was "one of the magic nights of my life", so Starr's handwritten note to Carl afterwards would attest. If not as "pure" as it could have been, and flawed at times by the egos of some involved, the show was a joy because everyone wished it to be. Judicious editing would decimate a lot of the tedium – mainly the interminable extrapolations that Edmunds had to curtail – before the New Year's Day broadcast.

When Dave's group and Carl had warmed up, Ringo was first out of the wings. Not bothering with Ted rig-out, he was, apart from a grin, more a shifty bebop drummer – dark glasses, pink tie, black shirt – as he positioned himself behind the kit for an elongated 'Honey Don't' that he sang with more bite than when going through the scream-rent motions at *Another Beatles Christmas Show* in the Hammersmith Odeon almost exactly 20 years earlier. As its last cadence died, he gasped, "It's been a long time."

Obliquely advertising Clapton's recent authorised biography,[18] the continuity between Starr and Perkins that heralded the guitarist's walk-on was worthy of *Cilla*. Sharing the verses of 'Matchbox' with Carl, neither of the two Britons disgraced themselves before tolerant Teds who might have wished for a more traditional rendition. At a cracking pace, 'Matchbox' was triumphant rather than despondent in 1985, and onlookers were struck by Starr's obvious pleasure in performing again, even if just tapping tambourine when, after quenching his thirst during the intermission, he sat with the others in a devout horseshoe around Perkins' high chair as they were guided through a final rampage which included 'Big Train', 'Sure To Fall' and obscurer byways of rockabilly.

Onto the cutting-room floor would cascade George's plug for HandMade Films, but the company's turn would come three years later with a televised hurrah for its first decade in business, for which Perkins returned the *Rockabilly Special* favour by keeping 'em cutting a rug in the dancing area. With a renewed if fleeting taste for the roar of the crowd, Harrison allowed himself a stake in the proceedings, too. A few months earlier, he'd taken a more formal plunge into the limelight before 12,000 for each of two evenings at Wembley Arena in a package show for one of Prince Charles' charities. For many, Elton John's proclamation that Harrison "and Ringo Starr!" were about to play a short set rode roughshod over Level 42, Go West and all the rest of the synchronised frenzy that had gone before.

Although he merely backed George's nervous 'While My Guitar Gently Weeps' and was thwacking indistinguishably between Phil Collins and Big Country's drummer during the finale on the first night, Ringo brought the house down the next day when, stepping down from his rostrum, he clasped the central microphone to trigger the audience and assembled cast's responses and choruses as, with voice in finer – and deeper – fettle than imagined, he prodded the right festive nerve with a rough-and-ready 'With A Little Help From My Friends', going the distance with workmanlike pitching shorn of any sticky extemporisation. To the relief of those wincing as the coda's perilous high C – "friiieeends" – approached, he was steered out of danger by both the participatory unison and an almost palpable wave of goodwill that continued to wash over him on the play-out when, uttering Arthur Askey's nasal "I thang yew" catch-phrase, he rattled a tambourine while shuffling off with a jaw-dropping flicker of Billy Preston-like dancing. At 47, who'd have thought that the old boy still had it in him?

With Ultravox's Midge Ure (on bass) the exception, only other elder statesmen – Elton John, Eric Clapton, Jeff Lynne – had been chosen for George – and Ringo's – slot at Wembley. Predictably, rumour abounded that, subtracting Ure and adding Julian Lennon, these had decided at Friar Park rehearsals to form less *ad hoc* a supergroup, but the most that transpired was that some of its *dramatis personae* made themselves useful during George's unhurried contradiction of his 1982 "retirement" statement with a new album, *Cloud Nine*. Perhaps we ought to be thankful, because, according to Ringo, "the worst band I ever played with in my life had Eric Clapton, Elton John, Keith Richards, Ronnie Wood and I all playing in my studio in Tittenhurst Park in 1985. Too many leaders. It just didn't work."[19]

Clapton had been on hand for *Old Wave*, which no US or British company whatsoever had been prepared to issue, but Hilary Gerrard's dogged country-by-country pursuit of contracts yielded pressings in Canada, Brazil and – most lucrative of all – West Germany, where its wing of Boardwalk was sufficiently enthused to risk a promotional 45 with 'In My Car', the weightiest of the "jammed" numbers. Within the record's remaining originals, there was hardly a tune, although 'Hopeless' came close to it and 'Be My Baby'[20] almost smokescreened its melodic pedantry with gimmicky vocal effects.

The fake effervescence of phasing and a lead-guitar section fattened with an Echoplex pedal polluted Starr's already dodgy cover of 1960s soul balladeer Chuck Jackson's 'I Keep Forgettin'', but more effective through its lack of artifice was a competent if pointless copy – bar contrived Dixieland interludes – of The Sir Douglas Quintet's wondrously dim 'She's About A Mover'. A synthesised orchestra with "trumpets" to the fore jutted from 'As Far As You Can Go', a forgettable *lied* by guitarist Russ Ballard, who, in sunglasses more perpetual than Ringo's, had journeyed through the previous two decades in Adam Faith's Roulettes, Unit 4 + 2, Argent and as a soloist, before concentrating on the possible as a jobbing composer. Another "professional'" piece as inappropriate to Starr's pipes as 'Easy For Me' from *Goodnight Vienna*, 'Picture Show Life' – describing flashes of Hollywood *demi-monde* – was, nevertheless, the album's strongest opus, although against the challengers that's no great accolade.

Ringo himself vetoed the release of a follow-up to *Old Wave* that had been born of a Christmas holiday in the Bahamas, where he bumped into "Chips" Moman, a proficient rather than brilliant US producer with a fast mouth. A southerner, Moman had gained some recent prestige in "outlaw" country-and-western circles via his ministrations to Waylon Jennings and Willie Nelson, who appealed to both rednecks and the newer country consumers who – scorning the form's rhinestoned tackiness but not its down-home maturity – adhered to the leaner, more abandoned approach of Nelson, Jennings and younger entertainers like The Sweethearts Of The Rodeo, Randy Travis and kd lang, with her spiky hair-do and artlessly laddered stockings. For Starr, another point in Moman's favour was his previous reputation for reactivating waning stars such as Tommy Roe, Paul Revere And The Raiders and The Boxtops.

Theoretically, he was just what Ringo needed, and after initial misgivings "because we didn't understand each other's accents"[21] the two spoke eagerly of cutting no fewer than three albums together, with Ringo's input much the same as it had been for *Beaucoups Of Blues*. The first of these got under way in the Three Alarm complex in Memphis one afternoon in February 1987. Without the safety net of a record-company advance, Chips agreed to meet studio costs ($150 per hour), supply a core of musicians and grub around publishers for material. Starr, meanwhile, would pay his own expenses while in the sprawling industrial city beside the ugly Mississippi. The area resembled Merseyside in spirit, too, in that it had cradled – just as Liverpool had The Beatles and Mersey Beat – the nascent talents of Presley, Perkins, Jerry Lee, Orbison and others who flowered momentarily in their wake.

During a US tour, The Beatles had made hush-hush designs to record at Sun, the one-storey studio that was the shrine of rock 'n' roll, but exposure by a Memphis radio station had necessitated an enraged cancellation to avoid fan besiegement. Now that the screaming had abated, a contrasting vexation when intelligence of Ringo's presence at Three Alarm leaked was the *Memphis Commercial Appeal*'s insulting leader that "an ageing Beatle is yesterday's news".[22] As a result, Starr, supported by Barbara, was threatening to transfer the entire operation to Los Angeles. This was only prevented when Moman whistled up a hundred-strong picket outside the errant newspaper's offices and the city council, desirous to humour a majority of its electorate, rushed through a hasty resolution to honour their visitor's contribution to culture and extend an official welcome. Appeased, the Starkeys organised one of their parties for councillors and showbiz periphery on a riverboat shortly after the album was "90 per cent ready"[15] in April.

Because "it might be an historic moment",[21] Ringo had requested that specific sessions be videoed, especially the ones where Clapton, Edmunds, Perkins and, purportedly, Dylan had dropped by. Two Perkins numbers were reported to be in the can, as were Starr treatments of Billy Swan's 'I Can Help' smash from 1974, as well as two items shortlisted from proffered demos: 'Shoobedoo' and 'Whiskey And Soda'.

For all of Moman's later claims that no session was tainted with alcohol, there is small cause to doubt Ringo's allegations that "certain nights we were all under the influence" of wine, tequila "or whatever else we felt like drinking".[21]

After only one of the three mooted albums, Ringo had had his bellyful of Chips, with whom he "ceased to communicate"[21] on returning to England. Two years on, he was still umming and ahing about the LP, which, in the harsh light of day, "I began to think that maybe it was not my best shot. Maybe we could find some better songs."[21] With his ambivalence justified when only one major company – MCA – came close to taking it on, he was game enough to want to try again at London's Mayfair Studios, with Elton John in the chair, but the four-week block-booking in August 1987 had to be reallocated when Starr acknowledged finally that he was no more a serious pop recording artist.

Come 1988, the only album of his that most retailers considered worth stocking was *Starrstruck*, a "best of" compilation by Californian reissue specialists Rhino Records, who had rejected his suggestion that it include the unreleased 'Can't Fight Lightning' as a bonus track for Beatle completists.

If his career as a hit-parade entrant was spent, Ringo still had tinier fish to fry. With *Scouse The Mouse* a dry run, he addressed himself more to youngsters by succeeding the more expressive Johnny Morris in 1984 as narrator of the adventures of moveable models known to infant ITV watchers as *Thomas The Tank Engine And Friends*. From a misconception that children's hour was "all *Star Wars* and high technology",[15] it occurred to him what little traditionalists toddlers are when Thomas became Tatia Jayne's favourite programme, "more because she's into the action than because it's her grandad's voice on screen".[24] To Ringo, "It's just mind-blowing that Thomas is so big in this day and age. It used to be 'Look! There's Ringo' in the street. Now it's 'Look! There's Thomas.' Would you believe there's hordes of screaming three-year-olds outside the house?"[23]

As a Dingle urchin, he was "more a Beano man",[23] never to be among the eight million predominantly middle-class families who'd come into possession of one of the Reverend Wilbert Vere Awdry's books of railway stories that – set in the imaginary land of Sodor – had been originated in 1945 to enthrall his measled son, Christopher. "There's something about a steam train. Unlike diesels, they have their own personalities,"[23] deduced this wizened Gloucestershire cleric, who created his engines – all with boys' names – to haul anonymous female coaches.

Although in direct opposition to BBC1's *Postman Pat*, viewing figures for *Thomas* were heartening enough to warrant both more series and the manufacture of 26 re-recorded episodes on cassette/text packages – by Pickwick Records' Tell-A-Tale subsidiary – to keep the brats quiet throughout the Empire. It was also nominated as 1985's Best Animated Film in the British Academy Awards, along with *Rupert And The Frog Song*, with its Paul McCartney soundtrack. No more than old pop icons' complicity in TV commercials, there was no shame in them entertaining the pre-teens, either. Among Ringo and Paul's Merseyside predecessors in this sphere were, on ITV alone, Freddie Garrity as general factotum of *Little Big Time*, Billy J Kramer compering *Lift Off* and Gerry

Marsden a *Junior Showtime* regular. Each – Starr included – relied on
forthright but amiable impudence and, like every northern comic
from Askey to Tarbuck, the conveyance of a feeling that everyone
knew him and he them.

Unlike a campaigning politician recoiling inwardly at kissing
babies, Ringo genuinely enjoyed the company of children, "because I
used to be one".[24] Therefore, as well as attending to more orthodox
Thomas promotional duties, such as an interview on *Good Morning
Britain* (mitigated by his hearty guzzling of a speciality prepared during
the magazine's cookery spot), he gladly responded to a request by
Dreams Come True – a benevolence sponsored by ITV – to brighten a
day out for two seriously ill nippers – to whom he was the *Thomas*
man rather than a pop singer – by conducting them around the
Bluebell railway in Sussex. With his own desolations on hold, "Ringo
was smashing – a really nice guy," beamed the charity's co-ordinator,
Margaret Hayles. "When little Theresa had a relapse, he sent her
flowers." He charmed Margaret as he had Barbara in Durango, when
"he played with the children and teased them all the time".[23]

The New York Post pronounced him "the most likeable children's
TV host since Captain Kangaroo"[25] when Thomas was attuned in
1988 for the US market as *Shining Time Station*, seen by many
reviewers as on a par of quality with internationally popular *Sesame
Street*. Rather than use models, its makers had hired actors such as
Leonard Jackson (star of *The Color Purple*), Brian O'Connor
(*Beverly Hills Cop*) and – as "Mr Conductor" – Ringo Starr, who'd
be up for an Emmy award as Outstanding Performer In A Children's
Series. Another outcome of *Shining Time Station* was his role as the
Mock Turtle – with what was nearly a mid-Atlantic accent – in a
two-part dramatisation of *Alice In Wonderland* for coast-to-coast
transmission that autumn.

After his required month filming the *Shining Time Station* tales in
the Big Apple, he publicised it as he had *Thomas*, but was often
sidetracked onto less savoury issues, such as Albert Goldman's
morbid biographical portrayal of Lennon, which Starr hadn't read.
For all his monochrome garb and matching hair dye, he cut a smaller,

mousier, more vulnerable figure than anticipated when, on *Entertainment Tonight*, he made the surprising boast, "It's three months to yesterday that I haven't had a drink. Ninety days."[24]

Regarding his public activities nowadays, he admitted that, other than *Thomas'* US equivalent, "Lately, I haven't been doing much at all."[24] Nowadays, he and Barbara were merely famous for being famous, wanted and ever-present guests at every high-society shindig, club opening, after-dinner laudation, *et al*. Often they attracted more attention than those with better claim to it, such as David Hentschel, who – with Startling Music just a memory – had penned the incidental music for 1988's *Educating Rita*. He'd be seated behind the Starkeys at the première.

There they were, the Ringo Starrs, in fancy dress at the Chelsea Arts Ball in a cluster with Cilla, Pattie Harrison-Clapton-as-was, actor John Hurt and Cathy McGowan, or sharing a joke with Terry O'Neill at the Hamilton Gallery on the publication day of that photographer's folio. Wasn't that Ringo drumming on an interminable blues jam with Clapton and members of The Police at Island Records' 25th anniversary do? And again behind Harrison, Dylan and Jagger's "spontaneous" 'I Saw Her Standing There' at The Beatles' induction into the rock 'n' roll Hall Of Fame at New York's Waldorf-Astoria? Didn't we see him – and her – at the Variety Club luncheon in honour of Tommy Steele, and the party for Goldie Hawn, and God knows how many Elton John birthdays? With Elton and all the usual mob, Mr and Mrs Starkey piled onto Concorde to zoom to New York when, in 1988, George Harrison was suddenly at Number One in the Hot 100 for the first time in 15 years. "So he's inviting all his mates over to celebrate,"[26] explained Ringo into a stick mic at Heathrow.

Even Barbara was outshone by Fergie, twittering and pregnant in bright orange, for the first night of *White Mischief*; but she and Richard – and the McCartneys – had been everyone's darlings over drinks at the Hippodrome just before the London screening of *Give My Regards To Broad Street*. They'd also cut a dash at *The Mission*, and so had Johnny with them for *Dark Crystal*.

Extensions of these finger-fluttering entrances and exits included Ringo serving as host on an edition of *Saturday Night Live* and as mystery guest of blindfolded panellists on *What's My Line?*, where he was identified after only eight questions. Off the television, the most unique public stint of either of Ringo's or Barbara's career was joining a celebrity team – representing Parisian jewellers Cartier – in Nepal for the world elephant polo championship. Although "pretty sceptical when it began",[27] they were drawn into the spirit of the occasion, despite elimination in an early heat.

For profit as well as fun, Ringo warbled 'When You Wish Upon A Star' – eerie in a *Sentimental Journey*-esque way – amid other reinterpretations of Walt Disney film songs by such odd bedfellows as Sun Ra and Sinéad O'Connor on *Stay Awake*, an album masterminded by New Yorker Hal Willner, on the rebound from a preceding artistic knock-out with *Lost In The Stars*, a similar salute to Kurt Weill.

Ringo also banked a huge cheque for five days in the Bahamas for a Sun County wine commercial, the first and last he'd ever undertake for an inebriating beverage because, as he'd implied on *Entertainment Tonight*, he and Barbara had taken the pledge. It hadn't been a moment too soon, either. While denying that their alcoholism was critical, Barbara would "try to straighten us out every couple of months, but then we'd fall straight back into the trap. I knew I should be doing something to get help, but I just never got around to it."[28] Friends would suggest that they "sort of cooled it a bit"[28] and, waking up thick-tongued and red-eyed after another bender, they'd swear not to touch another drop; but, sinking three fingers of hair-of-the-dog spirits within half an hour of getting dressed, "You're powerless to do anything about it. You get to the point where there's no choice left. You're at the point where you say, 'Please, God, I have to stop living this way.'"[29]

Already, Viv Stanshall, Alice Cooper and – decisively – Harry Nilsson had or were sweating away the blue devils, with Cooper using his experiences in a clinic as the theme for a comeback album. When obliged by law, Keith Richards had kicked heroin by acupuncture, while – through the love of a good woman and a spell in a Manchester nursing home – Wayne Fontana had overcome his dependence on valium and was no longer a booker's risk.[30] Not so strong minded was Dennis Wilson, who had been suspended from The Beach Boys until such time as he weaned himself off the drugs and alcohol that had an important bearing on his professional unreliability. In 1983, he drowned in a Californian marina, his judgement of the water's temperature and his own fatigue impaired by too much vodka. Ringo featured in the pool of drummers that got the group through an eponymous 1984 album and existing stage dates.

Not as capable of such kindnesses by the later 1980s, he and his missus took steps to dry out under supervision but, unlike half-forgotten Nilsson, for an ex-Beatle to so do required decoy tactics, false names and secret destinations as much as spare underwear. Without these precautions, today's private hospital would become tomorrow's sea of faces and camera lenses outside the building. For that very reason, Ringo didn't search for a cure anywhere – especially in England – where "creative" scribes would disguise themselves as staff to get some sordid scoop. Instead, in October 1988, he and Barbara checked into an exclusive rehabilitation centre 20 miles across rugged Arizona crags from the nearest town.

Possibly, it was Ringo's own fault that the cover was blown because, at Tucson airport, "I landed as drunk as a skunk. I drank all the way and got off the plane totally demented. I thought I was going to a lunatic asylum."[28] The game was up, and so were the headlines as a flow-chart of the Starkeys' mutual unhappiness unfolded: Ringo And Wife In Booze Hell! Wife-Beater Ringo!! Shame Of Crazed Beatle!!! Starr's Vicious Secret!!!! Fodder for tabloid cartoons was his drumming driving other inmates to drink. Ha! Ha! Very funny.

From the clinic, Ringo telephoned Derek Taylor to blunt journalistic quills, but he was too late to stop one newspaper from making a mountain of George Harrison's mild remark, "I'm really glad he's sorting out his problems."[31] Its Sunday edition would carry

Tony Barrow's pessimistic assessment of Ringo's chances of beating the booze.[31]

During a five-week limbo, the Starkeys – sleeping apart – confronted and wrestled with their inner and unknowable conflicts. Jerked from slumber, dawn would seem a year away. Nevertheless, help was but the press of a buzzer away when phantoms of eddying imaginations threatened to engulf them.

Accosted by enquirers after her clinic's famous patients, vice president Judy Schieb fogged by expounding the basic tenet of its "Minnesota method", whereby it was understood that "it's a disease of the mind, body and spirit. We assist people in dealing with their feelings [and] they start seeing some of the reasons why they are not willing to face life on life's terms. We ask that they take a look at their family of origin and how that might have transferred into their adult life."[32] What else could have brought Richard Starkey from being "crawling drunk"[28] in 1949 to the hour when he was poured into Tucson?

From this unpromising beginning, "Eight days in, I decided I am here to get help because I know I'm sick, and I just did whatever they asked."[28] As well as counselling – much of it from recovered sufferers – treatment included detoxification, compulsory exercise, group therapy, confinement to the premises and no sex. In cold print, it reads like prison, but Starr interacted well within the orderliness of the regime: "You get so safe in the clinic. I didn't want to leave."[29]

Their ways changed, Barbara and Ringo re-encountered the outside world, knowing their "trigger points" – ie the places, people and circumstances conducive to relapses. If tempted, either could snatch up the telephone and dial a sympathetic Alcoholics Anonymous ear at their behest "any time of the night or day and say, 'I feel shaky. Can you help me?' You just worry about getting through 24 hours at a time, but living in the present is so simple. We've been given our lives back."[29]

Many would find themselves excluded from Starr's social affairs: "Now, if any of my friends can't deal with me being sober, then I just don't bother with them, because, for me, to live is more important than a friend getting uptight just because I won't have a drink."[28] Evangelical in their new sobriety, he and Barbara would quit parties at godly hours "when everyone else starts getting rocky"[29] – except ones they held themselves. At a celebration in Cannes of their first year on the wagon, they were toasted in fruit juice. They'd always be alcoholics, but, affirmed Ringo, "My intention is never to drink again."[33]

A bout of pneumonia and then the death of his mother had poleaxed him soon after his sojourn in Arizona, but, although Ringo still looked a little haggard, no one doubted him when he said he felt "a lot better than I have for ages",[33] least of all Zak, Jason and Lee, to whom he gave books on his condition, as the clinic had instructed him, because "statistics say children of alcoholics are more inclined to become alcoholics themselves".[33] They were also encouraged to attend AA programmes at the centre attached to a Chelsea church hall, their more even-tempered father's main resort when things got tough.

At least he hadn't died in hell like Elvis, and it wasn't as if he was on the same endless-highway dilemma as a rock 'n' roller or black bluesman of a pre-Beatle epoch, with singing and playing an instrument his only saleable trade. Nevertheless, inactivity was Ringo's worst enemy, but it was more the example of other still-stagestruck 1960s contemporaries that prompted him to think aloud about hitting the road again: "I didn't want to front a band. I wanted to have fun. I wanted to be with good players, and I wanted to be with friends."[18] No one who listened was sure whether to believe him or not.

17 "Now I Just Stay Nervous"

When Ringo Starr watched the video of a 'Beatles Movie Medley' single – a splice-up of old clips – on *Top Of The Pops*, it seemed so far away, almost like another life. Sometimes, he could scarcely credit that it had been him on those records, in those films, at those stadiums. Was it truly him that once conquered the world? Such a feeling may have been anticipated, as, back in 1965, he'd predicted, "I wouldn't go on tour as a rock 'n' roll drummer with a group if I was 30. I'd feel so old and out of it."[1]

In a then-undreamable future, he'd retract these sentences when pop's history was seized upon as an avenue for selling as many – and, often, more – goods as its present. With repackaging factories in full production as the end of the century rolled around, it made sense for mature artists – supported by saturation television advertising – to plug "greatest hits" collections of recordings up to 30 years old as heavily as a latest album. Sometimes, the plugging of singles was done for them via the kind of unsolicited snippet coverage in TV commercials and movie soundtracks that sent The Hollies, The Righteous Brothers and, for gawd's sake, The Steve Miller Band to the top of the UK charts in the late 1980s, when at one stage the Top Ten contained but one entry that wasn't either a reissue or the revival of an old chestnut.

As Ringo could have done with 'She's About A Mover', it was a common if generally unviable practice for veteran stars to attempt a relaunch with a single of a cover from the hit repertoire of a contemporary. In 1988, for instance, Dave Berry fired a splendid pot-shot with Chris Farlowe's 'Out Of Time', while Farlowe himself had tried with Long John Baldry's 1968 Number One, 'Let The Heartaches Begin'. There was also such as Sandie Shaw with Cilla's 'Anyone Who Had A Heart', and Alice Cooper's go at Love's 'Seven And Seven Is'.

A more successful strategy was that of combining with another – often unlikely – artist. Not raising an eyebrow were alliances by Kenny Rogers with Tammy Wynette, Buck Owens with Emmylou Harris and Queen with David Bowie, but also scrambling up Top Tens in the 1980s were a Christmas single by Bowie and Bing Crosby, a UK chart-topping reprise of Gene Pitney's 'Something's Gotten Hold Of My Heart' by Pitney himself and crypto-punk vocalist Marc Almond and BB King's blistering obligatos tearing at a 1989 ditty by U2.

In the March of that year, Buck Owens had been in London for the Wembley Country Music Festival and sacrificed some free time to meet Ringo at Abbey Road, the ex-Beatle – absent for 14 years – expressing his amazement that the complex now had a restaurant in its basement. If it added little to either Owens' solo blueprint or the version of *Help!*, the pair's duet in Studio Two of 'Act Naturally' would be the title track of Owens' next album and, as a 1990 single, would cross over from the US Country charts into its pop Top 40, aided by a video shot in a restored Wild West town just outside Los Angeles.

In the same month that 'Act Naturally' was taped, Brian Poole, Reg Presley, Tony Crane and others of the same vintage – known collectively as "The Corporation" – rehashed The Showstoppers' 'Ain't Nothing But A House Party'. Even that tip-toed into the lower marches of the British lists.

Teenagers were no longer pop's most courted consumers, having been out-manoeuvred by their Swinging '60s parents and young marrieds who had satiated hunger for novelty. A humble US provincial journal caught the mood by defining rock 'n' roll as "a type of music preferred by adults aged 13 to 60".[2] These days, it was not laughable for those with "good" foreheads, crow's feet and double chins to slice into the hit parade with a newly-recorded 45 – like Alice Cooper with 'Poison' in 1987 – or, after vanishing for years, embark on sell-out transcontinental tours, as did Paul Simon, Fleetwood Mac, The Grateful Dead and, in his 50s, Leonard Cohen. Words being cheap, even George Harrison had let slip the "possibility" of him doing so, too, during the *Cloud Nine* junket, although those in the know realised that he had no such intention, there being little point in further publicising a million-selling album.

With Harrison's Bangladesh grand slam and the Carl Perkins TV special being the outstanding examples, Ringo had kept a facile hand in as a stage performer but had never put himself out on a limb as George had in 1974 and, to a greater degree, Paul still did. Nevertheless, not long out of the clinic, Starr had sat in on a couple of numbers when Bob Dylan's 1989 world tour reached Frejus, a few miles down the coast from Monaco, which was now more home than tax-prohibitive England since the sale of Tittenhurst Park in January 1988.

Taking a leaf from George's book, he was scouting around for a domain in Hawaii, while maintaining a toehold in London with a hideaway in Kensington. On one visit to the old country, he'd attended a show in a Dylan season at Hammersmith Odeon which included an ad-libbed cache of iconoclastic non-originals like 'She's About A Mover' and Kyu Sakamoto's 'Sukiyaki'(!). Rose-tinted memories of his groundbreaking concerts with The Band in the salad days of *Blonde On Blonde* had blinded many critics to the quality of his performances in the late 1980s, which were far more fun than those of his now more fêted commercial rivals. Also, while The Beach Boys, The Troggs and others worked a passage of the past around the globe, each new Dylan release was still a special event.

A new album by Ringo wasn't, but he could still clean up in North America if ever he wanted to take a band out there, maybe – as he'd long considered – one along the lines of Dylan's "Rolling Thunder thing, with no big production at all".[3] With resilient fatalism, he was no more in such fear of arseholes with firearms and the lurking of death around the next bend of the highway – or in the skies. Contradicting an earlier dictum, he had attended the funeral of guitarist Stevie Ray Vaughan, lost in a Wisconsin helicopter mishap while on tour with Eric Clapton.

The likes not of Stevie Ray Vaughan but certainly Clapton, Fleetwood Mac, Steve Winwood, Dire Straits and similar purveyors of cultured adult-orientated pop will always find habitual buyers for their reassuringly more ordinary albums from among those who'd matured with them. If you hadn't, you sought diversion in musical realms that you couldn't have imagined yourself ever liking – opera, 1930s dance bands, Gregorian chant – or else you regressed to adolescence by submerging yourself in another netherworld where current chart status has no meaning.

While it frequently lent credence to Adam Faith's assertion that "the worst thing in the world is to be an ex-pop singer doing the clubs",[4] at least no 1960s relic grew old there any more. An old hit-parade entrant was still a legendary hero, who – like an updated Caesar deified by the Gallic peasants – would offend none by refusing to autograph a dog-eared EP cover depicting him with most of his hair still on his head.

Incorrigible old mods, rockers and hippies would now be in compulsory ties or smart casuals, as these garments were often the norm at Blazers in Windsor, Caerphilly's Double-Diamond, the '60s Club in Marbella and other citadels of "quality" cabaret where there were rarely less than capacity crowds for "Sounds Of The '60s" nights. Promoters raked in loot via the customers' punishment of pricey liquor, while a sunken orchestra sight-read discreetly before some buffoon of a compere regaled all with gags that would shock a drunken marine. Then it'd be, "Without further ado, ladies and gentlemen, I'd like to bring on a *grrrrrreat* entertainer I know you're all going to enjoy – well, my late grandmother was quite fond of him..."

To utilise onlookers' time interestingly, a grrrrreat entertainer was no longer obliged to forge a *vita nuova* as a third-rate Sinatra. As everyone from The Swinging Blue Jeans on the chicken-in-the-basket trail to the Stones packing out the Hollywood Bowl had proved, all an act still intact from the 1960s had to do was to become an archetypal unit of its own, spanning with differing emphases every familiar trackway of its professional career – all of the timeless hits, each change of image, every bandwagon jumped. Nevertheless, at Reading's

Top Rank Bingo Hall in 1990, even the most susceptible of the elderly ravers bopping round their handbags could not have pretended that this was what it must have been like down the Cavern when The Merseybeats – with only Tony Crane left from the old days – gave 'em more than they paid for between games.

With a solo star like Freddie Garrity, who cared about the identity of The Dreamers behind him, in their collarless suits, Chelsea boots and three-piece Ringo drum kit? However, where there was no demarcation line between group and singer, it was often not quite the full shilling – the travesty that was the 1989 Byrds, with only the drummer a direct link with the 'Mr Tambourine Man' hitmakers; Herman's Hermits minus Herman; Dozy, Beaky, Mick And Tich with Mick and Beaky too youthful and no Dave Dee. A social secretary had to be careful about which Searchers he'd be booking, because, as well as the ones with the most valid legal claim to be the genuine article, there was "Mike Pender's Searchers" and – also led by another who'd been on 'Sweets For My Sweet' – Tony Jackson And The Vibrations.

As some groups on the circuit consisted wholly of slim-hipped herberts for whom 'Love Me Do' antedated conception, it seemed that, in order to find work, you needed just the rights to an old name, no matter how obscure. Roaming Britain in 1991 were Joe Brown's old backing group, The Bruvvers, who got by with one original member and his son, and Barry Noble and his Sapphires, who – with a certain logical blindness – could make out that they'd "achieved a couple of minor hits".[5] What was true was that Barry's bunch contained all of its "chartbusting" school of '62, which is more than can be said of a Hedgehoppers Anonymous, formed by four blokes with no connection whatsoever with the 1965 one hit wonders.

No matter how legitimate the set-up, nothing would coax builder Johnny Hutchinson or Birkdale butcher Kingsize Taylor back into the fray, although ambulance driver Johnny Guitar was fronting a reformed Hurricanes at Merseyside venues, mostly on the strength of renewed fascination with the original quintet stoked up since the mid 1980s by no less than two locally presented plays – *The Need For Heroes* and *The King Of Liverpool* – centred on the character of Rory

Storm. With ex-Merseybeat Billy Kinsley as lead vocalist, Pete Best, too, was no longer kicking against going the whole hog. Although his most recent single, 'Heaven' (penned by Rick Wakeman), had been attributed uncontroversially to "Kinsley and Best", Pete was, by 1991, quite blatantly calling the group after his now very collectable 1965 album, *The Best Of The Beatles*. Best of luck to him.

For a solitary charity engagement in 1989, Best had replaced the late John Banks in The Merseybeats. In that year, too, it was whispered that Ringo would likewise drum for Keith Moon in The Who's 25th anniversary tour. With no new LP in the shop, they were taking the States, in particular, for every cent that they could get by fixing solely and unashamedly on their back catalogue – even *Tommy*. Suddenly, their aficionados could not refute the suggestion that The Who were in the same bag as other huge but stagnant headliners like The Beach Boys and the reconstituted Monkees.

With another 20 episodes of *Shining Time Station* to be done, Ringo had shown that there was more to him than trying and failing to recapture chart glory. Having broken into the children's world without any trouble, why shouldn't he also provide entertainment as harmless for their elders by mining the same seam as The Beach Boys? Like their Brian Wilson, he was *compos mentis* again after an age of having "your brain all twisted in some way".[6] Nowadays, with hands no more a-tremble or nose enpurpled, he was eating regular meals, quaffing Adam's Ale and keeping daylight hours, even acquiring a tan – "And what happens? The doctors come along and say it's bad for you."[7]) He was also accepting studio sessions again, mostly in Los Angeles, where, for instance, he drummed for blues singer Taj Mahal on an album that emerged in 1991 on Private Stock, an independent company best known for its new age portfolio.

Happily persevering with teetotalism, Ringo was not, however, as voluble about its merits as Barbara, who, while sanctioning a bid for stardom by Francesca, had eschewed showbusiness herself, except when it provided a platform on which she could emphasise the horrors of alcoholism and appeal for cash to establish a Self-Help Addiction Recovery Programme (SHARP) centre in Britain offering the Minnesota Method. Her persistence paid off in the 1991 opening of such a clinic in London and hopes that treatment might be made available on the National Health one day. Against her former career, her commendable efforts in this direction had "more meaning – and, in the future, I'll probably do some counselling".[6]

He wasn't Maureen's "sodding great Andy Capp" any more, but Ringo's rise from his pit became most perceptible in 1989, when, no longer represented by Hilary Gerrard, he delegated day-to-day administrative responsibilities so that he could set about the clear-minded organisation of a show with a hand-picked "All-Starr Band", as the wheels for an autumn tour – with Barbara its official photographer – creaked into motion. It would take in the States, Canada and, lastly, Japan, embracing a concert at Tokyo's precious Nippon Budokan without any of the external antagonism that had blighted The Beatles' show there.

The logistics of shunting the show over to Europe were mulled over, but, as well as the distractions of the World Cup, there were tacit doubts about whether Starr could still pull the crowds there. After all, he wasn't Cliff Richard, who had recent smashes to slip in among the strolls down Memory Lane. If it was any yardstick on Beatle terms, a trudge around its concert halls by Yoko Ono a couple of years before hadn't broken even, not even out of sympathy or morbid inquisitiveness. While it might have been standing room only for a fortnight – possibly a whole month – at Blazers for Ringo, it might have been unwise for him to take on Wembley, even if he, too, had just come back from hell.

"The honest truth," as he perceived it, "is that I would not have been able to manage the rehearsals, let alone the tour, if I was still drinking."[7] Enforcers of their own order, bandleaders like John Mayall and *avant-garde* jazzer Annette Peacock would not tolerate boozing by their employees, and God help you if they caught you with drugs. Although by no means such a killjoy, it was Ringo's wish that his All-Starrs behave themselves off stage: "I explained to the band that I'd just come out of a clinic, and I'd like the hotel rooms to be left as we found them; but, after the show, if some of the members liked to drink, I couldn't be in charge of that – and you could always spot the ones who'd had a night out, when we got up the next morning for the plane."[8]

Casting about pop's old boy network, he'd been seeking not so much an abstemious backing group than a merger something like a less heavy-handed Bangladesh band, in which all participants were capable of either handling a lead vocal or otherwise being cynosure of the spotlight while the rest took a back seat. Ringo's All-Starrs would be the first of this strain of supergroup – that most fascist of pop cliques – to tread the boards in the 1980s, for neither The Corporation nor The British Invasion All-Stars – a producer's throwing-together of various members of The Yardbirds, The Nashville Teens, Creation and The Downliners Sect – would be heard outside the studio.

Formed as casually for recording purposes only were The Traveling Wilburys: Harrison, Dylan, Jeff Lynne, Roy Orbison and Tom Petty, the latter a singing guitarist whose style had been determined by hard listening to The Byrds. After the completion of 1988's *Volume One*, the Wilburys had returned to individual projects, but, bound by their "brotherhood", each implemented services for the others. Dylan, for instance, wrote a track for an Orbison album, although this was never recorded, owing to the ill-starred Texan's sudden death that December.

Through George, Ringo drummed on 'I Won't Back Down', a 45 lifted from Petty's *Full Moon Fever*. He was also present on its video, although he was unable to make the final day's shoot, thus necessitating the employment of a lookalike.[9] Petty – with Lynne, Joe Walsh and Jim Keltner – had accompanied Starr on 'I Call Your Name' for Yoko Ono's Pier Head spectacular, and was a likely candidate for the All-Starrs. On the cards, too, were Peter Frampton, former Traffic guitarist Dave Mason – another who'd made his qualified fortune across the Atlantic – and, at tour co-ordinator David Fishoff's suggestion, bass player Jack Bruce, who in 1972 had been canny enough to shelve more ambitious labours for two dull albums and attendant tours with two members of Mountain – who'd been spoken of as "the new Cream" – in order to cash in on his old trio's reputation.

Whether or not Ringo asked him to be an All-Starr, Bruce preferred to coerce Ginger Baker into joining him on a trek around the US with a band that broke the ice each night with an hour's worth of old Cream numbers. For Starr, an equivalent coup would have been turns by McCartney and Harrison, who were both sent his itinerary, but this long-shot would result in only Paul – or someone who looked like him – hovering in the backstage disarray at one stop.

Two – or three – ex-Beatles for the price of one would have been a most delectable treat for the fans, as would the handful of Rolling Stones that – judging by stepped-up security precautions – were half expected when The All-Starrs appeared near the Connecticut settlement where Jagger *et al* were readying themselves for another global money-spinner. However, how few would have recognised Buck Owens, had he accepted his invitation to duet with Ringo on 'Act Naturally'? A year later, more might have done when the Owens-Starr recording of this was up for a Grammy as Best Country Vocal Collaboration.

Beatle diehards, nevertheless, would have still clapped harder after the drum roll heralding the main attraction's "long-lost daughter", Lee, who took a bow the night the Stones didn't bother to show up – and she'd be viewed dancing around the front row in the domestic laser disc video, edited mainly from two shows at Los Angeles' Greek Theater, where the US tour wound down. On both of these evenings, Zak Starkey sat in with his father's methuselahs. He might have managed more such performances, had he not been so busy with Ice, the group that succeeded Nightfly, in which he played "heavy"[10] guitar as well as drums. "Rough and ready with a dance groove,"[10] they'd been in Japan that summer and had notched up some radio sessions back in Britain.

The Band's Garth Hudson was at the Greek Theater, too, as was actor Gary Busey, star of a 1979 film portrait of Buddy Holly, singing along to 'With A Little Help From My Friends' in a set that had been flexible enough to allow for other guest appearances *en route* by such as comedian John Candy (on keyboards), Nils Lofgren's guitarist brother Tom, Brad Delp from hard-rockin' Boston (named after their home locality), Max Weinberg and – after The All-Starrs had spent the day at his New Jersey house – Bruce Springsteen, who flashed smiles, plucked at his guitar, wrinkled his nose, clenched his teeth and mouthed the words others sang before monopolising the central microphone himself for a busked 'Long Tall Sally'.

While presiding over these comings and goings, the ultimately all-American All-Starrs' cordiality was such that any upstaging during working hours provoked no friction. According to Ringo's band introduction, it was Jim Keltner[11] rather than himself who was "the greatest drummer in the world". Between them, Starr would admit to "no sense of competition. We have a rule: if I do one fill, he gets the next one."[12] At California's Pacific Auditorium, the outfit interrupted the proceedings for the community singing of 'Happy Birthday To You' for a damp-eyed Billy Preston, whose 'That's The Way God Planned It' was cut after the second show in favour of 'Get Back'. He was also allowed 'Will It Go Round In Circles?' and 'Nothing From Nothing' from the hat-trick of US million-sellers that he'd scored since Bangladesh. Although the last of these was long ago, Billy could still whip up the rabble with his soulman antics.

An anti-climax, therefore, was Nils Lofgren's bit, during which he usually emoted 'Shine Silently' and – while Ringo took five – Buddy Holly's 'Raining In My Heart'. He'd then over-reach himself with a new number, 'Being Angry Is A Full-Time Job'. It didn't have a prayer in the midst of an equilibrium of everyone else's biggest smashes, even Joe Walsh's 'Desperado' from The Eagles' songbook, itself an arresting choice as it pre-dated his period with them. Rather than bore 'em stiff with excerpts from his latest LP, *The Confessor*, Walsh pleased the audience by pleasing himself with nothing that hadn't already proved a showstopper for him.

Ringo had been lucky to procure Joe, who, contacted in New Zealand, was waiting for confirmation of a support spot on The Who's journey across America – possibly his belated reward for producing 1981's *Too Late The Hero*, John Entwistle's last solo album. After Starr's more enticing offer, however, he wriggled out of all prior commitments. So, too, did Mac Rebennack – announced by

Ringo as "the only doctor in the house" – who had rather diluted his
Night Tripper dread through compromising assistance in diverse TV
commercials, from milk to American Express cards, as Dolly Parton's
pianist, and in the non-sardonic title and evergreen content of his
newest album, *In A Sentimental Mood*. Nonetheless, he lugged his
feathered, beaded head-dress and the rest of his old Dr John stage
costume from its mothballs and reminded himself of the words of
'Iko Iko' (into which would be integrated the percussion interlude
'Right Place Wrong Time') – the nearest he ever came to a hit – and,
the most up-tempo excerpt from *In A Sentimental Mood*, Johnnie
Ray's intense 'Such A Night'. He wouldn't let Ringo down, and in 30
cities he'd pound his Yamaha grand, beat auxiliary drums in 'Back
Off Boogaloo' – the 1972 arrangement that was supplanted on the
second night by 'I Wanna Be Your Man' – and, for his ordained time
in the limelight, belt out the old magic, even if nobody was getting
any younger.

Almost without fail, too, Rick Danko and Levon Helm would
uphold the retrospective criteria of each evening with 'The Weight',
'Cripple Creek' and 'The Shape I'm In', just as they had in The Last
Waltz and Danko had continued to do in solo tours across Canada
and Australia. Since The Band, he and Helm had made separate
headway as film actors, although both were cast in a 1985 remake of
The Man Outside. The prolific Danko had also marketed an
instructional video on the intricacies of the electric bass.

Whereas The Band had employed a horn section for their final
romp, thrifty Ringo settled for Clarence Clemons alone with
whatever hi-tech device could fatten his saxophone sound when
required. His *A Night With Mr C* album was then current, but he
didn't push it with The All-Starrs, electing instead to embellish
overall effect, as he'd done with Springsteen.

If The All-Starrs' *de jure* leader, Starr had had the least recent
experience of the road. During weeks of rehearsals with all the most
advanced cordless radar equipment on a Los Angeles soundstage and
in the Park Central Amphitheater near Dallas, scene of the opening
night, "the great discovery was that I could still play at all. I

rediscovered the dream I'd had when I was 13 and which, in a haze of alcohol, I'd gradually forgotten. The others had to be very patient with me, because I had to learn all my songs again. I'd sung a tune like 'Yellow Submarine' on the record, but I'd never played it live."[8]

Likewise unaccustomed to singing for so long, George Harrison's 1974 tour had become even more harrowing when every battered nuance had been rasped from his inflamed vocal cords. Learning from George's misfortune, Starr hired recommended Californian voice coach Nate Lam, "not to turn me into Pavarotti, but more to show me the tricks of breathing, pacing myself and not just screaming. But that's another reason for having people who are not just musicians but also singers."[8]

After thrusting aside doubtful starters like 'Drumming Is My Madness' and 'In My Car' (in short, anything from *Goodnight Vienna* onwards) Ringo's lion's share of The All-Starrs' lead vocals – from the lower chest now, instead of the throat – boiled down to about ten "songs you know and love",[13] as he'd tell those who would nearly – but not quite – swamp his tutored singing, after his Max Miller cry of "all together now!" brought in the choruses. He'd lean down to direct his microphone at the lips of those congregated around the apron of the stage for responses, like John's nautical quips in 'Yellow Submarine'. Although its *Abbey Road* counterpart, 'Octopus' Garden', was missing as well as 'Don't Pass Me By', Starr did not renege on other set works that he'd recorded "a long time ago with those other chaps" by fracturing the emotional intent of, say, 'With A Little Help From My Friends' with any revision bar a brief Walsh solo, although on 'Honey Don't' – which didn't count as much – Clemons' sax was where Harrison's guitar had once been. Furthermore, the subject of the rapid-fire lyrics was not "steppin' around" any more but, let's face it, "sleepin' around". Minus its banks of strings, 'Photograph' came over more forcefully, too. Other minor changes littered the remaining mixture of Beatles items peculiar to himself[13] and a smaller amount of his 1970s smashes, but most were improvements when heard in arenas that were also designed for sport.

While the boys in the band sharpened the show's focus, blizzards of dollars subsided into wads in David Fishoff's office, where telephones rang with merchandising deals, advances against takings, franchises and estimates spewed out at a moment's notice to promoters in Nevada, Maryland and wherever. All of them were yelling, "Klondike!" at the prospect of a carnival of at least a quarter the magnitude of a Beatles *blitzkrieg*, albeit – as Brian Epstein had once promised – "not in the context of the previous terms".[14] All had signed cast-iron contracts guaranteeing that poor box-office receipts meant cancellation. There was, nevertheless, no cause for despondency, what with Pepsi Cola's sponsorship of the tour and the trusted capabilities of Fishoff, who'd handled The Monkees' second coming after water-testing tours since 1983 by The Association, The Turtles and other old groups wanting another bite at the cherry. Sniffing the wind, he'd written to Ringo with a similar proposal in as early as 1987, and the ex-Beatle's eventual affirmative was – so it'd read in the tour programme – "my most exciting, satisfying and biggest success yet".

This presumption would be corroborated by *Pollstar*, a trade magazine that estimated Ringo's average ticket sale at 7,000 to 8,000 per venue, with over 20,000 at New York's Jones Beach mitigating losses at half-empty stadiums in Buffalo and Sacramento. The total gross was reckoned to be in excess of $5 million. If modest compared to the dough amassed by the Stones, The Who and McCartney, $5 million was still impressive, as was the care taken to ensure customer satisfaction. For this "Tour For All Generations", children under seven were allowed in to minimise babysitting costs and facilitate a family atmosphere of picnics and deckchairs, weather permitting – which it didn't, at a lot of engagements. Thanks to soundchecks lasting hours and two gigantic video screens on either side of every stage, never had Ringo or any of the others – not to mention the local heroes who'd cornered the 30-minute second billings – been heard or seen so well by so many in the given setting.

Prominent at the official proclamation of the tour on 20 June 1989 at the New York Palladium, Ringo made sure that even more knew about it with further in-person plugs on *Good Morning America* and *The David Letterman Show*, going as far as inviting Letterman's band leader to play with The All-Starrs on any evening that he felt the urge.

At the Palladium press conference, he noted that, while The Beatles had played many of the auditoriums a quarter of a century earlier, others lined up by Fishoff were in "towns that weren't built the last time I did this".[15] He bemoaned the fact that there were so few All-Starrs dates below the Mason-Dixon line but hoped to remedy this "maybe next time".[15]

Both on and off stage, he'd refer to his new-found sobriety. Correspondents admitted to his inner sanctums would not be offered as much as a shandy, even at the knees-up to celebrate Ringo's first Canadian booking since The Beatles played Toronto in 1966. "I used to drink when I got nervous," he told them. "Now I just stay nervous."[7] It took some getting used to, as well: "For the first week it felt real strange to be playing, because I'm an old rocker so, after these shows, half of my brain was going, 'Let's go crazy!' and the other half was going, 'We don't do that now.'"[8]

Savouring every unclouded moment, he was quite tickled by the standing ovations that were his before he'd sung a crotchet. Prancing on, he'd wave good-humouredly while advancing stage centre. When he hit the prelusive "got to pay your dues if you want to sing the blues" of 'It Don't Come Easy', he'd already be hostage to the beat of its introductory fanfare that had been counted in while he waited in the wings and the tension mounted.

As the matrons in his worldwide fan club would ritually mob beanpole Johnnie Ray after every performance until the month of his death in 1990, so – like a parody of Beatlemania – libidinous middle-aged women rushed down aisles towards the little fellow "like Yasser Arafat impersonating a Krishna"[16] in his ponytail and the sunglasses that he'd declared were "from Elton's safe". For the second half, he'd steal on in a different jacket from a wardrobe that included ones in bright pink, silver lamé (with tails) and Chinese silk, all dragons and tassels.

From his acned years as a would-be Teddy Boy, he still believed that you wouldn't guess that he was no Mr Universe, if his apparel was sufficiently gaudy. His emergence up-front from behind the kit with The All-Starrs demonstrated that he was no Mick Jagger. However, neither was he a cosmic clown like Freddie Garrity. Even so, he got the giggles occasionally and effected a "champion" handclasp above his head whenever a number went down especially well.

Like his "keep it rollin'", "take me to heaven, Clarence" and similar mid-song yelps of encouragement, much of his patter became predictable to the syllable as every recital yielded "the best audience yet", particularly after they'd bought the badges, T-shirts and other durables that he'd always inform them were for sale during the interval. Charming some and sickening others, he'd enquire, "What do you think of it so far?" and, several times, "What's my name?", raising a titter with "I love that bit" when everyone bawled "Ringo!" back at him. When the entourage traversed the North Pacific, this question mutated to "*Watushi no namae wa nandeseuka?*" for the Japanese leg.

Because he was Ringo, he got away with these enthusiastic inanities and deporting himself as if he had all the time in the world. The *LA Times* critic rubbished him at first, but then concluded, "Ringo was a smiling, delightful neo-vaudevillian who capered about joyfully while making all the hokey moves that fell flat earlier seem somehow full of life."[17] Like some old ham in a musical, he talked rather than sang bits of the songs, but apart from the odd painful note his lessons with Nate Lam hadn't been in vain, although he attacked each opus "like a drummer by shifting his weight from side to side and singing each word on the beat".[15] Getting braver as the tour progressed, he began to experiment with diction and phrasing, but not enough to mar the good old good ones played in approximately the good old way, despite feet-finding false starts, cluttered middles and miscued endings. Yet, for all the carefree mistakes that only old pros could make, The All-Starrs went about their business without pomposity, "a little loose, a little ragged and a whole lot of fun".[18]

Johnnie Ray hadn't liked "the word *talent*. Talent is what Einstein had. What I do is communicate with the audience."[19] As shown by the full and lucrative cabaret workload that he enjoyed throughout his life, Ray was never found out. Neither was Ringo as he carved once more a deep niche across the heartland of North America. If he'd sometimes been as corny and gawky in his way as Ray in Uncle Sam's baseball parks, well, it was almost the point. Once, I arrived late at an anti-seal hunt rally in Trafalgar Square. Craning my neck, I couldn't make out who was on the podium in front of Nelson's column for, undeserving of the ensuing uproarious laughter, were the speaker's innocuous stabs at black humour. At one particularly fatuous *bon mot* involving a rude word, everyone but me became quite overcome with thigh-slapping mirth. When he stepped down, I discovered that I'd been listening to a famous comedian.

The moral of this fable – if it has one – could also be applied to others who'd sustained the momentum of public favour since shedding most of their artistic load. Some would adopt an "emperor's new clothes" technique by intimating that what they had could only be appreciated by the finest minds. In Ringo's case, it was roughly the opposite. To frantic applause in the States and – at a guess – an amused cheer in Britain, he seemed to imply with a wink that he wasn't a genius musician or, indeed, a genius anything, but that didn't matter, because he had an indefinable something else.

On the grounds of his light, friendly mood on and off the boards, he'd come to terms with his past and present situations by concentrating on the possible with what *The New York Times* lauded as "the better kind of nostalgia tour",[20] and although some of his antics had been a bit crass he hadn't milked audiences as much as some might have anticipated. Of course, he'd have been lynched if he hadn't done Beatles numbers, but he'd practised a grace-saving constraint exemplified by equating 'Honey Don't' with Carl Perkins – not *Beatles For Sale* – in its preamble and in his refusal of a big-time chauffeured ride to Vancouver's Pacific Colosseum from the airport in the psychedelic Rolls Royce that had once belonged to John.

He'd select only one Lennon-McCartney composition ('I Wanna Be Your Man') for the concert album issued by Christmas 1990 – by EMI, of all labels – to combat bootleggers who still profiteered from anything on which an ex-Beatle even breathed. All the same, The All-Starrs had been unable to cut a studio LP because, flying in the face of vigorous supplication from Ringo, "no one would take a chance on us. It was as if they didn't trust us any more. They still think we're a bunch of crazies. They kept saying things like, 'What kind of music are you going to do?'"[21]

Ringo Starr And His All-Starr Band came out in the same month as *Traveling Wilburys Volume Three*. Such a clash didn't drain revenue from each faction as it would have done in days of yore. Indeed, the borders between them had already dissolved when 'With A Little Help From My Friends' from the Greek Theater turned up as a bonus B-side on a pressing of the Wilburys' 'Nobody's Child' charity single and on a compilation LP of the same title for Olivia Harrison's Romanian Angel Appeal, following her shocked inspection of an orphanage near Budapest. Of the other Beatle wives in collusion with Olivia, Barbara was the most active in checking that the funds reached their target. Back in England, she was gratified to report, "It's made such a difference. In one orphanage I visited, the walls have been cheerfully painted with flowers and the alphabet, and there are sinks and toilets."[6] She and Mrs Harrison also tithed some of their time and money to the Parents For Safe Food campaign.

Inevitably, Barbara's warm-hearted voluntary work bred invasions of privacy by the media nuisance brigade with the same mind-stultifying questions. "Will The Beatles reform?" "Yes," snapped Barbara, "in heaven."[6] While this ultimate reunion had yet to come to pass, the principal liaison between any combination of ex-Beatles remains that of Ringo and George, who, with a left-handed bass guitarist dressed as a walrus, appeared together in the promotional video of 'When We Was Fab' from *Cloud Nine*. In keeping with this invocation of The Beatles, the two donned the *Sgt Pepper* uniforms that Jason and Lee had been borrowing for fancy-dress parties. Harrison and Starr also had walk-ons in the 1988 movie *Walking After Midnight*, starring James Coburn.

Ringo was also seen as himself with Jeff Beck and The Pink Floyd's Dave Gilmour in a promotional film of 'Too Much To Lose' by Czechoslovakian jazz-rocker Jan Hammer. His own All-Starrs video was shown at a trade fair in Cannes, which led to intermittent screenings on satellite TV, but negotiations for more taxing parts never got past a stray newspaper report that it was probably possible that Starr might be in a flick about pre-revolutionary China as Morris "Two Gun" Cohen, the Guevara to Chiang Kai-Shek's Castro. However, the sudden demise in 1987 of its producer, Tony Stratton-Smith – founder of Charisma Records – effectively finished it off, if it had been ever more than hot air.

Starr was perpetually "about to" get to grips with a US situation comedy, too, as an ageing pop singer and widower left in charge of the offspring in *The Flip Side* (directed by Don Johnson); as a club promoter in *Ringo's Rock Riot*; and as guest voice in *The Simpsons*. In December 1990, *TV Guide* had him procrastinating about another series: "I am English, and we don't want the show written for an American, because there'd be a difference in the humour and in the delivery."[22]

"I'm afraid the teenage roles are gone for me,"[22] he added, but he was well qualified to play the father of one in an Oldsmobile commercial, which obliged him – or a stunt man – to slide down a banqueting table, out of a twelfth-floor window and into a Cutlass car driven by Lee, now quite a late-20th-century young adult, with dyed-purple hair. In common with stepsister Francesca – not to say the likes of Moon Unit Zappa, Donovan Leitch Jnr and other scions of showbiz families – Lee's acting career was furnished with the best and worst start by her dad's long shadow both keeping her feet on the ground and creating pre-conceived ideas about her abilities.

Assumptions that Ringo would never feel his way out of his Beatles-nostalgia rut were strengthened as, one by one, reissues of his solo albums on compact disc were deleted. Nonetheless, the spectre of Chips Moman persisted in its haunting of him, despite a 1990 ruling by an Atlanta magistrate which thwarted plans for the issue of the Memphis album by Moman's own CRS firm. The prosecution had argued that CRS could not oversee its distribution and publicity "in a manner befitting an artist of Starr's stature".[23] Into the bargain, Moman was to surrender – in exchange for less than half of his demanded recording expenses – the Three Alarm master tapes to the plaintiff, who'd given a most diverting account of himself in the witness box.[24]

While there was written and taped evidence[25] corroborating that the resurrection of the record to coincide with the All-Starrs tour – as well as a mooted out-of-court financial settlement – had crossed Ringo's mind, he'd been disconcerted by the expedient Moman's endeavours to "blackmail" him into rush-releasing it, ignoring his desire to overdub drums "to get more of my personality on it".[23] Moreover, in the light of his late victory over the demon drink, Starr would also feel uncomfortable about endorsing an opus entitled 'Whiskey And Soda'.

There'd been little point in Ringo putting out even a single in 1990, as, despite the pencilling-in of dates in Europe, he postponed another All-Starrs adventure until the following August amid rumours that Todd Rundgren and Keith Emerson had been drafted in to replace those unavailable from the 1989 personnel. Scheduled to perform in Fishoff's good ol' US of A "in the same places",[21] Starr advocated for this market consolidation a prudent change of format, with probably 'Octopus' Garden' and other favourites excluded from 1989, plus a track or two from a brand-new album. Because he'd shown that he meant business by his willingness to reach his public again – even if it was the same public as last time – someone had finally seen no harm in "taking a chance on us" in the form of a 1991 recording deal with Private Stock, signed largely because Ringo had got on well with Taj Mahal's producer, Skip Drinkwater, who ventured forth on an immediate quest for songs for his new client, before being superseded by Jeff Lynne, who had steered both George Harrison and Roy Orbison back into the charts.

Thus Ringo's life settled into the next stage of what has become almost a set pattern for biographies of famous 1960s pop musicians. After the years of struggle, the climb to fame, the consolidation, the decline and the "wilderness years" comes, hopefully, the qualified comeback. In nearly all examples, too, the repercussions of the initial breakthrough – in Ringo's case, the flush of chart strikes with The Beatles – yet resound, having gouged so deep a wound on pop that it gives the decades left to the artist a certain irrelevance, regardless of latter-day commercial or artistic windfalls.

Ringo Starr was to have a necessary hand in an excavation and even a surprise exhumation of The Beatles, but other than that his professional undertakings in the 1990s and since have stemmed, more or less, from that first nostalgia trek with The All-Starr Band. Certainly, there have been no more films ("No one's asked me, and I'm not interested right now"[26]), although he drummed on Little Richard's remake of 'Good Golly Miss Molly' for *King Ralph* and was the voice on middle-of-the-road 'You Never Know' from the soundtrack of a flick entitled *Curly Sue*; and, of course, there was his "appearance" in US cartoon series *The Simpsons* in 1991.

No, I haven't seen either *King Ralph* or *Curly Sue*, but if you're the type who finds nothing about The Beatles too insignificant to be intriguing then you probably have. Furthermore, you may have discovered already *Beatlefan*, the journal that chronicles all things to do with the Fab Four, together and apart. Otherwise, if you think you'd derive deep and lasting pleasure from studying and comparing, say, on-stage utterances of each concert Starr has played since 1989, write to *Beatlefan* at PO Box 33515, Decatur, GA 30033, USA.

Well, that's the Yanks for you. Where would the world be without them? More to the point, where would Ringo and The Beatles be? What about the all-important personage of Alan Clayson, too? Thanks to *Straight Man Or Joker*, *The Quiet One: A Life Of George Harrison* and *Backbeat* – the latter essentially a biography of Stuart Sutcliffe – I've been an honoured guest at many US Beatlefests, where I've met some interesting people, several of whom I would now regard as close friends. That any given Beatlefest in the States dwarfs even the Merseybeatle event puts us and them into perspective. This is a silly analogy, but, if Beatlemania lasts a lifetime for British devotees, it's for all eternity for their US counterparts.

That may be why the second phase of Ringo's world tour with his All-Starr Band in 1992 covered North America more extensively than any other territory. Keith Emerson didn't join him, after all, but Todd Rundgren did, along with Nils Lofgren and Joe Walsh from the old troupe. Further full-time newcomers included Zak Starkey (all pals with Dad, now), Dave Edmunds and Burton Cummings, a mainstay of The Guess Who, a Canadian outfit who, in around 1970, had racked up half a dozen US million-sellers but made far less impact in Europe.

When The All-Starrs crossed the Atlantic in summer 1992, perhaps the most eagerly anticipated stops were those at the Montreux Jazz Festival(!) for the recording of a second live All-Starrs album, the Stadtpark in Hamburg, London's Hammersmith Odeon and, especially, the Liverpool Empire, after Cavern City Tours announced limited weekend package trips to see him there. BBC Radio 4's early-morning magazine *Today* made a big fuss (although my bit was cut, blast their impudence), and the show was to be filmed for the Disney Channel, along with location sequences in the city centre. By one of these coincidences that occupy many an idle hour amongst Beatle disciples, Pete Best and his group were working the new Cavern on the very evening – 6 July – that The All-Starrs were on at the Empire.

Although McCartney – with and without Wings – had been back a lot, this was Ringo's first home game, so to speak, since The Beatles. For a few, therefore, it was more than just entertainment by a pop singer. Veiled in flesh, the Local Boy Made Good was re-appearing before his people like Moses from the clouded summit of Mount Sinai to the Israelites. Others were more level headed, but, while no one expected the waters of the Mersey to part, the show was on the scale of a cup final or Muhammad Ali's last hurrah in Las Vegas.

Although a roaring ovation brought him back for 'Act Naturally' and 'With A Little Help From My Friends' – encores he'd done throughout the entire expedition – only a miracle could have rescued the performance from anti-climax. A disaffected onlooker's angle might have been that, other than a few local references during announcements and Ringo dedicating an opus to his mother, it was just like any other evening on the tour. Although Starr rattled the traps as expected, he was more like a featured singer than anything else, sometimes vanishing into the wings as one of the others took over with an item, often half remembered at most by the audience.

Give him credit, though. Ringo wasn't playing it so safe this time around. Mixed in with the yellow submarines and help from his friends – and a bold instrumental version of 'Lady Madonna' – were items from the new studio album, *Time Takes Time*, recorded in Los Angeles for Private Stock. As well as a high calibre of hired musicians and arrangers at his disposal, there were star appearances by such as Brian Wilson and Tom Petty and a moveable feast of top producers: Jeff Lynne, Phil Ramone (who'd also worked with Paul McCartney and Julian Lennon), Don Was and Peter Asher[27] (also involved in the taping of 'You Never Know').

Among tracks shortlisted were a Lynne original ('Call Me'), Rick Suchow's 'What Goes Round' (picked as the singalong finale), a version of Elvis Presley's 'Don't Be Cruel' and songs written by Ringo either alone, with Paul McCartney (the remaindered 'Angel In Disguise') or with Johnny Warman, the principal source of new material, with no fewer than three selections: catchy 'Don't Go Where The Road Don't Go', similarly autobiographical 'All In The Name Of Love' and the social commentary 'Runaways' – a bawled audience request at Hammersmith.

As Ringo had aged, so had most of the topics tackled by either him or his wordsmiths. In a realistic conversational flow, parenthood (in 'Golden Blunders'), the passing time, regrets about past foolishness *et al* were filtered through clever arrangements and technological jiggery-pokery that somehow made the LP too pat, too dovetailed, too American for my taste, but that's the feeling of someone who would far prefer to find some scratchy old 45 by The Troggs in an Oxfam shop to receiving, say, the latest CD by Bruce Springsteen as a Christmas present.

What the hell do I know? A million Bruce Springsteen fans can't be wrong. Nor could a million fans of Ringo Starr back in 1973. However, moving the clock forward nearly 20 years from 'Photograph' and 'You're Sixteen', was either *Time Takes Time* or its spin-off single, 'Weight Of The World', a hit? You guessed it. However, its failure probably had less to do with its polished quality than with a chart climate that begs the question, who wants proper songs any more – even those as unremarkable (if pleasant) as 'Weight Of The World', with its Byrds-like jingle-jangle? Catch me in full philistine rant about virtually all of the major rap executants and any new Boyzone-type boy band, and I sound just like some middle-aged dad *circa* 1966 going on about The Rolling Stones. Nevertheless, if I'd gone to an All-Starrs recital, what would I have wanted to hear? Ringo didn't become a contemporary challenger again partly because his fans, old and new, will always clap loudest for the sounds of yesteryear.

George Harrison's understanding of this was apparent when, at a few days' notice, he performed at the Royal Albert Hall in 1992, doing nothing that wasn't in either The Beatles' or his solo repertoire of smashes. Not missing a trick, he waved in Ringo for the encores: 'While My Guitar Gently Weeps' and a 'Roll Over Beethoven' that incorporated a drum battle with other percussionists present.

Ringo had never been averse to special guests, either. In 1992, he'd got Harry Nilsson – another bit-part player on *Time Takes Time* – to be an All-Starr for one evening only in Las Vegas. Once well known for never singing in public, Nilsson also appeared that August at a Chicago Beatlefest for a question-and-answer session on stage and to give 'em a set that included 'Without You', backed by the house band, Liverpool. At the hotel, his was the room next to mine. My acquaintance with him got off to a bad and unknowing start when I telephoned the front desk to request them to ask what turned out to be Nilsson's two children to turn down their bloody video as I was trying to sleep off jetlag. However, when formally introduced, he and I got on well, possibly because, frankly, I'd never been impressed with many of his records. This meant that I wasn't fawning over him like nearly everyone else. During a chat on songwriting methodology, we exchanged demo tapes[28] and a promise to meet up when either he was next in England or I in California. We also discussed me penning his biography.

Some say that he was an inconsistent genius while others dismiss him as a tiresome *bon viveur*, but I liked Harry Nilsson because, for some reason God alone knows, he liked me. After all, I'd never been over-complimentary about him in either *The Quiet One* or *Straight Man Or Joker?*, the latter of which he'd scrutinised in my presence. Nevertheless, I felt that, as long as his painfully obvious poor health improved, some kind of return to prominence was not entirely out of the question for him, although one of his parting sentences lingers with me still: "I'm not as sure of my tomorrows as I used to be."

Harry Nilsson died in January 1994, and a few months later Harry Graves passed away at the age of 87. Shortly after his stepson attended the funeral in Liverpool, another with a principal role in the Ringo Starr story was gone, too. Despite a bone-marrow transplant from her elder son, leukaemia took Maureen Tigrett – Starkey as was – in a cancer-research clinic in Seattle in December. Her children and their respective fathers were all present at the final moments.

Tragedy almost struck the family again when Ringo interrupted an All-Starr tour that August after Lee – diagnosed as hydrocephalic – was rushed from the London garden flat that she shared with Jason[29] to an operating theatre, where keyhole surgery relieved the pressure of excess fluid on the brain and thus saved her.

Ticket-holders were sympathetic rather than angry about the cancelled dates of what was – for the US faithful, at least – the most value-for-money All-Starrs thus far, containing as it did Billy Preston, Felix Cavaliere from The Young Rascals, Grand Funk Railroad's Mark Farner, Randy Bachman – whose Bachman-Turner Overdrive had risen from the ashes of The Guess Who – and, on bass, John Entwistle, The Who's second-string composer. His taciturn stage presence belied a love of performing, expressed earlier in his fronting of Who splinter groups in the 1970s, as well as his bellowing of 'Twist And Shout' with the latter-day Who.

In an *NME* interview in 1966, John's colleague Pete Townshend had discussed which members were the equivalents of John, Paul, George or Ringo – for The Who, like many other mid-1960s outfits, had boiled down to The Beatles' blueprint as much as certain Britpop acts did later. Indeed, the notion of the self-contained beat group had been instilled from the cradle for Oasis, Pulp, The Bluetones, Supergrass and all the rest of those regarded by tidy-minded (or lazy) journalists as modern equivalents of whatever 1960s group they could be seen to resemble, however superficially.

Yet arguments that Oasis were first today's Rolling Stones and then today's Beatles – with leader Noel Gallagher its Lennon *and* McCartney – do not hold water because of radical changes in economic, sociological and technological atmospheres over the past 30 years. Being in a pop group is, for example, a much more acceptable career option to those parents who, when children of the 1960s, had been victims of repressions epitomised by short hair and long hem-lines.

You may dismiss this as a too-sweeping generalisation but, after escaping the clutches of those who didn't understand, former Mods, Rockers and hippies were much more liberal with their own offspring, buying synthesisers as birthday presents for teenagers who could even con grants out of the government to form a band – even if, in the same defeated climate, record companies were no longer chucking huge advances about, as they had when the wheels of the universe came together for The Sex Pistols in 1976, as vital a watershed year as 1962 or 1967.

Cemented together by the joys and sorrows of their heyday – and the opportunity to make an easy fortune – the Pistols reconvened in 1996 for a world tour. This included an appearance on *Top Of The Pops* that was, to me, as touching in its way as an occurrence in the previous autumn, when the surviving Beatles embodied the truism articulated by John McNally of The Searchers: "You don't have to be young to make good records."[30]

The perpetual to-ing and fro-ing of rumours had intensified with the runaway success of *Live At The BBC*, a collection of early broadcasts ("a really cool album," reckoned Ringo[31]) and an official announcement of an anthology of further Beatles items from the vaults being compiled by Starr, Harrison and McCartney themselves. These were to be released over the period of a year on nine albums (in sets of three) and linked to a six-hour documentary film spread over three weeks on ITV and presented likewise on foreign television.

Next came talk of the Fab Three recording new material for the project. When asked to participate in a connected news feature for London's Capital Radio, I ventured the opinion that all they'd be doing was incidental music. Writing in *The Daily Mail*,[32] the late Ray Coleman[33] hoped that it wouldn't go any further than this, arguing – with none to disagree – that it wouldn't be the same without Lennon and fuelling Ringo's truism, "There were four Beatles and there are only three of us left."[31]

After a fashion, Starr, McCartney and Harrison's efforts weren't without Lennon. Sessions at Paul's studio in Sussex and George's in Oxfordshire yielded the grafting of new music onto stark performances of 'Free As A Bird' and other compositions by John on home tapes provided by his widow after Paul's conciliatory embrace of her at a Rock 'n' Roll Hall Of Fame award ceremony. "It was just a natural thing which gradually evolved," explained Ringo. "It actually took about three years for all this to happen."[31]

Isn't it wonderful what they can do nowadays? Precedents had been forged in the 1960s by the respective superimposition of accompaniment onto the sketchiest demos by Buddy Holly[34] and Jim Reeves. In 1981, Nashville producer Owen Bradley's skills with sampler, varispeed and editing block had brought together Reeves and Patsy Cline on record with a duet of 'Have You Ever Been Lonely'. Ten years later, there arrived an international smash with 'Unforgettable', a similar cobbling together of Nat "King" Cole and daughter Natalie's voices over a state-of-the-art facsimile of Nat's original 1951 backing track.

With Jeff Lynne as console midwife, 'Free As A Bird' took shape as near as dammit to a new Beatles record, complete with Ringo's trademark "pudding" drums, a 'Let It Be' bottleneck-guitar passage from George and Paul emoting a freshly composed bridge as a sparkling contrast to John's downbeat verses, The effect was not unlike that of a mordant 'A Hard Day's Night'. Although it was 'Ticket To Ride' that he was describing as "uplifting and sad at the same time",[35] Beatles admirer (and imitator) Noel Gallagher could have said the same about 'Free As A Bird'.

"It's great, and I'm not just saying that because I'm on it,"[36] enthused Ringo. Well, to quote Mandy Rice-Davies, he would say that, wouldn't he? However, it was certainly better than 'Can't Buy Me Love' and 'The Ballad Of John And Yoko', A-sides issued by The Beatles when Lennon was alive. Yet, for all the accumulation of expectation via no sneak previews, a half-hour TV special building up to its first spin over a remarkable video and the multitudes willing it to jump straight in at Number One, 'Free As A Bird' stalled at second place in Britain's Christmas list when up against Michael Jackson's 'Earth Song' and an easy-listening overhaul of Noel Gallagher's 'Wonderwall' by the amazing Mike Flowers Pops. The follow-up, 'Real Love', made the Top Ten more grudgingly, dogged as it was by exclusion from Radio 1's playlist of Britpop, boy bands and chart ballast from the turntables of disco and rave.

Who couldn't empathise with Ringo's mingled disappointment and elation when the million-selling *Anthology* albums demonstrated that almost but not quite reaching the top in the UK singles chart was but a surface manifestation of enduring interest in The Beatles that made even their out-takes a joy forever?

Then there was the money. Revenue from every aspect of the *Anthology* project certainly swelled the participants' bank accounts. Well before 1996 was out, Starr would be indexed among Britain's richest 500 in an annual survey conducted by *The Sunday Times*.

In deference to the years before the coming of Ringo, the first *Anthology* package contained items with Beatles who had left the fold one way or another before 1962. Such inclusions did not benefit Stuart Sutcliffe, mouldering in Huyton parish cemetery these past 35 years, but Pete Best could foresee that these were to earn him what Derek Taylor had estimated as "a decent amount of money"[37] – decent enough, at least, for Pete to resign from the civil service and concentrate fully on being *de jure* leader of Best Of The Beatles now that *Anthology* had helped to broaden its work spectrum to a busy 1996 schedule covering 18 countries, as well as bigger UK venues than before – Margate Winter Gardens, London's Bottom Line, Southport Floral Hall, Barnsley Civic, Sutton Secombe Theatre, you name 'em.

Like Ringo does with The All-Starrs, Pete employs a close relation – brother Roag – as second drummer and takes on board Beatles numbers and the livelier crowd-pleasers from his latest album. While *Back To The Beat* spotlights his ensemble's reworkings of 1960s classics, Pete has since composed some numbers of his own. Interviewed by a national newspaper just prior to the uncaging of 'Free As A Bird', he said, "They're like what The Beatles would sound like if they were around in the 1990s."[38]

18 "I'll Be Fine Anywhere"

For the past five years, it's been more or less business as usual for Ringo – and quite big business, too. In spring 1996, for instance, he banked half a million pounds for uttering just one line in a Japanese television commercial for Ringo Suttar natural juice. Into the bargain, he didn't even have to go to Japan to do it, merely board a first class flight to Vancouver to be filmed in front of a photograph of Mount Fuji.

Not so lucrative, however, would be Starr's hitherto-unissued revival of 1971's 'Power To The People', John Lennon's fourth solo 45, sharing vocals with Billy Preston and, apparently, Eric Burdon for the soundtrack of *Steal This Movie*, a biopic of 1960s political activist Abbie Hoffman. Ringo agreed to do it out of the goodness of his heart, because all that he had to do these days was sit back and let the royalties from the ongoing Beatles industry roll in.

Rather than his customary million pounds or so per annum from his cut of sales of the four's back catalogue, dividends from 1996's renovated *Yellow Submarine* – with additional footage, remixed soundtrack CD, video and DVD and associated clothing, memorabilia and toys – reduced even the Ringo Suttar money to a sideshow. More was to come – up to £5 million more in a single tax year via the publication of The Beatles *Anthology* autobiography[1] in 2000. Despite a £35 cover price, this accrued enough advance orders to slam straight in at Number One in *The Sunday Times*' book chart, a feat duplicated across the world.

With its weight on a par with that of a paving slab, this de luxe

"Beatles story told for the first time in their own words and pictures" had been several years in its gestation. Transcriptions of recent ruminations and fallible reminiscences by Harrison, Starr and the lately knighted McCartney and archive spoken material by Lennon – plus a treasury of photographs, documents and further memorabilia – were edited by Genesis in consultation with fellow travellers of the ilk of Klaus Voorman, Sir George Martin and, until his death in 1997, Derek Taylor.

Overall, a likeable and sometimes courageous account – and an intriguing companion volume to this one – passed the litmus test of any pop life story, in that it provoked a compulsion in the reader to check out the records. Nevertheless, it was flawed, mainly because there is little if any anchoring text for that Tibetan monk who still hasn't heard of the wretched group, and while the surviving Beatles were often painfully honest about events that occurred up to 50 years earlier it was an autobiography aimed at fans who prefer not to know too much about what kind of people their idols are in private life. Too many illusions will be shattered, and the music may never sound the same.

As serious a fault was that, like the televisual *Anthology*, it lacked the perspectives of other living key *dramatis personae*, such as Pete Best, Tony Sheridan, Kingsize Taylor, Cilla Black – you name 'em. But where do you draw the line? By including all of the acts on the same label? Everyone who ever recorded a Beatles song? The factory hands who pulped the trees to make the paper on which they were written?

Anthology remained a best-seller while, with 60-year-old Neil Aspinall still at the helm, a four-strong team at Apple – now run from one of the white townhouses encircling central gardens in Knightsbridge – helped co-ordinate EMI's biggest-ever marketing campaign. Its budget was between £1 million and £2 million in Britain alone, and eight million copies of *1* – titled originally *Best Of The Beatles*, a compilation of The Beatles' 27 UK and/or US chart-toppers – were shipped around the world.

The fastest-selling CD ever, *1* was just that in Britain, Japan, Spain, Germany and Canada within a week of its issue in autumn

2001, with over 400,000 customers stampeding into Japanese record shops during the first day. At home, it outsold the latest by Oasis four to one.

Whether looking forward to the past is a healthy situation for any artist is open to conjecture, but it was hard fact that Joe Average was more intrigued by the corporate Beatles than Ringo Starr or any other individual locked in their orbit.* If Paul and George weren't yet ready to go gently into that good night, Ringo's acceptance of the situation was manifest in his continued trans-continental treks with The All-Starr Band and the first twelve-track volume of *The Third All-Starr Band Live*, with all of the usual suspects delivering their vintage goods, notably US Number Ones in The Rascals' 'People Got To Be Free' and – all from 1974 – Billy Preston's 'Nuthin' From Nuthin'', Bachman-Turner Overdrive's 'You Ain't Seen Nothing Yet' and Grand Funk's rehash of Little Eva's 'The Locomotion'. Britain held her own, however, with John Entwistle doing creepy 'Boris The Spider' (the discerning Jimi Hendrix's favourite Who opus) and new recruits Simon Kirke – once Free's drummer – giving 'em 'All Right Now' and Procol Harum's Gary Brooker 'A Whiter Shade Of Pale', 'Conquistador', 'The Devil Came From Kansas' and 'A Salty Dog'.

Although his portfolio bulged with more crowd-pleasers than any of them, the All-Starrs' leader understood, too, that few – apart from regular readers of *Beatles Monthly*, *Beatlefan* and suchlike – could speak with any authority or interest about a cossetted life divided domestically between Monaco, California and – for however many weeks per annum ordained by Britain's tax laws – a country estate in Cranleigh, Surrey. These days, Ringo Starr's name was far less potent an incentive to hold the front page, unless he pulled some eye-stretching stroke such as getting half killed, like George Harrison would be by some Beatlemaniac (from Liverpool, of all places) late in 1999. That had been far bigger news than any new or recycled disc by any ex-Beatle that a journalist might or might not have been aware as he cobbled together an editorial tirade about the government's vacillation about curbing the increase of violent crime in these distracted times.

---

* This may be illustrated by the raw statistic that, while there are nigh on 200 Beatles tribute bands in Liverpool alone, only one throughout the entire globe is known to be devoted to Ringo alone.

Slotted somewhere towards the backs of most national newspapers in May 1998 was a story concerning the most successful of Ringo, George and Paul's attempts to contain the industry of illicit Beatles merchandise, which was thriving as if the *Anthology* albums had never been. There was even a US magazine – *Belmo's Beatleg News* – devoted solely to unforgiving hours of everything (and I mean everything) on which The Beatles, together and apart, ever breathed. Germane to this discussion is an item like *Lost And Found*, which contained the Chips Moman sessions and, rubbing salt in the wound, an excerpt from Ringo's spell in the witness stand during the hearing in Atlanta to stop their over-the-counter release.

At what sort of lunatic were such products targeted? Who had the patience to sit through six takes of the same backing track, a fractionally shorter edit of some Italian B-side, a false start of 'Act Naturally', one more fantastic version of 'It Don't Come Easy' and then spend infinitely less time actually listening to something like *Lost And Found* over and over again than discussing how "interesting" its contents were?

The overall effect of eavesdropping on such conversations was akin to overhearing a prattle of great aunts comparing ailments. Yet, to The Beatles' most painfully committed fans, the intrinsic worth and high retail price of a bootleg hardly mattered and, displayed between, say, *The Koto Music Of Japan* and *Aznavour Sings Aznavour Volume Three*, it serves as a fine detail of interior decorating and a handy conversational ice-breaker.

Beatles talk became more animated among the faithful in 1998, when a borderline case – *The Beatles Live At The Star-Club, Germany, 1962* – reared up again when Lingasong, a company of no great merit, announced its intention to reissue it on lavishly packaged CD. Reviewing it the first time round, a now-defunct UK pop journal had noted contemporary implications in the back-cover photograph of 1962 teenagers congregating beneath the club's attributive neon sign, "Treffpunkt Der Jugend" ("youth rendezvous"), before concluding waspishly, "The Beatles couldn't play, either." That's as may be, but Billy Childish, a leading light of the 1980s Medway Town's pop scene, had considered it "their finest LP". The artists concerned, however, lacked Billy's objectivity about both the alcohol-fuelled playing and a muffled sound, despite further expensive studio doctoring.

So it was that, on a midweek day in May 1998, The Beatles and Apple forced Lingasong before the High Court in London. Leaving his Southport butcher's shop to take care of itself for the day, Kingsize Taylor would swear that he'd been granted verbal permission by John Lennon to immortalise The Beatles' late shift at the Star-Club, "as long as I got the ales in". Lennon's go-ahead meant – so Taylor had assumed – that it was OK by the others, too. The judge decided that it wasn't, and the mutton-dressed-as-lamb press-packs of the CD that had been distributed by Lingasong in false anticipation of victory became instant prized rarities.

While Starr, McCartney and Harrison presented a united front against Lingasong, team spirit wasn't as pronounced on their return to individual activities. George, for example, was to slide some bottleneck on an overhaul of Kitty Lester's 'Love Letters' on *Double Bill* by Bill Wyman's Rhythm Kings, but had been less inclined to do so on in-one-ear-and-out-the-other 'I'll Be Fine Anywhere' and pleasantly funereal 'King Of The Broken Hearts' during sessions for Ringo's album of summer 1998, *Vertical Man*.

"He wasn't in the mood," sighed Ringo. "Two weeks later, I phoned him up from LA just to say, 'Hi,' and, 'What are you doing?'

"'Oh, I'm in the studio, playing with the dobro.'

"I go, 'Oooh, a dobro would sound good on my album.'

"So he goes, 'Oh, all right. Send it over, then.' I really wanted that slide guitar. His soul comes out of that guitar. It just blows me away."[2]

Produced by Mark Hudson, singing guitarist with The Hudson Brothers – a US act signed to Casablanca in the mid 1970s – 13-track *Vertical Man* embraced what Beatle-ologists might have interpreted as more than a little offhand breast-beating. Was its very title a reference to Ringo's recovery from alcoholism, or to Atouk the *Caveman* becoming Homo erectus when, inadvertently, he cracks his bent spine into an upright position? Furthermore, for unmitigated audacity alone,

Starr's trundling and artistically pointless retread of 'Love Me Do' – with Aerosmith's Steven Tyler on harmonica – deserved attention.

"I think I've got the hang of it now,"[2] laughed Ringo. Perhaps it was a symbolic laying to rest of the ghost of Andy White, now aged 71 and a resident since 1983 of New Jersey, where he teaches children to play in Scottish-style pipe-and-drums bands. As he was on the same land-mass at the same time as Starr, maybe he should have been hired for the new 'Love Me Do' to please the more perverse amongst us. Instead, Ringo stuck with more negotiable studio guests such as Brian Wilson, Tom Petty, Steve Cropper, Alanis Morrisette – a young Canadian whose debut album, 1995's *Jagged Little Pill*, had sold millions – and, crucially, Paul and George.

Paul was loud and clear on 'What In The World', one of the majority of items co-written by Ringo himself. Conspicuous among the exceptions was his 'Drift Away', a US smash in 1973 for Dobie Gray, best known previously for Mod anthem 'The In Crowd'. 'Drift Away' was also tried by The Rolling Stones early in 1974, but it wasn't included on their then-current LP, *It's Only Rock 'n' Roll*, probably because, like Ringo's version, it wasn't up to the fighting weight of the original, partly because Starr chose to hover in the background of what amounts to a duet by Alanis Morrisette and Tom Petty, both technically more proficient but less distinctive vocalists.

When to the fore and singing his own lyrics, Ringo comes over as a kind of Scouse Socrates in the sloganising optimism of 'Minefield' and the title track, although he's not quite so chirpy on ambitious 'Without Understanding', with passages scored for a fusion of operatic contralto with tablas and wiry sitar. A breath of the Orient is exhaled for two bars only in 'Minefield', which, while alluding to Dylan, actually mentions the Maharishi. Similar biographical references crop up more subtly in period "pudding" tom-toms throughout; psychedelic babble in 'I Was Walkin'', embracing possibly the most delightful drum fill in Starr's entire career; 'I Am The Walrus'/'Fool On The Hill' mellotron peeping out on 'King Of The Broken Hearts', along with George's fretboard careen; 'Free As A Bird' *blat-blat* snare to kick off 'Vertical Man' itself; and a 'She's

Leaving Home'-esque string arrangement for 'I'm Yours', a ballad as uxorious in its way as any of Lennon's paeans to Yoko.

Elsewhere, you can pick out a riff reminiscent of the early Kinks in 'What In The World' and respective touches of Cropper's Booker T And The MGs and Elvis Presley's 'Got A Lot O' Livin' To Do' in 'Puppet' and 'I'll Be Fine Anywhere' – but, welded together, the contents of *Vertical Man*** were more absorbing than any Starr album since *Ringo*. However, so counter was it to the turn-of-the-century pop climate of rap and interchangeable boy bands that it begged the question, who wants proper songs any more? Least of all ones like *Vertical Man*'s first spin-off single, 'La De Da'?

While the libretto to this lightweight but attractive ditty was *a propos* of nothing in particular, that was fine by me. 'La De Da' certainly sounded like a hit, and I should imagine that Ringo would have had no trouble working it up into a rowdy singalong with All-Starrs audiences. Yet it wasn't considered a worthwhile marketing exercise in Britain, and its promotion in the United States was dogged by ill luck. A planned video shoot at Shea Stadium at a convenient moment during a major-league baseball match was scrubbed when rain stopped play. Undeterred, Ringo and the camera crew then took to the sidewalks of New York with Hanson, a blond trio, then the latest pre-teen sensation.

The resulting clips were seen in North America on *Entertainment Tonight* and *MTV News*, and Ringo was there in person on other programmes, such as a sofaing beneath sweaty arc lights on *The Regis And Kathie Lee Show* and on ABC TV's *The View*, actually giving 'em 'La De Da', 'Photograph' and – over closing credits – 'With A Little Help From My Friends'. 'La De Da' alone was intended for the more prestigious *Tonight* show with Jay Leno (a sort of US Terry Wogan), along with a pre-recorded interview with both Ringo and Paul during a break in the *Vertical Man* sessions. Even if

---

* Remaindered *Vertical Man* numbers 'Good News' (notable for yodelled backing vocals), 'Every Day' (nothing to do with either the 1957 Buddy Holly song or a UK Top-50 entry for The Moody Blues in 1965), rockabilly 'Mr Double-It-Up' and C&W-tinged 'Sometimes' were saved for selection as B-sides for spin-off singles 'La-De-Da' and 'King Of Broken Hearts'. Trivia freaks will be fascinated to learn that 'Sometimes' was the US B-side of 'La De Da', although 'Love Me Do' was on the back of the German single and, with 'Mr Double-It-Up', 'Every Day' turned up among bonus tracks on the Japanese pressing of *Vertical Man*.

the black carnival in the immediate wake of Frank Sinatra's sudden death – the US equivalent of that of the Queen Mother – in Los Angeles on the day of transmission hadn't put paid to this, Ringo Starr still couldn't have got a hit with 'La De Da' to save his life, partly because the USA's love affair with British pop was now at its most distant since Sinatra's optimum Hot 100 moments in the 1950s.

Two days before the passing of Old Blue Eyes, Ringo had fronted The Roundheads at New York's Bottom Line on 12 May 1998, his first club date since The Beatles. As the presence on the boards of Joe Walsh and Simon Kirke indicated, outlines dissolved between The Roundheads – centred on Mark Hudson and his brothers – and the latest incarnation of The All-Starr Band, although this time Starr monopolised the lead vocals, giving 'em all the expected favourites plus highlights from *Vertical Man*.

With the promptness of a vulture, this recital was made available on CD straight away by Mighty Fishy Records. It was less a roots-affirming engagement – similar to those to which the Stones were partial in the midst of global stadium tours – than a dress rehearsal for the next day's filming of *Storytellers* at Sony Studios for VH-1 television. This special concert spawned a damage-limiting official album, but this was less important than the broadcast itself, the heftiest push there'd ever be for *Vertical Man* and 'La De Da'.

Neither were mentioned a week later when Ringo attended an auction in aid of Elizabeth Taylor's AIDS charity in the Moulin De Mougins restaurant as part of the Cannes Film Festival. His on-stage spot with Elton John and actress Sharon Stone was memorable for someone pledging $90,000 if the three would perform 'Great Balls Of Fire'. Capping this, another pudgy millionaire – carried away by the jubilee atmosphere but unsure which member of that English combo everyone used to talk about was up there – promised a further $90,000 if they did 'Twist And Shout'.

The next two months were filled with preparations for the next All-Starr Band tour. The mid-August agenda included the Moscow Sports Complex on 25th August 1998 – when Starr became the first

Beatle to chance a performance in Russia* – and London's Shepherd's Bush Empire, which was poignantly appropriate, given that the All-Starrs now contained the highest percentage of Britons thus far, namely Peter Frampton, Simon Kirke, Gary Brooker and Jack Bruce. Putting his more *avant-garde* leanings on hold, Bruce – Cream's former bass player – replaced John Entwistle, who, with Zak Starkey now on drums,† was embroiled in Who projects.

If not as constant a travelling minstrel as Bob Dylan, forever on the road with his appositely named Never Ending Tour, Ringo – finding the pace energising – had an All-Starrs on the road for each subsequent year, mostly back and forth across the Land of the Free.

It was to US consumers only – or, perhaps more specifically, to watchers of repeats of *Shining Time Station* and those too tough to admit that they did – that Ringo's last album to date was pitched. Out in time for 1999's December sell-in, *I Wanna Be Santa Claus* was a perennial record-industry strategy. The tradition stretched back to the very dawn of 33rpm long-players. Since Bing Crosby shifted a million of his *Merry Christmas* in 1947, the disparate likes of Mantovani, Elvis Presley, The Beach Boys, The Partridge Family and Max Bygraves have been among countless artists trying their luck with albums freighted with seasonal evergreens.

On paper, Ringo seemed no different from everyone else, in his commandeering of 'Rudolf, The Red-Nosed Reindeer', 'Little Drummer Boy' (as inevitable, as Valentino's recording of 'Kashmiri Song') and all the rest of them. He even exhumed 'Christmas Time Is Here Again', doggerel from a Beatles fan club flexidisc disguised as a "proper" song (with bagpipes), and dared to take on 'Blue Christmas', an Elvis Presley A-side from 1964. Nevertheless, Ringo and his team clothed these in idiosyncratic musical vestments such as a quasi-military Gary Glitter-ish drive to 'Winter Wonderland', a pseudo-reggae jerk and Hawaiian guitar solo on 'White Christmas' and a spoken interlude in 'Rudolf...'.

There were also a commendable number of cleverly arranged Starkey-Hudson, originals including 'Christmas Eve' (albeit

---

* Where, incidentally, Ruth McCartney, Paul's stepsister, has made impressive headway as an entertainer.

† Zak was also working with guitarist Johnny Marr, founder member of The Smiths.

expressing the same downbeat sentiments as 'Blue Christmas'); charitable 'Dear Santa'; 'The Christmas Dance', which veered from an ostinato on loan from Elvis via Arthur Crudup's 'My Baby Left Me' to an ersatz Viennese waltz; and the finale, 'Pax Um Biscum (Peace Be With You)', in which a tuning-up orchestra segues into lyrics as succinct as a *haiku* and backing that emulates a celestial Indian *bhajan*.

Although he acquitted himself admirably on *I Wanna Be Santa Claus*, Ringo's non-Beatle income hinged mainly on earnings on the road with the All-Starrs. While the troupe was to reach Australasia in 2000, it was for North America that it was always designed. Sponsored by something called the Century 21 Real Estate Corporation, the last tour was 29 US cities long and began with a press conference in New York's Plaza Hotel, where The Beatles had been under siege prior to their *Ed Sullivan Show* debut in 1964. Now there was no shrieking tumult kept at bay by mounted policemen outside but, instead, a few dozen journalists and fans unscreened by security, receiving a sober greeting from besuited Steve Salvino, senior vice president of marketing, who introduced the firm's next TV commercial – in which Ringo (in cameo, as part of the deal) spoke two lines – and pointed out that proceeds of century21.com's online auction of artefacts donated and autographed by the stars would be donated to charity.[3] To help him keep abreast of this and other matters – such as a series of real-time web chats from various stops – to do with the tour, Ringo was presented with a laptop computer with Internet access, but confessed, "I've sent three emails in my life, and my wife, Barbara, typed two of them."[4]

When Salvino unveiled the 2000 edition of the All-Starrs, the most famous new face – in New York, anyway – was Eric Carmen. Four years after his Ohio garage band, The Choir, warmed up for The Yardbirds in 1966, he'd formed the more prosperous Raspberries. On leaving the group in 1974 – that year again – he scored a global million-seller in 'All By Myself' and a two year run of lesser US hits but hits all the same. While his stint with the All-Starrs was "an honour, a wonderful thing",[4] it was also an avenue of welcome exposure for his latest album, *I Was Born To Love You*, which, if not adventurous, was at least competent. The same could be said of nearly every disc by another member of the entourage, Dave Edmunds, both before and after the Carl Perkins *Rockabilly Special*.

Commensurate with this was Ringo's promise that the band would be "out there doing the songs that people know and love. That's what the All-Starrs is all about. We go out for a couple of months, have a lot of fun and do all the hits. We've more or less settled on 90 per cent of what we're going to be doing. For me, the rehearsal part is always the worst. We all have to get to know each other again so that I'm really comfortable when we do the show."

Epilogue
"I Go Along With Whatever Is Happening"

Ringo himself once agreed that, "If I hadn't taken the chance and gone to Butlins and then joined The Beatles, I'd still be on the shop floor as a fitter. I'm not really a strong-willed person. I go along with whatever is happening."[1] Possibly, he'd have stuck with Rory Storm to the bitter end or else joined some luckier local outfit, thereby recouping more than golden memories from the Mersey Beat craze before drifting back to Liverpool, privately relieved, perhaps, to return to normality.

What if King Harold had won the Battle of Hastings? What if Adolf Hitler had been strangled at birth? What if Elvis had been cross-eyed? What if The Beatles had passed their Decca audition? Let's concern ourselves with facts. When the graph of Richard Starkey's life gave a sharp upward turn in 1962, he blossomed as if made for the success that, in the long term, denied him maturity. In the teeth of the uncritical adulation of Beatlemania, never was his character tested more thoroughly and found sound. More important to The Beatles than his drumming, acting and certainly his singing was his graduation from passenger to the one who kept them on the rails. To Bob Wooler, he was their "only working-class hero. That lad was still living in the Dingle when he was a hit parader. Lennon, on the other hand, was a very privileged person.[2]

With his millions, Ringo behaved much like any other disadvantaged lad who'd won the Pools: the Rolls, the flashy clothes, the diamond rings, the champagne, the sexy model, the tax exile in Monte Carlo. When The Beatles went sour, he spent less time on anything constructive than on just mucking about – albeit "with extraordinary panache"[3] – becoming but a footnote in social history.

If it matters to him, he can die easy in the knowledge that his will remain the name most likely to trip off the tongue whenever pop percussionists are discussed by lay people – and, if ever a ballroom is built on Mars, you can bet even money that soundchecking drummers there will still be hailed "Oi, Ringo!" by its janitor.

Notes

In addition to my own correspondence and interviews, I have used the following sources, which I would like to credit:

Prologue: "I've Never Really Done Anything To Create What Has Happened"

1. *Confidential*, August 1964
2. *Rave*, March 1969
3. Atlanta press conference, 5 April 1986
4. This expression was coined obliquely by Eartha Kitt in her self-composed 'I Had A Hard Day Last Night', B-side of 1963's 'Lola Lola' (Columbia BD 7170)
5. New Musical Express, 23 March 1968

Chapter 1: "I Was Just One Of Those Loony Teddy Boys"

1. *Rave*, March 1969
2. Beatles Monthly, December 1986
3. *Sunday Post*, 9 November 1969
4. *Step Inside* by C Black (Dent, 1985)
5. *New Musical Express*, 14 October 1976
6. *Sunday Express*, 9 March 1969
7. To Billy Shepherd
8. *Melody Maker*, 3 September 1964
9. *TV Times*, 9 October 1984
10. *Daily Mirror*, 29 November 1969
11. *Melody Maker*, 15 January 1966
12. Mr S Roberts' report (1952)
13. *The Oxford School Music Book* (OUP, 1951)

14. Sun Day, 1 October 1989
15. *The David Essex Story* by G Tremlett (Futura, 1974)
16. *Melody Maker*, 8 January 1966
17. To Hunter Davies
18. *News Of The World*, 6 October 1977
19. A pre-1970 euphemism for fondling (desert sickness = wandering palms)
20. *The History Of Rock*, volume one, number five (Orbis, 1982)
21. *Rolling Stone*, 30 April 1981
22. *Picturegoer*, 1 September 1966
23. *New Musical Express*, 23 March 1968
24. *Melody Maker*, 29 March 1958
25. *New Musical Express*, 24 February 1956
26. *Disc*, 16 December 1972
27. *New Musical Express*, 1 November 1957
28. *Melody Maker*, 15 January 1966

Chapter 2: "Well, I Thought I Was The Best Drummer There Was"

1. I must pass on the raw information that, despite having a voice like Piers Fletcher-Devish of ITV's *The New Statesman*, Hamilton had a 1957 million-seller with 'We Will Make Love'. Its B-side, 'Rainbow', reached Number Seven in the US charts
2. Murphy/Rogers was not Paul Rodgers, the Middlesbrough vocalist who was a founder member of Free in 1968
3. *Melody Maker*, 1 August 1964
4. *New Musical Express*, 1 November 1957
5. *Beatles Monthly*, December 1986
6. The kit used by the first rock 'n' roll drummers was a standard dance-band set, which, by the mid 1950s, was bass drum and pedal (right foot), small tom-tom (mounted on bass drum), floor tom (right hand), snare drum for the off-beat (right hand), two cymbals (crash [for sudden accentuation] and ride [for continuous playing]) mounted on stands. To the left, the hi-hats (two cymbals facing each other) are brought together with a snap by a left foot pedal to provide a matching but more unobtrusive offbeat to the snare. Later, the hi-hat stand was heightened to be within easy reach of the stick. The drum shells were usually of wood. Throughout the 1950s, US drums could not be imported because of government trade embargos to protect Premier, Carlton and other British makes
7. To Billy Shepherd
8. *Melody Maker*, 7 August 1971
9. *Skiffle* by B Bird (Robert Hale, 1958)
10. *New Gandy Dancer*, undated (*circa* 1984)
11. *Mersey Beat*, 3 September 1964

12. *Melody Maker*, 2 October 1976
13. *Disc*, 16 December 1972
14. *Melody Maker*, 12 April 1975
15. *Melody Maker*, 14 November 1964
16. Miles would, however, return to the stage as a member of Hank Walters' Dusty Road Ramblers
17. *Mersey Beat*, 18 July 1963
18. *Daily Mirror*, 29 November 1969
19. *Step Inside* by C Black (Dent, 1985)
20. *New York Times*, 21 June 1989
21. The "look at that caveman go" hook line of 'Alley Oop' was adapted by David Bowie for his 1973 hit, 'Life On Mars'
22. *Creem*, October 1976
23 *Melody Maker*, 8 January 1966

Chapter 3: "I Took A Chance And I Think I've Been Lucky"

1. *New Musical Express*, 12 December 1959
2. Polydor press release, 1962
3. Later in 1960, it was re-opened as the Blue Angel, a cabaret night club much frequented by showbusiness folk visiting Liverpool. As a yardstick of its exclusiveness, Judy Garland would be ejected from the Blue Angel for not paying for her drinks
4. *Mersey Beat*, 3 September 1964
5. *Sunday Post*, 9 November 1969
6. *Sun Day*, 3 November 1985
7. An unnamed Liverpool local newspaper, 25 August 1960
8. To Spencer Leigh
9. *Melody Maker*, 17 April 1965
10. To Billy Shepherd
11. *Mersey Beat*, 18 July 1963
12. These programmes also introduced many young Hollywood actors to the general public. Among these were Clint Eastwood, Lorne Green and, later to share a girlfriend with Ringo Starr, James Coburn
13. *Melody Maker*, 14 November 1964
14. To Charles Hamblett and Jane Deverson
15. *Acker Bilk* by G Williams (Mayfair, 1962)
16. *Brum Beat*, December 1989
17. Quoted in *The Quiet One* by A Clayson (Sidgwick & Jackson, 1990; Sanctuary, 1996; 2001)
18. *Melody Maker*, 28 March 1964
19. *Fabulous*, 15 February 1964
20. *Beatles Monthly*, October 1982

21. Dave Dee on Radio Bedfordshire, 29 December 1985
22. *Sunday Times*, 27 February 1983
23. *The Beat Goes On* number five, April 1991
24. *Daily Mirror*, 3 November 1987
25. For this celebration (which fell on a Sunday), Rory Storm And The Hurricanes returned from Pwllheli to live it up with around 70 guests that included Sam Leach, Cilla White, The Big Three, Joey Bower, Billy Hatton, Gerry and all his Pacemakers
26. *Love Me Do* by M Braun (Penguin, 1964)
27. *Melody Maker*, 16 December 1962
28. *Mersey Beat*, 6 December 1962

Chapter 4: "I Had To Join Them As People, As Well As A Drummer"

1. Sue Evans' diary, 3 February 1963
2. Unconnected with *Mersey Beat* newspaper
3. *Mersey Beat*, 15 February 1962
4. Whose band included 15-year-old organist Billy Preston, who'd be seen playing with The Beatles in 1970's *Let It Be* movie
5. Polydor press release, 1962
6. *Mersey Beat*, 19 April 1962
7. To Spencer Leigh
8. *Sunday Post*, 9 November 1969
9. *Melody Maker*, 6 January 1966
10. *Mersey Beat*, 15 August 1963
11. But not for long. Within a year, Sutcliffe would die at the age of 21 of a cerebral haemorrhage
12. *Good Day Sunshine*, November 1989
13. *Mersey Beat*, 1 August 1963
14. Who, in parentheses, shared the same birthday as Ringo Starr
15. Ashdown had just finished a role in the 1962 film drama *The Loneliness Of The Long-Distance Runner*
16. *Sunday Times*, 30 September 1971
17. Harrison's letter to a fan named Jenny (sold at Sotheby's, December 1981)
18. *Beatles Monthly*, August 1983
19. *Love Me Do* by M Braun (Penguin, 1964)
20. *The True Story Of The Beatles* by B Shepherd (Beat, 1964)
21. When, in the late 1970s, Pete Best's drumming brother formed The Watt Four, Neil Aspinall was prominent in the campaign to find the group a recording contract. He also attended Mrs Best's funeral in 1987
22. To Glenn A Baker
23. *Melody Maker*, 14 November 1964

24. George Harrison to *Fabulous*, 15 February 1964
25. To Jan Wenner
26. To Ray Coleman
27. *Disc*, 24 November 1962
28. *Barbara Walters Special* (US TV, 31 March 1981)
29. *Beatles Monthly*, December 1986
30. *Disc*, 12 November 1963
31. *Melody Maker*, 28 March 1964
32. To G Pawlowski
33. *Mersey Beat*, 12 November 1962
34. *All You Need Is Ears* by G Martin and J Hornsby (St Martin's Press, 1979)
35. A troupe of choreographed singers recruited from amongst employees of Liverpool Football Pools company
36. Although the White and Starr takes became so similar as to be interchangeable, it is believed that White's drumming is heard on the 45 and Starr's on the album version of 'Love Me Do'
37. *Melody Maker*, 7 August 1971
38. *The Beat Goes On*, April 1991
39. *Rolling Stone*, 15 July 1976
40. *Mersey Beat*, 3 January 1963
41. *Melody Maker*, 7 May 1963
42. *New York Times*, 3 August 1963
43. Quoted in *Sunday Times*, 27 February 1983

Chapter 5: "I'm Happy To Go On And Play Drums – And That's All"

1. *Beatles '64* by A Royl and C Gunther (Sidgwick & Jackson, 1989)
2. *Sunday Times*, 27 December 1963
3. *Sunday Times*, 27 February 1983
4. *Confidential*, August 1964
5. *Melody Maker*, 23 November 1964
6. *Here Are The Beatles* by C Hamblett (Four Square, 1964)
7. *Melody Maker*, 14 November 1964
8. *Melody Maker*, 2 November 1971
9. *Melody Maker*, 8 September 1971
10. In Ken Colyer's Studio 51 Club in London's Great Newport Street, Lennon and McCartney offered The Rolling Stones 'I Wanna Be Your Man' as a follow-up to their minor hit treatment of Chuck Berry's 'Come On'. The Stones' 'I Wanna Be Your Man' (released in November 1963) reached Number Twelve in the UK charts. The *With The Beatles* version was their first to be taped on four-track equipment
11. To David Sheff

12. Once a lead vocal by Lennon but surrendered to Starr circa August 1963, 'Honey Don't' was also notable as the first Beatles recording to namecheck a member of the group, ie Starr's cry of "Rock on, George – one time for Ringo!" just before the guitar solo. The Beatles' arrangement of 'Honey Don't' was "covered" by Liverpool's Rhythm And Blues Incorporated on Fontana in January 1965
13. *Sunday Mirror*, 13 November 1988
14. This 1964 composition by Lennon and McCartney had been a B-side for Billy J Kramer And The Dakotas. The Kramer arrangement was cloned by The Beatles on their 'Long Tall Sally' EP in 1964
15. A cylindrical metal shaker containing peas or lead shot
16. *Melody Maker*, 16 November 1963
17. *Melody Maker*, 17 April 1965
18. Wellington (New Zealand) press conference, 23 June 1964
19. *Top Gear* (BBC Light Programme), 16 June 1964
20. *Beatles Monthly*, July 1988
21. *Saturday Club* (BBC Light Programme), 4 April 1964
22. *Mersey Beat*, 1 January 1963
23. *Melody Maker*, 28 March 1964
24. *Fabulous*, 5 February 1964
25. Extract from Johnny Guitar's diary, September 1962-January 1963
26. *Beatles Monthly*, October 1982
27. Hartley and a later Storm drummer, Aynsley Dunbar (also an ex-Mojo), would each garner a greater celebrity with first John Mayall's Bluesbreakers and then as bandleaders, while Trevor Morais, formerly of Paten's Flamingos, who could also claim a brief stint as a Hurricane, came up trumps as one of The Peddlars, who made the UK Top 20 in 1969. Yet, for every famous ex-Hurricane, there was a Brian Johnson, an Ian Broad, a Carl Rich...and a Jimmy Tushingham
28. A version by Gerry And The Pacemakers reached Number 15 in the British charts in 1965
29. Storm quoted in NEMS press release, November 1964
30. To George Tremlett
31. *Juke Box Jury* (BBC television), 7 December 1963
32. *Mersey Beat*, 13 February 1964
33. *Sunday Express*, 9 March 1969
34. *Huyton And Prescott Reviewer*, 14 November 1963
35. *Radio Luxembourg Record Stars* (Souvenir, 1965)
36. *Woman's Own*, December 1969
37. *16*, December 1964
38. Elsie Graves to Mersey Beat, 30 July 1964
39. *Boyfriend* annual (Trend, 1966)
40. *New York Times*, 20 December 1964
41. *Melody Maker*, 2 December 1967

42. *Scene And Heard*, 3 January 1973
43. Beatles Monthly, September 1963
44. *Sunday Post*, 9 November 1969
45. 18- and 20-inch cymbals plus 15-inch hi-hats. Later, he switched to Zildjian 22-inch bass drum, 16-inch snare and 13-inch hanging floor toms. Starr would eventually own three Ludwig kits – a Super Classic and two of the Downbeat variety (with bass drums modified to 20 inches)

Chapter 6: "Over In The States, I Know I Went Over Well"

1. Italian Broadcasting Company, *circa* autumn 1963
2. *News Of The World*, 21 October 1977
3. Milwaukee press conference, 4 September 1964
4. *Melody Maker*, 8 January 1966
5. *Love Me Do*, by M Braun (Penguin, 1964)
6. Because George Harrison had mentioned publicly that he was partial to jelly-babies, this practice had started during 1963 in Britain. To The Beatles' consternation (and discomfort), it was continued in the USA with jelly-beans – as different from jelly-babies as hailstones to snow
7. *Beatles Unlimited*, July 1976
8. Whose hit 45 'She's About A Mover' of 1965 was later recorded by Ringo Starr. At the time of its release, however, it was covered in Britain by Buddy Britten And The Regents, who'd known The Beatles and Rory Storm And The Hurricanes in Hamburg
9. So much so that it fooled most of the people (well, me, anyway) when presenter Spencer Leigh announced it as a Beatles out-take during an April Fool's Day edition of his Radio Merseyside show in 1989
10. Not the British instrumental group of the same name
11. *History Of Rock* volume three, number 35 (Orbis, 1982)
12. *Beatles Unlimited*, July 1976
13. Not the journalist who wrote for *Disc* in the mid 1960s
14. Covered in Britain by television string puppets Tich and Quackers
15. *Melody Maker*, 14 November 1964
16. *Beatles '64* by A Royl and C Gunther (Sidgwick & Jackson, 1989)
17. "We went to Greenland and took a left turn," replied Ringo. Quoted in *Rock Explosion* by M Bronson (Blandford, 1986)
18. *Beatles Monthly*, August 1988
19. Washington press conference, 11 February 1964
20. *Cincinnati Enquirer*, 28 August 1964
21. Toronto press conference, 7 September 1964
22. *Record Songbook*, June 1964
23. When faced with untrained thespians with thick accents, it was common for

directors to make them act with ear-plugs, thereby obliging them to speak louder and pronounce their lines more clearly. This practice might not have been applied to any Beatle, but it was certainly the case with members of The Dave Clark Five in John Boorman's *Catch Us If You Can* (1965)

24. *A Cellarful Of Noise* by B Epstein (Souvenir, 1964)
25. Then at the height of his fame in the BBC television comedy *Steptoe And Son*. He and his co-star, Harry H Corbett, performed in 1963's Beatles' Royal Command Performance
26. *Melody Maker*, 6 June 1971
27. To Ray Coleman
28. *Mersey Beat*, 30 July 1964
29. A suburb of Liverpool
30. Including a schoolgirl named Barbara Goldbach, who had a more-than-incidental bearing on Ringo Starr's later life. She was chaperoning her younger sister "because she was a Beatle freak. I wasn't." (*Playboy*, January 1981)
31. *Melody Maker*, 1 August 1964
32. In 1974, Little Jimmy Osmond climbed to Number Eleven in the British charts with his rehash of 'I'm Gonna Knock On Your Door'. Two years earlier, this pint-sized Mormon had reached Number One with 'Long-Haired Lover From Liverpool', composed by Christopher Dowden during the zenith of US Beatlemania
33. *Playboy*, February 1964
34. *New Musical Express*, 20 March 1964
35. London press conference, 31 March 1964
36. Copenhagen press conference, 4 June 1964
37. *Beatles Down Under* by GA Baker (Wild & Wooley, 1982)
38. *Disc*, 27 June 1964
39. To Glenn Baker
40. Mascot airport press conference, 13 July 1964
41. *Top Pop Stars* (Purnell, 1964)
42. San Francisco press conference, 13 June 1964
43. *Melody Maker*, 20 June 1964
44. To Ernie Sigley
45. In their ranks then was Trevor White, who was destined to play Ringo Starr in the Australian production of the *Lennon* musical in 1988
46. Spector produced 'Ringo I Love You', a 45 by a Bonnie Jo Spears, alias the "Cher" in Sonny And Cher. Without Sonny, she continued to enjoy a successful recording career, but also became well known as a film actress
47. *TV Times*, 14 May 1988
48. *Quant On Quant*, by M Quant (Cassell, 1966)
49. *Mersey Beat*, 13 February 1964
50. *Beatlefan*, Dec 1981
51. *Sunday Express*, 9 March 1969

52. To Billy Shepherd

53. Sunday Post, 9 November 1969

54. Daily Express, 12 March 1981

55. Radio WROD, 3 September 1964

56. Confidential, August 1964

57. Daily Express, 3 December 1964

58. Melody Maker, 12 April 1975

59. Midland Beat, May 1966

60. Melody Maker, 7 August 1971

61. Sunday Express, 7 December 1969

62. Q, January 1991

Chapter 7: "I've Been Thinking And Wondering Where It's All Going"

1. Melody Maker, 20 February 1965

2. Woman, December 1969

3. Not the BBC presenter of the same name

4. Beatles Monthly, February 1988

5. A controversial new BBC television comedy. However, like Z-Cars and Top Of The Pops had been, Till Death Us Do Part would be accepted as part of mid-1960s Britain's social fabric

6. Rave, March 1969

7. Melody Maker, 2 December 1967

8. Sun Day, 3 November 1985

9. Melody Maker, 17 April 1965

10. Daily Mirror, 5 November 1987

11. In whose Blue Flames Jimmy Nicol did not re-enlist after The Shubdubs. On 29 April 1965, Nicol was declared bankrupt. Later, he emigrated to South America

12. Where To Go In London And Around, 27 October 1966

13. New Musical Express, 25 June 1966

14. The ultimate Mod group, The Small Faces' coiffure emphasised the cult's solidarity in the mid 1960s as the moptop had earlier. It involved a centre parting to the crown and a bouffant back-combing the rest of the way, with the sides brushed straight over the ears

15. Mark Radford's letter to Melody Maker, 10 April 1965

16. To David Sheff

17. Melody Maker, 14 August 1966

18. Music Echo, 5 April 1969

19. Like one from The Beatles' first in-person appearance on Ready, Steady, Go! (4 October 1963), when Dusty Springfield read out a fan's postcard inquiring why Starr wore so many rings on his fingers. "Because I can't get them through my nose," he replied

20. *Melody Maker*, 14 August 1966
21 *Melody Maker*, 7 May 1966
22. From a Richard Condon novel. After The Beatles rejected the film, it was directed for 1969 release by Richard Quine and starred Richard Widmark, Genevieve Page, Topol and Cesar Romero
23. *Beatlefan* volume IV, number three, April 1982
24. *Radio Luxembourg Record Stars Book* (Souvenir, 1965)
25. Thus prompting a Manchester costumier to market fake ones with 'side-pieces' so those without the wherewithal to sprout their own could still "Make The Scene With These Fantastic New Raves!"
26. 'Step Lightly' on 1973's *Ringo* would be "Featuring The Dancing Feet Of Richard Starkey, MBE"
27. *New Musical Express*, 25 June 1966
28. *Disc*, 23 July 1966
29. *Disc*, 16 July 1966
30. *Just Rest* by L McKern (Methuen, 1983)
31. *Melody Maker*, 11 December 1965
32. *New Musical Express*, 25 June 1966
33. *New Musical Express*, 23 March 1968
34. Rotterdam Beatles Convention, 12 April 1985

Chapter Eight: "They More Or Less Direct Me In The Style I Can Play"

1. *New Musical Express*, 31 December 1966
2. *New Musical Express*, 23 March 1968
3. *Woman*, 7 December 1969
4. *Disc*, 22 March 1969
5. *Melody Maker*, 7 August 1971
6. Roy C Smith of accountants Comins & Son Ltd, who were employed by The Rolling Stones (*Q*, March 1989)
7. *Daily Express*, 5 November 1987
8. In 1968, it would be the title theme to the full-length cartoon movie depicting the group in a surreal "modyssey" from Liverpool to "Pepperland". The negotiation of its release with United Artists would be Brian Epstein's last major service as The Beatles' manager
9. And possibly because the recording of marching feet that accompanied this passage might have also been used on 'Crusader', a recent LP track by The Hollies, who incidentally were recording with The Everly Brothers in the next studio during the 'Yellow Submarine' session
10. *Melody Maker*, 9 July 1966
11. Joe Brown's cover reached Number 32 in the UK charts and Number Eleven in Australia. There was also a version issued before the *Sgt Pepper* release date by a duo called The Young Idea which got to Number Ten in the British hit parade

12. *New York Times*, 21 June 1989
13. Although attributed to "Lennon-McCartney", there have been rumours that the song 'Sergeant Pepper's Lonely Hearts Club Band' was actually composed by McCartney with assistance from Mal Evans
14. *Melody Maker*, 9 July 1966
15. *Melody Maker*, 31 July 1971
16. Originally titled 'Aerial Tour Instrumental'
17. Held every Sunday afternoon at the Marquee from February 1966
18. *Disc*, 16 December 1967
19. Excerpt from Yoko Ono's opening address at her exhibition at the Everson Museum of Art, 9 October 1971
20. *Melody Maker*, 31 March 1973
21. *Melody Maker*, 1 February 1975
22. *Beatlefan* vol II, number six, October 1980
23. *New Musical Express*, 16 December 1967
24. *Weekend*, 14 July 1967
25. Gregory's original estimate had been £2,500, but he apparently asked for £8,000 more before the job was completed. Starr refused to pay and the matter went to court
26. *Rolling Stone*, 30 April 1980
27. *Rolling Stone*, 14 December 1967
28. Rotterdam Beatles Convention, 12 April 1985
29. Of complications arising from an operation to remove his appendix
30. *Radio Luxembourg Record Stars Book* (Souvenir, 1965)
31. *Melody Maker*, 25 May 1968
32. *Disc*, 3 September 1967
33. *Melody Maker*, 3 September 1967
34. *Daily Mirror*, 29 November 1969
35. *Melody Maker*, 8 January 1966
36. With whom Varma would tour the USA in the summer of 1968
37. *Melody Maker*, 16 March 1968. This remark also inspired a *Sunday Express* cartoon (4 March 1968) in which the Maharishi enquires of Lennon, "This Butlin guru that Ringo speaks of. What's he got that I haven't?"
38. *Disc*, 16 March 1968

Chapter 9: "I Suppose I Seem Fairly Straight"

1. *Disc*, 23 March 1968
2. *Sunday Post*, 9 November 1969
3. *Melody Maker*, 16 March 1968
4. *Rave*, March 1969
5. *TV Times*, 14 May 1987
6. *Sunday Express*, 9 March 1969
7. *Scene And Heard* (Radio 1), April 1972

8. *New York Times*, 21 June 1986
9. *Newcastle Evening Chronicle*, 8 December 1971
10. *Disc*, 13 January 1968
11. *Melody Maker*, 2 December 1967
12. *Melody Maker*, 24 July 1971
13. *Music Echo*, 5 April 1969
14. *Daily Express*, 7 December 1969
15. *Daily Mirror*, 27 June 1969
16. *Rolling Stone*, 18 November 1976
17. *Sunday Times*, 27 February 1983
18. *Music Echo*, 19 April 1969
19. *Melody Maker*, 7 August 1971
20. *Daily Mirror*, 8 November 1968
21. *Daily Express* (date obscured)
22. *Chicago Tribune*, March 1981
23. *Rolling Stone*, 27 August 1987
24. *Melody Maker*, 31 July 1971
25. *Rolling Stone*, 15 July 1976
26. *Woman*, 7 December 1969
27. *Modern Drumming*, December 1981
28. *New Musical Express*, 9 November 1968
29. *Sunday Times*, 24 February 1971
30. *Rolling Stone*, 30 April 1981
31. Ron Richards to Mark Lewisohn
32. However, Brymon Estates Ltd's good name was to be further besmirched – if that's the word – when, at 34 Montagu Square in 1974, Mama Cass Elliott died of debilities not unrelated to drug abuse
33. *Daily Mirror*, 29 September 1969
34. *Sunday Express*, 7 December 1969
35. *Sun*, 23 September 1982
36. *Radio Times*, 15 May 1969
37. *New Musical Express*, 11 November 1966
38. *Rolling Stone*, 9 July 1970
39. *Morning Star*, 21 May 1970
40. George Harrison to Anne Nightingale
41. Former guitarist with Earl Royce And The Olympics and then The Fourmost
42. *Melody Maker*, 19 July 1969
43. To Ian Drummond

Chapter 10: "I Couldn't Believe It Was Happening"

1. *FAB 208,* 7 November 1969
2. *Melody Maker*, 6 June 1971

3. *Music Echo*, 5 April 1969
4. *Sunday Express*, 7 December 1969
5. *Films And Filming*, December 1969
6. *Melody Maker*, 24 July 1971
7. *New Musical Express*, 13 December 1969
8. *Disc*, 13 December 1969
9. *Daily Sketch*, 16 December 1969
10. *Daily Express*, 9 December 1969
11. *Melody Maker*, 31 July 1971
12. *Sunday Express*, 9 March 1969
13. *Daily Express*, 12 March 1972
14. Sleeve notes to *Celtic Requiem* (Apple SAPCOR 20)
15. To Peter Doggett
16. *Sunday Post*, 9 November 1969
17. *Melody Maker*, 19 July 1969
18 *Sunday Mirror*, 29 November 1969
19. *Melody Maker*, 7 August 1972
20. *New Musical Express*, 14 October 1976
21. *Daily Express*, 17 July 1971
22. Difford to *Rolling Stone*, 16 February 1984
23. *Scene And Heard* (Radio 1), 3 January 1973
24. *New Musical Express*, 28 March 1970
25. *Circus*, November 1976
26. An Apple spokesperson to *New Musical Express*, 14 March 1970
27. *Melody Maker*, 31 March 1973
28. *Melody Maker*, 2 October 1976
29. *Melody Maker*, 16 May 1970
30. Russell to *Rolling Stone*, 30 January 1970
31. *Rolling Stone*, 30 April 1981
32. *Woman*, December 1969
33. *New Musical Express*, 12 February 1970
34. *Melody Maker*, 7 February 1970
35. *New Musical Express*, 21 February 1970
36. *Daily Mirror*, 3 October 1970
37. To Ray Coleman
38. *Melody Maker*, 6 April 1973

Chapter 11: "I Love It When They Let Me Go Off On My Own"

1. *Disc*, 16 December 1972
2. Rotterdam Beatles Convention, 12 April 1985
3. *Special Pop* (French), November 1972

4. Unidentified London tabloid
5. *Step Inside Love* by C Black (Dent, 1985)
6. I'm not certain whether the plural of Elvis should be Elvi or the second declension, Elves. What do you think?
7. *Daily Express*, 21 July 1971
8. *Melody Maker*, 31 July 1971
9. To Jan Wenner
10. Quoted in *The Wit And Wisdom Of Rock And Roll*, compiled by M Jakubowski (Unwin, 1983)
11. *Melody Maker*, 19 February 1972
12. *Melody Maker*, 6 August 1972
13. As *A Fistful Of Dollars* was derived from *Yojimbo*, so *Blindman* was from *Zatoichi* (about a blind swordsman)
14. *Daily Express*, 21 July 1971
15. *Melody Maker*, 6 June 1971
16. *Music Echo*, 17 July 1971
17. *The David Essex Story* by G Tremlett (Futura, 1974)
18. *Scene And Heard* (Radio 1), 3 January 1973
19. *Melody Maker*, 6 May 1972
20. Marc Bolan to John Blake
21. *New Musical Express*, 24 March 1972
22. *Morning Star*, 15 December 1972
23. *The Marc Bolan Story* by G Tremlett (Futura, 1975)
24. To Margaret Nicholas
25. *Rolling Stone*, 30 July 1981
26. Frank Sinatra to Tony Scaduto
27. *Melody Maker*, 12 October 1974
28. *Disc*, 17 March 1972

Chapter 12: "I Can't Wait To Go Half The Time"

1. *Scene And Heard* (Radio 1), 3 January 1973
2. *The David Essex Story* by G Tremlett (Futura, 1974)
3. *Circus*, November 1974
4. *New York Times*, 11 November 1971
5. Kaylan uttered the deplorable sentence, "Emanuel the gardener thrust his mutated member up her slithering slit."
6. *Beatles Unlimited*, 14 December 1976
7. *Melody Maker*, 6 December 1975
8. *Rolling Stone*, 23 May 1974
9. *Rolling Stone*, 30 April 1981
10. Ringo Starr to Bob Woffinden

11. To John Tobler
12. *Melody Maker*, 31 March 1973
13. *Melody Maker*, 4 December 1971
14. *Daily Express*, 20 March 1972
15. Quoted in *The Record Producers* by J Tobler and S Grundy (BBC Publications, 1982)
16. *Beatles Unlimited*, 14 December 1976
17. *Making Music*, May 1987
18. Originally recorded under the working title of 'Hold On'
19. *Creem*, October 1976
20. *Tomorrow* (US television chat show), 28 April 1975
21. Nothing to do with Eric Maschwitz and George Porford's pre-war operetta of the same title but a north of England expression meaning, "I'm getting out of here"
22. Not the same Joe Walsh who was in Lee Curtis And The All-Stars
23. Not the British beat group but a US soft-rock act whose *Greatest Hits* would be in *Billboard*'s album chart for most of 1976
24. *Sun*, 23 September 1982
25. *Melody Maker*, 12 April 1975
26. To John Blake
27. *Q*, January 1991
28. In 1978, Frampton would be among the stars in a musical film based on *Sgt Pepper's Lonely Hearts Club Band*
29. *Melody Maker*, 23 November 1974

Chapter 13: "Wherever I Go, It's A Swinging Place, Man"

1. *Melody Maker*, 7 August 1965
2. To John Blake
3. *Daily Mirror*, 4 November 1987. Maureen's reference in the same report to "Andy Capp" is an allusion to a beer-swilling, womanising cartoon character in the same newspaper
4. *Melody Maker*, 23 November 1974
5. *Daily Telegraph*, 6 November 1987
6. It was worth nearly £500,000 in 1986, when Starr appealed against an order backdating an increase in his alimony payments to his ex-wife. In the following year, she sued her solicitors for not wringing enough money from Ringo to allow her to live in the manner to which she had become accustomed before the divorce. Mr Justice Bush threw out the case, leaving Maureen with a six-figure bill for costs
7. *Paris Match*, 3 May 1976 (translation: "for financial reasons")
8. *Weekend*, 24 February 1984
9. *Melody Maker*, 2 October 1976
10. *Sun*, 20 February 1991

11. *Sunday Mirror*, 23 July 1989
12. *Scottish Weekly News*, 28 March 1987
13. *Creem*, October 1976
14. *New Musical Express*, 14 October 1976
15. *Pebble Mill At One* (ITV), 4 January 1977
16. Merseybeatle '90 programme, August 1990
17. *Rolling Stone*, 18 November 1976
18. Andy White was heard on the re-release of 'Love Me Do', as the master with Ringo's drumming had been mislaid. However, demand was such that the Starr version was taped for pressing from a pristine original Parlophone single to appear on a twelve-inch issued later in 1977
19. *Time*, 21 May 1976
20. *Rolling Stone*, 30 April 1981
21. *Beatles Unlimited*, March 1977
22. *Beatles Unlimited*, December 1976
23. *Melody Maker*, 26 May 1973
24. To Spencer Leigh
25. *Circus*, October 1976
26. Originally titled 'Birmingham'
27. Including 'Wild Shining Stars', 'Out In the Streets', 'It's No Secret', 'The Party' and 'Lover Please'
28. 1948's *Easter Parade*. The line in question was Judy Garland's "You'll find my picture in the *Rotogravure*" (a journal)
29. *Special Pop* (French), October 1976
30. *News Of The World*, 16 October 1977
31. Ring O' Records press release
32. *Rolling Stone*, 18 November 1976
33. It was 'Danny' that Presley recorded for (but that did not feature in) 1958's *King Creole*. It was also the B-side of Marty Wilde's 'Teenager In Love' in 1959
34. Alias Eric Idle from the *Monty Python's Flying Circus* team and latter-day Beach Boy Rikki Fataar. Both starred in *All You Need Is Cash*, a spoof Beatles film, with Dirk as the "Paul" figure, and Stig as "George"

Chapter 14: "If I Don't Get You, The Next One Will"

1. *Beatles Unlimited*, 14 December 1976
2. *Circus*, November 1976
3. *New Musical Express*, 14 October 1976
4. In 1988, Ringo (and Barbara Bach) spoke about Queen in *Live Killers In The Making*, volume two of *Queen: Magic Years*, a set of three one-hour videos by Picture Music International
5. *Sun*, 18 March 1981

6. *Scene And Heard* (Radio 1), 4 April 1972

7. *Scene And Heard* (Radio 1), 5 April 1972

8. Starr's musical association with Guthrie Thomas continued. In 1983, for example, he appeared on another Thomas album, *Like No Other*

9. Pete Best at Rotterdam Beatles Convention, 12 April 1985

10. *Daily Express*, 23 April 1981

11. *Sunday Mirror*, 23 August 1989

12. *Sun*, 23 September 1982

13. To Simon Kinnersley

14. To Paul Connew

15. New York Beatlefest, 24 February 1979

16. *Beatlefan*, September 1985

17. *News Of The World*, 6 October 1977

18. To John Blake

19. *New Musical Express*, 10 December 1978

20. *Rolling Stone*, 30 April 1981

21. *Loose Talk* compiled by L Botts (Omnibus, 1980)

22. Mae West had recorded Lennon-McCartney songs and had been delighted to be included on the *Sgt Pepper* sleeve photo montage

23. The illustrations were by Gerald Potterton, who'd also worked on the *Yellow Submarine* film animations

24. Not the Abba hit, nor the Manhattan Transfer album track, on which Starr drummed

25. Push-a-lone (lead guitar), Git-ar (rhythm guitar), Hamish Bissonette (synthesisers) and Diesel (bass) were probably musicians who appeared in the Ringo TV special. These included Dr John, Dee Murray (Elton John's bass player), Lon Van Eaton and Jim Webb

26. *Rolling Stone*, 5 April 1978

27. Starr returned the favour by drumming on 'Hold On', a track on McLagan's 1979 *Troublemaker* album. *Troublemaker* was, allegedly, also the title of a film Ringo intended to make with Nancy Andrews

28. Not the Larry Williams composition of the same title that was covered by The Beatles

29. By US scriptwriters Pat Proff and Neil Israel

30. *Playboy*, January 1981

31. *Western Evening Herald*, 29 November 1978

32. *Beatlefan*, August 1979

33. *Chicago Tribune*, 18 April 1981

34. *New York Times*, 13 April 1981

35. *Village Voice*, 18 April 1981

36. *Newsday*, 14 April 1981

37. *Washington Post*, 18 April 1981

38. Weekend, 24 April 1984
39. *Beatlefan*, June 1980

Chapter 15: "I Knew I'd Had This Problem For Years"

1. *Whatever Happened To...* by J Brunton and H Elson (Proteus, 1981)
2. *Q*, January 1991
3. Chicago press conference, April 1991
4. For example, on 10 May 1979 at the World Music Awards in Monte Carlo, he represented The Beatles by receiving their award for Outstanding Contribution To Pop
5. *The Aspel Show* (ITV), 5 March 1988
6. *Rolling Stone*, 30 April 1981
7. *Daily Express*, 23 April 1981
8. *Circus*, November 1976
9. *Beatlefan*, (August 1983)
10. *Club Sandwich* number 26, 1982
11. A steel-guitar obligato was edited from this recording, probably because this instrument also dominated another track, 'Sure To Fall'
12. *Melody Maker*, 2 October 1976
13. New York press conference, March 1981
14. *Yoko Ono* by J Hopkins (Sidgwick & Jackson, 1987)
15. *Barbara Walters Special* (US television), 31 March 1981
16. *Daily Star*, 18 December 1981
17. *Weekly News*, 14 March 1981
18. *Playboy*, January 1981
19. To John Blake
20. *Daily Express*, 28 April 1981
21. *Weekend*, 24 April 1984
22. Fulton County Superior Court (Atlanta) statement, 15 November 1989
23. *New York Times*, 21 June 1989
24. Opened in 1982 by Michael Heseltine, MP, for Henley-on-Thames, where in 1986 George Harrison would be campaigning against the demolition of the town's Regal Cinema to make room for a shopping mall. Heseltine was, reportedly, unmoved by Harrison's lobbying
25. *The Man Who Gave The Beatles Away* by A Williams and W Marshall (Elm Tree, 1975)
26. *Rolling Stone*, December 1981
27. *Toronto Star*, 21 December 1981
28. For example, a line from Bowie's 1975 US smash 'Fame', co-written with John Lennon and guitarist Carlos Alomar
29. Possibly the title may have been inspired by 'Drums Are My Beat', a 1962 single by Sandy Nelson, whom Nilsson may have known during his earliest days as a professional songwriter

30. Wood had also composed with George Harrison, notably 'Far East Man', which was heard on both Harrison's *Dark Horse* and Wood's *I've Got My Own Album To Do*, each released in 1974

31. *Beatlefan*, June 1982

32. *Sunday Mirror*, 23 July 1989

33. *Sunday Mirror*, 13 November 1988

34. *Sun Day*, 1 October 1989

35. "The wish to be cured is the first step towards health" (Seneca)

36. Seen as a documentary on British television in April 1991

Chapter 16: "Please, God, I Have To Stop Living This Way"

1. *Sun*, 23 September 1982

2. *New Musical Express*, 12 December 1984

3. Later, Hardin, like Jim McCarty, became an exponent of new age music, elements of which were present in *Musical Version Of Wind In The Willows*

4. Once Joe Feegan of The Strangers, who were active if hitless before and during the Mersey Beat boom

5. *Sun Day*, 3 November 1985

6. Including Kim Wilde, Brian Wilson, Johnny Warman (of Ring O' Records "fame"), the B52s, Kate Bush, Belinda Carlisle, Andy Fairweather-Low, Richie Havens and LL Cool J

7. Chicago press conference, March 1981

8. Lofgren recorded a version of The Beatles' 'Anytime At All' on his 1981 album *Night Fades Away*

9. *People*, 9 December 1990

10. *Beatles Monthly*, February 1983

11. For example, he mentioned that 'I'm Down' was the opening number at 1965's Shea Stadium performance when it was actually the finale

12. *Sunday Mirror*, 23 July 1989

13. New York press conference, 23 June 1988

14. *Beatlefan*, April 1982

15. *New York Times*, 21 June 1989

16. *Club Sandwich* number 35, 1984

17. *Club Sandwich* number 34, 1984

18. *Survivor* by R Coleman (Sidgwick & Jackson, 1985)

19. *Q*, January 1991

20. Penned by Walsh alone, this was not The Ronettes' 1963 hit of the same title

21. Fulton County Superior Court (Atlanta) statement, 15 November 1989

22, Memphis Commercial Appeal, 9 March 1988

23. *TV Times*, 14 May 1988

24. *Entertainment Tonight* (US television), 6 January 1988

25. *New York Post*, 6 January 1988
26. *Daily Mirror*, 21 January 1988
27. *Beatlefan*, December 1985
28. *Sun Day*, 1 October 1989
29. *Woman's Own*, 10 December 1990
30. In 1991, Wayne was back in business, backed by a new set of Mindbenders (alias Manchester's Mike Sweeney And The Thunderbyrds)
31. *Daily Mirror*, 6 October 1988
32. *Sunday Mirror*, 12 October 1988
33. *Sunderland Echo*, 25 November 1988

Chapter 17: "Now I Just Stay Nervous"

1. *Melody Maker*, 17 April 1965
2. *Wink Bulletin*, 8 December 1988
3. *Melody Maker*, 2 October 1976
4. *Evening Post*, 23 June 1986
5. *The Beat Goes On*, February 1991
6. *Woman's Own*, 10 December 1990
7. *Sunday Mirror*, 23 July 1989
8. *Q*, January 1989
9. A Jack Lee Elgood from Hampshire
10. *Beatles Monthly*, January 1989
11. Keltner's brother Eric was drum technician for the tour
12. *New York Times*, 21 June 1989
13. Although there were instances of brief singalongs of the main refrain of 'She Loves You'
14. Brian Epstein to Murray the K on WORFM, April 1967
15. New York press conference, 20 June 1989
16. *San Francisco Chronicle*, 2 September 1989
17. *LA Times*, 3 September 1987
18. *Las Vegas Review*, 31 August 1989
19. *Daily Telegraph*, 31 March 1990
20. *New York Times*, 6 August 1969
21. *Beatlefan*, April 1991
22. *TV Guide* (US), December 1990
23. Fulton County Superior Court (Atlanta) statement, 15 November 1989
24. Beginning when he tapped the microphone on the stand and asked, "Is it rolling, Bob?"
25. The principal exhibit was a letter from Starr to Moman. There was also Ringo's statement at the New York press conference (see note 15) that "we may do a number from [the Memphis album] just to promote it"
26. To Allan Kozinn

27. Sister of Paul McCartney's ex-fiancée, Jane Asher, and half of Peter And Gordon, his portfolio as a producer includes albums by James Taylor, Linda Ronstadt, Tony Joe White and Bonnie Raitt
28. Nilsson's tapes were of a proposed 1993 album containing a huge helping of comic songs and a rediscovered duet with John Lennon of The Platters' – and Ringo's – 'Only You'
29. Now following in his father and brother's footsteps as a drummer
30. *Sunday Times*, 5 May 1990
31. *Beatles Monthly*, July 1995
32. *Daily Mail*, 24 June 1994
33. Former editor of *Melody Maker* and biographer of both Lennon and Brian Epstein
34. Most recently – and aptly – by The Hollies
35. *Sunday Times*, 15 January 1995
36. *Guardian*, 21 October 1995
37. *People*, 29 October 1995
38. *Guardian*, 2 October 1995

Chapter 18: "I'll Be Fine Anywhere"

1. Published by Cassell, 2000
2. *Mojo*, August 1998
3. Inner-City Games, a non-profit organisation "dedicated to providing enrichment opportunities for inner-city youth"
4. *Daytrippin'* (US Beatles fanzine), issue eleven, summer 2000

Epilogue: "I Go Along With Whatever Is Happening"

1. *Sunday Express*, 3 September 1969
2. *Sunday Times*, 22 February 1983
3. *The NME Encyclopaedia Of Rock* compiled by N Logan and B Woffinden (Star Books, 1976)

Index

Walters, Hank (And His
  Dusty Road Ramblers)
  30, 31
Walters, Lou (*né* Walter
  Egmond) 43, 45, 48, 53,
  56, 63, 68, 70, 76, 81,
  84, 110, 127, 154, 168
Ward, Clifford T 267
Warhol, Andy 190, 298
Warman, Johnny 271,
  273, 360
Warwick, Dionne 145
Was, Don 360
Waters, Muddy 275
Watt Four, The 261
Watts, Charlie 136, 137,
  204, 320
Waugh, Evelyn 176
Wax, Ruby 287
Wayne, John 31
Weather Report 255
Webb, Jim 240, 271
Weill, Kurt 63, 287, 335
Weinberg, Max 319, 348
Weissleder 81, 283
Welch, Raquel 194, 210,
  292, 298
Weld, Tuesday 139
West, Mae 177, 285, 286
Weston, Kim 113
Whatham, Claude 229
White, Alan 205, 255
White, Andy 87, 96, 97,
  129, 137, 372

Whitesnake 316
Whitfield, David 34
Whitman, Slim 30, 165
Who, The 116, 136, 163,
  188, 193, 197, 228,
  237, 251, 275, 316,
  344, 351, 362-3, 369,
  375
Wild Ones, The 82
Wilde, Marty (And The
  Wildcats) 37, 44, 45, 52
Williams, Allan 53, 54,
  61, 63, 64, 85, 262,
  307
Williams, Andy 193, 239
Williams, Hank 31, 208
Williams, Robin 290
Willie And The Poor Boys
  320
Willner, Hal 335
Wilson, Brian 344, 360,
  372
Wilson, Dennis 336
Wilson, Harold 100, 119,
  150, 154
Wings 243, 248, 267, 275,
  284, 300, 302, 359
Winters, Bernie 103, 234
Winters, Mike 103, 234
Winwood, Steve 271, 276,
  281, 316, 342
Wisdom, Norman 18
Wonder, (Little) Stevie
  113, 145

Wood, Ronnie 310, 311,
  329
Wooler, Bob 49, 50, 73,
  86, 91, 378
Wordsworth, William
  25
Worley, Joanne 210
Wreckers, The 67
Wyman, Bill 276, 320-1,
  371
Wynette, Tammy 340
Wynter, Mark 75

Yalor, Kingsize 85
Yamash'ta, Stomu 197,
  271
Yardbirds, The 103, 219,
  282, 346
Yes 255
Yogi, Maharishi Mahesh
  169, 170-1, 173, 372
York, Pete 83, 113, 136,
  137
Young Rascals, The 362
Young, Neil 207
Young, Roy 81

Zappa, Frank (And The
  Mothers Of Invention)
  234-6, 237
Zappa, Moon Unit 356
Zeros, The 68
Zodiacs, Ian And The 38,
  49, 214